北美高端留学考试系列丛书

New SAT
非官方指南

丛书主编：潘 磊

本册主编：何智孝 邹燕萍 李

中国科学技术大学出版社

内 容 简 介

本书挑选 SAT 2005～2016 年的真题,对考试的四个部分,即英语、数学、阅读和科学一一进行了剖析。本书的讲解部分主要介绍了各部分的答题要求,对典型例题进行解析,进一步归纳知识点。本书的习题部分也是从真题中精心挑选出来的,考生在对知识点有初步认识之后,可以进行题目的自我检测。此外,非常重要的是,考生将在书中获得宝贵的词汇合集。词汇合集是从所有真题中提炼出来的四个科目高频词汇,方便考生备考,突破词汇难关。

本书可作为参加美国大学入学考试 SAT 考生的备考用书。

图书在版编目(CIP)数据

New SAT 非官方指南/何智孝,邹燕萍,李琼主编. —合肥:中国科学技术大学出版社,2018.1
(北美高端留学考试系列丛书)
ISBN 978-7-312-04218-8

Ⅰ. N… Ⅱ. ①何… ②邹… ③李… Ⅲ. 英语—高等学校—入学考试—美国—自学参考资料 Ⅳ. H310.471.2

中国版本图书馆 CIP 数据核字(2017)第 093167 号

出版	中国科学技术大学出版社
	安徽省合肥市金寨路 96 号,230026
	http://press.ustc.edu.cn
	https://zgkxjsdxcbs.tmall.com
印刷	合肥华苑印刷包装有限公司
发行	中国科学技术大学出版社
经销	全国新华书店
开本	787 mm×1092 mm 1/16
印张	22.5
字数	576 千
版次	2018 年 1 月第 1 版
印次	2018 年 1 月第 1 次印刷
定价	58.00 元

前　言

2015年，我们见证了SAT(Scholastic Assessment Test)的改革。在改革后的一年多时间中，现行的新的SAT已经形成了一套完整的考试体系。但在教学过程中，教学资源除了官方指南(The Official SAT Study Guide)外，就是一些知名机构的模考题目。这些官方样题和模考题目虽然有答案和一些解析，但是知识点分散、技巧讲解稀疏，没有一个强有力的归纳和总结，而这些正是大部分中国考生在备考过程中最需要的。通过几年老SAT的教学积累与一年新SAT的教学沉淀，通过各方的筹措，2017年年初，我们完成了对SAT真题进行分析和总结的材料——《New SAT非官方指南》。之所以取这个名字，除了这是我们一系列出版教材的姊妹篇之外，更是因为我们研究透了官方的资料，全盘托出我们的教学心得。

对于准备参加SAT考试的考生而言，本书是有效的辅助性教材。结合SAT的官方指南和Khan Academy的相关练习，本书针对SAT的四个科目，即阅读、语法、数学和写作进行剖析，快速介绍每个科目的答题要求，并且通过对典型例题的解析来分类归纳知识点。同时，本书中的习题精选自官方指南与Khan Academy，让考生能够在阅读完知识点后进行自测。

本书是一本国内较早针对新SAT进行研发的教材。我们借助丰富的培训经验，提炼出有效的做题技巧和方法，帮助考生快速解码SAT。更重要的是，我们在补充技巧的同时，并没有忘记获得SAT高分的本质在于提高基本功。因此，在这本书中，我们补充了必备的语法知识，尤其是国内考生相对比较陌生的领域，比如标点的正确使用和官方指南第一套至第四套的全套文本翻译，帮助考生从根本上提高英语阅读与语法实力。我们在本书中针对官方指南的题目进行了详细的解析，真正让考生做到一本在手，考试无忧。

编　者
2017年2月

目　　录

前言 ·· (i)

第 1 部分　New SAT 阅读

第 1 章　New SAT 阅读技巧总览 ··· (1)
　1.1　文章技巧纵览 ··· (2)
　1.2　题型应对技巧 ··· (10)
第 2 章　New SAT 阅读重点篇章演练 ··· (71)
　2.1　Literature ··· (71)
　2.2　Social Science ·· (87)
　2.3　History ·· (101)
　2.4　New SAT Official Guide Test 1 解析 ··· (114)
　2.5　New SAT Official Guide Test 2 解析 ··· (136)
　2.6　New SAT Official Guide Test 3 解析 ··· (158)
　2.7　New SAT Official Guide Test 4 解析 ··· (179)

第 2 部分　New SAT 语法

第 3 章　New SAT 语法考点总览 ··· (199)
　3.1　标点符号 ·· (199)
　3.2　词汇 ··· (209)
　3.3　主谓一致 ·· (212)
　3.4　固定搭配 ·· (216)
　3.5　代词 ··· (219)
　3.6　语境理解 ·· (223)
　3.7　时态 ··· (232)
　3.8　平行原则 ·· (236)

第 3 部分　New SAT 数学

第 4 章　New SAT 数学全解 ·· (239)
第 5 章　重点知识点精讲 ·· (241)
　5.1　解线性方程 ··· (241)

- 5.2 解线性函数 ·· (243)
- 5.3 线性方程应用题 ·· (246)
- 5.4 线性不等式应用题 ·· (248)
- 5.5 画线性方程 ··· (251)
- 5.6 线性函数应用题 ·· (255)
- 5.7 线性不等式组应用题 ··· (258)
- 5.8 解线性方程组 ··· (263)
- 5.9 线性方程组应用题 ·· (265)
- 5.10 解二次方程 ··· (268)
- 5.11 表达式的结构 ·· (270)
- 5.12 分离变量 ·· (272)
- 5.13 函数表示法 ··· (275)
- 5.14 比例与百分比 ·· (280)
- 5.15 百分数 ··· (283)
- 5.16 单位 ·· (285)
- 5.17 列表数据 ·· (288)
- 5.18 散点图 ··· (292)
- 5.19 图像信息 ·· (298)
- 5.20 线性及指数增长 ··· (304)

第 4 部分　New SAT 写作

第 6 章　New SAT 作文整体介绍 ·· (307)
- 6.1 New SAT 作文介绍 ··· (307)
- 6.2 评分标准 ··· (307)

第 7 章　New SAT 作文评分标准实例 ·· (309)
- 7.1 阅读策略 ··· (311)
- 7.2 分析 ··· (311)
- 7.3 范文分析和评分标准 ··· (312)

第 8 章　New SAT 作文写作框架 ·· (315)
- 8.1 流水账型写法分析 ·· (316)
- 8.2 层次性写法分析和实例 ·· (320)

第 9 章　New SAT 作文高阶篇 ··· (326)

第1部分 New SAT 阅读

第1章 New SAT 阅读技巧总览

New SAT 阅读相较于之前的 SAT 阅读而言,更考察考生对于文章细节和作者隐含观点的把握。考试题目由 67 道减少至 52 道,而考试时间则由 70 分钟减少至 65 分钟,只缩短了 5 分钟。这意味着考生在面对 New SAT 的时候必然要花更长时间在语篇的阅读上,想要在没看懂文章的基础上做题,其正确率无疑会大打折扣。那么 New SAT 阅读究竟在考验考生哪些方面的能力呢?我们从下文中可以窥见一斑。

1. 对文章的整体理解能力

相对于之前的 SAT 阅读考试,New SAT 的阅读部分不再有 sentence completion 题了,而是用 vocabulary in context 题的形式来考察考生对于词汇的掌握。这是因为,前一类题型更多关注考生对于词汇的本身含义的理解,而现行的题型则将侧重点更多地放在了考生对于常用词汇在语境运用上的细微差别。College Board 意识到,认识专业性较强的高阶词汇,虽然在一定程度上对学生的研究类学习有所帮助,但对生活、学习中更为常用的文章理解意义不大。因此,在 New SAT 的阅读中,这一类新型词汇题的出现旨在让考生们走出死记硬背的范式,而是更多关注文章上下文(包括一些修辞手法,如类比、比喻、对比、举例说明等)对于词汇含义及理解的影响。

2. 对于文章结构和论据的逻辑推理能力

New SAT 阅读中的"Find the Evidence"问题(即循证题)是之前从未出现过的题型。在这一类题型中,考生被要求在四条文中语句里找到最能解释之前一题答案的选项。这一类问题要求学生对于之前一题进行验证思考,并通过"在文章中找到证据"的方式加强考生的逻辑推理能力,而这一能力对于综合类文章的理解大有裨益。

3. 识图能力

New SAT 阅读中还首次引入了图表题,要求考生在理解文章的基础上对于图表中的数据进行分析,并理解其对于文章论点的意义。这一新题型考察的是考生对于可视化信息的理解能力,即文字与数字的逻辑转换。

针对这一系列改变,我们建议考生在进行 SAT 阅读时可以参考以下顺序:

(1) 首先快速阅读文章。

快速阅读文章是指仅仅阅读文章的标题、首尾段和每一个段落的首尾句。这能够让考生对于整篇文章的主要观点和大意有所了解,而无须花费过多时间阅读整篇文章。

(2) 阅读问题,如有需要再重新阅读文章。

一般情况下,在对于文章主旨和作者主要论点有一定了解的基础上,很多文后的问题已经能够迎刃而解了。如果在题型中出现了图表题,那么建议考生先从这些图表题入手。因为这一类题型有图表的辅助,所以有一些题目可以直接从图表中得出答案。

(3) 切勿基于已有知识判断。

由于 New SAT 阅读的文章内容相较于 Old SAT 而言,更贴近社会热点或者考生生活,因此在阅读的过程中要更为仔细,以免被自己在这方面的刻板印象或者原有概念所误导,基于自己的个人情感对文章内容进行解析。

1.1 文章技巧纵览

New SAT 阅读共分为 5 篇文章,每篇 500～750 个单词,答题时间共 65 分钟。文章题材涉及一篇文学类文章、一篇社会科学类文章、一篇美国建国文档或重大全球问题讨论文本以及两篇科学类文章,每篇阅读文章均设有 10～11 个问题。在评分方面,除了与语法部分一起占 800 分以外,阅读部分还单独报告分数(10～40 分),而且报告下列方面的小分:

- 掌握证据(Command of Evidence)。
- 上下文词汇的掌握(Words in Context)。
- 历史/社会研究方面的分析能力(Analysis in History/Social Science)。
- 科学方面的分析能力(Analysis in Science)。

由于阅读量大,做题时间紧,考生们在研读文本的过程中不仅会受到时间上的压力,还会遇到难以理解文章内容的压力。下面我们就每一类 New SAT 阅读将会涉及的文章类型进行剖析,谈谈不同文章分别适用的解题技巧。

1.1.1 文学类文章(Literature)

1.1.1.1 小说类文章概述

小说类文章是 New SAT 阅读考试中考生面临的第一篇文章,选自 U.S./World literature(英语)。尽管 New SAT 阅读的文学类文章选取似乎更青睐近代小说,但 18～19 世纪的文学经典也是考试热门。这就意味着考生要对各个时期文学作品的写作手法和写作风格有所了解。

1.1.1.2 阅读技巧

1. 阅读引言部分(Introduction Information)

在每一篇 New SAT 阅读文章之前,都会以一两句话的形式告诉考生这篇文本的出处。在小说类文章中,这一段引言部分的作用格外重要,因为我们可能会从中发现一些帮助我们理解文中设定以及人物角色的背景信息。同时,出版日期也是一个重要线索,通过这一时间信息我们能够快速定位到作者所处的时代,对其文章的写作手法或者表现主题也会有所预期。

2. 关注人物描写(Description of Characters)

随着阅读的深入,文中的人物关系会慢慢显现,而我们要做的就是画出表现人物性格的语句或词语。通常,这些词句会以描绘人物动作、神态、外貌等形式出现。在注意到这些关键词汇的同时,不妨思考一下:这些词句表现了该人物怎样的性格特征或行为动机?作者为什么要用这个单词来形容他/她?这是否能体现作者对于该人物正面、负面或中立的态度?

3. 关注人物关系(Description of the Relationships between the Characters)

在文学类作品中,人物之间的"冲突"是很重要的组成部分,这能让整个小说更具有可读性和张力。因此在阅读这类文章时,要有意识地从字里行间建立起对人物关系的理解,也就是文中的人物对于对方行为的反应。这种反应同样不仅会通过动作、神态描写出现,有时也会出现在人物对话或人物的独白中。

4. 写下人物笔记(Notes about the Characters)

在阅读过程中不妨写下人物与其对应的性格,例如:Mary—mean-spirited, Lily—mild & indecisive 等。这些笔记并不需要过于详细,只需记下其最主要的性格特点即可。这会在之后做题的过程中提醒考生排除一些答案。以 Mary 为例,既然在文中其性格较为刻薄,那么在选项中如果出现对于其赞扬或者正面的褒义词,就需要考生多多警惕了。

5. 注意文中转折(Turning Points)

基本上每一篇 SAT 阅读中出现的文学作品里都会涵盖一个"turning point"(转折点),即文中人物遇到了某件事、回忆起曾经发生的某件事,或者曾做过的事被曝光。这一转折点对于理解文章是非常重要的,因为往往我们能够从中发现作者写文章的真正意图。当遇到这样的重要事件时,可以在旁边做记号,便于自己在做题时快速定位。

6. 关注人物对话(Conversations)

当文中出现人物对话,或者人物独白时,我们往往能够从中发现该人物的性格:是趾高气扬,还是唯唯诺诺?而从对方的回应中,我们也能看出他人对该人物的态度:是唯命是从,还是不屑一顾?这些要点对于我们理解人物有很重要的作用。

1.1.1.3 实战演练

• 选自 Khan College New SAT 阅读文章 Literature Level 3 Passage 3

> This passage is excerpted from Nathaniel Hawthorne, *The House of the Seven Gables*. Originally published in 1851. In this scene, set in the American Colonies when they were still governed by England, Colonel Pyncheon holds a party at his home for a visiting English dignitary.

One inauspicious circumstance there was, which awakened a hardly concealed displeasure in the breasts of a few of the more punctilious visitors. The founder of this stately mansion—a gentleman noted for the square and ponderous courtesy of his demeanor, ought surely to have stood in his own hall, and to have offered the first welcome to so many eminent personages as here presented themselves in honor of his solemn festival. He was as yet invisible; the most favored of the guests had not beheld him. This sluggishness on Colonel Pyncheon's part became still more unaccountable, when the second dignitary of the province made his appearance, and found no more ceremonious a reception. The lieutenant-governor, although his visit was one of the anticipated glories of the day, had alighted from his horse, and assisted his lady from her side-saddle, and crossed the Colonel's threshold, without other greeting than that of the principal domestic.

This person—a gray-headed man, of quiet and most respectful deportment—found it necessary to explain that his master still remained in his study, or private apartment; on entering which, an hour before, he had expressed a wish on no account to be disturbed.

"Do not you see, fellow," said the high-sheriff of the county, taking the servant aside, "that this is no less a man than the lieutenant-governor? Summon Colonel Pyncheon at once! I know that he received letters from England this morning; and, in the perusal and consideration of them, an hour may have passed away without his noticing it. But he will be ill-pleased, I judge, if you suffer him to neglect the courtesy due to one of our chief rulers, and who may be said to represent King William, in the absence of the governor himself. Call your master instantly."

"Nay, please your worship," answered the man, in much perplexity, but with a backwardness that strikingly indicated the hard and severe character of Colonel Pyncheon's domestic rule; "my master's orders were exceeding strict; and, as your worship knows, he permits of no discretion in the obedience of those who owe him service. Let who list open yonder door; I dare not, though the governor's own voice should bid me do it!"

"Pooh, pooh, master high sheriff!" cried the lieutenant-governor, who had overheard the foregoing discussion, and felt himself high enough in station to play a little with his dignity. "I will take the matter into my own hands. It is time that the good Colonel came forth to greet his friends; else we shall be apt to suspect that he has taken a sip too much of his Canary wine, in his extreme deliberation which cask it were best to broach in honor of the day! But since he is so much behindhand, I will give him a remembrancer myself!"

Accordingly, with such a tramp of his ponderous riding-boots as might of itself have been audible in the remotest of the seven gables, he advanced to the door, which the servant pointed out, and made its new panels reecho with a loud, free knock. Then, looking round, with a smile, to the spectators, he awaited a response. As none came, however, he knocked again, but with the same unsatisfactory result as at first. And now, being a trifle choleric in his temperament, the lieutenant-governor uplifted the heavy hilt of his sword, wherewith he so beat and banged upon the door, that, as some of the bystanders whispered, the racket might have disturbed the dead. Be that as it might, it seemed to produce no awakening effect on Colonel Pyncheon. When the sound subsided, the silence through the house was deep, dreary, and oppressive, notwithstanding that the tongues of many of the guests had already been loosened by a surreptitious cup or two of wine or spirits.

"Strange, forsooth! —very strange!" cried the lieutenant-governor, whose smile was changed to a frown. "But seeing that our host sets us the good example of forgetting ceremony, I shall likewise throw it aside, and make free to intrude on his privacy."

He tried the door, which yielded to his hand, and was flung wide open by a sudden gust of wind that passed, as with a loud sigh, from the outermost portal through all the passages and apartments of the new house. It rustled the silken garments of the ladies, and waved the long curls of the gentlemen's wigs, and shook the window-hangings and the curtains of the bedchambers; causing everywhere a singular stir, which yet was more like a hush. A shadow of awe and half-fearful anticipation—nobody knew wherefore, nor of what—had all at once fallen over the company.

通过以上分析我们不难看出,文中的人物关系并不复杂,我们可以做一下笔记:
- Pyncheon: ponderous and accountable; weird behavior this time
- Servant: respectful and afraid of his master
- High Sheriff: impatient and rude
- Lieutenant-governor: overbearing and arrogant

这篇文章说的正是 Pyncheon 老爷在宴请显贵人物时(Introduction 中的信息:Colonel Pyncheon holds a party at his home for a visiting English dignitary)未能出席的奇怪行为,其他几位人物对这一行为的反应,以及最终陆军上尉破门而入的情节,进而了解了人物之间的关系,以及人物的突出性格之后,很多题目的难度就大大降低了。例如:

QUESTION 6 OF 11

The actions of the Colonel's servant can best be described as motivated by _____.
A. his over-eagerness to please the Colonel
B. the pretentiousness that his position requires
C. his confusion over the high-sheriff's request
D. a sense of duty to his employer

解析:通过管家的行为和话语我们不难看出他对于主人的尊敬("my master's orders were exceeding strict; and, as your worship knows, he permits of no discretion in the obedience of those who owe him service. Let who list open yonder door; I dare not, though the governor's own voice should bid me do it!"),即使是陆军上尉和警长这样身份远高于他的人对他提出要求,他也不愿违背主人的意愿,体现出 a sense of duty to his employer,因此我们就能选到正确答案 D。

1.1.2 科学类文章(Science)

1.1.2.1 社会科学类(Social Science)、自然科学类文章(Nature Science)概述

在文学类文章之后出现的是两篇科学类文章,其中包括一篇建国文献或全球对话文本。这两类文章的阅读技巧并不完全相同,但 Social Science 类和 Nature Science 类文章均属于说明文,阅读方法类似。

1.1.2.2 阅读技巧

社会科学类文章涉及的主题主要为社会科学、心理学、经济学和政治现象的讨论等，而自然科学类文章则关注生物、天文、气象、地理等方面。相较于文学类文章而言，这两类文章的主旨一般更加清晰，行文结构更有规律可循。阅读这两类文章，只要抓住以下几点就能基本完成相关题目。

1. 文章主要论点（Main Idea）

一般出现在文章首尾段，或在以转折词引导的分句中。因此文章的第一段和最后一段是阅读的重点。通过阅读这两个段落能够基本了解文章讨论的主要内容。

2. 对文章呈现主题的不同看法、理论（Different Theories or Perspectives on the Topic Presented）

可能会出现在大写的人名或转折词之后。通常，一个观点就是一个段落，因此要着重阅读每个段落的第一句话。当然，如果段落中有明显的转折或让步的词语，那么该转折句也是重中之重。很可能段首句只不过是过渡句，转折句才是该段真正的主题。

3. 支撑文章论点的例子（Examples Used to Support the Topic）

一般会紧跟在 topic sentence 之后，并夹杂举例信号词，如"for example""for instance""including""such as""i.e.""that is to say"等。

4. 作者对于文章主要论点或讨论主题的态度及结论（Author's Conclusion about the Topic）

一般可以通过对于反驳观点的语气词看出，或通过一些副词看出，如"luckily""greatly"等。同时，作者也常常会在文章最后段落表明自己的立场。

1.1.2.3 实战演练

• 选自 Khan College New SAT 阅读文章 Social Science Level 3 Passage 1

> This passage is adapted from Jan Delhey and Christian Kroll, *A 'Happiness Test' for the New Measures of National Well-Being: How Much Better than GDP Are They?* © 2012 by WZB Berlin Social Science Center.

There is currently a broad global movement away from considerations of mere economic success towards a new public policy goal involving a broader notion of quality of life. This movement has also spurred a rethinking of which statistics inform us best about a country's situation and how its citizens are faring. For decades, the gold standard was a macroeconomic indicator: the GDP-gross domestic product, calculated per capita. This is the most prominent yardstick that the media, politicians and the public consider when they try to assess how a country is performing. However, this measure was never meant to be a measure of the welfare of nations (as its creator Simon Kuznets warned in the 1930s) and so there is growing skepticism about the GDP's usefulness as a measure of national well-being. Slogans such as "beyond GDP" or "redefining progress" challenge the preoccupation with the GDP.

Three key strategies have been employed to develop a better measure of well-being: healing the GDP, complementing the GDP, and replacing the GDP...

The first group of initiatives tries to deal with the downsides of the GDP by attempting to fix the indicator itself...

One key aim of this group of measures is to account for sustainability and the environmental damage associated with GDP growth. For example, the Index of Sustainable Economic Welfare and the Genuine Progress Indicator are both based on the consumption of private households. However, they also reflect additional social factors such as household labor and education with a rising value, while air pollution and environmental damage lower the score. As a consequence, the downsides of economic growth and modernization ought to be accounted for whilst retaining the benefits of the GDP, namely a single figure that captures different entities and is comparable across nations...

The second group of measures moves further away from the GDP as a yardstick than the previous approaches but does not abandon the sum of goods and services altogether. Instead, this group of measures seeks to assess national well-being by complementing the GDP with a number of key social indicators...

For example, the Human Development Index comprises the three dimensions health, education, and material living conditions, which are measured by life expectancy, years of schooling, and GNI (gross national income), respectively...

While the method of complementing the GDP with further indicators is able to overcome the controversial monetization from which the measures that try to "heal GDP" suffer, the standardization of different units is also controversial. In particular, merging different units into a single standardized index is methodologically challenging and again requires value judgements by the researcher...

The most radical departure from the GDP is embodied by the third group of measures, which seeks alternative indicators of well-being without accounting for the sum of goods and services produced in an economy. The logic behind this approach is that the GDP has always been and remains a means to an end rather than the end itself...

Famous examples include the Happy Planet Index calculated by the New Economics Foundation. The index comprises life expectancy, life satisfaction, and the ecological footprint and is therefore able to demonstrate how many resources countries need in order to produce a certain level of health and subjective well-being...

Replacing the GDP altogether is quite a drastic strategy for assessing national well-being, as not only is economic growth a prerequisite for many of the social goods that make life enjoyable but the metric of GDP is also highly correlated with such other factors. Thus, by arguing that the GDP is only a means to an end, these measures are in danger of making a conceptual assumption that is notable in theory but can be challenged in practice on the basis of actual causal mechanisms and empirical data.

Adapted from "The Unhappy Planet Index 2.0," © 2009 by the NEF (the New Economics Foundation)

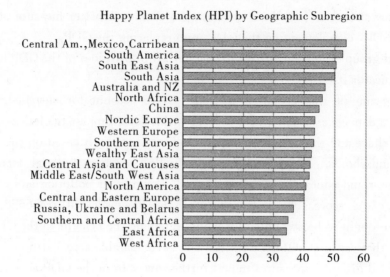

1.1.3 历史类文章(History)

1.1.3.1 历史类文章概述

与以往脱离日常课程教学的形象不同,College Board(即美国大学理事会)这次努力地把 SAT 与学校常规学习关联起来,鼓励学生通过长期的课程学习为 SAT 做准备。与"立国文档和全球性对话"这个主题相关的课程至少应该包括"美国历史""美国政府""世界历史"等。

对于大部分中国学生来说,新增加的这个 20% 并不是一个好消息。首先,大部分中国学生的美国史知识都比较薄弱,即使选修过,通常也只是些浅尝辄止的信息获取,很少会涉及诸如"The Federalist Papers"的细节知识,更别说讨论了。不经学习和讨论,要有深刻认识是很难的。下面我们就来一起看一下这类文章的阅读技巧。

1.1.3.2 阅读技巧

历史类文章或全球重要对话文本往往是以演讲类体裁出现的。这就意味着这类文章有明确的目标,即打动自己的听众。而要做到这一点,宣讲人往往需要调动起听众的情绪,同时明确表明自己的立场,同时还在文中有对于对手观点的揶揄或直接反驳。因此阅读这类文章,我们要特别注意以下几点:

1. 结尾段(尤其是全文最后一句话)的意义远大于第一句话

这是因为在演讲伊始,人们的情绪还没有被充分调动起来,这个时候就说出自己的观点并不能起到很好的效果。所以往往作者会在文章最后重申自己的主张,一方面听众的情绪在彼时达到了顶点,另一方面则能够对听众形成重复刺激。

2. 排比句或问句之后的话往往是核心观点

众所周知,排比句、反问句和设问句都是渲染情绪的良方。在一系列排比句之后,听众的情绪越发高昂。此时提出核心观点更易被人们所接受,也让人觉得更合情合理。

3. 关注例子中的感情色彩

在这类文章中,作者往往会大量运用典故。而在典故的运用过程中,作者通过一些副词或形容词所体现的感情色彩往往能够暗示其态度。考生可以通过作者对于例子的态度推断出作者对于相似事例的态度,即文章主旨。

4. 关注转折词

往往转折词之后是作者要强调的内容。

5. 关注 introduction

Introduction 中的信息对于考生理解文章所处的历史背景很有帮助。

1.1.3.3 实战演练

- 选自 Khan College New SAT 阅读文章 History Level 2 Passage 4

> This passage is excerpted from a published letter written by an author known only as the Federal Farmer.

Our object has been all along, to reform our federal system, and to strengthen our governments, but a new object now presents. The plan of government now proposed is evidently calculated totally to change, in time, our condition as a people. Instead of being thirteen republics, under a federal head, it is clearly designed to make us one consolidated government. Whether such a change can ever be effected in any manner; whether it can be effected without convulsions and civil wars; whether such a change will not totally destroy the liberties of this country—time only can determine.

The confederation was formed when great confidence was placed in the voluntary exertions of individuals, and of the respective states; and the framers of it, to guard against usurpation, so limited and checked the powers. We find, therefore, members of congress urging alterations in the federal system almost as soon as it was adopted. The first interesting question is how far the states can be consolidated into one entire government on free principles. The happiness of the people at large must be the great object with every honest statesman, and he will direct every movement to this point. If we are so situated as a people, as not to be able to enjoy equal happiness and advantages under one government, the consolidation of the states cannot be admitted.

Touching the federal plan, I do not think much can be said in its favor: The sovereignty of the nation, without coercive and efficient powers to collect the strength of it, cannot always be depended on to answer the purposes of government; and in a congress of representatives of sovereign states, there must necessarily be an unreasonable mixture of powers in the same hands.

Independent of the opinions of many great authors, that a free elective government cannot be extended over large territories, a few reflections must evince, that one government and general legislation alone, never can extend equal benefits to all parts of the United States: Different laws, customs, and opinions exist in the different states, which by a uniform system of laws would be unreasonably invaded. The United States contain about a million of square miles, and in half a century will, probably, contain ten millions of people.

1.2 题型应对技巧

1.2.1 New SAT 新题型——图表题

图表题是 New SAT 区别于原 SAT 的新题型，其特征就是题干中出现与图表相关的内容。这种题型需要通过读懂文章大意，然后根据文章的信息和图表中的信息，综合判断选项。相对而言，读图题一般较为简单，与托福文章类似。有些题目直接通过文章主旨和图表本身就可以做出来，有一些题目需要通读文章找到出题点才可以做出来。此类题型在一套题中可能会出现 1 到 2 次，主要在社会科学类和自然科学类文章中。

题型特点：题干中往往会出现：
- According to the chart/graph/diagram …（单图表题）
- Based on the chart/graph/diagram …（单图表题）
- Based on the passage and the information in the chart/graph/diagram …（图文结合题）

技巧总览

凡是读图，首先必须要看清楚这个图位置之上的标题，即说明这个图是做什么用的。其次，要看清楚图的各项指标，尤其是数字部分，要比较它们之间的不同、所代表的不同的特点，最重要的是，要发现图表所表示的一般规律。图下方的斜体字表明图表的出处，意义不是很大；如果这个斜体字部分很长，那可以适当看看，里面有可能含有重要信息。

图表题分为以下两类：

（1）单图表题——仅仅读懂图表不需要阅读文章就可以解答的题目。

（2）图文关系题——仅仅依靠图表信息无法找到正确答案，还需要依靠文章提供的信息辅助解题。做这类题的方法就是根据题干中的关键词进行定位，回到原文找到对应信息，并对照图表中的数据进行解题。

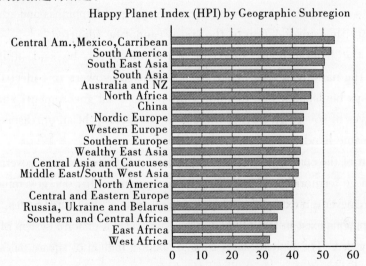

真题模拟

• 选自 Khan College New SAT 阅读文章 Social Science Level 2 Passage 1

Adapted from "The Unhappy Planet Index 2.0," © 2009 by the NEF (the New Economics Foundation)

QUESTION 9 OF 11

According to the graph, the region with the fourth-lowest HPI score is _____.
A. Russia, Ukraine, and Belarus   B. Central and Eastern Europe
C. South Asia   D. North America

解析：题干要求我们查找的是在 HPI 指数中排名倒数第四的地区，而图表中纵轴表示的是地区，横轴表示的是 HPI 指数。因此我们只需找到横轴上数字倒数第四的对应地区即可，可以选到 Russia, Ukraine, and Belarus，即选项 A。

QUESTION 10 OF 11

Based on the passage, which of the following is most likely to contribute to South America's HPI ranking?
A. A somewhat high duration of education
B. A moderately low gross national income
C. A fairly low production of services
D. A relatively high life expectancy

解析：题干中的定位词是 South America，因此我们可以定位到南美所对应的 HPI 排名在正数第二位。而显然题目中问我们的是造成南美这一 HPI 排名的原因，所以我们需要回到原文中用 HPI 进行定位，找到因果关系，可以看到在文中有如下这句话：

Line 57: Famous examples include the Happy Planet Index calculated by the New Economics Foundation. The index comprises life expectancy, life satisfaction, and the ecological footprint and is therefore able to demonstrate how many resources countries need in order to produce a certain level of health and subjective well-being.

很显然，在这一段对 HPI 指数的描述中，只提到了选项中的 life expectancy，而别的选项均未提及。因此我们就可以选到答案 D。这就是一道非常典型的图文结合题，需要根据图表中的关键词（往往是图表题目，或者横轴、纵轴，或者图下注释）回到原文中定位，找到对应的答案。

QUESTION 11 OF 11

The greatest number of geographic regions have an HPI score in which range?
A. 20~30   B. 30~40   C. 40~50   D. 50~60

解析：观察题目我们发现四个选项均为数字，也就是图表中横轴上的信息，因此锁定我们要找的就是地区。而这一地区在文中的限定为 greatest number，所以只要找到地区数包含最多的区间即可。而在 40~50 区间中的地区数明显大于其他几个区间，因此可以选到正确答案 C。

更多练习

• 选自 Khan College New SAT 阅读文章 Social Science Level 2 Passage 3

The effect of social network diversity on observed colds as verified through objective criteria.

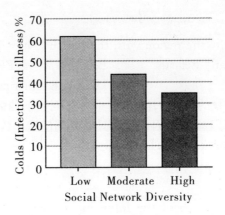

[Source: Cohen S, Doyle W J, Skoner D P, et al. Social Ties and Susceptibility to the Common Cold[J]. JAMA, 1997, 277(24): 1940-1944.]

QUESTION 9 OF 11

According to the graph, the average incidence of colds for participants who had low-diversity social groups was closest to _____.

A. 30%　　　　B. 40%　　　　C. 60%　　　　D. 70%

解析: 题目问的是 average incidence of colds（纵轴），而限定词是 low-diversity social groups，因此只需在图表中选定 Low 锁定的数值，即可选到正确答案 C。

• 选自 Khan College New SAT 阅读文章 Social Science Level 2 Passage 3

QUESTION 10 OF 11

According to the passage, the link shown in the graph between high social diversity and a strong immune system _____.

A. illustrates the "stress-buffering effect" of social support

B. proves the value of frequent hugs

C. shows that people with many social ties have less conflict in their lives than other people do

D. cannot be explained by science

解析: 题目中问的是 high social diversity 和 a strong immune system 之间的联系，而图表中并没有出现过 immune system，因此我们需要回到原文针对 social diversity 和 immune system 这两组关键词进行定位。可以看到在文中有如下句子：

Line 44：The most important results, however, were what the researchers deemed a "stress-buffering effect." Keep in mind that interpersonal conflict can cause people a lot of stress and thereby weaken their immune systems. Yet regardless of how much conflict they endured, participants with a strong sense of social support developed less severe cold symptoms than those who felt socially deprived.

最后一句中说 less severe cold symptoms 对应一个强健的免疫系统，同时也能够对应图表中纵轴的信息。而 a strong sense of social support 则可以对应图表中 social network diversity 的程度。而这一句话证明的是第一句中的"stress-buffering effect"这一概念，因此可以选到答案 A。选项 C 虽然内容并无错误，但在图表中并没有表现出 frequent hug 和 social network diversity 的关系，而是表现感冒和社会化程度的关系，因此与图表信息不符合，排除。所以在做这类题型时，我们还要注意选项正确但不对应图表的情况。

- 选自 Khan College New SAT 阅读文章 Social Science Level 2 Passage 4

Survey results of members with National Scrabble Association Ratings versus college students at a liberal arts college who have played Scrabble at some point but have never competed.

Variables	Scrabble experts	College students
Number of people	114	147
Ave. days per year spent playing scrabble	221.37	8.1
Questions	Scrabble experts answering yes	College students answering yes
Have you ever studied words from the Offcial Scrabble Player's Dictionary or a similar source?	99%	5%
Are there words that you know are legal in Scrabble, but you do not know what the word means?	89%	26%
When you play Scrabble do you always keep track of the letters that have been played, so you know if you are likely to get a rare letter that you might need?	80%	4.8%
When your opponent has the Scrabble board facing him or her, do you sometimes mentally rotate the board to imagine what it would look like if it were facing you?	17%	38%
When you think about the layout of Scrabble boards, do you know the point value for every square on the board (e. g. double or triple word/letter score tiles?)	70%	3%

QUESTION 9 OF 11

According to the chart, the question to which the smallest percentage of college students answered "yes" mainly tested the students' _____.

A. vocabulary knowledge B. critical thinking
C. working memory D. visuospatial reasoning

解析：根据题目，我们需要找的是百分比数值最小的且回答是"yes"的 college students 的信息，因此可以定位到最后一个问题，找到其中的关键词是 point value for every square，显然考察的是他们的记忆能力，可以选到答案 C。

• 选自 Khan College New SAT 阅读文章 Social Science Level 2 Passage 4

QUESTION 11 OF 11

According to the chart, elite scrabble players are most likely to do which of the following?

A. Study the definitions of words B. Keep track of letters played
C. Memorize point values D. Memorize words

解析：既然题目问的是 elite scrabble players are MOST likely 做的事，那么我们只要找到对应 elite player 数值最大的那一项即可，即第一个问题：have studied words，因此可以选到答案 D。而选项 A 则是一个混淆选项，似乎是 studied words 的近义词。但是仔细回看图表中的第二个问题，我们就会发现这个问题中的"what the word means"能更好地对应选项 A 中的"definition"，所以可以排除选项 A。

• 选自 Khan College New SAT 阅读文章 Social Science Level 3 Passage 3

The Similarity of Sun Dances Among Four Great Plains Tribes

	Arapho	Assiniboine	Gros Ventre	Blackfoot
Arapho	100%	30%	50%	41%
Assiniboine	30%	100%	32%	32%
Gros Ventre	51%	32%	100%	48%
Blackfoot	41%	32%	48%	100%

The table demonstrates the degree of similarity (with a maximum similarity of 100% when a group is compared to itself) between any given pairing among the four tribes.

QUESTION 9 OF 11

According to the table, which two tribes have the most similar Sun Dances, discounting each tribe's comparison to itself?

A. The Gros Ventre and Arapho tribes
B. The Blackfoot and Gros Ventre tribes

C. The Arapho and Blackfoot tribes

D. The Assiniboine and Gros Ventre tribes

解析：题目问的是哪两个部落之间有最相似的 Sun Dances，因此我们只需找到除了自身比较（100%）之外最大的数值所对应的两个部落即可，即 51% 所对应的 Gros Ventre 和 Arapho 部落，选到答案 A。

- 选自 Khan College New SAT 阅读文章 Social Science Level 3 Passage 3

QUESTION 10 OF 11

According to the passage, the similarities between the tribes' Sun Dances as shown in the chart can be best attributed to _____.

A. the close geographical locations that the tribes shared

B. similarities in the languages from which their present-day languages derived

C. patterns of similarity in design preferences among different tribes

D. selection biases that different tribes have exhibited

解析：分析题目可知这是一道图文结合题，而需要回答的是部落间 Sun Dances 相似的原因，因此我们可以根据 similarities 和因果词回到原文进行定位，可以看到如下句子：

Line 64：Ordinarily, this pattern might simply be attributed to the fact that tribes with more mutually comprehensible languages were able to more effectively transmit the behavioral variants among themselves.

这句话中的 be attributed to 为因果词，之后的内容就是这种相似性的原因。而 with more mutually comprehensible languages 则可以对应选项 B 中的 similarities in the languages，因此可以选到答案 B。

1.2.2 New SAT 新题型——循证题

循证题（Evidence-Based Question）是对文本论据的考察，要求为上一题的答案寻找论据或者为某个结论提供论据，在每个篇章中会出现两题，共 10 题。这类题型其实是要求学生形成一个习惯性的思维——提出一个观点，必有对此观点的证明；或者一旦进行推论，必有推论所依据的参照。在 New SAT 的阅读中，为什么选，为什么不选，都应该能从文章中找得到直接的证据佐证自己的观点。如果能在平时做题中形成这种思维，那么适应 New SAT 阅读的要求会相对轻松一些。

题型特征如下：

- Which choice provides the best evidence for the answer to the previous question?
- In lines ××××, what is the most likely reason for ...?

技巧总览

在最新的 New SAT 的官方样题文章中，涉及文本循证的题目分为以下两大类型：

- 两道题：分别对于观点及其证据的两重设问。
- 一道题：观点已明确，需要找到支持该观点的原文依据。

目前来看,绝大多数题属于第 1 类。尽管 New SAT 考试在设计之初就有减少考试 "trainable"的目标;但从目前来看,还是有规律可循的。就以文本循证(Command of Evidence)为例,至少有如下技巧:

1. 顺序性原则

一般而言,题目顺序与其在原文的对应位置顺序基本是一致的,例外的情况较少。这个原则可以辅助文本循证性题目的解答。利用该原则,甚至可以借助到前后题目对应的原文位置,从而大致确定文本循证题所对应的原文的位置范围。

2. 依据文本循证题选项中的行号辅助解答,反推观点

建议按照以下顺序解答——先观点,再证据。即先通过自己对于文章的理解,直接选出前一个观点性问题的答案,再来看下一道题中所提示的证据,即原文内容与此观点可以互相验证。之所以不去逐个看第二题中选项中对应的行号内容,从而推知观点,除了做题效率的考虑外,最主要的还是防止选项干扰。

3. 避免混淆选项

前文提到过,文本循证题目通常是两个一组设置的,即第一题考察观点性内容,第二题考察第一题所选答案的依据。因而,很容易在第一题设置错误选项的同时,在第二题设置与之相应的行号。这样,单纯从逻辑来看,即使错误的内容也就有了"依据"。所以,单纯地先依据、后观点,即先做第二题、再做第一题的解答顺序是有很大风险的。那么,我们可以通过先检验第二题的答案能否直接回答第一题的题干这一方法进行解题。

真题模拟

• 选自 Khan College New SAT 阅读文章 History Level 2 Passage 1

QUESTION 5 OF 11

Jefferson implies that the initial purpose of his walk was to _____.

A. better understand the physical geography around him
B. get out of the town in order to think more clearly
C. understand the condition of non-American laborers
D. avoid running into the king and his courtiers

QUESTION 6 OF 11

Which choice provides the best evidence for the answer to the previous question?

A. lines 8~12 ("But as this is not indispensably required, and my finances do not admit the expense of a continued residence here, I propose to come occasionally to attend the king's levees, returning again to Paris, distant 40 miles.")
B. lines 13~14 ("This being the first trip, I set out yesterday morning to take a view of the place.")
C. lines 16~18 ("As soon as I had got clear of the town I fell in with a poor woman walking at the same rate with myself and going the same course.")
D. lines 18~20 ("Wishing to know the condition of the labouring poor I entered into

conversation with her ...")

解析：第一题问的是 Jefferson 散步的本来目的是什么，因此我们要在第二题的选项中找到一个对于目的的说明，我们来一一分析第二题的选项：

选项 A 中说的是 Jefferson 往返于巴黎和该小镇的原因，并非散步的目的，没有回答第一问，因此排除。

选项 B 中 This being the first trip 解释了 Jefferson 散步的原因，而 to take a view of the place 则通过不定式表目的，回答了第一题的问题，因此第二题选到答案 B。

选项 C 已经阐述在散步过程中发生的事件了，因此也并非目的，可以排除。

选项 D 说的是和乡村妇女聊天的原因及目的，并非散步的初衷，文不对题。

我们在第二题确定答案为 B 之后回看第一题，发现只有选项 A 中的 better understand the physical geography around him 能够对应第二题选项 B 中的 this being the first trip 以及 to take a view of the place，因此第一题选 A。

• 选自 Khan College New SAT 阅读文章 History Level 3 Passage 4

QUESTION 4 OF 11

It can reasonably be inferred from the passage that both Paine and the Archbishop of Toulouse hope for _____.

A. a violent overthrow of the French monarchy
B. a peaceful resolution to the people's grievances in France
C. the creation of a multi-party democracy in France
D. stronger ties between the Church and the French monarchy

QUESTION 5 OF 11

Which choice provides the best evidence for the answer to the previous question?

A. lines 37~39 ("When I came to France, in the spring of 1787, the Archbishop of Toulouse was then Minister, and at that time highly esteemed.")

B. lines 39~42 ("I became much acquainted with the private Secretary of that Minister, a man of an enlarged benevolent heart; and found that his sentiments and my own perfectly agreed with respect to the madness of war ...")

C. lines 45~47 ("That I might be assured I had not misunderstood him, nor he me, I put the substance of our opinions into writing and sent it to him;")

D. lines 52~55 ("He answered me by letter in the most unreserved manner, and that not for himself only, but for the Minister, with whose knowledge the letter was declared to be written.")

解析：第一题问的是我们能从文中推断出 Archbishop of the Toulouse 和 Paine 对什么抱有共同的希望，带着这个问题我们来看第二题的选项：

选项 A 只说了 Paine 来到法国时的社会状态，并非 hope，可以排除。

选项 B 中的 his sentiments and my own perfectly agreed with 可以对应第一题题干中的 both，同时 agree 也可以对 hope 进行同义替换，因此该选项正确。

选项 C 中说为了确保自己没有误解他而写信，是说明写信的目的，而并非两人共同的 hope，同样可以排除。

选项 D 同样与 hope 无关，只写到了回信的事宜，可以排除。

在确定第二题的答案为 B 之后，就能发现两人在 the madness of war 上有一致的观点。由于第一题是一道推断题，所以说明答案不一定会像细节题那样在文中明确写出，可能需要我们通过作者语汇的运用或参考文中的比较，进行推理。从 madness 一词中，我们可以看出两人对于战争的负面情绪，结合上一句中 an enlarged benevolent heart，基本可以确定两人对战争是不满的，也就对应第一题选项 B 中的 peaceful resolution。

• 选自 Khan College New SAT 阅读文章 Science Level 2 Passage 2

QUESTION 7 OF 11

The authors imply that the response of various officials to attempts to measure their countries' carbon stock through field surveys has been _____ .

A. unhelpful, because they fear that jobs for their countries' scientists will be lost

B. helpful, because their countries have invested significantly in technology to allow studies to expand.

C. helpful, because their countries stand to benefit from universal carbon data that the studies will uncover

D. unhelpful, because they do not make their countries' land holdings readily available for study

QUESTION 8 OF 11

Which choice provides the best evidence for the answer to the previous question?

A. lines 63～65 ("Due to the constancy of the underlying measurements, both field and LiDAR data could provide the needed information if they covered every hectare on Earth.")

B. lines 66～68 ("The surveys that do exist measure a tiny amount of actual forest, and so what might be verified is widely spaced.")

C. lines 68～70 ("And to avoid fraud and protect landowners, many governments keep their plot locations secret.")

D. lines 70～73 ("Satellite LiDAR data remain sparse, providing only extrapolated, coarse-resolution carbon estimates with very high uncertainties, and there is no prospect of wall-to-wall coverage in the near future.")

解析：第一题问的是各政府对本国碳储量测量是否 helpful，以及支撑的理由，带着这一问题我们一起来看第二题的选项。

第二题的选项 A、选项 B 和选项 D 说的都是这种调查的普遍特征及缺陷，并没有提到第一题中所问的 officials，因此排除。

选项 C 中的 governments 与第一题题干中的 officials 相对应，因此可以保留。

确定第二题选项后，我们发现该选项说的是很多政府为了保护土地所有者，并没有将很多 plot locations 公开,对应第一题选项 D 中的 do not make their countries' land holdings readily available for study。既然需要调查的数据没有公开,这一测量的可靠性也就大大下降,因此 unhelpful 也是正确的表述。所以我们可以确定第一题答案为 A,第二题答案为 C。

更多练习

• 选自 Khan College New SAT 阅读文章 Science Level 2 Passage 1

QUESTION 7 OF 11

The author implies that the results of Sinclair's study will enable future scientists to _____.

A. reverse the aging process
B. diagnose patients with age-related illnesses from an earlier age
C. create mice that are essentially immortal
D. more effectively treat a number of age-related illnesses

QUESTION 8 OF 11

Which choice provides the best evidence for the answer to the previous question?

A. lines 45~50 ("SIRT is short for sir-2 homologue—a well-studied protein that is known to extend yeast cell longevity.")
B. lines 50~54 ("According to Sinclair, all of the mammalian SIRT genes (and their proteins) are possible drug targets for therapies aimed at extending life, as well as staving off age-related illnesses, such as Alzheimer's disease, cancers and metabolic disorders, like diabetes.")
C. lines 59~62 ("Sinclair's lab is now working on developing what he calls a possible "supermouse" with elevated levels of NAMPT to see if it lives longer and is more disease-resistant than normal mice.")
D. lines 67~69 ("If the NAMPT-overexpressing mice are long-lived and disease resistant, that will provide more support for this idea.")

解析: 第一题问的是 Sinclair 的研究能够给未来科学家们提供什么,因此我们预设 evidence 中应有 Sinclair 研究的结果或影响。带着这种预设我们来看第二题的选项:选项 A 说的是 SIRT 的特征,可以排除;选项 B 说的是 the mammalian SIRT genes 的可能用途 (possible drug targets),可以保留;选项 C 提到 Sinclair 的实验室正在研究提高 NAMPT 是否能够在老鼠身上起到延长寿命和抵抗疾病的作用,而并非其研究的结果或影响,因此可以排除;选项 D 说道如果 Sinclair 的实验对象活得比普通老鼠要久,那么就能够给这一想法提供支持,的确是其实验的结果或作用,可以保留。

到目前为止,我们已经初步排除了两个错误答案,而剩下的两个则需要我们回看第一题中的选项,通过上下两题选项中的对应关系进行排除,选到正确答案。我们来看第一题的选项 A:reverse the aging process,在第二题保留的选项 B 和选项 D 中只说到 lives longer,但活得久并不意味着逆生长,因此选项 A 显然是错误的。选项 B 中的 diagnose(诊断)在第二题的选项 B 和选项 D 中同样找不到对应,选项 C 中的 immortal mouse 更是无中生有,因此我们可以确定第一题的答案是选项 D。而在确定了这一题的答案之后,我们再来看第二题的选项 B 和选项 D,检验哪个选项与上一题的答案 D 有更多的对应关系。我们先来看第二题的选项 B:句中的 are possible drug targets for therapies aimed at extending life, as well as staving off age-related illnesses 与第一题答案 D 中的 treat a number of age-related illnesses 完美对应。而在第二题的选项 D 中我们则找不到这种对应,更多的是一种假设成立后的 outcome。因此第一题的答案为 D,第二题的答案为 B。

综上,在面对循证题时,如果我们第一步无法确定第二题的答案,不妨按照如下步骤解题:

步骤一,看第一题题干,带着预设去看第二题。

步骤二,排除第二题中与第一题题干无关的选项。

步骤三,如果能够直接选到第二题的答案(即排除掉所有的错误答案),那么可以根据第二题中的关键词匹配确定第一题的答案。

步骤四(如果步骤三不成立),如果仅能排除部分第二题的选项,则回看第一题的选项,将第一题中与第二题保留选项完全无关的内容进行排除。

步骤五,确定第一题答案,并根据第一题中的关键词匹配确定第二题的答案。

• 选自 Khan College New SAT 阅读文章 Science Level 2 Passage 3

QUESTION 2 OF 11

It can reasonably be inferred from passage 1 that, in humans, the existence of mental time travel _____.

A. begins before birth

B. continues to develop throughout adulthood

C. is universal

D. is limited to certain populations around the world

QUESTION 3 OF 11

Which choice provides the best evidence for the answer to the previous question?

A. lines 1~2 ("The ability to travel mentally through time sets humans apart from many other species...")

B. lines 6~9 ("From memories of lost loves to expectations about forthcoming vacations, mental time travel(MTT)makes it possible to revisit the past and pre-experience the future.")

C. lines 9~11 ("Present across cultures and emerging early in childhood, MTT is believed to serve a pivotal function in human cognition.")

D. lines 11~15 ("When confronted with complex and challenging judgments, simulating future outcomes (i.e., prospection) on the basis of prior experience (i.e., retrospection) is a tactic that optimizes decision-making and behavioral selection.")

解析:第一题问的是 mental time travel 存在的特点,带着这一预设问题我们来看第二题的选项：

选项 A 说 mental time travel through time 是人类区别于其他很多物种的一种能力,的确是其特点,因此可以保留。

选项 B 说 MTT 可能出现的内容,可以保留。

选项 C 说的是 MTT 出现的范围、时间和地位,可以保留。

选项 D 说的是人们面对问题的应对方法,与 MTT 无关,因此排除。

我们接着来看第一题的选项：

选项 A 中的 begins before birth 显然与第二题选项 C 中的 emerging early in childhood 相悖,直接排除。

选项 B 中的 develops throughout the adulthood 在第二题的保留选项中均未得以体现,因此排除。

选项 C 中的 universal 对应第二题选项 C 中的 across culture,因此保留。

选项 D 中的 is limited to certain populations 在文中没有提到,因此排除。

而第二题选项 A 中的 set human apart from many other species 则意味着这种现象是动物所不具备的,并不能很好地体现出这一能力是全球化的。综上,我们可以确定第一题的答案为 C,第二题的答案为 C。

• 选自 Khan College New SAT 阅读文章 Science Level 4 Passage 2

QUESTION 4 OF 11

It can reasonably be inferred from Passage 1 that, for most bird species, there is a certain size at which they _____.

A. are unable to fly
B. require less energy when flying
C. are more likely to attack other animals
D. do not have to compete with other birds for food

QUESTION 5 OF 11

Which choice provides the best evidence for the answer to the previous question?

A. lines 1~4 ("For reasons that are not entirely clear, when animals make their way to isolated islands, they tend to evolve relatively quickly toward an outsized or pint-sized version of their mainland counterpart.")
B. lines 15~18 ("Though Haast's eagle could fly—and presumably used its wings to launch brutal attacks on the hapless moa—its body mass (10~14 kilograms) pushed the limits for self-propelled flight.")
C. lines 19~21 ("As extreme evolutionary examples, these island birds can offer insights into the forces and events shaping evolutionary change.")
D. lines 25~27 ("Their results suggest the extinct raptor underwent a rapid evolutionary transformation that belies its kinship to some of the world's smallest eagle species.")

解析：第一题问的是当大多数鸟类达到一定的大小之后，其体型对它们的影响。我们带着这一预设问题来看第二题的选项：

选项 A 说鸟类在独立岛屿时一般会进化成比较大型的鸟类，与第一题所问无关，因此排除。

选项 B 说尽管 Haast's eagle 能飞，但其体重给其飞行设了限，的确体型对鸟类有影响，因此保留。

选项 C 说的是对这些鸟类的研究的作用，与第一题所问无关，可以排除。

选项 D 说的是鸟类进化的问题，也与第一题所问无关，因此我们可以确定第二题的答案为 B。

我们接着来看第一题的选项：

选项 A 中的 unable 对应第二题选项 B 中的 pushed the limits。而第一题选项 B、C、D 中的 require less energy、attack other animals 和 compete for food 则均没有在第二题的选项 B 中有所体现。

综上，我们能够确定第一题的答案为 A，第二题的答案为 B。

- 选自 Khan College New SAT 阅读文章 Social Science Level 3 Passage 2

QUESTION 3 OF 11

The author implies that cyber-optimists view the use of new media technologies by minor parties as _____.

A. the only solution to the problem of unfairness in elections

B. useful tools that may be dangerous in the wrong hands because of the limited understanding most people have of them

C. platforms that have been carefully developed by politicians in order to serve the needs of special interests

D. an opportunity to make the electoral process more democratic

QUESTION 4 OF 11

Which choice provides the best evidence for the answer to the previous question?

A. lines 10~12 ("The first area of debate to be considered here is to what extent new media are able to put minor parties on a par with their larger counterparts, in terms of exposure.")

B. lines 12~14 ("Minor parties are able to make use of new media technologies to disseminate information and promote themselves.")

C. lines 18~20 ("However, cyber-pessimists argue that a higher number of communication channels does not equate with more democracy.")

D. lines 20~24 ("Both minor and major parties tend to approach the Internet in utilitarian terms, using it as a tool to provide information about policies rather than as a new platform for the promotion of interaction and interorganizational links.")

解析：第一题问的是 cyber-optimists 对于小党派使用新媒体的看法，因此第二题的选项中应出现小党派新媒体使用的后果或影响(同时,要注意第一题是推断题,所以在第二题中可能会出现帮助考生推断的逻辑桥梁,如对比、逻辑关系、比较等)。我们来看第二题的选项:

选项 A 更多讨论的是新媒体从何种程度上作用于其在公众面前的曝光率,与 new media technologies used by minor parties 的作用并没有直接的对应关系,因此排除。

选项 B 说少数党能够利用新媒体传播信息并推广自己,对应第一题所问,可以保留。

选项 C 阐述了 cyber-pessimists 的观点,认为更多传播渠道并不意味着更多民主。虽然在这句话中并没有直接提到第一题题干中 cyber-optimists 的观点,但因第一题是推断题,且在文中 cyber-optimists 和 cyber-pessimists 是明显有对立立场的,所以可以视作帮助推断的依据。而句中的 more democracy 也的确是 new media use 的结果,因此可以保留。

选项 D 中说的是 both parties,因此与第一题所问不符,可以排除。

我们接着来看第一题的选项:

选项 A 中出现了 only 这一绝对词,同时 solution to the problem of unfairness 在第二题的选项 B 和 C 中并没有对应,因此排除。

选项 B 中的 dangerous in the wrong hands 在第二题的选项中也没有对应,因此同样可以排除。

选项 C 中的 special interest 在第二题中没有对应(第二题选项 B 中的 disseminate information 和 promote themselves 是每一个党派都会有的正常需求),因此排除。

而选项 D 中的 more democracy 对应第二题选项 C。既然 cyber-pessimists 认为御用新媒体并不等同于更多民主,我们可以推断 cyber-optimists 与之持相反意见。

综上,我们可以确定第一题的正确答案是 C,第二题的正确答案是 D。

- 选自 Khan College New SAT 阅读文章 Social Science Level 3 Passage 2

QUESTION 6 OF 11

The author uses the Pew Research Center findings to imply that _____.

A. Barack Obama's victory was possible only because of social media usage

B. new media users influence real-world political events to some degree

C. cyber-optimists take an overly positive stance towards new media

D. cyber-pessimists do not understand how new media outlets are used

QUESTION 7 OF 11

Which choice provides the best evidence for the answer to the previous question?

A. lines 25~28 ("However, political cyber-optimists have criticized cyber-pessimists for being too extreme and maintain that new media might be the decisive element in pushing the democratic agenda of elections nowadays.")

B. lines 28~33 ("For instance, based on data published by the Pew Research Center, sixty-six percentage of social media users have participated in at least eight online political activities, such as encouraging people to vote or posting their comments on politics through social media.")

C. lines 33~37 ("Thus, Internet voters may shape election campaign agendas to some extent. The fact that Barack Obama obtained an electoral victory following a triumphant grassroots campaign and successful use of social media such as Facebook and MySpace is a case in point.")

D. lines 38~44 ("The third area of the debate to be considered here is the phenomenon of citizen (micro) blogging. Citizens are using social media, such as blogs, Facebook, Twitter, and Weibo, as a channel for participation in political discussions, aiming to directly or indirectly influence public concerns or even reshape the public agenda, promoting the democratic public sphere.")

解析：第一题问的是 Pew Research Center 的研究结果在文中的意义，是一种举例目的题，因此我们可以预设这一例子的使用是为了支撑之前的总起句或之后的总结句的。我们带着这个问题来看第二题的选项：

选项 A 说的是 cyber-optimists 的一种对于 new media 能够推进民主进程的乐观态度，可以作为一种总起的观点，予以保留。

选项 B 是 Pew Research Center 的研究结果，从中我们无法看出其在文中的意义，因此排除。

选项 C 中的 thus 明显预示着对于上文例子的总结，可以保留。

选项 D 已经开始讨论关于新媒体使用的第三个方面了，因此直接排除。

我们接着来看第一题的选项：

选项 A 中 only 是一个绝对词，同时第二题的选项 C 中也并没有说 Obama 的成功仅仅是因为 social media，因此排除。

选项 B 中 influence 可以对应第二题选项 C 中的 shape，而 real-world political events 对应 Obama 成功的例子，to some degree 则对应 to some extent，可以保留。

选项 C 中的 an overly positive stance 在第二题的选项中没有对应，因此排除。

选项 D 中的 do not understand 也同样没有对应（第二题选项 A 中只说到 cyber-pessimists 因太过极端的观点而受到抨击），予以排除。

综上，我们可以确定第一题答案为 B，第二题答案为 C。

• 选自 Khan College New SAT 阅读文章 Literature Level 2 Passage 3

QUESTION 7 OF 11

In the passage, Dan is characterized as someone who is _____.

A. honest B. foolish
C. stubborn D. distrustful

QUESTION 8 OF 11

Which choice provides the best evidence for the answer to the previous question?

A. lines 16~20 ("Dan had never told a conscious falsehood in his life he never even exaggerated.")

B. lines 21~22 ("Julius, beholding Dan's solemn face, was seized with a perfectly

irresistible desire to "fool" him.")
C. lines 34~35 ("Yet Dan, credulous as he was, could not believe it all at once.")
D. lines 53~54 ("Oh, but Dan had been easy!")

解析：第一题问的是 Dan 的性格，因此第二题应有 Dan 的行为、言语等方面的描述。我们来看第二题的选项：

选项 A 说 Dan 从来没有有意地撒过谎，也从来不会夸大其词、添油加醋，的确能够对应到 Dan 的性格，因此保留。

选项 B 说的更多的是 Julius 想要愚弄 Dan 的动机，尽管提到了 Dan's solemn face，但与 Dan 性格的直接对应关系不大，因此排除。

选项 C 说的是 Dan 对于 Julius 所告知信息的反应，可以对应性格，因此保留。

选项 D 说的是 Julius 对于 Dan 的看法，而非直接对于 Dan 的描写，因此排除。

我们来看第二题的选项：

选项 A 中的 honest 对应第二题选项 A 中的 never told a conscious falsehood 和 never seen exaggerated，因此保留。

选项 B 和 C 中的 foolish 和 stubborn 在第二题的选项中没有对应，因此排除。

选项 D 中的 distrustful 与第二题的选项 A 直接说反。选项 C 中也仅仅说到 Dan 较为轻信，并不能对应 distrustful，因此排除。

综上，我们可以确定第一题的答案为 A，第二题的答案为 A。

1.2.3 细节题

细节题目考察考生是否理解文章中的一段细节。细节题一般会给出行号信息，因此只需要回到原文用下划线或者括号划出相关语句，但答案很可能会出现在该关键句的前后两句中。试着用自己的话把关键句进行同义转述（paraphrase）。

题型特征：无明显特征。

技巧总览

1. 定位关键词

在绝大多数 SAT 阅读细节定位题中，都提供了行数（例如：In line 25，In lines 20~25），这样可供我们快速回到原文中去定位。

2. 利用顺序性

大多数情况下，SAT 阅读细节定位题给出的定位信息是遵循文章脉络的，即细节题是有顺序性的：第一道题的答案往往在文章前部，中间的细节题往往可以定位到文章中部，以此类推。

3. 根据关键句进行解题

定位题的解题线索均来自于定位部分的一小段上下文，甚至就来自于定位信息的本身，只要对于该关键句进行同义转述即可选出答案。

4. 排除错误答案

细节题型的干扰选项一般有以下几种形式：

• 以文章其他地方的叙述来混淆视听。

- 使用了与原文相近的词汇，却歪曲了原文的意思。
- 与原文的叙述相矛盾。
- 所说的内容在原文中并没有表述出来，而且也不能从原文的逻辑中推导出来。
- 使用了极端化的叙述。

真题模拟

- 选自 Khan College New SAT 阅读文章 Literature Level 2 Passage 1

QUESTION 6 OF 11

According to the passage, Catherine is "uncomfortable" because _____.

A. it is too noisy, crowded, and warm
B. they do not know anyone at the ball
C. they have arrived at the ball very late
D. their dresses are at risk of being torn

解析：我们根据定位词 uncomfortable、because（因果词）回到原文进行定位，可以看到如下这句话：

Line 31："How uncomfortable it is," whispered Catherine, "not to have a single acquaintance here!"

显然，句中 not to have a single acquaintance 就是 Catherine 感到不适的原因，对应选项 B 中的 do not know anyone at the ball，因此 B 为正确答案。

- 选自 Khan College New SAT 阅读文章 Science Level 3 Passage 3

QUESTION 2 OF 11

Based on the passage, the significance of Jeffrey Bada's experiment rests mainly on his success at _____.

A. confirming that the production of amino acids on early Earth was possible
B. explaining the critical function of nitrites to the production of amino acids
C. verifying the presence of nitrites in Earth's atmosphere as well as in comets and meteors
D. tracing the development of different types of amino acids on Earth

解析：我们根据题干中的 experiment 进行定位，回原文找其成功的意义，可以看到如下这句话：

Line 15：Their experiment produced a brown broth rich in amino acids, the building blocks of proteins.

这句话中的 produce 对应选项 A 中的 production，amino acids 与选项 A 中的表达完全对应，因此选项 A 是正确答案。

• 选自 Khan College New SAT 阅读文章 History Level 3 Passage 3

QUESTION 5 OF 11

The main relationship Hamilton highlights between the Northern and the Southern states is in terms of their _____.

A. incompatible philosophies B. disproportionate production
C. ongoing hostilities D. complementary economies

解析：我们根据 Northern 和 Southern 进行定位，回原文找它们之间的关系，可以看到如下这句话：

Line 27：Ideas of a contrariety of interests between the Northern and Southern regions of the Union, are in the Main as unfounded as they are mischievous.

从这句话中我们可以看到南北方之间的 contrariety of interests 是 unfounded 的，也就是没有根据的。因此 Hamilton 认为南北双方之间并没有相悖的利益，因此可以排除选项 A、B、C。那 complementary economies 的 evidence 又在哪里呢？我们可以根据选项进行定位，看到文中如下这句话：

Line 56：If the Northern and Middle states should be the principal scenes of such establishments, they would immediately benefit the more Southern, by creating a demand for productions; some of which they have in common with the other states, and others of which are either peculiar to them, or more abundant, or of better quality, than elsewhere.

这句话中的例子说明了南北双方在经济上的互补性，即：南方生产的作物满足了北方的需求，北方则对南方的经济做出了贡献，对应了选项 D 中的 complementary economies，因此 D 为正确答案。

更多练习

• 选自 Khan College New SAT 阅读文章 Science Level 2 Passage 5

QUESTION 4 OF 11

The author of Passage 1 claims that the Milky Way and the Andromeda Galaxy will collide mainly because _____.

A. they are bound together by gravity
B. they show signs of impact from billions of years ago
C. one is much denser than the other
D. one is a spiral galaxy and the other an elliptical galaxy

解析：我们根据题干中的关键词 the Milky Way 和 the Andromeda Galaxy 进行定位，同时注意到题目问的是原因，因此在阅读原文的过程中还要注意寻找因果词，可以看到如下这句话：

Line 16：Galaxies that had been pulled together before the universe began accelerating still have the chance to collide. Collectively they form overdense patches of the universe in which gravity still 20 reigns. In our neighborhood the Andromeda galaxy, our largest companion, is actually falling toward us, and we will have our first close encounter with it in just a few billion years' time.

在这段话中作者说明了 the Milky Way 和 the Andromeda Galaxy 即将会相撞的原因，即：这是两个在宇宙开始加速之前就 had been pulled together 的星系。其中 been pulled together 对应选项 A 中的 are bound together，而这一将两个星系捆绑在一起的力量则在第一段中就有所说明，即 gravity，因此可以选到正确答案 A。选项 B 中的 from billions of years ago 是无中生有的信息；选项 C 中 much denser 的比较在原文中无从体现；选项 D 中对于两个 galaxy 的特征归纳在文中，也并非作为碰撞的理由出现。

• 选自 Khan College New SAT 阅读文章 Science Level 4 Passage 3

QUESTION 10 OF 11

The scientists who conducted the study claim that the South American opossum _____.

A. descended directly from the kangaroo rather than the other way around
B. evolved in Australia at approximately the same time it evolved in South America
C. branched off from a common ancestor before the kangaroo did
D. migrated from South America to Australia through Gondwana

解析：我们根据题干中的 the South America opossum 进行定位，可以看到如下句子：

Line 67: They then searched through the DNA of 20 marsupial species—including the wallaroo, the common wombat, and the marsupial mole—to see which of these markers they carry. It hadn't been clear which lineage of marsupials split off first, but the new study found this first branch gave rise to the Didelphimorphia lineage, which includes several species of opossums of South America.

从这段话中我们可以看出，opossums of South America 对应题干中的 the South America opossum，而这一分支则是包含在 Didelphimorphia lineage 中的。又从第一句话中分析得知，产生（give rise to）这一分支的是 marsupial species（包括 wallaroo、the common wombat 和 the marsupial mole）。但在这段话中我们并没有看到选项 B 中的有关进化时间的比较，因此可以排除选项 B。也没有看到选项 D 中的 Gondwana 一词，因此同样排除。而选项 A 和选项 C 中均出现了 kangaroo，根据相似选项容易得出正确答案的规律，我们将 kangaroo 作为定位词再次回到该段落进行定位，可以看到如下句子：

Line 74: All of today's Australian marsupials appear to have branched off later, all arising from a single lineage that branched from a South American microbiotherian-like ancestor to form varied forms—kangaroos, the rodent-like bandicoots, and the Tasmanian devil.

从这句话中我们得出 kangaroos 和现今 Australian marsupials 的祖先都是一样的，对应选项 C 中的 common ancestor，而 branched off later 则对应选项中的 before，因此选项 C 为正确答案。而选项 A 与原文所述相反。

• 选自 Khan College New SAT 阅读文章 Science Level 4 Passage 1

QUESTION 11 OF 11

The author acknowledges that the study leaves which question unanswered?
A. When marsupials arrived in Gondwana
B. When the kangaroo split off from the Didelphimorphia lineage
C. Why the oppsum and the kangaroo have a similar genetic structure
D. Why marsupials split into two distinct branches

解析：我们根据关键词 question unanswered 进行定位，又因为该题是最后一题，依据阅读细节题顺序性的原则，答案应该对应到文章最后一部分，很快就能在最后一段的第一句中找到 question unanswered 的对应词 mystery——

Line 80：It's still a bit of a mystery, Nilsson, Schmitz, and colleagues say, why the marsupial family tree sorted out so cleanly. They found two distinct branches …

句中的 sorted out 对应 split，而 two distinct branches 则原词对应，因此可以选到正确答案 D。其他选项均为无中生有。

• 选自 Khan College New SAT 阅读文章 History Level 2 Passage 1

QUESTION 5 OF 11

According to the passage, the main objection to immediate passage of the Constitution is that it is _____ .
A. unpopular   B. despotic   C. imperfect   D. partisan

解析：我们根据 main objection 进行定位，发现整个第三段（In these sentiments …）都在叙述反对通过宪法的理由，其中包含了大量 because 引导的排比句。为了找到其核心总结句，我们跳过排比句，直接看段尾句，可以看到如下句子：

Line 32：For when you assemble a number of men to have the advantage of their joint wisdom, you inevitably assemble with those men, all their prejudices, their passions, their errors of opinion, their local interests, and their selfish views.

显然，这句话中的 prejudices、errors of opinion、local interests 和 selfish views 都能对应到选项 D 中的 partisan。而选项 C 只是反对理由中的具体一点，因此是一个迷惑选项，不具有总结性。

• 选自 Khan College New SAT 阅读文章 History Level 2 Passage 1

QUESTION 9 OF 11

Which choice best describes Jefferson's attitude towards socio-economic conditions in France?
A. He approves of the king's policies on most, but not all, issues.
B. He sees France as an isolated case, with unique conditions not applicable to other

countries.

　　C. He is affronted at the few opportunities given to the poor.

　　D. He is pleased that the United States does not experience the same conditions as France.

解析：我们根据题干中的 Jefferson、socio-economic conditions、France 进行定位，可以看到如下句子：

　　Line 37：The property of this country is absolutely concentered in a very few hands, having revenues of from half a million of guineas a year downwards ... But after all these comes the most numerous of all the classes, that is, the poor who cannot find work.

　　其中 property 和 classes 对应题干中的 socio-economic conditions，而 the poor who cannot find work 则可以对应选项 C 中的 the few opportunities given to the poor。选项 A 是一个无关选项，因为在发表自己的论点时，Jefferson 并未提到国王；而用本段段首句中对应的内容就可以排除选项 B，可以看到如下句子：

　　Line 33：This little attendrissement, with the solitude of my walk led me into a train of reflections on that unequal division of property which occasions the numberless instances of wretchedness which I had observed in this country and is to be observed all over Europe.

　　句中 to be observed all over Europe 明显与选项 B 中的 isolated 相反。

　　选项 D 中的 the United States 在文章最后才有所提及，且作者也并未在文中体现出 pleased 的情绪，因此我们可以选到正确答案 C。

• 选自 Khan College New SAT 阅读文章 History Level 2 Passage 4

QUESTION 6 OF 11

Which choice best explains Roosevelt's praise for the workers?

　　A. He appreciates them for their determination to prove the United States' superiority.

　　B. He admires them for their success at rekindling national pride.

　　C. He respects them for their selfless service to the nation.

　　D. He values them for their contribution to the world's economy.

解析：我们根据细节题顺序性原则，以及关键词 Roosevelt's praise 进行定位，可以看到如下句子：

　　Line 44：So you men here, in the future, each man of you, will have the right to feel, if he has done his duty and a little more than his duty right up to the handle in the work here on the Isthmus, that he has made his country his debtor; that he has done more than his full share in adding renown to the nation under whose flag the canal is being built.

　　这段话中的 more than his full share 对应选项 C 中的 selfless service；选项 A 中的 superiority 并没有在文中有所体现；选项 B 中的 admire 和 success 虽然正确，但 rekindling national pride 是无中生有的信息（并未提到 national pride 在之前有所低迷，因此 rekindle 一词是没有根据的推断）；选项 D 中的 the world's economy 并非全文重点，也没有提到，因此可以排除错误选项，选到正确答案 C。

1.2.4 推断题

推断题的特征非常明显,即在题干中会出现 imply、infer、suggest、most likely、probably true、assumption 等词。推断题的考法是需要根据文章信息和逻辑,推理出一种可能的情况,所推理出的内容(选项内容)在文章中并没有明述。

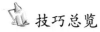 技巧总览

1. 通过关键词定位

在做推断题的时候,首先可以通过关键字找定位句,然后进行推理,在99%的情况下,选项是不会完全重复原文信息的,这样等于没有考察推断能力。

2. 通过细节描写推断

这类推断题往往在 literature 文中出现,要求考生通过文中人物的对话或神态、动作的描写而对人物的性格或对某人某事的态度进行一定程度的推理。因此,做好充足的心理态度形容词汇储备也是应考的一大法宝。

3. 通过比较进行推断

文中往往会出现 unlike、compare、similar、differ、contrary、same、as … as … 等表示比较的信号词,要求考生通过与文中已知事物性质、特点的比较进行推理。常见的比较推理涉及时间推理及特征推理。

4. 避免过度推理

很多考生思维较为跳跃,往往在推理的过程中会出现跨步骤推理的现象。因此,要注意在范围上不要随意扩大,也不要缩小,在内容上不能随意增加或减少。

5. 通过文章态度进行判断

如果本句及上下句没有答案,则答案应与本段的态度一致。

6. 排除错误答案

如果通过对原文的正向理解(没有正向印证)解不出题来,则采取"非正即反"的原则,找到原文当中表示态度或定性的形容词或副词等,找其相反的意思。

真题模拟

• 选自 Khan College New SAT 阅读文章 Social Science Level 3 Passage 5

QUESTION 8 OF 11

It can reasonably be inferred from the discussion of the thousands of acres of Sequoia Forest (lines 37～39 "For the thousands of acres of Sequoia forest outside of the reservation and national parks, and in the hands of lumbermen, no help is in sight.") that _____.

A. lawmakers have been slower to protect natural sites in California than in other states

B. laws have already been established to protect natural sites in some areas of the state
C. citizens have won legal battles against loggers and milling companies
D. the Sequoias in Calaveras Grove have been classified as endangered

解析：这道题已经给了行数提示，因此我们根据这句话进行推断。这句话说在伐木工人的手上，没法看到对于 Sequoia Forest 的任何帮助。通过这句话中的参照物，即在 the reservation and national parks 之外的 Sequoia Forest，我们可以作出比较。既然保护区外的森林是 no help，那么显然保护区内是有一定的保护措施的，对应选项 B 中 in some areas of the state。选项 A 将加州与其他州进行了比较，而我们并不能从该句中看出这一比较，因此排除。选项 C 中的 citizens 在这一句中更无体现。选项 D 中的 classified as endangered 也没法合理推断出，因此可以选到正确答案 B。

• 选自 Khan College New SAT 阅读文章 Literature Level 2 Passage 2

QUESTION 11 OF 11

It can be inferred that Tom is "in something of a temper" because he _____.
A. feels exasperated by Julius' tendency to gossip
B. believes Adelia doesn't want to marry him
C. is agitated that he is the subject of a rumor
D. has too many errands to run in Valley View

解析：我们通过题干中引号内的关键词回到原文进行定位，可以看到如下句子：
Line 77：He drove home at last in what was for him something of a temper. How on earth had that fool story started? With such detailed circumstantiality of rugs and quilts, too?

从两个连续的问句我们可以推断出 Tom 不满的情绪，对应选项 C 中的 be agitated。而这种情绪是这个 fool story 引起的，与选项 C 中的 rumor 对应，因此可以确定正确答案 C。

• 选自 Khan College New SAT 阅读文章 Literature Level 3 Passage 2

QUESTION 3 OF 11

Based on lines 7~8 ("I was young and ignorant, and I envied my brother"), it can reasonably be inferred that the narrator's perspective is one of _____.
A. critical reflection upon his past views
B. objective analysis of his prior actions
C. fond recollection of his recent adventures
D. regretful remembrance of his past mistakes

解析：通过句中 young and ignorant，我们可以推断出主人公对于从前的自己并非赞扬有加，因此可以把 C 选项排除。而在这句话之后的 envied my brother 则说明了自己 ignorant 的表现，对应选项 A 中的 past views，而非选项 B 中的 actions，也并不能推断出之前的嫉妒是一种 mistake，因此确定正确答案 A。

更多练习

• 选自 Khan College New SAT 阅读文章 Literature Level 4 Passage 3

QUESTION 9 OF 11

It can be inferred that Lily does not want to go to Sherry's because she _____.

A. thinks she will not find the company there engaging
B. is worried she won't make it to her destination on time
C. is sure that it will be too hot and crowded to enjoy
D. believes she is too old to enjoy the atmosphere

解析：我们根据 Sherry's 回到原文进行定位，可以看到如下内容：

Line 57："Shall we go over to Sherry's for a cup of tea?"

She smiled assentingly, and then made a slight grimace.

"So many people come up to town on a Monday—one issue to meet a lot of bores. I'm as old as the hills, of course, and it ought not to make any difference; but if I'm old enough, you're not," she objected gaily. "I'm dying for tea—but isn't there a quieter place?"

分析这段对话，我们发现当 Seldon 邀请 Lily 去 Sherry's 喝杯茶后，Lily 先是 smiled assentingly，代表她对这一提议的认可，紧接着却又 made a slight grimace，与之前的态度形成了对比。那么我们可以推测，Lily 在下文中对 Seldon 提议的回应里一定会有这一态度转变的解释，即本题的答案。在她的回答中，one is sure to meet a lot of bores 对应选项 A 中的 will not find the company there engaging。选项 B 和选项 C 无中生有。选项 D 是混淆选项，虽然 Lily 的确说她 old enough，但这显然是一句谦辞，因此可以选到正确答案 A。

• 选自 Khan College New SAT 阅读文章 Literature Level 4 Passage 3

QUESTION 5 OF 11

It can be reasonably inferred that Fenella's father "looked tired and sad" (line 48) because he _____.

A. has a long journey ahead of him
B. feels concerned about his family's tickets
C. is going to miss his family
D. senses something is wrong

解析：我们回到原文，可以看到如下内容：

Line 43："And your other tickets?"

Grandma felt for them inside her glove and showed him tips.

"That's right."

He sounded stern, but Fenella, eagerly watching him, saw that he looked tired and sad.

"Miaoooooo!" The second whistle blared just above their heads, and a voice like a cry shouted, "Any more for the gangway?"

在这段对话中,我们发现在 Fenella's father 询问 grandma 船票是否带齐时,grandma 的回答是肯定的,说明他并不需要为此担忧,因此可以排除选项 B。而选项 A 与原文信息相反,并非 Fenella 的爸爸要出远门,而是他去为家人送别,同样可以排除。而在这段话中,作者将催促人们上船的叫声比作 a cry,体现出一种悲伤的情绪,对应句中 sad 一词。结合当时送别的情景,我们就能推断出 Fenella's father 是因为家人即将离去而 looked tired and sad,即选项 C。选项 D 似是而非,在原文中其实并没有相关信息,因此选项 C 为正确答案。

- 选自 Khan College New SAT 阅读文章 Science Level 2 Passage 5

QUESTION 3 OF 11

It can reasonably be inferred from the passage that, like a bar magnet, the nucleus of a hydrogen atom _____.

A. spins in a counter-clockwise direction
B. is responsive to external magnetism
C. attracts metallic substances
D. is surrounded by electrons

解析:我们根据题干中的关键短语 like a bar magnet 回到原文进行定位,同时要注意题干中的 the nucleus of a hydrogen atom 在第一段中就有其解释(a single proton),因此这可以作为关键词在文中的同义替换,可以看到如下内容:

Line 7: In this respect it behaves like a small bar magnet. Under normal circumstances, these hydrogen proton "bar magnets" spin in the body with their axes randomly aligned. When the body is placed in a strong magnetic field, such as an MRI scanner, the proton's axes all lined up. This uniform alignment creates a magnetic vector oriented along the axis of the MRI scanner.

这段话的意思是,在普通情况下,hydrogen proton 的排列是 random 的,而当被放置在一个强磁力场中时,其排列就会变得 uniform。在这里我们找到了一组明显的反义词(random-uniform),而往往出现这种对比关系的地方会是考点(因为这为考生提供了推断的依据,类似于实验中的对照组)。在这组关系里,唯一的变量就是 hydrogen proton 放置的位置,因此这种排列上的变化正说明了磁力场对 hydrogen proton 的影响,对应选项 B。选项 A、C 和 D 都没有形成合理推断的依据,因此选项 B 为正确答案。

- 选自 Khan College New SAT 阅读文章 Social Science Level 2 Passage 1

QUESTION 4 OF 11

The authors imply that the "first group of initiatives" would primarily _____.

A. change the measurement approach to encompass only social factors
B. take both positive and negative factors into account universally
C. show the positive effects of modernization in its new measurements

D. shift the measurement of GDP so that it is calculated per capita

解析：我们根据题干中的关键词 first group of initiatives 回到原文进行定位可以看到如下内容：

Line 20：The first group of initiatives tries to deal with the downsides of the GDP by attempting to fix the indicator itself...

句中的 downsides 对应选项 B 中的 negative factors，说明这一种方法旨在将 GDP 未能反映出的经济发展的 downsides 也纳入考虑范围，因此选项 A 中的 only social factors 过于绝对，选项 C 只提到了 positive effects，明显偏离这一方法的核心，而选项 D 则完全是无中生有，因此均可以排除。而选项 B 中的 positive 本身就是 GDP 所能反映出来的，因此我们可以推断出选项 B 为正确答案。

• 选自 Khan College New SAT 阅读文章 History Level 4 Passage 1

QUESTION 8 OF 11

According to Passage 2, the failure of the Senate to pass the Civil Rights Act would suggest that the _____.

A. public is not yet ready for the passage of civil rights legislation
B. Senate is either uninterested in or unable to enact reform
C. Senate recognizes that civil rights issues cannot be dealt with all at one time
D. President of the United States must lead the way in enacting reform

解析：我们根据题干中的 failure 和 pass 进行定位，可以看到如下内容：

Line 71：But, insofar as the majority leader is concerned, he must state to the Senate that it would be a tragic error if this body, as a whole, were to elect the closed-eyes course of inaction.

That course, Mr. President, would disclose a cavalier disinterest or a legislative impotence on this issue, and either would be completely inconsonant with the serious domestic situation which now confronts us.

第一句中的 inaction 对应 failure... to pass，而第二句中的 disinterest 对应选项 B 中的 uninterested，句中的 legislative impotence 则对应 unable to enact reform，因此可以选到正确答案 B。选项 A 是张冠李戴的信息，原文并没有说是民众缺乏通过这一议案的准备。选项 C 中的 cannot be dealt with all at one time 并非天河 Senate 意识到的，而是作者意识到的。选项 D 中的 President 则答非所问，与 Senate 无关，均可以排除。

• 选自 Khan College New SAT 阅读文章 Literature Level 2 Passage 3

QUESTION 11 OF 11

The passage suggests that Edna views Mademoiselle Reisz as someone who is _____.

A. intimidating but profound
B. cold and uninviting
C. motherly and inspiring
D. misguided but irresponsible

解析：我们回到原文找 Edna 对 Mademoiselle Reisz 的态度，可以看到如下内容：

Line 2：Of course Edna would like to hear Mademoiselle Reisz play; but she feared it would be useless to entreat her.

Line 59：She trembled, she was choking, and the tears blinded her.

Line 66："Well, how did you like my music?" she asked. The young woman was unable to answer; she pressed the hand of the pianist convulsively. Mademoiselle Reisz perceived her agitation and even her tears.

从这几句话中我们看出，虽然 Mademoiselle Reisz 对他人的态度是不屑一顾，但对 Edna 是区别对待、格外和蔼的，而 Edna 在听完 Mademoiselle Reisz 的演奏后深受感触地哭泣也从侧面印证了她对 Mademoiselle Reisz 的尊敬之情。结合第一句中的关键词 fear，我们可以判断出 Edna 对 Mademoiselle Reisz 的态度是非常矛盾的，既认为 Mademoiselle Reisz 是一个让人 fear 的女性，又对她关照有加，因此我们可以排除完全正向或完全负向的形容词，如选项 B、C 和 D。而 fear 则对应选项 A 中的 intimidating，agitation 则对应 profound，所以正确答案即是选项 A。

1.2.5 修辞目的题

众所周知，无论是在文学作品或研究著作中，英语语言的运用都是多种多样的。为了突出人物性格或证明一种论点，作者都会独具匠心地引入大量修辞手法。这些修辞手法一方面丰富了文章的层次结构，另一方面更突出了作者逻辑的缜密，而鉴别这些修辞手法是我们阅读、分析文本中必备的能力之一。

在 College Board 针对 New SAT 的官方指南中对这一类题型明确写道：You will have to think abstractly about the text—not just understanding what the text says but also what the author is trying to achieve.

因此，这类修辞目的题与我们之前所提到的、考察文本信息的细节题有所区别。修辞目的题更多的是考察作者写作的意图，仅仅分析文本本身所传递的信息是不够的。

题目特征如下：

- The author refers to ××× in order to…
- In lines Y, the author refers to ××× primarily in order to…
- Which best describes the function of the statement in lines Y?
- Why does the author mention…
- … mention … in order to …

 技巧总览

1. 非小说类(Non-Fiction)文章

无论是议论文还是说明文，我们首先要把握的是这篇文章到底想要告诉我们什么信息。而这类文章的根本目的就是论证或反驳某个观点，或者发表对某事物的看法，再者就是向读者介绍某种事物或观点。因此，文章中提到的具体的细节、例子和事实通常是为了这样的观点服务的。

2. 观察例子所在位置

回顾议论文或说明文的写作手法我们不难发现，一般这类文章的结构均为"总—分"或

"总—分—总"结构。因此,如果修辞手法出现在文章开始,往往是为了引入话题或主旨;如果出现在文章中部,则是为了对某种观点进行佐证。出现在文章最后的修辞则通常是对全文的总结,或者话锋一转,对文中话题提出建议或指出其不足之处。

3. 定位前后的总起、总结句

既然是为了说明 general statement,那么我们只需在这一例子的前后找到总起句或总结句即可。做题的时候,首先看例子,再看前后的总起句或总结句,对其进行同义改写;如果没有答案,则选择和本段主旨相关的句子;如果依然没有答案,则选择与全文主旨相关的答案。

4. 小说类(Fiction)文章

小说的首要目的不再是证明观点,而是讲故事,即通过人物的特点和人物之间的关系、矛盾展开情节与故事,然后在故事中继续体现人物的特点。所以小说中文本的目的可能会比较多样。比如,提供人物所在的文化环境和社会环境可能是为情节的进行提供背景;描述人物外貌可能是为了体现人物的性格;开篇的句子可能是为了提供一个视角和观点,为后文情节的展开做出铺垫;人物的内心描写可能是为了体现人物的想法和情绪等。所以需要考生对文章具体的文本进行分析。编者在此为考生整理了以下较为常见的修辞手法:

(1) 插入语(Parenthesis)

通常以插入语、括号或破折号作为标志,对之前的内容进行补充说明。这种修辞手法通常有以下两种作用:

- To provide some contexts for a statement.
- To creates the effects of immediacy.

(2) 增益(Amplification)

通常以重复之前词语的形式出现,并在重复的基础上增加更为细节化的描述,如添加形容词,或用定语从句进行进一步修饰等。这种修辞手法通常有以下作用:

To make sure the reader realizes its importance or centrality in the discussion.

(3) 设问(Hypophora)

以提出问题并在文中作出解答的形式出现,常见的例子是在段首提出设问,并用该段对这一问题进行回答并论证。这种修辞手法通常有以下作用:

- To help to maintain curiosity and interest of readers.
- To introduce material of importance, but which the reader might not have the knowledge or thought to ask for himself.
- To act as a transitional or guiding device to change directions or enter a new area of discussion.

(4) 反问(Rhetorical Question)

与设问的修辞手法不同,反问的答案往往非常明显。其主要作用如下:

- To draw a statement from the facts at hand.
- Its implied answer will lead to further discussion.
- To be used for effect, emphasis, or provocation.

(5) 夸张(Hyperbole)

对文中的信息进行明显的夸大处理。其主要作用如下:

- To evoke strong feelings or create an impression which is not meant to be taken literally.

• To show how really different it is from something supposedly similar to which it is being compared.

（6）悖论(Paradox)

通常由两种截然相反的观点组成，如大文豪狄更斯在《双城记》中的名句：It was the best of times, it was the worst of times. 又如：It is a paradox that such a rich country should have so many poor people living in it. 其主要作用如下：

• To make statements that often sum up the main ideas of the work.

• To emphasize or arouse reader's attention to the main ideas of the work.

（7）类比(Analogy)

对部分相似的两种事物、人或理论进行比较。类似的修辞手法有明喻(simile)、暗喻(metaphor)及拟人(personification)等，其特征虽然有所不同，但主要作用有相似之处。其主要作用如下：

• To explain or clarify some unfamiliar or difficult idea or object by showing how the idea or object is similar to some familiar one.

• To establish the pattern of reasoning by using a familiar or less abstract argument which the reader can understand easily and probably agree with.

（8）用典(Allusion)

在文中引用古代故事或有来历出处的词语。其主要作用如下：

• To explain something difficult by reminding readers of something they are familiar with.

（9）讽刺(Sarcasms/Irony)

用含蓄的褒义词语来表示其反面的意义，往往是正话反说或反话正说。其主要作用如下：

• To provoke the reader into thinking harder and analyzing a situation.

• To emphasize a central idea.

真题模拟

• 选自 Khan College New SAT 阅读文章 History Level 2 Passage 2

QUESTION 10 OF 11

The main purpose of Franklin's comment about the French lady (line 19) is most likely to _____.

A. ridicule the arrogance of the lady
B. allude to the division of public opinion
C. point out a universal truth in a humorous way
D. convey the futility of further dispute

解析：我们根据行数提示回到原文进行定位，可以看到如下内容：

Line 17：But though many private persons think almost as highly of their own infallibility as of that of their sect, few express it so naturally as a certain French lady, who in a dispute with her sister, said "I don't know how it happens, Sister but I meet with no body but myself, that's always in the right"...

很显然,在 French lady 与其姐妹的对话之前是 Franklin 的 comment,也是 French lady 这一例子所支撑的总起句。这句话中说很多人都认为他们是永远正确的,但没有一个像这位法国女士说得那么明显罢了,因此可以对应选项 C 中的 universal truth,而这位法国女士话语中的"I don't know how it happens"则体现出一种幽默感,对应选项 C 中的 in a humorous way。作者并没有轻视这位女士(选项 A),而是想通过这位女士的话对自己之前的 statement 进行论证。

- 选自 Khan College New SAT 阅读文章 Social Science Level 2 Passage 1

QUESTION 2 OF 11

In the first paragraph, the reference to Simon Kuznets mainly serves to _____.

A. emphasize that the GDP is a respected and valid tool

B. underscore a common concern about the GDP by citing a critic

C. clarify an abstract point about the development of the GDP by mentioning its creator

D. strengthen the argument that the GDP does not adequately measure well-being

解析:我们根据 Simon Kuznets 回到原文进行定位,可以看到如下内容:

Line 10:However, this measure was never meant to be a measure of the welfare of nations (as its creator Simon Kuznets warned in the 1930s) and so there is growing skepticism about the GDP's usefulness as a measure of national well-being.

Simon Kuznets 出现在括号中,是一种 Parenthesis 的修辞手法,其作用是为之前的论点提供背景,而之前的主句中说这一测量方法(GDP)从来就不是用来测量国家福利的,对应选项 D 中的 not adequately measure well-being,因此可以确定选项 D 为正确答案。

- 选自 Khan College New SAT 阅读文章 Literature Level 2 Passage 2

QUESTION 9 OF 11

Lines 57~58 ("At this point Julius and Danny drop out of our story, and Young Thomas enters.") serves mainly to _____.

A. introduce a new character and setting to the story

B. show the resulting impact of the rumor Julius started

C. add a surprising twist to the story

D. create a sense of suspense for the outcome of the prank

解析:这个句子明显是过渡句,说一个主人公退场了,而另一个主人公则登场了。选项 A 中的 a new character 与文章内容不符,因为 Young Thomas 在上文就在 Julius 和 Dan 的对话中出现过,可以排除。同时,这句话并未真正说明 Julius 所开玩笑的后果,同样可以排除。选项 C 看似正确,但往下文读我们就会发现该 rumor 是按照 Julius 预想的那样得以传播的,而并没有出现选项 C 中的 surprising twist。最后,联想到过渡句的修辞作用(引出下文,总结上文),我们可以对应到选项 D 中的 outcome of the prank。同时因为这句话中并未对 outcome 进行详细说明,更为读者设置了一种悬念,即选项 D 中的 a sense of suspense。因此可以选到答案 D。

更多练习

- 选自 Khan College New SAT 阅读文章 Science Level 3 Passage 2

QUESTION 6 OF 11

The "rock", line 29, primarily serves to provide an example of an item that _____.

A. is closer in substance to a metabolically active sack than is a virus
B. functions exactly like a virus
C. has a form similar to that of a virus
D. is easy to classify, unlike a virus

解析:我们回到原文,可以看到如下句子:

Line 27:But a spectrum may exist between what is certainly alive and what is not. A rock is not alive... But what about a seed? A seed might not be considered alive. Yet it has a potential for life, and it may be destroyed. In this regard, viruses resemble seeds more than they do live cells.

题干中的 rock 所在的句子并不能说明什么问题,因此我们需要往前找作者举例子的目的,即该例子支撑的总起句。在第一句话中,作者称在 alive 和 not alive 之间可能是存在明确界限的,而 rock 显然就是 not alive。但到这里我们仍然看不出该例子与题目中四个选项里的关键词 virus 之间的关系。因此我们往下看,发现在这个例子中又出现了一个 but 引导的转折,与 rock 形成对比。这句话说 seed 可能是 not alive,却有 a potential for life。而 viruses 又 resemble seeds,意味着在 viruses 是否为 alive 的问题上也很难下定论,与 rock 这样明确 not alive 的物体形成对比,因此对应选项 D 中的 unlike。选项 A 中的 metabolically active 无中生有;选项 B 中的 functions 也没有提到;选项 C 中的 similar 更是无关紧要的。因此我们可以选到正确答案 D。

- 选自 Khan College New SAT 阅读文章 Science Level 3 Passage 5

QUESTION 3 OF 11

The word "Now" (line 5) primarily serves to _____.

A. highlight the recent nature of the scientific findings
B. interject a note of informality into a formal passage
C. suggest that humans no longer perform the activity mentioned in the first paragraph
D. create a sense of urgency in the passage

解析:我们回到原文,可以看到如下内容:

Line 5:Now, salicylic acid may also offer relief to crop plants by priming their defenses against a microbial menace known as "potato purple top phytoplasma".

这句话显然是一个论述，又因为这是一个段首句，因此我们可以通过找到该段落与上一段之间的逻辑关系来确定 now 在文中的意义。在上一段中，作者写道——

Line 1：Willow trees are well-known sources of salicylic acid, and for thousands of years, humans have extracted the compound from the tree's bark to alleviate minor pain, fever, and inflammation.

在这句话中，我们发现 for thousands of years 可以与题干中的 now 形成对比。在过去几千年中，人们都是用 salicylic acid 来减轻疼痛、缓解发烧等症状的；而现在人们发现 salicylic acid 还能 offer relief to crop plants，对应选项 A 中的 recent nature。选项 B 中的 informality 和选项 D 中的 urgency 在这句话中无从体现。选项 C 是一个迷惑选项，在这个选项中出现了与第一段落的联系，粗心的考生很容易直接就选择了这个答案。但是仔细分析选项我们就会发现，在文中并没有说 humans no longer perform the activity，人们现在用 salicylic acid 继续缓解疼痛的可能性仍然存在，作者并没有就该问题进行说明，因此该选项是一个无中生有的推断，可以排除，选到正确答案 A。

- 选自 Khan College New SAT 阅读文章 Science Level 4 Passage 2

QUESTION 7 OF 11

In Passage 2, the image of a barcode mainly serves to _____.

A. trivialize the complexity of a particular research practice
B. use a familiar concept to communicate an idea
C. question the novelty of a scientific phenomenon
D. inject a note of levity into an otherwise serious argument

解析：我们根据题干中的 barcode 回到原文进行定位，可以看到如下句子：

Line 43：Because of its age, the DNA was highly fragmented, so they focused in on three DNA "mini barcodes"—small sections of DNA which are unique for most bird species.

在关键词 barcodes 之后，作者很快就用 small sections of DNA which are unique for most birds species 对其进行了补充的解释说明，这是科学文中一个常见的手法，即用生活中常见的例子来类比一个较为复杂的、不为人们所熟知的概念，往往在这种情况下，被类比的例子一定能够体现概念的一个或多个特征。只要我们能找到对应的特征，就可以基本确定作者是在运用这种 familiar concept 类比的修辞手法了。而在这句话中，对应的特点就是 unique。因为 barcodes 指的是商品的条形码，而每个商品的条形码显然都是独一无二的，因此可以对应 unique，选到答案 B。选项 A 中的 trivialize 和选项 D 中的 levity 两种手法在科学文中都是比较少见的，文中也显然没有体现；选项 C 中的 quesiton 与文章内容不符，因此均可排除。

- 选自 Khan College New SAT 阅读文章 Social Science Level 4 Passage 1

QUESTION 6 OF 11

The author's discussion of the "Green Revolution" in paragraph 4 (line 34) primarily serves to _____.

A. provide a positive contrast to the dire predictions made elsewhere in the passage

B. reassure readers that unexpected agricultural inventions mean they have nothing to fear

C. offer evidence that alternative outcomes to overpopulation and famine are possible and likely

D. warn readers not to be lulled into a false sense of security by a small number of beneficial agricultural advances

解析：我们根据句中的行数提示回到原文，可以看到如下句子：

Line 32：But the 1970s surprised population watchers. Instead of being a period shadowed by calamitous famine, the new crop strains introduced by the "Green Revolution" (especially grains such as rice, wheat, and maize) caused a dramatic increase in the global production of cereals, the main source of energy in the global diet.

这个例子说的是 the "Green Revolution" 所带来的新作物使全球粮食产量大大提升，其总起句是这段的段首句。但我们发现段首句是由转折词 but 引导的，显然是与上一段形成转折的逻辑关系。因此我们需要回看上一段的最后一句——

Line 30：George H. W. Bush was also sympathetic to this view, prior to becoming vice president in 1981.

在这句话中出现了代词 this view，因此我们还需往上找这一观点的具体内容——

Line 17：By the 1960s, concerns of a mismatch between global population and global food supply peaked—expressed in books such as Paul Ehrlich's 1968 *The Population Bomb*.

综上，全球人口的增速会远超 food supply，导致供不应求。但 1970 年代的 Green Revolution 带来了粮食产量的大幅提升，因此 surprised population watchers 对应选项 A 中的 positive contrast 和 dire prediction。选项 B 中的 reassure 并未提到，且 have nothing to fear 也过于绝对和主观。选项 C 中的 alternative outcomes 虽然提到了，但并非 famine 的 outcome，且作者也没有 imply 这些结果是 likely 的，因此是答非所问的选项。选项 D 中的 warn 与原文所表达的内容不符合，因此正确答案为 A。

- 选自 Khan College New SAT 阅读文章 History Level 4 Passage 1

QUESTION 2 OF 11

In Passage 1, the quotation from Victor Hugo mainly serves to _____.

A. reveal that Victor Hugo would lend his support to civil rights reform

B. illustrate the author's assertion that the Senate is eager to enact civil rights reform

C. offer criticism of the United States military for failing to enforce civil rights reform

D. introduce the author's argument that civil rights reform should not be postponed

解析：我们根据题干中的 Victor Hugo 回到原文进行定位，可以看到如下句子：

Line 9：It is said that on the night he died, Victor Hugo wrote in his diary, substantially this sentiment：

"Stronger than all the armies is an idea whose time has come."

The time has come for equality of opportunity in sharing in government, in education, and in employment. It will not be stayed or denied. It is here.

显然，在引用的雨果名言中，whose time 对应下文中的 the time，即争取平等机会的时机。而这一时机不仅已经到来了，并且就如雨果所言，是 stronger than all the armies。因此，作者是化用了雨果的话来显示争取平等权益的时刻已经到来、不应被拖延，对应选项 D 中的 should not be postponed。选项 A 是无中生有的选项。选项 B 与文章明显说反。选项 C 中的 offer criticism 和 military 也并没有在这一段落中有所提及，因此可以排除错误选项，得到正确答案 D。

- 选自 Khan College New SAT 阅读文章 Literature Level 2 Passage 2

QUESTION 5 OF 11

The description of Mrs. Allen in lines 26~30 primarily serves to _____.

A. illustrate her unruffled personality　　B. highlight her scrupulousness

C. show her expensive tastes　　D. establish her sense of vanity

解析：我们根据行数提示回到原文进行定位，可以看到如下句子：

Line 26：Mrs. Allen congratulated herself, as soon as they were seated, on having preserved her gown from injury. "It would have been very shocking to have it torn," said she, "would not it? It is such a delicate muslin. For my part I have not seen anything I like so well in the whole room, I assure you."

从 Mrs. Allen 的话语中，我们能够看出她对于自己衣着的重视：congratulated herself ... on having preserved her gown from injury、shocking to have it torn、delicate muslin 中的 preseve、injury、shocking 等词一般都是用来描述极为珍贵的物品的，而 Mrs. Allen 却用这些词汇来描述她的裙子。显然，作者在这里用了一种夸张的语气体现出这条晚礼服对她的重要性，凸显 Mrs. Allen 性格中的虚荣和空虚，对应选项 D 中的 sense of vanity。选项 A 中的 unruffled personality 明显与原文说反。选项 B 中的 scrupulousness 指的是小心谨慎，是较为褒义的描述，与文中所体现的作者情感不符。选项 C 中的 expensive tastes 是无中生有的推断，因此我们可以选到正确答案 D。

1.2.6　对比题

在对比题中，考生需要对两篇就同一主题发表看法的文章进行比对（往往在 social science 或 history 中出现），这两篇文章一定相互支持、相同和求异，即：第二篇完全反对第一篇的观点，或第二篇部分反对第一篇的观点，或第二篇完全支持第一篇的观点。对于 New

SAT 阅读中的对比题,要点是快速通读文章,把握文章的主要内容和主要观点。

题型特征如下:
- What choice best describes the relationship between the two passages?
- What's the author's view in Passage Ⅰ on line X in Passage Ⅱ?
- Passage Ⅰ and Ⅱ shared which trait?
- Is the main conclusion presented by the author of Passage Ⅱ consistent with the one described in Passage Ⅰ?

技巧总览

对比阅读的难点之一是文章内部观点的交叉度高,往往作者叙述他人观点和论据中间交织着自己的观点和论据,并且作者的论点常常不是开门见山。做这类题目的方法如下:
- 阅读每篇 passage 的段首句和全文最后一句,找到重复出现的关键词,以理清文章大意。
- 找到每个观点对应的人物——是作者的观点? 还是作者引用的他人的观点?
- 抓住作者态度,开始做题。
- 如果题干中问的是两篇文章针对某一方面的观点,那么需要用定位词回到原文进行定位,而不能直接通过两位作者的态度进行做题,因为文中可能出现部分反对或部分支持的情况,需要具体分析。

真题模拟

- 选自 Khan College New SAT 阅读文章 History Level 2 Passage 4

QUESTION 10 OF 11

How would the author of Passage 2 most likely respond to the author's ideas about consolidation of power in lines 33~41 ("Independent of the opinions of many great authors, that a free elective government cannot be extended over large territories, a few reflections must evince, that one government and general legislation alone, never can extend equal benefits to all parts of the United States: Different laws, customs, and opinions exist in the different states, which by a uniform system of laws would be unreasonably invaded. The United States contain about a million of square miles, and in half a century will, probably, contain ten millions of people.") of Passage 1?

A. With disapproval, because they contradict his argument.
B. With approval, because they help support his argument.
C. With caution, because while the authors agree on some points, they do not agree on all.
D. With support, because they bring up a new idea about the debate.

解析: 我们首先通过阅读两篇文章的首尾句了解其 main idea——

Passage Ⅰ: Our object has been all along, to reform our federal system, and to strengthen our governments, but a new object now presents.

Different laws, customs, and opinions exist in the different states, which by a uniform system of laws would be unreasonably invaded. The United States contain about a million of square miles, and in half a century will, probably, contain ten millions of people.

Passage Ⅱ: Let us now consider how far [the new system] is consistent with the happiness of the people and their freedom.

All that part, therefore, of the new system, which relates to the internal government of the states, ought at once to be rejected.

显然,两篇文章的作者对于联邦体制的建立都持反对态度,从 be unreasonably invaded、ought at once to be rejected 等词组中就能看出。同时,两人都认为因为美国疆域辽阔、人口复杂,联邦政府只会损害人们的利益。这从第二篇的倒数第二句中就能看出——

Line 71: The idea of an uncompounded republic, on an average, one thousand miles in length, and eight hundred in breadth, and containing six millions of inhabitants all reduced to the same standard of morals, or habits, and of laws, is in itself an absurdity, and contrary to the whole experience of mankind.

其中对于美国疆域、人口的描述与题干中的 that a free elective government cannot be extended over large territories 对应,而态度也一直 cannot be extended over 对应 be rejected。因此可以选到正确答案 B。

• 选自 Khan College New SAT 阅读文章 History Level 3 Passage 2

QUESTION 9 OF 11

The author of Passage 2 claims that public liberty is threatened by the majority's abuse of power. This claim most clearly contrasts with the claim in Passage 1 that public liberty is threatened by _____.

A. an ambitious minority
B. an overactive majority
C. an immoral citizenry
D. an oppressive government

解析: 我们通过关键词 public liberty 回到 Passage Ⅰ中进行定位,可以看到如下句子:

Line 1: Guard with jealous attention the public liberty. Suspect every one who approaches that jewel. Unfortunately, nothing will preserve it but downright force.

这句话的意思是"(我们要)精心守护公共自由,警惕任何一个觊觎它的人。不幸的是,只有彻底的权力才能保护它。一旦你放弃这种绝对权力,毋庸置疑,你将会被摧毁"。但这句话中并没有说到底是什么危害了 public liberty。因此我们需要根据选项进行定位,选项 A 中的 ambitious minority 在文中有所出现——

Line 20: Take longer time in reckoning things; revolutions like this have happened in almost every country in Europe; similar examples are to be found in ancient Greece and ancient Rome—instances of the people losing their liberty by their own carelessness and the ambition of a few.

很显然,在这句话中作者阐述了人民失去 liberty 的原因是 their own carelessness 以及 the ambition of a few。其中 a few 对应选项 A 中的 minority,因此选项 A 是正确答案。

• 选自 Khan College New SAT 阅读文章 History Level 3 Passage 2

QUESTION 11 OF 11

The authors of both passages would agree that the Constitution could provide _____.

A. public liberty
B. moral restraint
C. increased democracy
D. legal protection

解析：通读两篇文章的首尾句我们可知第一篇文章的作者对于联邦体制是反对的态度，并认为其会损害 public liberty。而第二篇文章的作者则认为联邦体制应该受到推崇。题干中的 the Constitution 明显是联邦体制的代表，因此，若要找到第一篇文章作者对于 the Constitution 的正面评价，则之前必定会出现 although、thought、despite、in spite of、while 等让步、转折的信号词。因此我们可以根据这类信号词回到第一篇文章中进行定位，可以看到——

Line 26：I acknowledge that licentiousness * is dangerous, and that it ought to be provided against：I acknowledge, also, the new form of government may effectually prevent it；yet there is another thing it will as effectually do—it will oppress and ruin the people.

这句话中的 yet 充当了转折词，大意为：尽管 licentiousness（道德的缺失）是危险的，也应该被阻止，新政府也能有效阻止这一点，但新政府也会镇压人民。因此作者承认联邦政府能够 prevent licentiousness，对应选项 B 中的 moral restraint，因此选项 B 为正确答案。

更多练习

• 选自 Khan College New SAT 阅读文章 Science Level 4 Passage 1

QUESTION 9 OF 11

The authors of both passages would likely agree that, in the field of evolutionary biology, genetic testing is _____.

A. a helpful tool when trying to decipher the evolutionary history of a species
B. only possible if the DNA sample originated in a cell's mitochondria
C. useful when analyzing the evolutionary history of birds, but not other animals
D. an imperfect practice that should only be used as a last resort when analyzing a species' evolution

解析：我们根据题干中的关键词 evolutionary biology 和 genetic testing 回到两篇文章中进行定位，可以看到如下内容：

Passage Ⅰ：

Line 19：As extreme evolutionary examples, these island birds can offer insights into the forces and events shaping evolutionary change. In a new study, Michael Bunce et al. compared ancient mitochondrial DNA extracted from Haast's eagle bones with DNA sequences of 16 living eagle species...

从这句话中我们可以看出，对 island birds 的研究至于 evolutionary biology 的意义重大（从 offer insights ... shaping evolutionary change 的表述中就能看出）。而这一研究采取用的方法则是比对 DNA，即是题干中的 genetic testing，因此 Passage Ⅰ 的作者在 genetic testing 与 evolutionary biology 的问题上态度是正面的。

Passage Ⅱ：

Line 36：The mysterious spotted green pigeon (Caloenas maculata) was a relative of the dodo, according to scientists who have examined its genetic make-up.

这篇文章的首句写道，科学家们根据检测 Caloenas maculata 的 genetic make-up（对应题干中的 genetic testing），得出了有关于该生物的结论。换言之，genetic testing 是支持这一结论的有力证据，因此 Passage Ⅱ 作者的态度应该也是正面的。

综上，我们可以排除选项 B、C 和 D。选项 B 中的 only possible 太过绝对。选项 C 中的 not other animals 是随意推断，在这篇文章中并没有说这一研究方法仅对鸟类适用。选项 D 中的 impractical 是明显的贬义词，与作者观点不符。而选项 A 中的 decipher 对应文中一系列有关鸟类进化历史的讨论，a useful tool 则对应作者态度，因此可以选到正确答案 A。

- 选自 Khan College New SAT 阅读文章 Science Level 2 Passage 3

QUESTION 9 OF 11

The authors of passage 1 and passage 2 would likely agree about which of the following characteristics of mental time travel?

A. That it is similar to the concept of semantic memory
B. That it is a sophisticated cognitive ability
C. That it is present throughtout the animal kingdom
D. That it can affect the positioning and movement of the body

解析：我们根据 mental time travel 回到两篇文章中进行定位，而由于 Passage Ⅰ 全篇都在讨论 mental time travel，因此我们先看 Passage Ⅱ 中出现这一概念的句子——

Passage Ⅱ：

Line 65：The ability to represent oneself and one's action in the mind's eye—both in the past [and] in the future—is what scientists refer to as "mental time travel."

这是 Passage Ⅱ 中唯一提到 mental time travel 的句子，而在这个句子中我们可以排除选项 A 和选项 D，因为无论是 similar to the concept of semantic memory，还是 affect the positioning and movement of the body，在该句中都无从体现。而选项 B 和选项 C 都是两个相对中性的评价，不能贸然地仅通过这一句话就排除。接着我们再来看 Passage Ⅰ 中有关于 mental time travel 的表述——

Line 1：The ability to travel mentally through time sets humans apart from many other species, yet little is known about this core cognitive capacity.

显然，该句中的 sets humans apart from many other species 与选项 C 中的 present throughout the animal kingdom 说反,因此选项 C 也可以排除,从而确定正确答案 B。

• 选自 Khan College New SAT 阅读文章 Science Level 3 Passage 1

QUESTION 11 OF 11

Which type of evidence is used extensively in passage 2 but not passage 1?
A. Summaries of scholarly opinion.　　B. References to historical sources.
C. Judgments of renowned scientists.　　D. Results from a study.

解析:自然科学类、社会科学类的文章时常会出现这类题型,为了节约时间,我们可以在初读原文的过程中就在文中所运用到的研究手法旁做记号,便于之后的查找和整理。我们先来看 Passage Ⅰ——

在 Passage Ⅰ中,我们没有找到一处对于科学研究的引用(results from a study),或对于某位著名科学家言论的判断(judgments of renowned scientists),因此可以初步确定正确答案会在选项 C 和选项 D 中。我们接着来看 Passage Ⅱ——

Line 49:"Our study found these common massive galaxies do form by mergers," Van Dokkum explains.

这是科学家在介绍其研究结果,对应选项 D 中的 results 和 study,因此可以选到正确答案 D。选项 C 是迷惑选项,虽然提到了 Pieter van Dokkum,但文中他的身份是 astronomer,且也没有选项中说的 scientists(复数),因此可以排除。

• 选自 Khan College New SAT 阅读文章 Science Level 4 Passage 2

QUESTION 10 OF 11

Which of the following is a main idea in Passage 1 but NOT in Passage 2?
A. The dodo originated from "island hoppers" that lived on islands in Southeast Asia.
B. The dodo and the Haast's eagle both originated from a common ancestor that lived in New Zealand.
C. The geographic isolation of a species can significantly affect the average size of that species over time.
D. Bones and other types of connective tissues are excellent sources of DNA for genetic testing.

解析:由于题干中关键词较少,我们可以根据选项中的关键词回到原文找到关键句,并先排除肯定错误的答案。显然,定位词最为明显的是选项 A,因此我们根据"island hopping"回到原文进行定位——

Line 36:The mysterious spotted green pigeon (Caloenas maculata) was a relative of the dodo, according to scientists who have examined its genetic make-up. The authors say their results, published in the open access journal *BMC Evolutionary Biology*, support a theory that both birds are descended from "island hopping" ancestors.

这是 island hopping 一词在两篇文章中唯一一次出现,且出现在 Passage Ⅱ 中,显然与题干所问相反,可以直接排除选项 A。我们紧接着用选项 B 中的 New Zealand 进行定位——

Line 11: New Zealand also had avian giants, now extinct, including the flightless moa, an ostrich-like bird, and Haast's eagle (Harpagornis moored), which had a wingspan up to 3 meters.

虽然在 Passage Ⅱ 中并没有提到 New Zealand，但 dodo 的祖先却并非来自 New Zealand。我们从下面的句子中就可以看出——

Line 5: Perhaps the most famous example of an island giant—and, sadly, of species extinction—is the dodo, once found on the Indian Ocean island of Mauritius. When the dodo's ancestor (thought to be a migratory pigeon) settled on this island...

显然 dodo 的祖先是在印度洋的一个岛上定居的，并非大洋洲的 New Zealand，因此选项 B 与原文事实不符，可以排除。

选项 D 中的 bones 一词显然更好定位，因此我们先来看选项 D——

Line 21: In a new study, Michael Bunce et al. compared ancient mitochondrial DNA extracted from Haast's eagle bones with DNA sequences of 16 living eagle species to better characterize the evolutionary history of the extinct giant raptor.

从这句话中我们可以看出，选项 D 中的 tissues 一词并未出现，且这明显是一个细节信息，因此选项 D 也可以排除。

而既然是 Passage Ⅰ 的主旨，文章的首尾句中一定会有所体现——

Line 1: For reasons that are not entirely clear, when animals make their way to isolated islands, they tend to evolve relatively quickly toward an outsized or pint-sized version of their mainland counterpart.

在这句话中 iolated islands 对应选项 C 中的 geographic isolation，outsized or pint-sized version 则对应 affect the average size of that species。而这一主旨在 Passage Ⅱ 中则无从体现，因此我们可以选到正确答案 C。

同时，面对这样主旨型的对比题，考生可以考虑直接判断两篇文章的主旨，直接进行正向选择。

• 选自 Khan College New SAT 阅读文章 History Level 2 Passage 4

QUESTION 5 OF 11

Both passages argue that individual states _____.

A. would not benefit from following the same set of laws
B. are becoming too unwieldly due to lack of one unifying government
C. run the risk of engaging in multiple civil wars over time
D. duplicate functions and should be eventually consolidated

解析：我们根据题干中的 individual states 回看两篇文章——

Passage Ⅰ：

Line 37: Different laws, customs, and opinion exist in the different states, which by a uniform system of laws would be unreasonably invaded.

句中的 a uniform system of laws 对应选项 A 中的 the same set of laws，而 be unreasonably invaded 则对应 will not benefit。

Passage Ⅱ：

Line 71：This new system is, therefore, a consolidation of all the states into one large mass, however diverse the parts may be of which it is to be composed.

句中的 the parts 对应题干中的 individual states，而 a consolidation of all the states into one large mass 则对应选项 A 中的 the same laws。同时 however 一词体现出作者不满的情绪，对应 will not benefit，因此我们可以确定正确答案为选项 A。选项 B 的态度明显说反。选项 C 是通过新政的结果，而非现实情况。选项 D 则同样与原文信息相反，均可排除。

- 选自 Khan College New SAT 阅读文章 History Level 4 Passage 1

QUESTION 10 OF 11

In their discussion of civil rights, the authors of Passage 1 and Passage 2 both claim that the issue _____.

A. must be addressed, although they would prefer to postpone debate until a later time

B. will not be resolved by the bill under discussion, though the bill remains necessary

C. must be dealt with immediately through direct action in the Senate

D. should not be discussed until controversy surrounding the bill has died down

解析：这其实是一道变相考察全文主旨的题目，因此我们会看两篇文章的中心句即可——

Passage Ⅰ：

Line 13：The time has come for equality of oppotunity in sharing in government, in education, and in employment. It will not be stayed or denied. It is here.

从这句话中我们可以看出作者对认为 civil rights issue 就是当下最为重要的问题，不该被 postponed，因此我们可以排除选项 A 和选项 D。

Passage Ⅱ：

Line 82：In these circumstances, I cannot believe that this Senate will abdicate its constitutional responsibilities.

这句话中同样能够体现出 urgency，对应选项 C 中的 immediately。而选项 B 仅在 Passage Ⅱ 中被提到，因此可以排除选项 B，选到正确答案 C。

1.2.7 主旨题

主旨题包括全文主题和局部主题。在 College Board 针对 New SAT 的官方指南中对主旨题进行了一下说明：Proposition questions require you to think about the "big ideas" in the passage and how they can be refined to better clarify and structure the writer's message.

题型特征如下：

- Mainly discuss.

- Main idea/Point/Purpose/Title/Topic.
- Answer which of the following questions.

技巧总览

1. 针对段落大意或全文行文结构提问

- 如果问的是某段的大意,则通过阅读该段落的第一句、第二句和最后一句,并对这三句进行归纳、同义改写即可得出答案。
- 如果问的是全文的大意,则阅读文章每一段的段首句和全文最后一句即可。
- 如果问的是全文的行文结构,则在阅读文章段首句和全文最后一句的基础上,更多关注转折词(but、however、yet、nevertheless、in spite of、despite)所引导的句子。

读者要注意以下问题:

- 段首句中反复出现的词一定是文章的重点或主要概念,需要在答案中有所体现。
- 转折词往往意味着之前的句子只不过是过渡句,而转折词引导的句子才是该段落的核心所在。
- 不要过分纠结于细节信息,如果该信息只在文中出现过一次,那么并不能代表文章的主旨。

2. 排除错误选项

- 选项含有明显属于文中细节的内容,而缺少全文的写作对象(例如只出现过一次的人物、例子等)。
- 选项表述明显与作者的全文态度相悖。
- 选项超出了文章的范围,过于宽泛。
- 选项过于极端,超出了文章的叙述范畴。

3. 一般最后做

在做完有行数提示以及循证题之后,我们自然会对全文有一个较为全面的了解,这个时候再来选择全文主旨就会更有效率,正确率也会更高。

真题模拟

- 选自 Khan College New SAT 阅读文章 Science Level 2 Passage 3

QUESTION 1 OF 11

Over the course of passage 1, the main focus shifts from _____.

A. a scientific study about mental time travel to an example of how humans use mental time travel in their daily lives

B. a description of the evolution of mental time travel to an evaluation of its limitations in humans

C. an explanation of mental time travel to a description of a study about its neurological basis

D. an argument in support of the existence of mental time travel to a counter-argument refuting its existence in humans

解析：我们回到原文阅读一下全文段首句和最后一句，可以看到如下内容：

• The ability to travel mentally through time sets humans apart from many other species, yet little is known about this core cognitive capacity.（我们对于 travel mentally through time 知之甚少。）

• A core facet of conscious experience is that one's mind periodically wanders from the here-and-now.（对于 travel mentally through time 进行介绍。）

• However, remarkably little is known about the actual process of MTT and how it impacts people's behavior.（说明 MTT 会影响 travel mentally through time，但我们对其具体机制缺乏了解。）

• The results revealed that the temporal locus of MTT did indeed influence the direction of people's movements—whereas retrospection was accompanied by significant backwards sway, prospection yielded postural movement in an anterior direction.（同上。）

很明显，文章前半部分是对 travel mentally through time 进行了介绍，而后转向了对 MTT——一个影响因素的研究，最后指出该研究的成果和局限性，因此对应选项 C。

- **选自 Khan College New SAT 阅读文章 Social Science Level 3 Passage 3**

The author's central claim is that _____.
A. cuteness provokes the same emotional responses around the world
B. encountering a cute object may lead to changes in behavior
C. studies of cuteness should include tasks that involve social interaction
D. cuteness elicits feelings of tenderness in test subjects

解析：我们回到原文阅读一下全文段首句和最后一句，可以看到如下内容：

• Cute things are popular worldwide.（引入"可爱的事物"这一主题。）

• Cute objects are assumed to be characterized by baby schema.（引出 baby schema 和 cute objects 之间的关联。）

• Sherman, Haidt, and Coan reported two experiments showing that performance in a fine motor dexterity task (the children's game Operation) improved after participants viewed a slide show of cute images (e.g., puppies and kittens) more than after they viewed images that were not as cute (e.g., dogs and cats).（说明看到 cute objects 对人可能会产生的影响。）

• Recently, Sherman and Haidt challenged the classic view that cuteness is an innate releaser of parental instincts and caregiving responses.（对于 cute objects 如何影响人类的理论的新见解。）

• If cuteness-induced behavioral carefulness is caused by a heightened motivation for social interaction, the effect would not be found in simple perceptual-cognitive tasks that do not suggest social interaction.（说明看到 cute objects 所引发的行为与其他 social interaction 的区别。）

这些句子中反复出现的关键词有：cuteness、behavior、response、cause 等，对应选项 B 中的 encountering a cute object 以及 changes in behavior，因此可以选到正确答案 B。

• 选自 Khan College New SAT 阅读文章 History Level 2 Passage 3

QUESTION 1 OF 11

The main purpose of the speech is to _____.
A. stress the importance of the Panama Canal
B. report on the progress of the Panama Canal
C. inspire the Panama Canal workers
D. proclaim the Panama Canal project a success

解析: 我们回到原文阅读一下全文段首句和最后一句——

• It was without precedent for a president to leave the United States, but this work is without precedent. (说明该项目的伟大。)

• I want to say this word to you men,—right through,—to all of you who are engaged in the work of digging this canal, whether you are here as superintendent, foreman, chief clerk, machinist, conductor, engineer, steam-shovel man (and he is the American who is setting the mark for the rest of you to live up to, by the way), whoever you are, if you are doing your duty, you are putting your country under an obligation to you just as a soldier who does his work well in a great war puts the country under an obligation to him. (对项目实施者进行鼓励、赞扬。)

• Those were the things they talked about a good deal of the time. (过渡句,主要重点在之后转折词引导的句子上。)

• But when the war was done—when they came home, when they looked at what had been accomplished—all those things sank into insignificance, and the great fact remained that they had played a part like men among men; that they had borne themselves so that when people asked what they had done of worth in those great years, all they had to say was that they had served decently and faithfully in the great armies. (尽管并非段首句,但转折词引导的句子非常重要。用战争来类比运河项目,突出能为该项目效力是一件荣耀的事,同样是对项目实施者进行鼓励。)

• You are doing the work the like of which has not before been seen in the ages, a work that shall last through the ages to come, and I pledge to you as President of the United States, every ounce of support and help and assistance, that it is in my power to give you, so that we together, you backed by the people of the United States, may speedily bring this greatest of works to a triumphant conclusion. (突出美国对他们的支持,再次鼓励项目参与者。)

纵观全文,我们发现这些句子都在突出这些项目实施者有多么伟大,并对他们进行鼓励,告诉他们美国人民对他们的支持,因此可以对应选项 C 中的 inspire,选到正确答案 C。

更多练习

• 选自 Khan College New SAT 阅读文章 History Level 3 Passage 2

QUESTION 1 OF 11

The author's central claim in the passage is that _____.
A. since bordering nations are naturally competitive, the U. S. should avoid division
B. since Britain is experienced in the art of war, the U. S. should imitate their policies
C. since the North is stronger than the South, multiple confederacies are inevitable
D. since unity is critical to the future of the U. S., a new form of government is needed

解析： 我们回到原文阅读一下全文段首句和最后一句——

• The history of Great Britain is the one with which we are in general the best acquainted, and it gives us many useful lessons.（用美国人熟悉的英国历史事件为下文的讨论做铺垫。）

• Should the people of America divide themselves into three or four nations, would not the same thing happen?（用反问句的形式引出作者对于 dividing America into several parts 的观点。）

• The most sanguine advocates for three or four confederacies cannot reasonably suppose that they would long remain exactly on an equal footing in point of strength, even if it was possible to form them so at first; but, admitting that to be practicable, yet what human contrivance can secure the continuance of such equality?（用 but 引导的转折句突出作者观点。）

• Whenever, and from whatever causes, it might happen and happen it would, that any one of these nations or confederacies should rise on the scale of political importance much above the degree of her neighbors, that moment would those neighbors behold her with envy and with fear.（重申作者观点。）

• The North is generally the region of strength, and many local circumstances render it probable that the most Northern of the proposed confederacies would, at a period not very distant, be unquestionably more formidable than any of the others.（叙述 confederacies 对于北方的威胁。）

• They who well consider the history of similar divisions and confederacies will find abundant reason to apprehend that those in contemplation would in no other sense be neighbors than as they would be borderers; that they would neither love nor trust one another, but on the contrary would be a prey to discord, jealousy, and mutual injuries; in short, that they would place us exactly in the situations in which some nations doubtless wish to see us, viz., formidable only to each other.（but 之后作者重申自己的观点，即分裂国家是 formidable 的。）

从上述这些句子中，我们可以看出作者对于 new government 的态度是非常负面的，因此可以直接排除选项 C(multiple confederacies are inevitable)和选项 D(a new form of government is needed)。选项 B 中的 Britain 仅仅在第一段中出现,因此并非全文中心。通过排除错误选项我们可以得出正确答案 A,同时选项 A 在以下句子中也能够找到对应——

Line 23:Hence, like most other bordering nations, they would always be either involved in disputes and war, or live in the constant apprehension of them.

既然 bordering nations 很可能会有 disputes and war,美国就更应该 avoid division,对应选项 A。

- 选自 Khan College New SAT 阅读文章 History Level 3 Passage 2

QUESTION 2 OF 11

The main purpose of the passage is to _____.

A. warn against a potential form of government
B. argue for a particular diplomatic decision
C. defend a current form of government
D. explain a way in which science relates to politics

解析:我们回到原文阅读一下全文段首句和最后一句——

- The history of Great Britain is the one with which we are in general the best acquainted, and it gives us many useful lessons.(用美国人熟悉的英国历史事件为下文的讨论做铺垫。)

- Should the people of America divide themselves into three or four nations, would not the same thing happen?(用反问句的形式引出作者对 dividing America into several parts 的观点。)

- The most sanguine advocates for three or four confederacies cannot reasonably suppose that they would long remain exactly on an equal footing in point of strength, even if it was possible to form them so at first; but, admitting that to be practicable, yet what human contrivance can secure the continuance of such equality?(用 but 引导的转折句突出作者观点。)

- Whenever, and from whatever causes, it might happen and happen it would, that any one of these nations or confederacies should rise on the scale of political importance much above the degree of her neighbors, that moment would those neighbors behold her with envy and with fear.(重申作者观点。)

- The North is generally the region of strength, and many local circumstances render it probable that the most Northern of the proposed confederacies would, at a period not very distant, be unquestionably more formidable than any of the others.(叙述 confederacies 对北方的威胁。)

- They who well consider the history of similar divisions and confederacies will find abundant reason to apprehend that those in contemplation would in no other sense be neighbors than as they would be borderers; that they would neither love nor trust one another, but on the contrary would be a prey to discord, jealousy, and mutual injuries; in short, that they would place us exactly in the situations in which some nations doubtless wish to see us, viz., formidable only to each other.（but 之后作者重申自己的观点，即分裂国家是 formidable 的。）

综上，作者的主要观点是反对 diving America into several parts，因此选项 B 中的 diplomatic decision 和选项 D 中的 science 与文义不符，可以排除。选项 C 是一个迷惑选项，看上去似是而非。但仔细看首尾句我们发现，作者并没有对现行政府发表自己的看法，只是在警告如果采取一种新的政治架构就可能会引起 disputes，这与选项 A 中的 warn against 显然更为对应，因此该题的正确答案为选项 A。

• 选自 Khan College New SAT 阅读文章 History Level 2 Passage 4

QUESTION 1 OF 11

The main purpose of Passage 1 is to _____.

A. provide information about plans to reform the federal system
B. highlight inconsistent government principles across multiple states
C. introduce plans for a new kind of government that differs greatly from the current one
D. question a proposal to consolidate power in a single federal system

解析： 我们回到原文阅读一下全文段首句和最后一句——

• Our object has been all along, to reform our federal system, and to strengthen our governments, but a new object now presents.（引出作者想要讨论的议题，即 a new object。）

• The confederation was formed when great confidence was placed in the voluntary exertions of individuals, and of the respective states; and the framers of it, to guard against usurpation, so limited and checked the powers.（介绍 confederation plan。）

• Touching the federal plan, I do not think much can be said in its favor…（点明作者观点，即反对 federal plan。）

• Independent of the opinions of many great authors, that a free elective government cannot be extended over large territories, a few reflections must evince, that one government and general legislation alone, never can extend equal benefits to all parts of the United States…（阐明反对 federal plan 的理由。）

• The United States contain about a million of square miles, and in half a century will, probably, contain ten millions of people.（再次重申反对 federal plan 的理由。）

从上述这些关键句中我们可以看出，作者对 federal plan 是明确反对的，因此选项 A 中的 provide information 和选项 C 中的 introduce plans 都太过于中性，可以排除。作者的确提到了 individual states 有各自的法律、习俗，但并非批评这种个性，因此选项 B 中的 inconsistent 一词的态度有误。而选项 D 中的 question 一词与作者态度一致，consolidate power in a single federal system 则对应上述第四句中的 a free elective government cannot be extended over large territories，因此该题正确答案为选项 D。

- 选自 Khan College New SAT 阅读文章 History Level 2 Passage 1

QUESTION 3 OF 11

Over the course of the passage, the main focus shifts from _____.
A. a description of the locale to a broader discussion of principles
B. a humorous anecdote to a position on a popular U. S. debate
C. an analysis of the king's situation to an analysis of an unemployed person's
D. Jefferson's experiences in France to Madison's experiences in the U. S.

解析: 我们回到原文阅读一下全文段首句和最后一句——

• Seven o'clock, and retired to my fireside, I have determined to enter into conversation with you; this [Fontainebleau] is a village of about 5000 inhabitants when the court is not here and 20000 when they are, occupying a valley through which runs a brook, and on each side of it a ridge of small mountains most of which are naked rock. (介绍文章背景情况,引出下文事件发生的地点。)

• This being the first trip, I set out yesterday morning to take a view of the place. (为下文遇见乡村老妪做铺垫。)

• This little attendrissement, with the solitude of my walk led me into a train of reflections on that unequal division of property which occasions the numberless instances of wretchedness which I had observed in this country and is to be observed all over Europe. (从典型事例延伸到对于一个现象的观点阐述。)

• I am conscious that an equal division of property is impracticable. But the consequences of this enormous inequality producing so much misery to the bulk of mankind, legislators cannot invent too many devices for subdividing property, only taking care to let their subdivisions go hand in hand with the natural affections of the human mind. (第二句是转折词 but 引导的,因此更为关键,意在引出作者对于 division of property 的观点。)

• If, for the encouragement of industry we allow it to be appropriated, we must take care that other employment be furnished to those excluded from the appropriation…(通过阐述他国的例子,警醒美国切勿重蹈覆辙。)

综上,作者首先通过法国见到的事例(a description of the local)引出自己的观点,然后将其延伸扩展到更大范围的讨论中(a broader discussion of principles),因此对应选项 A。选项 B 中的 humorous 与原文不符,且文中也并未提到在美国的 debate。选项 C 中的 king's situation 和 an unemployed person 均是细节,并非文章中心内容。选项 D 中的 Madison's experience in the U. S. 在文中也完全没有提到,因此均可排除,选到正确答案 A。

- 选自 Khan College New SAT 阅读文章 History Level 4 Passage 2

QUESTION 1 OF 11

The main purpose of the passage is to _____.
A. delineate the course of industrial progress

B. question the practicality of democratic ideals
C. encourage support for individual liberties
D. highlight the uselessness of social reform

解析：我们回到原文阅读一下全文段首句和最后一句——

• It will not probably be denied that the burden of proof is on those who affirm that our social condition is utterly diseased and in need of radical regeneration. （引出下文想要讨论的议题。）

• When anyone asserts that the class of skilled and unskilled manual laborers of the United States is worse off now in respect to diet, clothing, lodgings, furniture, fuel, and lights; in respect to the age at which they can marry; the number of children they can provide for; the start in life which they can give to their children, and their chances of accumulating capital, than they ever have been at any former time, he makes a reckless assertion for which no facts have been offered in proof. （通过除去长难句中的并列修饰成分，我们不难发现这个句子的核心在于最后——he makes a reckless assertion，这是作者对于他人的反驳。）

• Nine-tenths of the socialistic and semi-socialistic, and sentimental or ethical, suggestions by which we are overwhelmed come from failure to understand the phenomena of the industrial organization and its expansion. （支撑作者观点，指出反对的声音源于他们对于工业扩张和发展的不了解。）

• The advance of a new country from the very simplest social coordination up to the highest organization is a most interesting and instructive chance to study the development of the organization. （从正面支撑自己的论点。）

• Now the intensification of the social organization is what gives us greater social power. （重申观点。）

• Our life is bounded on every side by conditions. （再次支撑论点。）

综上，我们不难发现通篇作者都在描述并分析美国从最简单的社会协作阶段步入最高机构阶段的发展历程，而第三句中的关键词 industrial organization and its expansion 和第四句中的 the advance 则可以对应选项 A 中的 industrial progress，因此选项 A 为正确答案。选项 B 中的 democratic ideals、选项 C 中的 individual liberties 和选项 D 中的 uselessness 在文中均作为主要内容有所提及，因此可以排除。

• 选自 Khan College New SAT 阅读文章 History Level 4 Passage 2

QUESTION 2 OF 11

Over the course of the passage, the main focus shifts from _____.
A. an overview of industrial advancement to a clarification of the problem
B. an acknowledgement of the problem with industrial advancement to the proposal of a solution
C. an assembling of arguments against industrial advancement to a justification of its effects
D. an explanation of industrial advancement to an admission of the drawbacks

解析: 我们回到原文阅读一下全文段首句和最后一句——

• It will not probably be denied that the burden of proof is on those who affirm that our social condition is utterly diseased and in need of radical regeneration. (引出下文想要讨论的议题。)

• When anyone asserts that the class of skilled and unskilled manual laborers of the United States is worse off now in respect to diet, clothing, lodgings, furniture, fuel, and lights; in respect to the age at which they can marry; the number of children they can provide for; the start in life which they can give to their children, and their chances of accumulating capital, than they ever have been at any former time, he makes a reckless assertion for which no facts have been offered in proof. (通过除去长难句中的并列修饰成分,我们不难发现这个句子的核心在于最后——he makes a reckless assertion,因此是作者对于他人的反驳。)

• Nine-tenths of the socialistic and semi-socialistic, and sentimental or ethical, suggestions by which we are overwhelmed come from failure to understand the phenomena of the industrial organization and its expansion. (支撑作者观点,指出反对的声音源于他们对于工业扩张和发展的不了解。)

• The advance of a new country from the very simplest social coordination up to the highest organization is a most interesting and instructive chance to study the development of the organization. (从正面支撑自己的论点。)

• Now the intensification of the social organization is what gives us greater social power. (重申观点。)

• Our life is bounded on every side by conditions. (再次支撑论点。)

从上述句子中我们看出,作者首先提出了各种对于当前工业社会现象的不满(从第一段段首句中的 our social condition is utterly diseased and in need of radical regeneration、第二段段首句中的 worse off 均可以看出),紧接着则对这些反对的声音进行了一一驳斥,从 most interesting and instructive chance、what gives us greater social power 中便能看出,因此对应选项 C 中的 assembling of arguments against 和 justification of its effects。选项 A 中的 overview of industrial advancement 与文章前半段说反。选项 B 中的 proposal of a solution 在文中没有提及。选项 D 中整体说反。因此我们可以排除错误选项,得到正确答案 C。

1.2.8 态度题

态度题主要分为全文态度题和细节态度题。全文态度题指的是作者对整篇文章所讨论内容的态度,因此,通过快速阅读法能基本判别出作者的写作态度。而细节态度题则涉及具体词汇的运用。

题型特征如下:

• Attitude.

• Reaction.

• Tone.

技巧总览

1. 全文态度题
- 做法与全文主旨题一致：通过全文首尾句判断文章主要观点。
- 判断作者态度：通过一些带有主观色彩的形容词和副词以及有感情色彩的动词，来判断作者态度。

2. 细节态度题
只需定位原句，找出含有感情色彩的形容词、副词、动词即可。

3. 常见的态度词
编者为考生整理了以下 New SAT 阅读中较为常见的态度词：

正面情绪（positive）

喜悦
delight, please, excite, exhilarate, cheerful, ebullient, enthusiasm.

赞赏
appreciate, admire, celebrate, espouse, champion, commend, endorse.

同情
sympathetic, compassion.

诙谐幽默
humorous, witty, amusing, jocular.

客观
detached, objective, impartial, analytical.

其他
enlightening, cautious, reflective, nostalgic.

负面情绪（negative）

嘲讽
deride, derision, jeer, mock, scorn, sarcasm, irony, satire, scoff, ridiculous, ludicrous, comical, facetious.

贬低、轻视
disparage, disdain, disrespect, contempt, devalue, defy/defiance, depreciate, despise.

悲伤
sorrow, wrench, bitterness, grief, distress.

吃惊
amaze, astonish, astound, surprise.

忧郁
anxiety, insecurity, apprehensive, somber, gloomy, depressing, dreary, melancholy, glum, sullen, wistful, distress, uneasy, upset, sentimental, annoying.

怀疑
distrust, doubt/dubious/doubtful, skeptical, incredulous, suspicious, disbelief.

批评

criticize, condemn, reject, disapprove, reprove, admonish, deny, denounce, repudiate, refute.

尴尬

embarrass, abash, humiliate, mortify.

沮丧

frustrated, disappointed, dismay.

恐惧

fear, alarm, trepid, panic.

屈尊、恩赐

condescending, patronizing.

疑惑

puzzle, baffle, confuse, perplex, dumbfounded.

嫉妒

jealous, begrudge.

傲慢

arrogant, insolent, haughty, impertinent.

贪婪

greedy, avaricious, grasping.

冷漠

indifferent, lukewarm, unsympathetic, nonchalant, apathetic, callousness.

真题模拟

- 选自 Khan College New SAT 阅读文章 History Level 2 Passage 10

QUESTION 7 OF 11

What main effect does the phrase "flower of the country," line 40("the flower of the country"), have on the tone of the passage?

A. It lightens the tone by providing a metaphor of beauty in an otherwise bleak narrative.

B. It provides an impassioned tone to describe the discrepancy between the relative privilege of the few and the hardship of the many.

C. It creates a tone of praise by comparing the workers of France to those in the U.S.

D. It creates an optimistic tone by showing that the people of France are variously employed.

解析：我们来阅读这个句子——

Line 40：These employ the flower of the country as servants, some of them having as many as 200 domestics, not labouring.

这句话说祖国的花朵被当作了家仆，而不是真正地让他们去劳动。Flower 作为一个正面的褒义词,与之后的 servants 形成了明显的对比,因此作者绝非抱有一种积极的语调,可以排除选项 A、C、D。而选项 B 中的 the many 与句中的 some of them 对应,discrepancy 则与句中的对比形成对应,为正确答案。

• 选自 Khan College New SAT 阅读文章 Literature Level 4 Passage 3

QUESTION 2 OF 11

Over the course of the passage, Selden's attitude shifts from _____.
A. bewildered to curious　　　　　B. dismayed to apprehensive
C. amazed to anticipatory　　　　　D. incredulous to indifferent

解析:我们回到原文阅读一下全文的首尾句,在阅读的过程中着重注意表现人物神态、动作的形容词、副词或动词——

• Selden paused in surprise.(起初是惊喜的情绪。)

• In judging Miss Bart, he had always made use of the "argument from design."(因缺乏对引号内内容的了解,我们往前再看一句。)

• Her discretions interested him almost as much as her imprudences: he was so sure that both were part of the same carefully-elaborated plan.(最后是被女主人公性格上的双面性所吸引。)

显然,起初的 surprise 对应选项 A 中的 bewildered,因为他不太明白为什么女主人公会出现在那里。而之后的 interested 则更多解释为选项 A 中的 curious,因为他对于女主人公展现出的、与其印象中不同的性格感到好奇,所以可以选到正确答案 A。

• 选自 Khan College New SAT 阅读文章 Science Level 3 Passage 2

QUESTION 11 OF 11

Which choice best describes the author's tone in describing the research described in paragraph six?
A. Analytical　　　B. Ambivalent　　　C. Biased　　　D. Objective

解析:我们来阅读一下第六段的第一句、第二句和最后一句——

• In fact, in October [2004], French researchers announced 50 findings that illustrate afresh just how close some viruses might come.

• Didier Raoult and his colleagues at the University of the Mediterranean in Marseille announced that they had sequenced the genome of the largest known virus, Mimivirus, which was discovered in 1992.

• As the research team noted in its report in the journal *Science*, the enormous complexity of the Mimivirus's genetic complement "challenges the established frontier between viruses and parasitic cellular organisms."

这些句子并没有带着明显的感情色彩,同时因为这是一篇说明文,作者带有强烈主观色彩的可能性不大,因此可以排除选项 C。而选项 B 中则是一个混淆选项——如果作者的态度是模棱两可的,那就根本没有写这篇文章且提出自己观点的必要了,因此也可以排除。同时，说明文基本上的语调都是客观的，没有选择的必要，因此选项 D 也是干扰项。而最后一句话引用了他人的话对该 research 进行了评价，称其对已有理论发起了挑战，明显带有分析色彩，因此可以选到答案 A。

> 更多练习

- 选自 Khan College New SAT 阅读文章 History Level 2 Passage 4

QUESTION 2 OF 11

What main effect does the phrase "nation's picked sons," (line 6), have on the tone of the passage?
　　A. It creates an historical tone that recalls past traditions.
　　B. It creates an uplifting tone that boosts confidence in the project.
　　C. It creates a presidential tone that reinforces Roosevelt's authority.
　　D. It creates a patriotic tone that stimulates pride.

解析：我们根据行数提示回到原文——
　　Line 4：I am profoundly thankful that I shall be able to take back to the United States the message that the nation's picked sons are carrying themselves so well here that I can absolutely guarantee the success of the mighty work which they are doing.

从这句话中我们能够看出 the nation's picked son 对应副词 profoundly 和之后的 can absolutely guarantee the success of the mighty work，体现出罗斯福对于这些 picked sons 的自豪和自信之情，极大地鼓舞了人们的士气，对应选项 D 中的 a patriotic tone 和 pride。选项 A 中的 recalls the past traditions 在这句话中无法体现。选项 C 中的 reinforces Roosevelt's authority，显然也并没这句话想要表达的内容。选项 B 是一个迷惑选项，因为选项中的 an uplifting tone 与这句话中的情绪同样是对应的，但要注意的是，罗斯福更多的是赞扬 picked sons。虽然句中也提到了 guarantee the success of the mighty work，但这种 confidence 是因为有这些 picked sons 而存在的，因此重点仍然在 picked sons 上，而非为了 project 而 boost confidence。

当出现具有上述迷惑性质的选项时，我们更要注意去找对应词。显然在这道题中，句中的 nation's picked sons、profoundly thankful 和 take back to the United States 均与选项 D 中的 a patriotic tone 和 stimulates pride 能更好地对应，因此该题正确答案为 D。

- 选自 Khan College New SAT 阅读文章 Science Level 2 Passage 7

QUESTION 4 OF 11

What effect does the word "monsters" (line 48) have on the tone of the passage?
　　A. It creates a heightened tone that reinforces the massive size of black holes.
　　B. It creates a frightening tone that suggests that black holes are something to fear.
　　C. It creates an alarming tone that implies that measuring black holes is impossible.
　　D. It creates a menacing tone that hints at the destructive power of black holes.

解析： 我们根据行数提示回到原文进行定位——

Line 48："These monsters, with masses from millions to billions of times that of the sun, are formed as small seeds in the early universe and grow by swallowing stars and gas in their host galaxies, merging with other giant black holes when galaxies collide, or both," said the study's lead author, Guido Risaliti of the Harvard-Smithsonian Center for Astrophysics in Cambridge, Mass, and the Italian National Institute for Astrophysics.

因句中的 monsters 一词前有代词 these，因此我们要回到上一句找到其指代的内容。

Line 45：Measuring the spin of a supermassive black hole is fundamental to understanding its past history and that of its host galaxy.

在这句话中，我们能看出 these monsters 指代的是 supermassive black holes。我们接着看 monsters 所在句中对于该词的补充说明，发现句中的 swallow 与 monsters 一词明显是对应的，体现出 black holes 吞食 host galaxies 中其他行星并自行壮大的过程，其中 masses、swallow、merge 等词对应选项 A 中的 massive size。选项 B 中的 something to fear 和选项 C 中的 measuring black holes is impossible 则在句子中无从体现。选项 D 中的 menacing tone 态度过于极端，且句中也并未体现出 black hole 的破坏力，而只是突出（heightened）巨大的黑洞的形成过程。因此我们可以排除错误答案，选到正确答案 A。

• 选自 Khan College New SAT 阅读文章 Literature Level 3 Passage 1

QUESTION 11 OF 11

In the description of the boat's movements, the words "walked" and "walking" primarily serve to establish a tone of _____.

A. humor B. foreboding C. strangeness D. awe

解析： 我们根据句中的 boat's movement、walked 和 walking 回到原文进行定位，可以看到——

Line 50：No record is left in my mind, now, concerning it, but a confused jumble of savage-looking snags, which our boat deliberately walked over with one wheel or the other; and of reefs which we butted and butted, and then retired from and climbed over in some softer place; and of sand-bars which we roosted on occasionally, and rested, and then got out our crutches and sparred over.

Line 57：In fact, the boat might almost as well have gone to St. Jo. by land, for she was walking most of the time, anyhow—climbing over reefs and clambering over snags patiently and laboriously all day long.

第一句中的 walked 指的是船在 a confused jumble of savage-looking snags 中穿梭，而 walked 的方式则是 with one wheel or the other，显然是在用比喻的手法凸显出船在这样障碍重重的水道中穿行的艰难和缓慢。同时，walked 所在的分句是一系列排比句，因此 walked 一词还与之后 butted、retired、rested、roosted 等词有所对应，反映出一种缓慢行进、走走停停的状态，凸显出作者百无聊赖的心情，即选项 B 中的 foreboding。

而第二句中的 walking 则与之前 have to St. Jo by land 对应，显示船行之慢。而补充修饰这种状态的副词 patiently and laboriously all day long 则同样体现出无聊之感，与作者在出发前的高昂兴致形成鲜明对比,因此我们可以确定正确答案为选项 B。选项 A、C 和 D 均为无关选项。

• 选自 Khan College New SAT 阅读文章 Science Level 4 Passage 3

QUESTION 2 OF 11

What effect does the word "murky" (line 6) have on the tone of the passage?

A. It creates a pessimistic tone that implies that finding conclusive evidence is unlikely.

B. It creates a judgmental tone that alerts the reader to possible bias.

C. It creates an exuberant tone that shows the author's passion for scientific research.

D. It creates an engaging tone that suggests a problem to be solved.

解析:我们根据行数提示回到原文进行定位——

Line 5: Exactly how these various marsupials, both living and extinct, are related has been murky. There are marsupials found today in both Australia and the Americas, with the opossum the most familiar to Americans.

显然,第二句具体说明了这些 marsupials 之间的联系是非常 murky 的状态,而 murky 一词本身解释为"昏暗的",在这里可以引申为"尚不明确的",因此与选项 C 中的 an exuberant tone、author's passion 并不符合,可以排除;同时,选项 B 中的 alerts readers to possible bias 在句子中并没有体现。而尽管作者的确写到了这一问题尚待解决,但却并没有说将来也无法找到解释这一问题的证据,因此选项 A 中的 finding conclusive evidence is unlikely 也是无中生有的推断。相较之下,选项 D 中的 suggests a problem to be solved 更符合文章行文逻辑——作者通过 an engaging tone 引起读者的兴趣,并为下文对这一问题的深入分析埋下了伏笔。通过验证下文内容,我们发现通篇都在讨论各地 marsupials 的联系,因此从侧面印证了选项 D 的正确性。

• 选自 Khan College New SAT 阅读文章 Literature Level 4 Passage 4

QUESTION 4 OF 11

What main effects do the words "timid" and "quivering," used in the first paragraph, have on the tone of the passage?

A. They create an ominous tone that foreshadows Fenella's separation from her father.

B. They create a solemn tone that contrasts with Fenella's emotions about leaving.

C. They create an uncertain tone that reflects Fenella's relationship with her father.

D. They create a sinister tone that implies Fenella's wariness of the situation.

解析:我们根据题干中的关键词 timid 和 quivering 进行定位,可以看到——

Line 9: Here and there on a rounded wood-pile, that was like the stalk of a huge black mushroom, there hung a lantern, but it seemed afraid to unfurl its timid, quivering light in all that blackness; it burned softly, as if for itself.

从这个句子中我们可以看出,timid 和 quivering 修饰的是在黑暗中的 lantern 光线,作者用这两个词描绘出码头灯光的昏暗。而 timid 和 quivering 本身都有羞怯、颤抖之意,暗指灯光在黑暗中忽明忽暗,营造出一种不安和不确定感。同时,通过阅读文章第一句我们可知文章背景是在码头送别,因此这种不安与选项 A 中的 separation 是对应的,为之后的送别做铺垫(foreshadows)。选项 B 中的 solemn tone 与文义不符。选项 C 中的 an uncertain tone 虽然有所对应,但这种态度并非体现在 Fenella 与她爸爸之间的关系上(从文中我们能看出这对父女之间的感情是很深的)。选项 D 中的 a sinister tone 太多极端,且在文中也无法找到 Fenella's wariness of the situation 的对应,因此均可以排除,选到正确答案 A。

• 选自 Khan College New SAT 阅读文章 Science Level 3 Passage 3

QUESTION 11 OF 11

Which choice best describes the author's attitude towards potential uses of salicylic acid in agriculture?

A. Unreservedly enthusiastic B. Generally wary
C. Cautiously optimistic   D. Resolutely opposed

解析: 我们根据题干中的关键词 potential uses of salicylic acid 进行定位,但全文都在讨论 salicylic acid 的 potential uses。这种情况下,我们可以锁定文章的首尾段查找作者的态度(要注意区分作者的态度和其他研究者的态度)——

Line 57:Why salicylic acid had this effect isn't known. Other questions remain as well, including how treated plants will fare under field conditions. Nonetheless, such investigations could set the stage for providing growers of potato, tomato, and other susceptible crops some insurance against phytoplasmas in outbreak-prone regions.

这段话中出现了明显的转折——前半部分中的 isn't known 和 other questions remain as well 体现出作者对于 salicylic acid 运用的不确定性。但后半部分中的 set the stage 则体现出了褒义。而选项 A、B 和 D 均是全然的肯定或全然的否定,因此不符合文中作者双面的态度,可以排除。相较之下,选项 C 中的 cautiously 对应句中的 question,optimistic 则对应句中的 set the stage,因此选项 C 为正确答案。

1.2.9 词汇题

词汇题主要牵涉两类:熟词僻意和生僻词汇。熟词僻意指我们熟悉的单词往往有多种解释,在不同语境中有不同的含义。New SAT 阅读中更为常见的是这种词汇题,对生僻词汇的考察相对较少。

题型特点如下:

As used in line X, "_____" most nearly means:

技巧总览

1. 利用前后文的补充说明

如果这句话前后有同位语或有例子,那么往往这个词语之前的例子是有联系的,如归纳或总结。

2. 把握平行结构

如果词汇题的定位点出现了平行结构,则去这个平行结构的其他部分找相对应词性的单词,并且在选项中找一个与这个对应单词的同义词。

3. 代入法

选择语气、语义都符合的选项。

4. 把握构词法

利用构词法找到选项中与考察词汇相同的词根和词缀,选出正确答案。

5. 把握文章态度

如果在本句及上下句中均找不出答案,则可通过该定位句所属段落的主旨或作者态度进行做题。

真题模拟

• 选自 Khan College New SAT 阅读文章 Social Science Level 3 Passage 2

QUESTION 3 OF 11

As used in line 22 ("elemental"), "elemental" most nearly means _____.
A. inner   B. chemical   C. partial   D. essential

解析:我们回到该定位句——

Line 20:Lorenz assumed that responses to baby schema are innate processes and are triggered by elemental features of the stimuli.

根据韦氏词典,elemental 的基本含义如下:

• basic and important
• having the power of a force of nature
• of or relating to a chemical element

因此我们可以排除选项 A 和选项 C,而这句话中 elemental 修饰的是 features of the stimuli,如果将 chemical 代入则不成逻辑,应解释为重要的、基本的。所以选项 D 为正确答案。

• 选自 Khan College New SAT 阅读文章 Social Science Level 3 Passage 3

QUESTION 2 OF 11

As used in line 12 ("mediated"), "mediated" most nearly means _____.
A. resolved   B. influenced   C. intervened   D. reconciled

解析:我们回到该定位句——

Line 11:Moccasin decorations exhibit a pattern consistent with geographically-mediated between-group interaction.

根据韦氏词典,mediated 的基本含义如下:

• occupying a middle position
• acting through an intervening agency

- exhibiting indirect causation, connection, or relation

显然，mediated 并没有选项 A 的含义。而地理上的干预（intervened）或调解（reconciled）都是说不通的，排除选项 C 和选项 D。而选项 B 中的 influence 对应第三个解释，指地理对于两个部落之间文化所产生的影响，所以 B 为正确答案。同时，该题我们还能这样理解：

在这个句子中，geographically-mediated 修饰的名词是 between-group interaction，而选项 A 中的 resolved 并不需要 interaction 的参与，因此没有对应关系，可以直接排除。选项 D 中的 reconciled 代入句子中不成逻辑，因此排除。选项 C 中的 intervened 有干预、干扰的意思，带有贬义。而回看原文的句子显然是一句较为中性的句子，并没有明显的倾向性，因此选项 B 中的 influence 更为合适，技能对应句中的 interaction，又较为中立。

- 选自 Khan College New SAT 阅读文章 History Level 3 Passage 2

QUESTION 7 OF 11

As used in line 48 ("abridgment") of Passage 2, the word "abridgement" most nearly means _____ .

A. abbreviation　　　　　　B. concentration
C. summarization　　　　　D. reduction

解析：我们回到该定位句——

Line 44：He has suggested that licentiousness has seldom produced the loss of liberty; but that the tyranny of rulers has almost always affected it. Since the general civilization of mankind, I believe there are more instances of the abridgment of the freedom of the people by gradual and silent encroachments of those in power, than by violent and sudden usurpations ...

根据韦氏词典，abridgment 的基本含义如下：

- the action of abridging : the state of being abridged
- a shortened form of a work retaining the general sense and unity of the original

四个选项似乎均有可能，但句中 abridgment of the freedom 的方式是 encroachments（侵蚀），因此 freedom 肯定不可能是 concentration（选项 B）或 summarization（选项 C）的。而用 abbreviation 形容 freedom 也不合理，因此选项 D 为正确答案，指自由地减少。

更多练习

- 选自 Khan College New SAT 阅读文章 Literature Level 2 Passage 3

QUESTION 4 OF 11

As used in line 19, "veracity" most nearly means _____ .

A. candor　　　B. truthfulness　　　C. verisimilitude　　　D. impartiality

解析：我们根据行数提示回到原文进行定位——

Line 17：He seldom smiled, never joked, and had a Washingtonian reputation for veracity.

在这个句子中，veracity 对应的是 a Washingtonian reputation、never joked 和 seldom smiled，因此显然是褒义的，并有"严肃的、正直的"之意。而选项 A 中的 candor 指的是 frankness(坦白)，与 never joked 并没有对应，因此排除。选项 B 中的 truthfulness 对应 never joked，选项 C 中的 verisimilitude 意为逼真，选项 D 中的 impartiality 意为公正，均没有对应。因此此题正确答案为 B。

• 选自 Khan College New SAT 阅读文章 Social Science Level 3 Passage 2

QUESTION 2 OF 11

As used in lines 1～2, "concerned with" most nearly means _____.
A. worried about   B. interested in
C. motivated by   D. uneasy about

解析： 我们根据行数提示回到原文进行定位——

Line 1：Political communication scholars are keenly concerned with the extent to which new media is affecting politics...

这是一句全文的总起句，而全文并没有仅仅阐述 new media affecting politics 的好处或者坏处，而是均有所提及，因此纯褒义或纯贬义的答案均可以直接排除。根据这一逻辑，选项 A(贬)、选项 D(贬)被排除。而选项 C 与 concerned with 的原意不符，因此排除，选到正确答案 B。

• 选自 Khan College New SAT 阅读文章 Social Science Level 4 Passage 1

QUESTION 5 OF 11

In line 30, "sympathetic to" most nearly means _____.
A. caring for   B. agreeable with
C. supportive of   D. compassionate toward

解析： 我们根据行数提示回到原文进行定位——

Line 30：George H. W. Bush was also sympathetic to this view, prior to becoming vice president in 1981.

句中的 also 提示我们可以从之前的句子中找到与 sympathetic 同义的参考词——

Line 26：Johnson was part of an unbroken series of US presidents concerned with the harmful effects of rapid population growth in developing countries. This line extended (at least) from John F. Kennedy to Jimmy Carter.

从这个句子中我们发现 sympathetic 修饰的是 the harmful effects of rapid population growth in developing countries，对应句中的 concerned with。因此我们可以排除纯褒义的选项，即选项 B、C。而选项 D 中的 compassionate toward 与 concerned with 的含义不符，因此可以排除，选到正确答案 A。

• 选自 Khan College New SAT 阅读文章 Social Science Level 4 Passage 2

QUESTION 2 OF 11

As used in line 8, "track" most nearly means _____.
A. carry　　　　B. assign　　　　C. monitor　　　　D. linger

解析：我们根据行数提示回到原文进行定位——

Line 7：Participation in PA in youth is of great importance as PA may track into adulthood where adequate levels of PA are protective against many chronic diseases.

在这个句子中，track 修饰的是 youth to adulthood，因此对应的是一个过程，即选项 D 中的 linger(逗留)。如果将选项 A 中的 carry 代入则与原句中的 track into 的主语无法吻合（应为 be carried），因此排除。选项 B 中的 assign 和选项 C 中的 monitor 与原句中的含义不符合，因此我们可以选到正确答案 D。

• 选自 Khan College New SAT 阅读文章 History Level 2 Passage 2

QUESTION 8 OF 11

In line 40, "invaded" most nearly means _____.
A. infringed　　　　　　　　B. usurped
C. trespassed　　　　　　　D. permeated

解析：我们根据行数提示回到原文进行定位——

Line 33：Independent of the opinions of many great authors, that a free elective government cannot be extended over large territories, a few reflections must evince, that one government and general legislation alone, never can extend equal benefits to all parts of the United States：Different laws, customs, and opinions exist in the different states, which by a uniform system of laws would be unreasonably invaded.

"invade"一词所在的句子是对之前观点句进行的补充，因此我们可以在之前一句句子中找到对应关系。例如，后一句中的 a uniform system of laws 可以对应第一句中的 one government，different states 对应 all parts of the United States 和 large territories。因此，invaded 对应 never can extend equal benefits，即权益无法得到保证，也就是选项 A "infringed"中的"侵犯"之意。而选项 B、C、D 在代入后无法吻合 be invaded 的承受方 (different laws, customs and opinions)，因此我们可以确定该题答案为 A。

• 选自 Khan College New SAT 阅读文章 History Level 2 Passage 4

QUESTION 4 OF 11

As used in line 24, "enterprise" most nearly means _____.
A. establishment　　B. business　　C. invention　　D. undertaking

解析：我们根据行数提示回到原文进行定位——

Line 22：I am weighing my words when I say that you here, who do your work well in bringing to completion this great enterprise, will stand exactly as the soldiers of a few, and only a few, of the most famous armies of all the nations stand in history.

句中的 you 与 the soldiers of a few … of the most famous armies of all the nations 是类比关系,因此这些人所完成的 great enterprise 也可以类比到 the soldiers 所做的事。而选项 A、B 和 C 均与 soldiers、armies 能完成的事情没有对应关系,只有选项 D 中的 undertaking 在作 cause 之意时能够涵盖 soldier 对于国家的贡献。而在这篇文章中,enterprise 对应的明显是建造巴拿马运河的任务,因此选项 D 是正确答案。

第 2 章　New SAT 阅读重点篇章演练

2.1　Literature

2.1.1　Passage Ⅰ

答案解析

1. Over the course of the passage, the main focus shifts from _____.
A. a description of one woman to a detailed characterization of a group of people
B. a depiction of a place to a statement of one character's opinions about that place
C. opinions shared by many laypeople to opinions held by a great artist
D. the setup of a situation to one character's reaction to that situation

答案:D

解析:文章从计划听 Mademoiselle Reisz 弹钢琴,转向 Edna 对于听她演奏情感的反应。选项 A 错在文章不是转向主要写一群人的特点,而是主要写 Edna。选项 B 错在文章一开始不是主要描述一个地点,也不是转向对于这个地点的观点。选项 C 错在文章一开始不是写很多外行的观点,之后也不是写一个伟大的艺术家的观点。

2. In paragraph 4 (lines 22~28), the words "satisfaction" and "expectancy" serve mainly to _____.
A. show that those in attendance have fixed ideas about Mademoiselle Reisz's performance
B. characterize Mademoiselle Reisz's feelings about being asked to play for the group
C. indicate that Edna has been waiting for Mademoiselle Reisz to acknowledge her presence
D. demonstrate that the listeners anticipate that Mademoiselle Reisz will not be able to play the pieces well

答案:A

解析:satisfaction 是听众的感受,而不是 Mademoiselle Reisz 或者 Edna 的感受,选项

B、C错误。satisfaction 和 expectancy 又都是正面词,选项 D 表示听众希望 Mademoiselle Reisz 不会演奏好这个乐章,错误。选项 A 表示听众们的 satisfaction 和 expectancy 是因为他们原本就知道 Mademoiselle Reisz 很会弹钢琴,有 fixed ideas,正确。

3. The primary purpose of paragraphs 2 and 3 (lines 5~21) is to _____.

　　A. characterize Mademoiselle Reisz as someone who delights in making people uncomfortable solely for her own amusement

　　B. emphasize that Mademoiselle Reisz has changed a great deal in the time Edna has known her

　　C. describe Mademoiselle Reisz's interaction with Robert, which reflects her general interest in social pleasantries

　　D. establish Mademoiselle Reisz's unpleasant attitude and appearance, which contrast with the beautiful music she makes

答案:D

解析:文章中未提及 Mademoiselle Reisz 的不令人开心的行为的原因,只说她有"a temper which was self-assertive(自信)",选项 A 错误。文章中未提及 Edna 一开始是怎么认识 Mademoiselle Reisz 的,所以也无从判断 Edna 有没有观察到她的任何变化,选项 B 错误。文章这两段的确展示了 Mademoiselle Reisz 与 Robert 的互动,但不是主要内容,这些互动也没有展示她的个性,选项 C 错误。这两段写到 Mademoiselle Reisz "disagreeable"还"no taste in dress",与题目中"unpleasant attitude and appearance"对应,选项 D 正确。

4. It can be reasonably inferred that Edna refuses to choose the music that Mademoiselle Reisz will play because she _____.

　　A. feels that her musical education is insufficient for the honor of making the selection

　　B. is uncomfortable with being treated differently than the other guests

　　C. does not know what music the other guests would prefer to hear

　　D. wants to hear "Solitude" but doesn't know how to ask for it

答案:B

解析:我们回到原文——

Line 28: Edna was a trifle embarrassed at being thus signaled out for the imperious little woman's favor.

其中"embarrassed"对应"uncomfortable","being signal out"对应"being treated differently",故选项 B 为正确答案。选项 A 错在文章中没有提及 Edna 的 musical education。选项 C 无根据。选项 D 不构成因果关系。

5. Which choice provides the best evidence for the answer to the previous question?

　　A. lines 28~30 ("Edna ... favor")　　B. line 32 ("Edna ... music")

　　C. lines 34~35 ("She ... practiced")　　D. lines 35~37 ("One ... strain")

答案:A

解析:选项 B、C 确认了 Edna 喜欢音乐,但不表明是她拒绝挑选弹奏的音乐的原因;选项 D 藐视了 Edna 曾经听到的并喜欢上的一首音乐,但也不表明是她拒绝挑选弹奏的音乐的原因。

6. As used in line 33, "rendered" most nearly means _____.
A. covered B. made C. provided D. performed

答案：D

解析：要填入"良好_____的音乐旋律可以让她头脑中浮现画面"中的空格，选项 A 表示"覆盖"，选项 B 表示"制作"，选项 C 表示"提供"，选项 D 表示"演奏"，选项 A、C 排除，而文章中说的都是演奏钢琴曲，而不是制作钢琴曲，所以选项 D 更好。

7. The imagery in paragraph 5 (lines 38～42) mainly serves to _____.
A. show that Edna's imagination is not influenced by her surroundings
B. demonstrate Edna's inability to distinguish reality from fantasy
C. characterize the vivid scenes music brings to Edna's mind
D. make it clear that Edna longs to be alone in an isolated environment

答案：C

解析：作者表述了 Edna 听到音乐想象的场景，选项 C 正确。选项 A，第五段的这些行描述的是 Edna 的想象受到她听到的音乐的影响，所以相矛盾。选项 B 在文中未提到。选项 D，文中没有提到 Edna 希望独自一人，只是说 Edna 听到音乐想象到一个男人站在海岸上的一块荒芜的石头旁边。

8. The "dainty young woman clad in an Empire gown" (lines 43～44) is best understood to be _____.
A. a member of the group
B. someone about whom Mademoiselle Ratignolle is singing
C. an imaginary woman
D. Edna as a child

答案：C

解析：题目上提到的部分之前提到："another piece called to her mind"，也就是说同上题提到的场景一样，这个也是想象的，所以选项 C（一个假想的女人）正确。

9. It can be reasonably inferred that Mademoiselle Reisz considers Edna to be worth playing for because _____.
A. only Edna has received enough training to fully appreciate the music
B. Edna feels passionately and deeply about the music
C. Edna has never had the opportunity to hear her play before
D. only Edna understands how it feels to be a musician

答案：B

解析：见下题。

10. Which choice provides the best evidence for the answer to the previous question?
A. lines 50～51 ("It was ... piano")
B. lines 54～55 ("She ... imagination")
C. lines 63～64 ("As she ... shoulder")
D. lines 67～68 ("Mademoiselle ... tears")

答案：D

解析：选项 A 指的是 Edna 对听音乐的观点，选项 B 展示了 Edna 对于 Mademoiselle

Reisz 演奏的音乐的反应,都没有解释为什么 Mademoiselle Reisz 认为 Edna 是唯一值得为之演奏的。选项 C 尽管表达了 Mademoiselle Reisz 对 Edna 的喜爱,但也没有直接的解释。通过选项 D 所在行中 agitation 和 tears 都表示 Edna 对音乐的深沉的爱,可得知上题选项 B 正确。上题中选项 A,文章没有提到 Edna 的音乐训练,错误。选项 C,文章中没有提到 Edna 之前是否听过 Mademoiselle Reisz 演奏,错误。选项 D,文章中没有提到 Edna 知道作为一个音乐家的感觉,错误。

11. The passage suggests that Edna view Mademoiselle Reisz as someone who is _____.

A. intimidating but profound   B. cold and uninviting
C. motherly and inspiring   D. misguided but irresponsible

答案:A

解析:Mademoiselle Reisz 对别人的态度是吓人的,但她的音乐影响是深远的,这个人有两面性,选项 A 正确。选项 B 未反映出这种两面性。选项 C motherly 错误。选项 D 两个词都不准确,Mademoiselle Reisz 在音乐上对于 Edna 的引导很正确,而不是 misguided 或者 irresponsible。

译文

"你想听雷西小姐弹琴吗?"罗伯特走到她所在的廊前问她。爱德娜当然想听,但又担心请求她没用,请不来她。

"我去跟她说,"他说道,"我去跟她说你想听她弹琴。她很喜欢你。她会来的。"罗伯特转身急匆匆地赶到远处的一栋别墅。雷西小姐正在那里踱着步子。她拖着一把椅子从屋里搬进搬出的,时不时地对一个婴儿的哭声表示抗议。隔壁别墅里,一个保姆正在努力哄这个婴儿睡觉。她是一个难相处的小个子女人,年纪不轻了;她自负,脾气坏,性情古怪,无视别人的权利,她几乎跟这里的每个人都吵过架。可罗伯特没费很大劲就说服了她。

在跳舞的间歇,雷西小姐跟他一起进入了大厅。她进来时很别扭地轻轻鞠了一躬,给人感觉很专横跋扈的样子。她是一个相貌平平的女子,脸孔和身体都很干瘦,眼睛发亮。她对穿着打扮绝对没有品位,穿着一套褪了色的黑色花边衣裙,头发一侧别着一小束假紫罗兰花。

"去问一下蓬迪里埃夫人想听我弹什么?"她要求罗伯特道。罗伯特走到窗前给爱德娜传口信的时候,她就极其安静地坐在钢琴前,没动琴键。当人们看到这位钢琴家进来的时候,都非常地惊喜和满足。大家都安静下来,大厅里弥漫着期待。受到这个傲慢的小女人的特别钟爱,使爱德娜感觉稍稍有点尴尬。她不敢挑选,而是请雷西小姐自己随意选曲弹奏。爱德娜,用她自己的话说,是非常喜欢音乐的。弹奏得好的乐曲能在她脑海中激起一幅幅回忆的画面。她有时喜欢在早上坐在房间里听拉蒂诺尔夫人弹奏或练习。那位小姐弹奏的一支曲子,爱德娜把它称为《孤独曲》。这是一支很短、很哀婉的小调。其实这支曲子另有其名,但爱德娜就把它称为《孤独曲》。当她听到这支曲子的时候,她的脑海中就会浮现出一个人影,站在海滩上一块荒凉的岩石旁;当他看着远方的一只小鸟拍打着翅膀飞离开自己时,他是无奈而绝望的。

另一支曲子使她脑海里浮现出一位身穿帝国时期长袍的优雅的年轻女子,迈着矫饰的舞蹈步伐,沿着一条夹在两排高高的篱笆之间的长长的林荫道走来。还有一支曲子,使她想起了正在玩耍的孩子,以及另一支曲子在她眼前呈现出一位娴静的小姐在爱抚一只小猫的画面。除此之外,大地上一片白净。雷西小姐弹出的最初几个弦音便使蓬迪里埃夫人的脊背从上到下感到一阵强烈的颤抖。她并非第一次听到艺术家弹奏钢琴,但也许这是第一次有心理准备,渴望接受这一永恒的真理。

她期待着脑海中的这些真切的图画在她的想象中聚集并大放光彩,可她的等待是徒劳的。她没看到任何孤独、希望、渴求或绝望的画面。而这些情感却在她的灵魂深处被唤起,支配并鞭打着她的心灵,正如浪潮每天拍击她曼妙的身体。她颤抖着、抽泣着,泪水模糊了她的视线。

雷西小姐弹完了。她站起来,生硬而又傲慢地略鞠一躬就走了,没有因为大家的感谢与掌声而做任何停留。她路过长廊的时候,轻轻地拍了拍爱德娜的肩膀。

"哦,你喜欢我的演奏吗?"她问道。这位年轻的夫人没能做出回答,只是猛劲地按住了这位钢琴家的手。雷西小姐看出了她的激动情绪,甚至看到她噙着泪水,又拍了拍她的肩膀说道:"你是唯一值得我为之弹奏的人。其他那些人?呸!"说完就拖着步子侧身穿过长廊回自己房间了。

2.1.2 Passage Ⅱ

答案解析

12. Over the course of the passage, the main focus shifts from _____.

A. an explanation of a city's layout to a description of one particular street

B. the description of a character's personality to the introduction of a life-changing event

C. an interaction between two characters to the effects of that interaction on one of them

D. a character's thoughts to the depiction of him acting upon those thoughts

答案:B

解析:文章最先从 Marc 的个性开始说起,之后转向 Marc 发现了一条在人们记忆中一直被遗忘的一条路,符合选项 B。选项 A 错在一开始并没有很详细地介绍一个城市的布局。选项 C 错在文章没有转向这两个角色的互动。选项 D 错在文章最开始没有集中介绍一个角色的想法,所以之后也没有描述他对这些想法是怎么行动的。

13. The imagery in lines 2~5 ("city ... lanes") primarily serves to _____.

A. characterize the mysterious nature of Montreal

B. demonstrate the intricacy of Marc's memory

C. show that nobody else could understand the map

D. emphasize Marc's exceptional sense of direction

答案:B

解析:这四行说的是 Marc 可以在他的头脑里形象化这个城市所有的街道,与选项 B Marc 的记忆力很好一致。这四行说的主体并不是 Montreal,而且也并没有说 Montreal 很神秘,只是说了 Montreal 有很多街道,所以选项 A 错误。这四行也只是说 Marc 很了解城市的布局,但没有说其他人都不能够理解地图,所以选项 B 错误。选项 D 是易错选项,Marc 可以在他的头脑里图像化所有的街道,只能表明记忆力,而无法证明他的方向感,所以选项 D 错误。

14. The situation described in paragraph two (lines 6~11) is most like _____.
    A. a cook who is an expert on a specific dish but who has never tasted it
    B. a travel agent who makes a living describing destinations to clients
    C. a librarian who catalogues and organizes books for the general public
    D. a student who is interested in a particular artist but never seen any of her work

答案:A

解析:Marc 从未去过的地方却知道那些地方,就像一个从未尝过菜却知道怎么做的厨师,选项 A 正确。选项 B 错在 Marc 并不贩卖他的知识。选项 C 错在 Marc 确实存档,但这些记录并不是为了大众的消费。选项 D 错在 Marc 不是一个学生,已经是一个专家了。

15. Which statement best characterizes Marc's relationship with his job?
    A. He enjoys his job but dislikes certain tasks he must perform.
    B. He is good at his job but does not enjoy it.
    C. He is consumed by his job and believes it to be all-important.
    D. He finds his job fun but does not realize how significant his work is.

答案:C

解析:我们回到原文——

Line 24:He tried to explain the meaning of his existence once to a fellow tenant …

选项 A 错在文中没有说 Marc 不喜欢他必须做的有些任务。选项 B 错在 Marc 看上去是享受他的工作的,或者说,是骄傲于他的工作的。选项 D 错在 Marc 知道他工作的重要性,并且想解释给其他人。

16. Based on the passage, the other workers in the engineering department view Marc as _____.
    A. valuable but looked-down-upon   B. intelligent but underused
    C. superior but shy   D. inferior but quick

答案:A

解析:我们回到原文——

Line 18:They might despise him as a lowly clerk, but they needed him all the same.

其他的工作人员需要 Marc,尽管有的时候鄙视他,与选项 A 吻合。选项 B 的 underused(未充分利用)在文中未体现。选项 C 的 shy 在文中未体现。选项 D 为易错选项,Marc 的确快,也的确可能会被鄙视,但说其他工作人员认为 Marc 是 inferior(较差的),这是无根据的,Marc 只是被认为地位低下,而不是能力差。

17. It can be reasonably inferred that Marc and Louis differ primarily because _____.
    A. Marc is poetic and Louis is unimaginative
    B. Marc is delusional and Louis is realistic
    C. Marc is productive and Louis is lazy
    D. Marc is kind and Louis is brusque

答案:B

解析:见下题。

18. Which choice provides the best evidence for the answer to the previous question?

   A. lines 34～37 ("How ... said")   B. lines 37～39 ("You ... hall")
   C. lines 39～40 ("The post ... to")   D. lines 40～44 ("If ... muttered")

答案：D

解析：选项A只提到了Louis，没有描述Marc。选项B、选项C只提到了Marc的观点，没有描述Louis。提到Marc和Louis两个人的只有D选项。通过D选项所在行，上题中B说Mar是喜欢幻想的，Louis是现实的，符合描述，正确。上题中，文章中没有提到Mac和Louis关于他们的效率或者友善程度的描写甚至比较，所以选项C、D排除。选项A说Marc是诗意的，Louis是没有想象力的，第一，诗意的不准确，而是有想象力的，第二，Louis不一定没有想象力，只是没有跟着Marc去想象，所以选项A错误。

19. As used in line 54, "exploring" most nearly means _____.

   A. traveling   B. inquiring
   C. examining   D. evaluating

答案：C

解析：explore原意为"探索"，在文中指Marc把抽屉拉到底后觉得有东西，想进一步往里面找找、探探。选项A表示"旅游"错误。选项B表示"询问"，不是进一步询问，而且也没有询问的人，错误。选项C表示"检查"，指Marc进一步检查抽屉后到底有什么东西，正确。选项D表示"评价"，无法进一步评价去发现，错误。

20. At the end of the passage, the narrator implies that Marc is _____.

   A. confused as to why he forgot to file a particular street
   B. curious about what the street contains
   C. anxious about the quality of the street inspections
   D. terrified by the discovery he has made

答案：D

解析：见下题。

21. Which choice provides the best evidence for the answer to the previous question?

   A. lines 64～66 ("It ... nothing")   B. lines 68～69 ("The date ... ago")
   C. lines 70～72 ("As ... so")   D. line 73 ("It ... street")

答案：C

解析：选项A讲的是Marc做的事去寻找道路名称的来源，错误。选项B讲的是卡片上的信息，未提到情感，错误。选项D说的是这个街道的位置，错误。选项C中的in horror对应上题中选项D中的terrified，选项C中的truth对应上题中选项D中的discovery，所以上题答案选D。而上题中，选项A、B、C中的情感都不正确。

22. Lines 73～76 ("It was ... water") mainly serve to _____.

   A. highlight the importance of a character's discovery
   B. illustrate the main character's unusual point of view
   C. describe a journey taken by the main character
   D. depict a new setting that a character will explore

答案：B。

解析：选项A，尽管Marc有一个发现，但这句话并不强调这个发现对除了他之外的人的重要性。选项C,这些行没有说主人公进行了一次旅行。选项D,从这句话中我们只能看出这条路不为Marc所熟知,并不能推出之后主人公要对其进行explore,因此可以排除该选项。而回看前文,我们发现正因为这条路是a stone in water,而Marc又是号称对这个城市所有道路都了如指掌的,所以Marc才会如此震惊,从侧面突出了他的unusual point of view。

译文

  Marc Girondin在市政大厅工程部门的档案室工作了这么久,整个城市脉络在他的脑海里,就像一张地图一样:所有的地方名称,所有交汇的要道,通向任何地方的小街,死胡同,蜿蜒的巷子……在Montreal,没有人具备这样的素质,12个警察加出租车司机都抵不上他1个。并不是说他真的认识那些像一连串咒语一样的路名的路,因为他很少去走过。他仅仅知道这些路的存在,它们在哪里,以及它们与其他道路之间的关联。

  但是,他要成为一位专家,那是绰绰有余了。他是档案陈列室里当之无愧的专家。对于从Abbott到Zotique的道路,纵横交汇延伸,他全都了如指掌。那些权贵、工程师、水管总勘察员等这类人,都会在紧要关头来向他咨询,问至细枝末节。可能在他们眼里,Marc就是个基层职工,但他们又都一样离不开他。

  尽管Marc的工作极度枯燥,但他仍然很喜欢自己的办公室,尤其是比起他在Oven大街的住所(从Sherbrooke东到St. Catherine,由北向南),他的邻居们很闹腾,有时候还比较粗暴,女房东往往也很粗暴。曾经有一次,他试着向另一个租客Louis解释他的存在是多么有意义的一件事情,但没有起到什么作用。Louis听完了大致,便开始报以讥笑。

  "Craig连着Bleury,Bleury又可以通往公园,所以呢?跟我有什么关系?请问哪里有意思了?"

  "我会让你明白的,"Marc说,"你先告诉我你住的位置。"

  "你是不是傻了?我们都住在Oven大街啊!你想说什么?"

  "你是怎么知道的?"

  "我是怎么知道的?我住在这里,我自己不知道?我交租金,对不对?我在这里可以收到信,对不对?"

  Marc很耐心地听完了这些,摇了摇头。

  "这些都不是关键。"他说着,"你住在这里,这儿是Oven大街,那是因为我市市政大厅档案室里面是这样记载的。你能够收到邮件,因为我的资料卡片索引决定了这些信件将发往哪里。如果我的这些卡片上不是按照这样去写的,那么你和Oven大街根本就不会存在了。朋友,这都是官僚机制的胜利。"

  带着一丝厌恶,Louis走开了。"去跟女房东讲这些去吧,"他嘟囔着。

  就这样,Marc继续着平凡的工作,他四十岁的生日匆匆而过,每天都过得平淡无奇。又一条大街被重新命名了,另外一条完建,还有一条拓宽;全新的纵横交错,都逐一被记入了档案资料里。

  之后发生的一件事,让Marc十分意外,他感到无比的震惊,整个档案室的柜子,从上到下,直到底部的钢架,都在随之一同震颤。

  一个8月的午后,当他想要将抽屉拉到底时,他觉得里面有样东西把抽屉卡住了。他伸手往里探了探,摸到了一张卡在抽屉底部中间的卡片。他将卡片摆了出来。这是一张旧索引卡片,脏脏的,有些破损,不过上面的字迹还是清晰可辨的。上面标注着:Bouteille Verte

大街/ Green Bottle 大街。

　　Marc 惊讶地盯着这卡片。他从来没有听说过这条大街,也从来没有听说过任何与这个诡异的名称相类似的东西。可以确定的一点是,这条大街已经应景地更了名。他仔细查看了历史信息,沉着地翻看着大街名册集,并没有找到这条大街。他又把资料柜里的资料翻了个遍,这一遍,他更为仔细,时间也更久。可是仍然一无所获,什么都没有。

　　他再次看了一眼这张卡片。卡片是没有问题的,上面记录的最后一次路名的核查时间定格在十五年零五个月十四天以前。

　　面对这样一个残酷的现实,Marc 手上的卡片掉落在了地上。他带着惊恐,转身伸手去抓……

　　这是一条被人们所遗忘了的、被弄丢了的街道。15 年来,它都存在于 Montreal,距离市政大厅只有短短一英里不到的路程,但是没有人知道这条街道的存在。它淡出了人们的视线,成为了一个谜。

2.1.3　Passage Ⅲ

答案解析

23. Over the course of the passage, the main focus shifts from _____.

A. a depiction of a family's strained dynamic to a character's wandering recollections of the distant past

B. one character's reception of new information to a frank discussion of money and inheritances

C. two characters' reactions to an unexpected message to a character's anticipation of a journey

D. a comparison between two characters to one character's thoughts about memories and aging

答案：C

解析：文章前半部分讲 Rachel 和她的父亲对于她阿姨第一次寄给 Rachel 的一封信的反应,后半部分结束于 Rachel 对于去伦敦的渴望,选项 C 正确。选项 A,尽管文章的确显示了一个家庭里的某种关系的紧张,但最后说到的是 Rachel 对于未来的想法,而不是回忆过去。选项 B,尽管钱和继承的确被提到了,但不是文章后半部分的重点。选项 D,Rachel 和她阿姨的比较不是文章前半部分的重点,而且 memories and aging 不是文章后半部分的重点。

24. Which statement best describes Rachel's perspective regarding her aunt?

A. She is curious about her similarities to her aunt and intrigued by the idea of meeting her.

B. She is disdainful of her aunt because she has ignored her family for years.

C. She is suspicious of her aunt's intentions but excited about the possibility of an inheritance.

D. She is puzzled by her aunt's sudden interest in meeting her.

答案：A

解析:我们回到原文——

Line 8:Moreover there was a likeness between her aunt's autograph and her own...

Line 44:She was excited at the thought of meeting this traditional, almost mythical aunt whom she had so often heard about.

可得出选项 A 正确。选项 B 错在文章中没有提到 Rachel 对她阿姨的鄙视。选项 C 错在文章中没有提到 Rachel 对她阿姨的怀疑,而且只是她的父亲提到了一下可能得到的遗产,但 Rachel 对此并不在意。选项 D 错在文章中没有提到 Rachel 困惑为什么阿姨突然想见她。

25. In line 7, "impugned" most nearly means _____.
 A. contradicted　　B. challenged　　C. opposed　　D. resisted
 答案:B

 解析:Rachel 的阿姨的名字与她的相同,_____ 了她的身份。选项 A 表示"反驳",选项 C 表示"反对",选项 D 表示"抵制"都太过于绝对,选项 B 挑战正确。

26. The narrator implies that Rachel's attitude towards her father is _____.
 A. overtly disrespectful　　　　　B. generally loving
 C. mildly contemptuous　　　　　D. wholly patronizing
 答案:C

 解析:见下题。

27. Which choice provides the best evidence for the answer to the previous question?
 A. lines 15~16 ("Rachel's ... remark")　　B. lines 22~23 ("She ... modern")
 C. lines 23~25 ("She had ... period")　　D. lines 32~33 ("I should ... said")
 答案:A

 解析:选项 B 说的是 Rachel 对她自己的看法,不是她对她父亲的看法。选项 C 展示了 Rachel 对一些过去的事情的感受,而不是她对她父亲的态度。选项 D 尽管显示了 Rachel 与她父亲的谈话,但并没有揭示她对她父亲的态度。通过选项 A 所在行可得知上题中选项 C 正确。上题中选项 A 错在尽管 Rachel 经常与父亲意见不同,但仍然"gentle in her answer",并没有公开地不尊重她的父亲。选项 B 错在 line 15 提到她需要压抑住对她父亲的无法容忍,而不是充满爱意的。选项 D 错在 wholly 太过绝对。

28. As used in line 24, "veneration" most nearly means _____.
 A. distaste　　B. reverence　　C. deference　　D. awe
 答案:B

 解析:她对更遥远的过去有一些_____,但对她父亲的时期一点_____也没有。选项 A"不喜欢"与 Rachel 对她父亲有不满矛盾。选项 C"遵从"与 Rachel 认为她是"ultra-modern"(line 23)相矛盾。选项 D"敬畏"对于更遥远的过去不适用。选项 B"尊敬"正确。

29. The primary purpose of paragraph 5 (lines 15~31) is to _____.
 A. establish Rachel's lack of interest in ethics and aesthetics
 B. detail the differences between Rachel's generation and her father's
 C. validate Rachel's sense that her father is untrustworthy
 D. provide insight into Rachel's view of the past
 答案:D

解析：选项 A，这一段说了 Rachel "had long since condemned alike the ethic and the aesthetic of the nineteenth century"(line 25)，但不是说她对 ethics 和 aesthetics 不感兴趣。选项 B，这一段说了 Rachel 认为她父亲那一代和她这一代很不同，但没有具体地说到哪些方面不同，错在 detail。选项 C，尽管这一段说到 Rachel 通常不同意她的父亲并且不相信他，但这一段没有证实 Rachel 的这种看法是正确的。选项 D，这一段主要讲了 Rachel 对于过去的观点，正确。

30. It can reasonably be inferred that the relationship between Rachel's father and her aunt _____.

A. has been damaged by a misunderstanding

B. is strained as a result of their past conflicts

C. has become less tense as time has passed

D. is uneasy due to their different financial situations

答案：B

解析：见下题。

31. Which choice provides the best evidence for the answer to the previous question?

A. lines 13~14 ("You're ... signature")

B. lines 33~36 ("How ... disagreed")

C. lines 61~64 ("He sighed ... speculations")

D. lines 68~72 ("There ... old")

答案：B

解析：选项 A 说 Rachel 的父亲认为她和她阿姨在某些方面很像，选项 C 说 Rachel 知道她父亲经常想起并后悔过去的经济决定，选项 D 讨论了 Rachel 的阿姨的年龄，这三个选项都没有提到 Rachel 的父亲与她阿姨的关系。通过选项 B，尤其是 Line 36 的 "We disagreed, we invariably disagreed"，可得知 Rachel 的父亲和她的阿姨超过 40 年没有见面是由于他们之间没能达成共识，选项 B 正确。上题中选项 A，文章中没有提到 Rachel 的父亲和阿姨之间有误解，错误。选项 C，文章中未提及，尽管 Rachel 的阿姨给她写信了，但并不能表明 Rachel 的阿姨和父亲之间的关系缓和了，错误。选项 D，尽管文章中提到 Rachel 的阿姨比她父亲更有钱，但没有提到他们之间关系不好是因为经济状况的原因，错误。

32. Which conclusion does Rachel make based on the letter from her aunt?

A. Her aunt's personality is consistent with her father's stories.

B. Her father has made up a great deal about her due to his forgetfulness.

C. Her aunt has taken pity on them and wants to leave them her fortune.

D. She and her aunt are remarkably alike in personality.

答案：A

解析：the letter 定位到文章 Line 49，具体定位到 53 行。

Line 53：It was all consistent enough with what her father had told her.

选项 A 完全照应 53 行，正确。选项 B，文章中既没有提到 Rachel 父亲健忘，也没有说 Rachel 认为她的父亲编造了她阿姨的故事。选项 C，尽管 Rachel 确实感受到了 "an air of pity"，而且她的父亲希望 Rachel 可以从她阿姨那里继承一些钱，但是没有得出她的阿姨想要给 Rachel 财富的结论。选项 D，尽管 Rachel 注意到了她和她阿姨的签名的相似性并且她父亲也说 Rachel 和她阿姨在某些方面很像，但 Rachel 并没有从信的内容中得出结论她和她阿姨在性格上很像。

33. In lines 56～60, the information about wealth serves mainly to _____.
  A. emphasize that Rachel's aunt makes strong demands of her family
  B. provide context for the disagreement between Rachel's aunt and her father
  C. illustrate why Rachel generally disregards her father's advice
  D. reveal that Rachel may benefit from building a relationship with her aunt

答案：D

解析：选项 A，这些行说的是 Rachel 父亲的希望，而不是 Rachel 阿姨的需求。选项 B，这些行没有说到 Rachel 父亲和阿姨的分歧。选项 C，尽管 Rachel 的父亲基本上没有什么留给 Rachel 做遗产，但不是 Rachel 不听她父亲建议的一个原因。选项 D，Rachel 父亲对于自己经济状况的评价和 Rachel 阿姨的经济状况说明，揭示了 Rachel 父亲认为她可能会从她阿姨那里继承钱财。

译文

这是有生之年，头一回，Rachel 收到来自她的阿姨的信。

"我觉得你的阿姨最终还是原谅了我。"她的爸爸说着，将这封信从桌子的另一头推向了 Rachel。

Rachel 先看了下署名。她很是惊奇，自己的"名字"居然会出现在那个位置。正如，她头一回意识到，这个世界上还有另外一个 Rachel Deanes 存在一样。另外，她阿姨的字迹和她的也很相似，尤其是连笔时候的笔锋回转都一样，透着一种坚毅不苟的特质。如果 Rachel 早个 50 年上学，那么她或许就完全用那样的风格去书写了。

"你在一些地方跟她很像。"她的爸爸说。Rachel 仍然在看着那签名。

她的眼帘下垂，神情中流露了些许对于她爸爸的言辞所表现出的隐隐的不耐烦。这件事，他重复说了很多次了，并且用的口吻也是一模一样的，以至于她自然而然地形成了一种习惯，去无视这些言辞确凿与否。他在她面前，总有些倚老卖老。他五十多岁生了 Rachel。从开始记事起，Rachel 就总是对爸爸说的话持狐疑态度。用她自己的话形容，她是一个"怀疑论者"，一个"超现代主义者"。她对先前过往的事存着一种敬畏，但她爸爸的除外。长久以来，她都对自己与爸爸所共同持有的"十九世纪伦理美学观点"很是"过敏"。甚至到现在，当 Rachel 的爸爸表达着他那与她极为神似的看法时，她仍然会本能地选择不相信这些。不过呢，她在回应上用的语气还是很谦卑的。她借着自己的年少气盛，来表达对年迈父亲的一种怜悯。

"爸爸，我想你一定已经不记得 Rachel 阿姨是个什么样的人了，"她问，"你们多少年没有见面了？"

"四十多年了，"她爸爸沉思道，"我们意见不合，向来不合。Rachel 总是觉得自己是超摩登的，并以此为傲。她读过达尔文等人的书。的确，我承认，她比我强。但是，我总觉得，无论如何，那些先前得来的经验才是历久弥新的，不管怎么样。" Rachel 舒展了一下肩颈，脸上露着不屑，不过言语中却丝毫未予显露："所以，那么，她想见见我是吧。"

一想到要去见这位听闻已久、带着些许神秘感的阿姨，Rachel 是兴奋的。有那么几次，她会想这位了不起的亲戚，她的性格是不是正如她的父亲所说的那样，而不是一种想象或者一种基于依稀过往而构建出来的虚幻。但是,早餐桌上放着的阿姨的这封来信,说明了一切。隐晦的措辞中包含了一丝傲慢、一丝戾气。她的信写得很客套,但是那种客套里带了一层同情。这些与 Rachel 爸爸所告诉她的如出一辙。

Deane 老先生从追忆中回过神来,叹了一口气。

"对对,她想见见你,我的女儿,"他说着,"我觉得你最好答应她,陪陪她。她很有钱,几乎可以用'富裕'来形容。而我呢,你知道,其实什么都没有能留给你的,真的什么都没有。如果她愿意……"

他又叹了一口气,Rachel 知道,那么多次,他都在悔恨着自己当年的无用。他在钱这方面是很愚蠢的,将过去很显赫的一笔资金投用到了漫无目的的投机生意当中。

"我当然会去,如果你可以给我两个星期。"Rachel 说道,"我很想见见这位厉害的阿姨。顺便问一句,她多大年龄了?"

"我们的年龄只差了 15 个月,"Deane 老先生答道,"所以,女儿啊,她应该是,对,她应该是 73 岁了。天哪,你阿姨居然已经 73 岁了! 我还总是觉得她跟你一样大。我从来没有意识到,原来,她的年纪居然已经那么大了……"

他继续沉思着,而 Rachel 没有再听。他希望子辈能够明白这些。他试图穿越世纪来触及女儿的理解与同情。而 Rachel 呢,已然决心去冒险一回,热切地期待着伦敦之行。这场旅程,除了更多地去了解这位久仰的神秘阿姨,还带着一种既定了的欢愉。

2.1.4　Passage Ⅳ

答案解析

34. Over the course of the passage, the main focus shifts from _____.
　　A. the narrator's view on his brother's job to the narrator's hopes for his own trip
　　B. the narrator's jealousy of his brother to the narrator's anxiety about his own trip
　　C. the narrator's expectations about the Far West to the reality of life in the Far West
　　D. the narrator's excitement about traveling west to the narrator's fear of leaving home

答案:A

解析:文章一开始集中写主人公兄弟的新工作,想象他的兄弟会经历的事情,然后转向他对他自己旅行的期待,选项 A 正确。选项 B 错在尽管主人公嫉妒他的兄弟的新工作,但没有表达任何对于他自己旅行的焦虑。选项 C 错在没有转向 Far West 生活的真相。选项 D 错在没有提到对于离开家的害怕。

35. As used in line 2, "majesty" most nearly means _____.
　　A. solemn royalty　　　　　　　　B. breathtaking beauty
　　C. impressive dignity　　　　　　D. extreme difficulty

答案:C

解析:majesty 形容的是主人公的兄弟的新工作,一个政府里的职位。选项 A"皇权"错误,选项 B"美丽"无法形容工作。选项 D"难的"在文章中没有依据。选项 C"有尊严的",正确,他的兄弟的工作是令人羡慕的。

36. Based on lines 7~8, ("I ... brother") it can reasonably be inferred that the narrator's perspective is one of _____.

A. critical reflection upon his past views
B. objective analysis of his prior actions
C. fond recollection of his recent adventures
D. regretful remembrance of his past mistakes

答案：A

解析：主人公说自己年轻并且无知,是对他之前观点的批判性的反思,选项 A 正确。选项 B,是一个主观性的判断,并不是一个客观性的分析,错误。选项 C,主人公是回忆他之前对他的兄弟的职位的观点,不是回忆最近发生的历险,错误。选项 D,文章中并没有直接说到主人公说自己年轻并且无知所以犯了错误。

37. Which statement best characterizes the narrator's relationship with his brother?

A. The narrator is disinterested in emulating his brother.
B. The narrator is solely motivated by his brother's wealth.
C. The narrator is generally unrealistic about his brother's situation.
D. The narrator is mostly critical of his brother's recent decision.

答案：C

解析：见下题。

38. Which choice provides the best evidence for the answer to the previous question?

A. lines 1~5 ("My ... absence")
B. lines 8~11 ("I ... explore")
C. lines 18~22 ("And ... hillside")
D. lines 27~28 ("What ... describe")

答案：C

解析：选项 A 描述的是主人公的兄弟的新工作,选项 B、D 描述的是主人公对他兄弟的处境的嫉妒,都没有说到主人公对此有不切合实际的想法。选项 C,说主人公想象他的兄弟会参观"the gold mines and the silver mines"并且每天收集很多有价值的东西,这种不切合实际的场景是主人公"young and ignorant"对他的兄弟的处境的观点。主人公解释他嫉妒他的兄弟的工作,并且贪求这个工作所能带来的优越、财富与旅游,但是也说他"young and ignorant",也就是说他在那时没有切合实际地考虑他的兄弟的处境,选项 C 正确。选项 A,主人公说他"envied"他的兄弟并且"coveted his distinction and his financial splendor",所以应该是 interested in 而不是 disinterested in。选项 B,solely 太过绝对,错误。选项 D,主人公羡慕和嫉妒他的兄弟,而不是批判他的兄弟,错误。

39. At the end of the first paragraph, the description of the brother's return mainly serves to _____.

A. demonstrate that the narrator is correct to be envious of his brother
B. call into question the idea that the Far West is a "curious new world"
C. suggest that the narrator's expectations about the Fair West are fantastical
D. support the narrator's view of his brother's job with specific examples of its glamour

答案:C

解析:选项 C,作者对他的兄弟在远东经历之后回来的场景充满了期待,正确。选项 A,第一段结尾主人公想象他兄弟回家会是什么样的,但不是叙述真实发生的事情,所以没有办法证实主人公是对的,选项 A 错误。选项 B,call into question(质疑)错误。选项 D,主人公是在描述很多远东的经历而不是聚焦在他的兄弟的工作上,错误。

40. It can be reasonably inferred from the discussion of Nevada in paragraph 3 (lines 33~43) that the narrator's stay was _____.

   A. less exciting than he had expected
   B. much longer than he had planned
   C. more pleasurable than he had anticipated
   D. more dangerous than he had expected

答案:B

解析:见下题。

41. Which choice provides the best evidence for the answer to the previous question?
   A. lines 34~37 ("Not ... apiece")   B. lines 38~40 ("I only ... that")
   C. lines 40~41 ("I meant ... business") D. lines 41~43 ("I ... years")

答案:D

解析:选项 A 是主人公对旅行的准备。选项 B 大致描述了主人公认为他会待在 Nevada 的时间,而没有说他真实花在那里的时间。选项 C 说的是作者的打算,而没有说到实际情况。选项 D 说明原来主人公认为他会待在那里 3 个月,而其实要待上 6~7 年,所以上题中选项 B 正确,是主人公的停留时间比计划的更长。

42. Which situation is most similar to the situation described in paragraph 4 (lines 44~46)?
   A. While paying his bills, a man daydreams about winning money in the lottery.
   B. The night before the school play, a boy worries that he will forget his lines.
   C. On her way to practice, a softball player pictures herself up to bat.
   D. As he prepares for a diving excursion, a diver imagines sunken treasure.

答案:D

解析:这一段描述的是作者想象他即将开始的旅行会经历一些什么,选项 D 正确。选项 A 更多的是直接受益,而不是经历一些事情。选项 B 错在文中是期待的而不是担心的。选项 C 更多的是想象之前已经做过无数次的一件日常性的行动而不是文中的从未经历的一件事。

43. As used in line 55, "roosted on" most nearly means _____.
   A. made a nest   B. lay down to sleep
   C. settled in a single place D. climbed to the top of

答案:C

解析:文中 roosted on 这个动作的执行者是 steamboat,选项 A 表示"做一个巢",选项 B 表示"躺下来睡觉",选项 D 表示"爬到高处",都无法是一个蒸汽船做出的动作,只有选项 C 表示"待在一个地方"可以是一个蒸汽船做出的动作,所以选项 C 正确。

44. In the description of the boat's movements, the words "walked" and "walking" primarily serve to establish a tone of _____.

A. humor　　　　B. foreboding　　　　C. strangeness　　　　D. awe

答案：A

解析：用"walk"而不是"sail"体现了一种幽默来表达船的进程，所以选项 A 正确，而不是一种 foreboding（预示）、strangeness（奇怪）或者 awe（敬畏）。

 译文

　　我哥哥刚被任命为内华达准州的州务秘书。这个职位集许多权力和尊严于一身：财政部长、审计员、州秘书，在州长缺席时，还是代理州长。1800 美元年薪和"秘书先生"头衔给这个职位蒙上一种至高无上的尊荣。我既年轻又少阅历，非常羡慕他。我垂涎他的显赫和豪富，更向往他即将进行的漫长而神秘的旅行，以及他要去探索的奇妙的新天地。他就要去旅行了！可我还从来没有出过门，"旅行"这个词儿对我来说有一种迷人的魅力。不久，他就会千里迢迢，在那广袤的沙漠和平原上跋涉——游历于远西地区的山中，看到印第安人、野牛、草原犬鼠和羚羊，经历种种冒险，过一种前所未有的愉快生活。他在家书里会给我们讲述这一切，成为我们的英雄。他还会看到金矿和银矿，公务之余，下午出去各处溜达，或许会捡到两三桶亮晃晃的金币和银币，在山里还会捡到金块和银块。用不了多久，他就会腰缠万贯，由海路还家，平心静气地讲起旧金山、海洋和"地眠"，似乎亲眼见过的那些天下奇观不过是区区小事。我眼红他的幸福，心中受尽折磨，用笔墨都难以描述。因此，当他郑重地提议让我做他的手下——令人尊敬的私人秘书时，我觉得世界骤然间消失了，苍穹像画轴一样被收去！这就是我最大的妄想，我完全心满意足了。两小时以后，我已整装待发。没有多少行李需要收拾，因为我们将要乘坐由密苏里边区至内华达的大陆驿马车，每个旅客只能携带少量行李。在 10～20 年前那美好的年代里，太平洋铁路还没有修筑，连一根枕木也没有。

　　我打算在内华达只住 3 个月——一点也没有想在那里多待，只想去尽量看看那里的新奇东西，然后便马上回家来干正经事。万万没想到，那 3 个月愉快的旅行，竟在六七年漫长的岁月之后才看到它的尽头。

　　整夜，我梦见印第安人、沙漠和银块。在第 2 天预定的时间内，我们在圣路易港登上一条开往密苏里河的汽船。

　　从圣路易到圣约走了 6 天——多么沉闷、乏味，使人昏昏欲睡的航程，在我的记忆中，它留给我的印象好像不到 6 分钟，而不是那么许多日子。关于那次旅行，我现在已经没有什么印象了，所记得的就只是水中那些形状丑恶、盘根错节的树根。船开到这里，得小心翼翼地时而开动这个轮子，时而开动那个轮子，一次又一次地碰到礁石，退回来，在平缓的地方又开过去；经常陷进沙滩，于是停下来，取出撑杆，撑了过去。实际上，这条船简直可以说是从陆地上开到圣约去的。因为大部分时间都在"走"——成天耐心而吃力地越过礁石，爬过树根。船长说，它是一条"出色"的船，它需要的只不过是更大的冲力和一个大些的轮子。我认为，它倒是需要一副高跷。但是我很聪明，没有说出口。

2.2 Social Science

2.2.1 Passage I

答案解析

1. The authors' central claim in the passage is that _____.

A. replacing the GDP outright may seem appealing, but its alternatives would be difficult and dangerous to implement

B. well-being and economics have not been shown to correlate to any significant degree

C. the GDP can only measure economics, while happiness must be considered primarily in terms of other factors

D. there is a growing movement to improve the way in which a country's well-being is measured

答案：D

解析：我们回到原文——

Line 1：There is currently a broad global movement away from considerations of mere economic success toward a new public policy goal involving a broader notion of quality of life.

Line 17：Three key strategies have been employed to develop a better measure of well-being …

选项A，作者的确看上去觉得换掉GDP很appealing，但是没有觉得它的替换方案是dangerous的。选项B，作者提到过well-being和economics是有联系的。选项C，作者提到GDP和"many of the social goods that make life enjoyable"是有联系的。

2. In the first paragraph, the reference to Simon Kuznets mainly serves to _____.

A. emphasize that the GDP is a respected and valid tool

B. underscore a common concern about the GDP by citing a critic

C. clarify an abstract point about the development of the GDP by mentioning its creator

D. strengthen the argument that the GDP does not adequately measure well-being

答案：D

解析：我们回到原文——

Line 12：However, this measure was never meant to be a measure of the welfare of nations …

选项A，文中warn表示负面，与选项A中的respected and valid的正面形象不符。选项B，Simon Kuznets是creator不是critic（评论家/批评家）。选项C，文中没有提到the development of the GDP。

3. As used in line 8, "prominent" most nearly means _____.
 A. pronounced   B. remarkable   C. recognized   D. projecting
答案：C
解析：prominent 本意为"著名的"；pronounced 解释为"明显的"，偏向于形容一件事情；remarkable 为"出色的"，与"著名的"涵义有所偏差；recognized 为"公认的"，正确；projecting 为"突出的"，偏向于形容一件物品。

4. The authors imply that the "first group of initiatives" would primarily _____.
 A. change the measurement approach to encompass only social factors
 B. take both positive and negative factors into account universally
 C. show the positive effects of modernization in its new measurements
 D. shift the measurement of GDP so that it is calculated per capita
答案：B
解析：见下题。

5. Which choice provides the best evidence for the answer to the previous question?
 A. lines 17～19("Three ... the GDP")
 B. lines 20～22("The first ... itself")
 C. lines 25～27("For example ... households")
 D. lines 30～34("As a consequence ... nations")
答案：D
解析：选项 A 的行数总体说有三种方法来改进，选项 B 只说了"downside"，选项 C 只与"consumption of private households"有关，选项 D 中"downsides ... ought to be accounted for whilst retaining the benefits"对应第 4 题选项 B 中的"positive and negative factors"。而上题中，选项 A 错在不是只有 social factors，还有像 air pollution and environmental damage。选项 C 错在不是只有 show the positive effects，还有 downsides of economic growth and modernization(line 31)。选项 D 在文中未提到。

6. As used in line 33, "figure" most nearly means _____.
 A. symbol   B. number   C. level   D. structure
答案：D
解析：GDP 是一个数字，而不是一种象征、层次或者结构。Figure 有数字的意思，所以选 B。

7. It can be inferred that the alternative approach to measuring happiness that is most different from the current approach is based on the belief that _____.
 A. GDP is a helpful measurement of how economics contribute to welfare in different countries
 B. the sum of goods and services produced by a country is not a necessary factor in determining a country's well-being
 C. material living conditions and life expectancy have no effect on individual happiness
 D. economic prosperity is a good predictor of life expectancy and is particularly useful for comparing life expectancies around the world
答案：B

解析:见下题。

8. Which choice provides the best evidence for the answer to the previous question?
   A. lines 52～55("The most ... economy")
   B. lines 55～57("The logic ... itself")
   C. lines 58～59("Famous ... foundation")
   D. lines 59～63("The index ... well-being")

答案:A

解析:选项 B 尽管评论了 GDP 与 well-being 的联系,但没有说这个方法与如今的方法怎么不同,选项 C、D 只举例了替换方法,也没有说怎么"most different"。选项 A 中 Line 53:... which seeks alternative indicators of well-being without accounting for the sum of goods and services produced in an economy. 对应上题选项 B,所以此题选项 A 正确,上题选项 B 正确。上题中,选项 A 是现在的方法,选项 C 的 no effect 与 line 59 "The index comprises life expectancy"矛盾,选项 D 中的"economic prosperity is a good predictor of life expectancy"错误。

9. According to the graph, the region with the fourth-lowest HPI score is _____.
   A. Russia, Ukraine, and Belarus　　B. Central and Eastern Europe
   C. South Asia　　　　　　　　　　D. North America

答案:A

解析:看图表,从下往上数第 4 个是"the fourth-lowest",也就是"Russia, Ukraine, and Belarus"。

10. Based on the passage, which of the following is most likely to contribute to South America's HPI ranking _____.
   A. A somewhat high duration of education
   B. A moderately low gross national income
   C. A fairly low production of services
   D. A relatively high life expectancy

答案:D

解析:我们回到原文——

Line 59:The index comprises life expectancy, life satisfaction, and the ecological footprint ...

选项 A、B、C 都没有在提到 Happy Planet Index 时出现,只有选项 D 出现,"relatively high"也对应图表中 South America 为第二高 HPI 指数地区。

11. The greatest number of geographic regions have an HPI score in which range?
   A. 20～30.　　　B. 30～40.　　　C. 40～50.　　　D. 50～60.

答案:C

解析:20～30 无地区,30～40 有 5 个地区,40～50 有 12 个地区左右,50～60 有 2 个地区左右,因此,40～50 最多。

译文

目前,全球都出现了一种公共政策目标的转变:从仅仅注重经济上的成就过渡到将更广泛意义上的生活质量纳入公共政策制定目标的考量范围。这种过渡也让人们开始反思,从数据中反映出来的一个国家的欣欣向荣与其国民(真正的生活状态之间的)差异。几十年来,(衡量一个国家实力的)黄金指标都是一个宏观经济指标——GDP,即由人均推算出的国民生产总值。这是媒体、政客和公众在试图衡量一个国家表现如何的时候会考虑到的标尺中最为突出的一个。然而,这一指标从来都不是用来衡量国家福利的,因此对于 GDP 是否能够有效衡量国家安康的怀疑声越来越大。诸如"超越 GDP"或"重新定义过程"的标语(不断)挑战着(人们对于)GDP 的执着。

要发展出一个更好的衡量指标要用到三种关键策略:修正 GDP、完善 GDP 或替换 GDP。第一种策略的最初目的在于试图通过修正 GDP 自身来解决这一指标的缺陷……这种策略的主要目标是为将 GDP 的增长与可持续性及环境损害相联系。例如,可持续经济福利指数和真实发展指数都是以家庭消费总量为基础的。然而,他们也反映了其他的社会因素,例如:家庭劳动力和教育会加分,而空气及环境的污染则会降低分数。这样一来,(GDP 在衡量)经济增长和现代化上的缺失就被解决了,同时还保留了 GDP 指标的优势,也就是用一个单独指标能抓取不同本质并能全国通行。

第二种策略较之前一种走得更远,却没有把生产总量和服务两个方面完全抛弃。这种策略转而寻求通过一系列重要的社会性指标来完善 GDP,从而评估一个国家。例如,人类发展指数包含了健康、教育和物质生活状况三方面。这些是由预期寿命、受教育年限和 GNI(国民收入总值)等组成。尽管用其他指标来对 GDP 进行补充的方法能够弥补上一种方式在货币化上的弊端,但是不同指标如何标准化同样饱受争议,尤其是将不同衡量指标合并成一个单独的标准化指数这一概念在方法上就很受质疑,同时也还需要研究者们的价值判断。

第三种方法离 GDP 最远,直接寻求另一个指标而不将经济生产中的商品和服务总量计算在内。这一策略背后的逻辑是,GDP 已经是并且将会一直是通向终结的道路,而非终结本身。著名的例子有由新经济基金会计算出的地球快乐指数。这一指数包括了预期寿命、生活满意度以及生态指标,因此,它能够显示国家需要多少资源才能维持一定程度的国民健康和国家安康……

把 GDP 这一指标整个替换掉是一个衡量国民幸福的较为激进的策略,因此经济增长不仅仅是社会商品的前提,这些社会商品让生活更加美好,更与其他(社会)因素息息相关。因此,认为 GDP 是一种通往结果的过程实际上有危险的。它做出了一个感念上的假设,这一假设在理论上很出名,但在实际中会被因果机制和经验主义的数据挑战。

2.2.2　Passage Ⅱ

答案解析

12. The authors' central claim is that _____.
A. cuteness provokes the same emotional responses around the world
B. encountering a cute object may lead to changes in behavior
C. studies of cuteness should include tasks that involve social interaction
D. cuteness elicits feelings of tenderness in test subjects

答案:B

解析：全文都在说遇到一个可爱的物体可能会导致行为改变。选项 A、C、D 不是文章重点。

13. The authors mention Pokemon and Hello Kitty in order to _____ .

A. provide examples of popular kawaii products from Japan

B. clarify an earlier statement by showing that some products use cuteness in their marketing

C. demonstrate that cute products are more likely to be exported than other products

D. support the claim that kawaii products are found in various fields

答案：A

解析：我们回到原文——

Line 4：... which are often described as kawaii ...

选项 B，作者之前没有提到"marketing"。选项 C，作者之前没有提到可爱的产品更可能被出口。选项 D，作者没有提及可爱的产品在很多领域能被找到，只是说"attract considerable attention from various fields"(line 6)。

14. As used in line 22, "elemental" most nearly means _____ .

A. inner　　　　B. chemical　　　　C. partial　　　　D. essential

答案：D

解析：elemental 本意为"基本的"，inner 指"内部的"，partial 指"部分的"，essential 指"必要的"。

15. The words "capture" and "induce" (lines 23～24) primarily serve to _____ .

A. ironically depict the unclear effects of cute images on test subjects

B. characterize the cute stimuli used in tests in unusually strong terms

C. indicate that cute stimuli can have a forceful impact on the viewer

D. provide a formal tone to contrast with the rest of the passage's informal tone

答案：C

解析：选项 A，这两个词不是为了 ironic(讽刺)，是强调可爱的形象可能有强大的影响。选项 B，不是 characterize(描绘)stimuli(刺激)，而是强调刺激的影响。选项 D，这两个词并不是正式的语气。

16. The authors imply that they see Sherman, Haidt, and Coan's experiments as mainly _____ .

A. interesting but unnecessary　　　　B. sloppy and inconclusive

C. suggestive but incomplete　　　　D. inventive and groundbreaking

答案：C

解析：见下题。

17. Which choice provides the best evidence for the answer to the previous question?

A. lines 43～45（"The ... actions"）

B. lines 45～46（"Sherman ... perspective"）

C. lines 46～48（"That ... state"）

D. lines 49～51（"Although ... reasons"）

答案：D

解析：选项 A、B 提到的是实验的方法，没有说明作者的观点。选项 C 提到的是实验的结果,没有说明作者的观点。选项 D 中 Line 49:Although the results are intriguing, the mechanism of performance improvement remains unclear…对应上题中选项 A,所以此题选项 D 正确,上题选项 A 正确。上题中,选项 A 中 unnecessary 错误;选项 B,尽管作者希望有进一步研究,但没有说这些实验是 sloppy(马虎的)或者 inconclusive(无说服力的);选项 D 在文中没有提及。

18. The authors imply that Sherman, Haidt, and Coan's Operation experiment would have been improved by changing the _____.

　　A. methodology　　　　　　B. test subjects
　　C. experimental setting　　　D. researchers

答案:A

解析:见下题。

19. Which choice provides the best evidence for the answer to the previous question?
　　A. line 56~59("If … task").
　　B. line 59~63("The … body").
　　C. line 63~64("Using … improvement").
　　D. line 67~69("Instead … tendencies").

答案:C

解析:选项 A 表示实验的一个推论而不是更改实验。选项 B 表示实验本身。选项 D 表示实验结果。选项 C 说明这个实验只集中于一类任务,用不同的任务会更好,而这个是改变了方法,所以此题选项 C 正确,上题选项 A 正确,这里没有改变测试对象、实验设定或者研究人员,所以上题选项 B、C、D 错误。

20. According to the graph, the second-highest overall score in the study was achieved by the participants who _____.
　　A. had just viewed pictures of baby animals
　　B. had just viewed pictures of adult animals
　　C. were about to view pictures of adult animals
　　D. were about to view pictures of baby animals

答案:B

解析:根据图表,最高的是 baby animal 的 post,第二高的是 adult animal 的 post,第三高的是 adult animal 的 pre,最低的是 baby animal 的 pre;pre 指前,图表中指看图像之前,题目中对应 were about to,post 指后,图表中指看图像之后,题目中对应 had just。

21. According to the passage, one explanation for the performance of the subjects in the graph's top-scoring is that the _____.
　　A. test took place under timed conditions, forcing the subjects to be more accurate
　　B. subjects had to perform several kinds of tasks, making them consider each one more carefully
　　C. tenderness elicited by viewing the images made them more careful in performing the task
　　D. subjects experienced a heighted motivation for social interaction

答案:C

解析:选项 A,文中提及"the time to complete the task was not measured"(line 51),与

timed conditions 矛盾。选项 B,实验对象只完成一种任务——playing a game,而不是多种任务。选项 C,文章中指出"the tenderness elicited by cute images"(line 47)。选项 D 不是实验对象表现的直接解释。

22. The average initial score of participants who were later shown the adult animal pictures was closest to which number?

A. 7.   B. 8.   C. 9.   D. 10.

答案:B

解析:图表显示大多数 score 都在 8 左右。

译文

可爱的事物在全世界都是流行的。尤其是日本的文化,更是从社会层面上接受并欣赏幼稚(这一属性)。多种多样的动画角色周边产品,例如常被描述为 kawaii 的皮卡丘和凯蒂猫,都被生产并出口至许多国家。这一现象吸引了各个领域的广泛关注,(甚至)包括美学及工程领域。Kawaii 在现代日语中是一个作定语的形容词,在英语中常被译作"cute"(可爱)。然而,这个单词本身是从古日语中的 kawa-hayu-shi(字面意思是脸红)派生出的描述情感的形容词,其原意"感到羞耻的、非礼勿视的、看到羞耻的"也(在历史上)变成了"不能留下某人独自一人、照顾"。现在,我们把这种喜爱的感觉称之为"可爱",典型的就是孩子、婴儿、小动物(给我们的感受)。

可爱的事物被认为处于婴儿模式。这指的是一系列通常见于小动物身上的特性:相对于躯干而言大大的头、高而突出的前额、大眼睛等。Lorenz 认为这些对婴儿模式的反应是一系列内在的反应,并会为一些刺激因素所引发。在人类中,这些刺激因素被认定是可爱的、引人注意的、能让观者微笑的且能诱发接近、照顾动机及行为的。婴儿模式在(人们)处理视觉信息的早期阶段就调节了人们的感知和注意,并激活了大脑中的奖励系统。从行为学的角度来说,可爱的事物总能得到优待是可以理解的。但是,(我们对于)遇到可爱事物是否会影响旁观者接下来的反应则知之甚少。因为可爱的东西会产生正面的情绪,其影响可能会延伸至行为的其他领域。

Sherman、Haidt 和 Coan 所做的两个实验显示,在被试观看了一些可爱的图片(小狗和小猫)所组成的幻灯片后,他们在完成精细灵巧动作时的表现比在观看了那些不怎么可爱的图片(狗和猫)后进步了更多。实验测量的是被试从游戏板上描绘的病人躯干上成功移走了多少塑料身体部件的数量。他们只能用镊子,而且不能触碰其他部分的边缘。被试在完成这项任务时准确度的提高可以被看作是对动作更高关注度及控制力的表现。Sherman 解释说这一效果代表了认知学的观点。也就是说,可爱的图片引发了喜爱的情感,但更多的是一种温柔的情绪。它能让人们在行为上更温和。尽管(实验)结果很令人感兴趣,但行为进步的机制仍然因以下两个原因而不明:第一,完成任务所用的时间并没有被测算。更精准的行为可能是通过很慢、不慌不忙的动作完成的,也可以是通过快且准确的动作完成的。测算行为速度能够帮助解释(该结果)潜藏的机制。第二,(实验)只用到了一种任务。如果看动物幼崽会引发保护性、照顾性的温和行为,行为上的进步可以是具体到照顾类的任务上。但 Sherman 实验中用到的这一任务则是看护任务,因为被试要扮演医生的角色,通过移除多余的身体部件来帮助游戏板上的病人。不同种类的任务能够(更好地)阐明行为进步的原因。

最近,Sherman 和 Haidt 对人们的普遍观点,即可爱是内在母性天性和看护反馈的内在释放器,发起了挑战。他们提出,感受到可爱促进了社会参与,并为相应的友善与温和做好了准备。这一态度上的变化被认为是与(人的)认知过程有关。而认知过程则又与心理活动有联系,进而导致更多关爱行为。如果因可爱而引发的谨慎行为是基于更高层次的社会互动动机,这一效果可能不会在简单的、没有社会互动参与的感知-认知任务中出现。

2.2.3 Passage Ⅲ

答案解析

23. The authors' central claim is that _____.
A. while there is disagreement about whether or not new media enhance democracy, all agree that they are changing politics
B. political candidates cannot influence elections without manipulating new media to benefit their campaigns
C. citizens must become more engaged in politics by blogging to truly exercise their democratic privileges
D. it is too soon to tell what new media's political effects will be, but they are generally thought to be positive

答案:A

解析:全文在讨论新媒体正影响着政治,但既有正面的也有负面的,与选项 A 吻合。选项 B,作者没有提出政权候选人在操纵新媒体。选项 C,尽管作者列出一些市民用博客参与政治的例子,但不是为了说要行使民主权利,公民必须利用更多的博客来参与政治。选项 D,作者提到新媒体的政治影响有"benefits and limitations"(line 63),与题目中"generally thought to be positive"矛盾,所以错。

24. As used in lines 1~2, "concerned with" most nearly means _____.
A. worried about   B. interested in   C. motivated by   D. uneasy about

答案:B

解析:Line 4 的"cyber-optimists"和"cyber-pessimists"说明 concern(关心)既有正面的也有负面的,因此选项 A、D 两个负面的词组排除,选项 C motivated by(被激励)与文章意思不符。

25. The author implies that cyber-optimists view the use of new media technologies by minor parties as _____.
A. the only solution to the problem of unfairness in elections
B. useful tools that may be dangerous in the wrong hands because of the limited understanding most people have of them
C. platforms that have been carefully developed by politicians in order to serve the needs of special interests
D. and opportunity to make the electoral process more democratic

答案:D

解析:见下题。

26. Which choice provides the best evidence for the answer to the previous question?

A. lines 10~12 ("The first ... exposure")

B. lines 12~14 ("Minor ... themselves")

C. lines 18~20 ("However ... democracy")

D. lines 20~24 ("Both ... links")

答案：C

解析：选项 A 总述争论的对象是 exposure，但并没有说 cyber-optimists 的观点。选项 B 说的是 minor party 通过新媒体可以做的事，但并没有说 cyber-optimists 的观点。选项 D 说的是 minor 和 major parties 通过新媒体可以做的事，但并没有说 cyber-optimists 的观点。上题问的是 cyber-optimists 的观点，且文中并未直接提及，而是用它的反面观点来说明，所以选项 C 正确，上题正确答案为 D。

27. The expressions "cyber-optimists" and "cyber-pessimists" (line 4) primarily serve to _____.

A. frame the debate surrounding new media and politics with familiar oppositional terms

B. legitimize the author's argument by creating a new kind of jargon to reference the players in this political field

C. clarify that there are only two possible positions to take regarding this issue, and they are opposed to one another

D. distinguish between major and minor parties with new terms that allow the reader to view them as positive and negative

答案：A

解析：大多数人对于 optimists（乐观主义者）和 pessimists（悲观主义者）这两个对立的术语熟悉，所以这两个表达说明了关于新媒体的争论。

选项 B 中"a new kind of jargon"错误。选项 C，作者并没有说只有两种可能的立场。选项 D，这两个表达不是为了区分"major and minor parties"，也不是为了让读者"view them as positive and negative"。

28. The author uses the Pew Research Center findings to imply that _____.

A. Barack Obama's victory was possible only because of social media usage

B. new media users influence real-world population

C. cyber-optimists take an overly positive stance towards new media

D. cyber-pessimists do not understand how new media outlets are used

答案：B

解析：见下题。

29. Which choice provides the best evidence for the answer to the previous question?

A. lines 25~28 ("However ... nowadays")

B. lines 28~33 ("For ... media")

C. lines 33~37 ("Thus ... point")

D. lines 38~44 ("The third ... public sphere")

答案：C

解析:选项 A 大致说的是"cyber-optimists"和"cyber-pessimists"的分歧。选项 B 是 Pew Research findings 的具体内容。选项 D 大致说的是微博的现象。上题中关键词 Pew Research Center 出现在 line 29,往后找,题目问作者用这个发现的目的,找到 Line 33:Thus, Internet voters may shape election campaign agendas to some extent,选项 C 中的 "shape"对应上题中选项 B 的"influence",选项 C 中的"election campaign agendas"对应上题中选项 B 的"real-world population",此题选项 C 正确,上题选项 B 正确。上题中,选项 A 错在"only",文中还提到除了 social media usage 的其他理由,例如 grassroots efforts;选项 C,文中没有说是"overly positive";选项 D 在文中未提及。

30. The author discusses Li Xiaode as an example of _____.
A. a new media user who made a political impact
B. an average person who misguidedly tried to change the world
C. a new kind of politician who began as an ordinary citizen
D. a scholar in political communications working to change the field

答案:A

解析:Li Xiaode 定位到文章 line 49,提及他是"the first successful case of using a blog as a 'watchdog' to expose numerous official corruptions... thereby broadening the channel of political participation through blogs."

选项 B 中"misguidedly"错误;选项 C 中说 Li Xiaode 是一个"politician"错误;选项 D 中说 Li Xiaode 是一个"scholar"错误,Li Xiaode 只是一个 ordinary citizen。

31. Which of the following choices represents the greatest number of people?
A. McCain's Facebook supporters   B. Obama's Twitter followers
C. McCain's MySpace friends   D. Obama's MySpace friends

答案:D

解析:McCain 有 627459 Facebook supporters,Obama 有 115623 Twitter followers, McCain 有 419463 MySpace friends,Obama 有 844781 MySpace friends,在这些数中, Obama 的 MySpace friends 的数最多。

32. According to the passage, Obama's comparatively high usage of social media as depicted in the chart is an example of _____.
A. the links between new media use and political success
B. early adopters of technology benefiting from their timing
C. the importance of micro-blogging to reach supporters
D. minor candidates gaining exposure through new media

答案:A

解析:文章中提到了社交媒体的运用会导致一个成功的竞选,图表表明 Obama 在社交媒体上更加活跃,所以选项 A 正确,选项 B、C、D 在图表中都没有体现。

33. We can infer from the chart that the majority of McCain supporters were _____.
A. active on Facebook   B. active on MySpace
C. active on Twitter   D. not active on any of these platforms

答案:A

解析:根据图表,McCain 在 Facebook 上有 627459 followers,在 MySpace 上有 219463

friends，在 Twitter 上有 4911 followers。

译文

　　政治交流学学者们正密切关注着新媒体对政治的影响程度。下面几个部分对应的就是网络乐观论者和网络悲观论者对于这场讨论中三个关键问题所持的相应立场。这三个问题是：新媒体是怎样让少数党获得更大（或更少）曝光率的？新媒体怎么能够增进公民的政治参与？公民是怎样通过（微）博来参与政治讨论的？

　　这场辩论的第一个问题就是：新媒体究竟在多大程度上能让少数党派获得与那些大党派一样的曝光率？少数党能够利用新媒体科技传播信息，并推广自己。最典型的优势就是这些新科技不仅仅为它们提供了更大的曝光率，还成为了它们额外能够挑战主流竞争对手且进行政治辩论的渠道。然而，网络悲观论则认为交流渠道多并不意味着更多民主（的可能性）。少数党和主流大党使用网络的态度都非常功利，（仅仅是）将网络作为一种传播政治信息的工具，而非推进互动以及组织间联系的新平台。

　　但是，网络乐观论者认为悲观论者（在这一问题上）过于极端，坚称新媒体可能在推动民主选举进程上会起到决定性的作用。例如，基于 Pew 研究中心发布的数据，66％的社交媒体用户都曾参与过至少 8 项线上政治活动，诸如鼓励人们参与投票，或将他们对于政治的评论发布通过社交媒体发布。因此，网络上的投票者可能会在一定程度上左右选举拉票（的安排）。巴拉克·奥巴马在草根拉票取得唤醒鼓舞的成绩，以及对于例如 Facebook 和 MySpace 之类社交媒体的成功使用后所获得的竞选胜利就很能说明问题。

　　辩论的第三个问题讨论的是公民的（微）博使用现象。公民正在使用博客、Facebook、Twitter 和微博这样的社交媒体，并将其作为一种参与政治讨论的渠道，意在直接或间接地影响公众所关心的事，甚至重建公众议程以推动民主的公众氛围。Voltmer 在他以观察或实验为依据的政治交流研究中指出，政客、公民和媒体之间存在着相互依赖关系，并强调了一些媒体是更适合民主化公共交流渠道的原因。Voltmer 以一位名叫 Li Xiaode 的博主为例。这位博主是首位将博客作为一种监督工具，并于 2004～2005 年间曝光了相关的腐败现象。这个事例显示了新媒体的潜在力量，这股力量已经开始挑战现有的政治体系了。

　　回看上文所列出的这一辩论中的三个关键问题，我们能明显发现新媒体自身并没有民主（的属性），它能在何种程度上被用于推动民主（进程）取决于谁在运用新媒体以及他们使用新媒体的意图……（但无论）新媒体科技是否推动了民主，它们都是一些政治上正在发生的根本性变化背后的推动力。这些变化毫无疑问将会（给社会）带来裨益，但也一定会有其局限之处。

2.2.4　Passage Ⅳ

答案解析

　　34. The main purpose of the passage is to _____.

　　A. defend an unpopular belief

　　B. confirm a previously untested hypothesis

C. summarize various studies of a social condition

D. debunk common misconceptions surrounding an issue

答案:C

解析:文章讨论了不同的研究关于童年时体育运动的效果,选项C正确。文章中说很多人都相信体育运动很有用,而不是 an unpopular belief,选项A错误。文章中没有说这是一个之前没有被测试的假设,选项B错误。文章并没有揭露常见的误解的真相,选项D错误。

35. As used in line 8, "track" most nearly means _____.

    A. carry   B. assign   C. monitor   D. linger

答案:D

解析:carry 表示运送,而体育运动无法主动运送到成年。assign 表示分配,表意不正确。monitor 表示监视,表意不正确。linger 表示逗留、留存,track 原意轨迹,身体活动留存到成年,选项D正确。

36. The statistics about UK children (lines 10~13) primarily serve to _____.

    A. encourage readers to become more active

    B. call attention to a particular situation

    C. transition to a discussion of unstructured and structured play

    D. introduce an argument that the authors will later contradict

答案:B

解析:这数据说的是很多英国小朋友没有达到每日推荐的运动标准,选项B认为这个数据是为了让我们重视某一情况,正确。选项A错在不是鼓励读者。选项C完全错,不是为了转向讨论play,而是还在讨论 physical activity。选项D错在作者没有反对这些数据。

37. The author implies that studies that have increased playtime physical activity are _____.

    A. accurate, because they depict the benefits of play across all social groups

    B. correct, because they have allowed for the purchase of playground structures and other equipment to help facilitate play

    C. faulty, because they ignore the importance of natural environments

    D. limited, because they do not study socio-emotional development

答案:D

解析:见下题。

38. Which choice provides the best evidence for the answer to the previous question?

    A. lines 29~32 ("A number ... structures")

    B. lines 32~33 ("However ... PA")

    C. lines 34~35 ("Unstructured ... playtime")

    D. lines 36~38 ("Natural ... playtime")

答案:C

解析:第一题问的是对于增加PA活动时间的研究是怎样的状态,因此我们带着这个问题来看这道题的选项。选项A中说的 playground structure 以及其他设备的运用,并未体现出与研究之间的关系,因此缺乏让我们做出推断的依据,可以排除。选项B说的是 playground structure 和其他设备在与 structured physical activities 之间的联系,而并非第一题中问的在与 unstructured physical activities 之间的联系,可以排除。选项 C 说的是 unstructured playtime 是 socio-emotional development 不可缺少的一环,能够体现出两者之间的关系,因此保留。选项 D 说的是自然环境和 unstructured playtime 之间的联系,因此排除。此题选到 C 之后,我们发现选项 C 中的 socio-emotional development 与上一题中的选项 D 对应,因为 unstructured playtime 是其中重要的一环,如果该研究中缺少这一项就会是 limited,因此上题选 D。

39. What does the author claim about "Green Exercise" (lines 53～54)?

A. It benefits adults' self-esteem but its effects on children have not been fully determined.

B. Looking at images of natural environments is the best way to improve self-esteem.

C. Adolescents do not benefit from green exercise in the same way that adults do.

D. Self-esteem can only rise through direct interaction with the environment.

答案:A

解析:我们回到原文——

Line 53:Green Exercise has also been demonstrated to provide improvements in self-esteem in adults.

Line 60:the only known study in children ...

得知选项 A 正确。选项 B 只是对于 adult 来说,而且不是文章的主要声称。选项 C,文章说了没有做足够的研究来确定一个答案。选项 D,没有限定到 natural environment 而不是任何环境。

40. What does the author imply about physical activity in a natural environment?

A. Scientific studies have determined that physical activity can only benefit self-esteem in adults.

B. The relationship between physical activity in nature and self-esteem requires further study.

C. Although it has been studied, effects of the physical activity in a natural environment's are unclear in both children and adults.

D. Physical activity in a natural environment benefits self-esteem in both children and adults.

答案:B

解析:见下题。

41. Which choice provides the best evidence for the answer to the previous question?

A. lines 57～60 ("Studies ... environments")

B. lines 60～62 ("However ... orienteering")

C. lines 62～64 ("The task-oriented ... effect")

D. lines 64～66 ("Unstructured ... self-esteem")

答案:C

解析:选项 A 指出了对幼儿和青少年的特定研究的结果,选项 B 提到了一个关于 orienteering 的研究,选项 D 给出了一个假设,但这三个选项都没有引出一个事实,也就是我们需要进一步地研究。通过选项 C,可得知上题中选项 B 正确。而上题中,尽管在自然环境下的体育运动被发现仅仅对成人有利，其他的关于体育运动的研究被发现对孩子的自尊也有利，选项 A 错误；在自然环境下的体育运动对成人的好处很清晰了，所以选项 C 错误；在自然环境下的体育运动没有被发现对孩子自尊有好处，选项 D 错误。

42. Which of author's claims about self-esteem does the chart best support?

 A. Unstructured PA in a natural environment may benefit self-esteem in children.

 B. Boys' self-esteem benefits less than girls' from PA in both structured and unstructured settings

 C. Studies of orienteering do not provide enough information to study effects on self-esteem.

 D. Structured PA on playgrounds provides greater benefits to self-esteem than other activities do.

答案：A

解析：图表显示当在一个田地里玩耍时孩子们的自尊心有上升趋势，选项 A 正确。图表没有显示体育运动是结构性的还是非结构性的，选项 B 错误；图表没有提到 orienteering，选项 C 错误；图表中没有显示其他的活动，选项 D 错误。

43. It can reasonably be inferred from the chart that _____.

 A. girls enjoyed playing more than boys

 B. playgrounds and fields are the only two viable options for physical activity in children

 C. boys are equally happy playing anywhere

 D. PA on playgrounds increased average self-esteem more than PA in fields

答案：D

解析：从图表中可得出，在操场上玩时自尊的平均增长接近 0.7，而在田野上时接近 0.6，选项 D 正确。尽管女孩比起男孩在自尊方面增长更多，但这并不意味着她们比男孩更享受玩耍，选项 A 错误；尽管图表只显示了 playground 和 field 在一个特定的研究中是仅有的两个选项，但这并不意味着对于体育运动，这两个是仅有的选择，选项 B 错误；尽管男孩们在两个场所玩耍时，自尊增长相同，但自尊不意味着快乐，选项 C 错误。

44. The difference between the average increase in girls' self-esteem and boy's self-esteem post-play is closest to _____.

 A. 0.3　　　　B. 0.5　　　　C. 0.68　　　　D. 0.83

答案：A

解析：女生的自尊增长为 0.8，男生为 0.5，两者相差 0.3。

译文

在儿时参加体育运动能够强健体魄、提高认知功能和骨骼健康，还能减少体脂、发展运动技能，并降低患心血管及代谢类疾病的风险。幼年时多运动还能提升个人自尊，并减少焦虑和抑郁的症状。在青少年时期参加体育活动是极其重要的，因为这在成年后能够有效减少慢性病的发生。然而在英国，有 75%~80% 的 5~10 岁之间的男孩和女孩并未达到推荐的每日 60 分钟中等到强度较大的体育运动(要求)。

非结构性游戏也是儿童时期的重要组成部分，(因为)它能让孩子们建立自身与周边环境之间的联系,并(帮助他们)增进社交技能、协调能力和力量。户外的环境便于(孩子们)嬉戏,与体育运动之间也有着越来越深的联系。因此,我们应让孩子们每天都有出门玩耍的机会。学校通过游戏时间提供了这样的机会。游戏时间通常在学校操场的水泥地上进行,每天持续至少 1 小时。然而,普遍意义上的游戏时间据说对所要求孩子们进行的每日活动总量的贡献相对较少。在英国,只有一项已知的调查报道了游戏时间在每日活动总量里的占比低至 4.5%。

很多研究都成功通过干预,例如运动、游戏设施、操场标记、休息时间以及操场结构等增加了游戏时间(进行的)体育运动。但是,这些干预的类型更有助于结构性体育活动,而不是非结构性活动。非结构性体育活动对于童年发展非常重要,因此(更)需要在(孩子们的)游戏时间(对非结构性运动)进行鼓励。

自然环境能促进非结构性活动,所以其对游戏时间内进行的非结构性体育活动也大有裨益。自然环境(能)提供大而开阔的场地,鼓励孩子变得积极活跃;而因为有限的空间,以及家长们对于犯罪和道路交通的担忧,非自然环境则可能会限制体育活动。孩子们也表现出对自然环境中游玩的偏好,(因为)这更便于他们开展富有想象力、创造性的游戏。

与此同时,那些居住在城市的青少年更能接触到大自然(比如公园),且身体更活跃。这表明各种形式的自然(元素)都能作为增进年轻人开展体育活动的工具。因此,如果校内的游戏时间是在田野上展开的,那么孩子们的体育活动(的参与程度)可能会有所增加。(然而)到目前,(我们仍)缺乏数据来量化自然环境对孩子们体育活动(参与程度)的影响,尤其是在校园环境中对他们的影响。

在自然环境中进行体育活动("绿色运动")也体现出对成年人自尊的增进作用。无论被试仅仅是在看大自然的景象,抑或是直接与自然环境进行接触(这种增进作用都是存在的)。而对青少年和孩子们的研究则表明,相较于在其他环境下进行的运动,绿色运动并没有(这种)对自尊的附加作用。但唯一已知的对孩子的研究(绿色运动)检验了定向越野这一绿色游戏时间干预的影响。这种以完成任务为目的、以结构性主导的活动可能并不能显示绿色运动的效果。在自然环境中的非结构性游戏能(有效)增进孩子与环境之间的互动,从而(更好地塑造)自尊。

2.3 History

2.3.1 Passage I

答案解析

1. The authors central claim in the passage is that _____.

A. the Constitution will have to suffice until it is proven to be inadequate

B. the objections to the constitution are trivial and should be disregarded by the Assembly

C. the objections to the Constitution can be dismissed unless they are unanimous

D. the Constitution is adequate and should be passed without objection

答案:D

解析:通过 author's central claim 定位到第一段。

Line 2:I confess that are several parts of this constitution which I do not at present approve, but I am not sure I shall never approve them. 这句话后面双重否定表示肯定,所以其实作者的意图是赞同的,所以选项 A、B 不符合,选项 C 作者的意图中没有提及,所以选择 D。

2. In the passage, Franklin characterizes himself as someone who is _____.
   A. sarcastic   B. experienced
   C. cynical   D. indecisive

答案:B

解析:通过 characterizes himself 定位到第一段。

Line 4:I have experienced many instance of being obliged by better information…这句话就是说作者从自身角度出发,认为自己已经经历了许多这样的情况。选项 A 表示"挖苦的、讽刺的",选项 C 表示"愤世嫉俗的、怀疑的",选项 D 表示"优柔寡断的"。因此,根据定位句,选项 B 是最合适的,即经验丰富的。

3. Which choice provides the best evidence for the answer to the previous question?
   A. lines 8~10("It is … of others")
   B. lines 23~26("I think … well administered")
   C. lines 44~46("Thus … the best")
   D. lines 59~62("I hope … Constitution")

答案:A

解析:通过上一题定位到第一段。

Line 8:It is therefore that the older I grow, the more apt I am to doubt my own judgment, and to pay more respect to the judgment。从上一题来看,只有选项 A 最接近,而且本句中还有 the older I grow,也是表明 experienced 的一种,因此,根据定位句,选项 A 是最符合的答案。

4. In line 35, the word "local" most nearly means _____.
   A. geographical   B. provincial   C. nearby   D. domestic

答案:B

解析:通过题目提示定位到 line 35。

Line 35:their passions, their errors of opinion, their local interests, and their selfish views。选项 A 表示"地理的",选项 C 表示"邻近的",选项 D 表示"国内的";因此,根据定位句,选项 B 表示"省的、州的",是说与他们的当地偏好相关。

5. According to the passage, the main objection to immediate passage of the Constitution is that it is _____.
   A. unpopular   B. despotic   C. imperfect   D. partisan

答案:C

解析:通过 the main objection 定位到 line 45。

Line 45:because I expect no better, and because I am not sure, that it is not the best. 选项 A 表示"不流行的",选项 B 表示"暴虐的、专横的",选项 D 表示"党派性的、偏袒

的"。因此,根据定位句,选项 C 表示"不完美的"。

6. Over the course of the passage, the main focus shifts from _____.

A. an acknowledgment of criticism to a dismissal of its validity

B. an admission of a problem to the proposal of a solution

C. an overview of inconsistencies to an explanation of their complexity

D. an argument for action to a summary of guiding principles

答案:A

解析:通过 the main focus shifts 定位到 line 53。

Line 53:and thereby lose all the salutary effects & great advantages resulting…提到了这个争论的有效性。因此,根据定位句,选项 A 是关于这项宪法的有效性。

7. Franklin attributes the Constitutions flaws to the fact that _____.

A. the document was written very quickly

B. the people who wrote it all had their own opinions

C. the citizens of the nation were not consulted

D. the writers were trying to appear unanimous when they were not

答案:B

解析:通过 the Constitution's flaws 定位到 line 32。Line 32:For when you assemble a number of men to have the advantage…提到了每个人都有自己的意见。因此,根据定位句,选项 B 是最合适的答案。

8. Which choice provides the best evidence for the answer to the previous question?

A. lines 2～4("I confess … them")　　B. lines 32～36("For when … views")

C. lines 38～39("It therefore … does")　　D. lines 46～49("The opinions … die")

答案:B

解析:通过上一题定位到 line 32。

Line 32:For when you assemble a number of men to have the advantage…,其实第 7、8 题可以连一起看,然后找最合适的答案。

9. The main comparison Franklin draws between the Assembly and the Churches is in terms of their members _____.

A. stubborn adherence to doctrine　　B. dedication to promoting the truth

C. unwillingness to accept failure　　D. blindness to their weaknesses

答案:D

解析:通过 Assembly and the churched 定位到 line 40。Line 40:with confidence to…就是说他们太过于盲目自信。因此,根据定位句,选项 D 是最合适的选项。

10. The main purpose of Franklins comment about the French lady (line 19) is most likely to _____.

A. ridicule the arrogance of the lady

B. allude to the division of public optimism

C. point out a universal truth in a humorous way

D. convey the futility of further dispute

答案:C

解析：通过题目我们定位到 line 19。Line 19：who in a dispute with her sister, said ... that's always right 中说到了这位女性认为自己一直是对的，所以作者其实是在以一种幽默的方式来指出一个普遍的现象。因此，根据定位句，选项 C 是最合适的答案。

11. As used in line 57, "general" most nearly means _____.
    A. overall   B. typical   C. customary   D. ordinary

答案：A

解析：通过题目提示定位到 line 57。

Line 57：Depends on opinion, on the general opinion of the goodness of the Government. 选项 B 表示"典型的"，选项 C 表示"通常的"，选项 D 表示"普通的、一般的"，与题意都不相符，因此选择选项 A，指所有人的整体意见。

译文

下文为本杰明·富兰克林于 1787 年 9 月 17 日在制宪会议上发表的演讲。该会议旨在决定是否正式批准美国宪法的最终版本。

主席先生，坦白地讲，这部宪法中有若干点是我目前所不能赞同的，但我不敢说将永远不赞成它。因为我活了这把年纪，有过许多经验。在这些经验中，因有了较充分的信息或经过较充分的考虑，在一些重大议题上，若我当初认为是正确的见解但实际是错误的，我愿意改正。我的年纪愈大，就愈倾向于怀疑自己的判断，同时更尊重别人的判断。实际上，世上大多数的人和宗教里的大多数教派一样，以为自己拥有全部的真理。凡是和他们意见不同，就认为是谬误。一个叫斯蒂尔的新教徒在一次献辞中对天主教教皇说过这样一句话："在对宗教教义的解释上，我们两个教会唯一不同的地方是罗马教会是'千真万确的'，而英国教会则是'永远不会错的'。"就连许多平民，也都像他们信奉的教派一样认为自己是"千真万确"的。这种自以为是曾被一位法国太太表现得极为自然。她在和妹妹发生争执时说："我也不明白这是怎么回事，妹妹，可是我从来也没有遇到过永远正确的人，除了我自己。"

先生，从这种感觉出发，我同意这部宪法，连同它所有的瑕疵，如果它们确实是瑕疵的话。因为我们的人民需要一个总体政府，而现在我们还没有。如果政府治理有方，对百姓来说也许是个福音。我甚至相信，这一次可能天下大治若干年，然后以专制收场，就像以前那些共和国一样。当世风堕落到其他任何形式的政府都无能为力时，就会需要专制政府。但我也怀疑，无论召开多少次制宪会议，也未必能制定出一部更好的宪法。当你集合一群人来利用他们的智慧时，你也就免不了集合了他们的偏见、他们感情上的冲动、他们观点中的错误、他们的地方性的利益观念以及他们自私的观点。

从这样的集合中，难道能期待完美的结果吗？因此，主席先生，让我惊讶的是，现在制定的这套方案，如此地近乎完美。我认为，这部宪法也会使我们的敌人大吃一惊的。他们正在那里自信地等着看我们的好戏呢，他们以为我们开会，也和巴比伦人造通天塔一样，每次都是劳而无功；以为我们各邦正处在分崩离析的边缘，此后每次见面都不过是为了彼此掐断对方的喉咙。所以，主席先生，我同意这部宪法，因为我不指望还有更好的，也没有把握说它就不是最好的。为了公众利益，我决定牺牲自己认为宪法中还有谬误的私人之见。我从未在外面窃窃私语。我的话语在此四壁之内诞生，也将在此消失。如果我们每个回到选民当中去的人，都向他们报告自己对宪法曾有过的反对意见，并努力获得党人对这些意见的支持，我们就可能阻挠宪法被普遍接受，从而失去所有的有益影响和巨大好处。这种影响和好处，是从世界各国和我们人民中间对我们自然的好感中产生的,而这种好感,只能从我们的全体一致中产生,不管这种一致是真实的还是表面的。任何政府,为了获得和保障人们的幸福必须有力量和效能。大部分力量和效能取决于民众对政府、对治理者智慧和人格的普遍印象。为此我希望作为人民的组成部分,为了我们自己,为了子孙后代,我们采取全心全意、高度一致的行动,尽我们所能去推荐这部宪法(如经国会批准、全国代表大会确认),以便将我们的思想和努力转向安邦治国。

最后,我希望制宪会议中每位对宪法或许还有异议的代表和我一起,就此机会略为怀疑一下自己的一贯正确,宣布我们取得一致,并在这个文件上签下自己的名字。

2.3.2　Passage Ⅱ

答案解析

12. The main purpose of the passage is to stress _____.
    A. the complementary nature of agriculture and manufacturing
    B. the importance of manufacturing to international trade
    C. the suitability of the country's resources to both agriculture and manufacturing
    D. the agricultural basis of economic imbalances within the States

答案:A

解析:考察作者的写作目的。定位于文中第二段第三行,"indeed they are perceived so often to succor and to befriend each other."可知,两个关键词"succor"和"befriend"可得出选项 A。选项 B,南北地区互帮互助,经常被看作一个整体。选项 C 在文中未提到。选项 D,文章主要讲制造业和农业相互影响。

13. How does Hamilton organize his argument?
    A. He ridicules an ongoing debate and then clarifies the issue behind it.
    B. He describes a current problem and then gives historical examples to explain it.
    C. He introduces a prevailing belief and then presents arguments against it.
    D. He proposes a course of action and then explains the problem with enacting it.

答案:C

解析:文章开头第一句"It is not uncommon to meet with an opinion that though the promoting of manufactures may be the interest of the Union, it is contrary to that of another part."首先介绍了一个非常普遍的观点。第二段用 "common error" 反驳这个观点,说明正确的观点。

14. What objection to his argument does Hamilton anticipate in the passage?
    A. The Northern sates and Southern states have an inequality of resources.
    B. The agricultural and manufacturing industries embrace conflicting goals.
    C. The escalation of agricultural production is both appropriate and inevitable.
    D. The development of a national economy is neither desirable nor practical.

答案:B

解析:考察作者是怎样论证自己的观点的。But it is nevertheless a maxim well

established by experience, and generally acknowledged, where there has been sufficient experience, that the aggregate prosperity of manufactures, and the aggregate prosperity of agriculture are intimately connected. 选项 A 表示"南北地区存在利益冲突"。选项 C 表示"制造业与农业共同发展促进经济增长"。选项 D 在文中未提到。

15. Which choice best supports the answer to the previous question?

   A. lines 1~3 ("It is not ... other part.") ("It is not uncommon to meet with an opinion that though the promoting of manufactures may be the interest of a part of the Union, it is contrary to that of another part.")

   B. lines 14~17 ("Particular ... manufacturers.") ("Particular encouragements of particular manufactures may be of a Nature to sacrifice the interests of landholders to those of manufacturers;")

   C. lines 24~26 ("Perhaps ... truth.") ("Perhaps the superior steadiness of the demand of a domestic market for the surplus produce of the soil, is alone a convincing argument of its truth.")

   D. lines 67~71 ("The wool ... of Europe.") ("the Wool of Virginia is said to be of better quality than that of any other state: a Circumstance rendered the more probable by the reflection that Virginia embraces the same latitudes with the finest Wool Countries of Europe.")

答案：A

解析：考察哪一个观点最能反驳作者的观点。第一段开头是大众的观点，作者先陈述，后反驳。所以，选项 A 最有说服力。Line 67：Flax and Hemp are or may be raised in greater abundance there, than in the More Northern states; and the Wool of Virginia is said to be of better quality than that of any other state: a Circumstance rendered the more probable by the reflection that Virginia embraces the same latitudes with the finest Wool Countries of Europe.

选项 B 表示"发展特殊制造业是以牺牲农业生产劳动的生产为代价的"。

选项 C 表示"国内市场对石油的大量需求，是一个说明事实的真相"。

选项 D 表示"维多利亚生产的羊毛比其他地区生产的都好"。

16. The main relationship Hamilton highlights between the Northern and the Southern states is in terms of their _____.

   A. incompatible philosophies   B. disproportionate production
   C. ongoing hostilities   D. complementary economies

答案：D

解析：细节判断。题干中考察南北各大洲的关系，定位于第三段第五行"mutual wants constitute one of the strongest links of political ... in the means of mutual supply."制造业与农业密切相关。

17. In the second paragraph, Hamilton implies that conflicts of interest among geographical regions _____.

   A. reflect an opposition to independence
   B. are unique to industrialized nations

C. interfere with the process of nation-building

D. lead to civil unrest

答案:C

解析:推断题。根据 line 14：Particular encouragements of particular manufactures may be of a Nature to sacrifice the interests of landholders to those of manufacturers。选项 A 表示"两地区的经济是相互联系的"。选项 B 表示"利益冲突对双方都有影响"。选项 D 表示"利益冲突会导致经济的不平衡"。

18. Which choice best describes Hamilton's perspective on agriculture?

A. Its uncontrolled growth tends to thwart economic progress.

B. Its advancement is guaranteed by industrial development.

C. Its expansion to the Northern states disadvantages manufacturers.

D. Its significance is overestimated by Southern landowners.

答案:B

解析:细节推断。根据问题定位于文章倒数第二段第二行"To fortify the idea, that the encouragement of manufactures is the interest of all parts of the Union.""If Northern and middle states …, they would benefit the more Southern, by creating a demand for production."可得出工业能保证农业的发展。选项 A 表示"农业迅速发展促进经济增长"。选项 C 表示"农业、工业发展前景"。选项 D 表示"南方低估了它的前景"。

19. Which choice provides the best evidence for the answer to the previous question?

A. lines 14～17 ("Particular … manufacturers.") ("Particular encouragements of particular manufactures may be of a Nature to sacrifice the interests of landholders to those of manufacturers;")

B. lines 19～21 ("The aggregate … connected.") ("The aggregate prosperity of manufactures, and the aggregate prosperity of Agriculture are intimately connected.")

C. lines 24～26 ("Perhaps … truth.") ("Perhaps the superior steadiness of the demand of a domestic market for the surplus produce of the soil, is alone a convincing argument of its truth.")

D. lines 31～33 ("Mutual … connection") ("Mutual wants constitute one of the strongest links of political connection,")

答案:B

解析:选项 A 表示"鼓励特殊产业的发展是以制造业为代价的"。选项 C 表示"国内对石油生产的需求是唯一的事实依据"。选项 D 表示"双方希望建立一个稳定的政治体系,扩大自然资源的比例"。

20. As used in line 29 ("mischievous."), "mischievous" most nearly means _____.

A. disobedient　　B. spirited　　C. spiteful　　D. damaging

答案:D

解析:根据 line 27：Ideas of a contrariety of interests between the Northern and Southern regions of the Union, are in the Main as unfounded as they are mischievous.

考察词语在文中的意思。Disobedient 表示违背、不服从,Spirited 表示生机勃勃的,Spiteful 表示恶意的,而 damage 表示有害的。根据文章内容,南北的利益冲突根源没有找到,似乎对双方是有害的。

21. Hamilton uses the term "National Resource" (line 53 ("National Resource.")) most likely to emphasize _____.

　　A. the benefits of an export economy
　　B. the interdependence of industry
　　C. the importance of industrialization
　　D. the superiority of the United States

答案:B

解析:根据 line 54:But there are more particular considerations which serve to fortify the idea, that the encouragement of manufactures is the interest of all parts of the Union. 选项 A 强调经济共同发展。选项 C 强调二者的重要性。选项 D 在文中未提到美国的优越性。

22. Hamilton compares the latitudes of Virginia to those of the finest wool countries in Europe (paragraph 5) mainly to support his assertion that _____.

　　A. the United States is capable of competing on the global market
　　B. the United States should focus on growing a limited number of crops
　　C. the agricultural prosperity of the South is limited by its geographical location
　　D. the South contributes directly to the prosperity of the nation

答案:D

解析:根据 line 67:Wool of Virginia is said to be of better quality than that of any other state; a Circumstance rendered the more probable by the reflection that Virginia embraces the same latitudes with the finest Wool Countries of Europe. 选项 A:文中未提到美国竞争全球市场。选项 B:作者在文中提到多种农业发展。选项 C:南部地区凭借地理优越性使得农业大大发展。

译文

本文摘自亚历山大·汉密尔顿出版于 1791 年的《关于制造业的报告》。

制造业只能让联盟内的一部分人受益,而与另一部分人的利益相悖,这一想法并不罕见。南方和北方有时会在这方面表现出对立利益。在这些农业国家里,这被称为制造业:一种在工业以及农业利益之间的假想存在的对立物种。

这两种利益之间存在对立关系的想法是各国早期都可能会犯的常见错误,但是随着经验的增加,这种想法会逐渐消除。实际上,人们会认为两种利益互帮互助,以至于其最终通常被视作一个整体:一个经常被滥用但是普遍不真实的假设。尤其对特定制造业的鼓励而言,本质上有可能是为了制造业者而牺牲掉土地所有者的利益。但它仍然是来自经验的至理名言,并且在经验丰富的情况下,人们公认为制造业总体繁荣与农业总体繁荣密切相关。在已经进行的讨论过程中,各种慎重考虑已被列举出来并为该至理名言提供了支持。或许国内市场对多余农产品需求所呈现出的较好的稳定性仅仅是这一真理中令人信服的一个论点。

联盟南部和北部利益相悖的想法在整体上是没有根据的,还是有恶意的。通常断言此类对立性的多样化条件,可以直接得出一个相反结论。共同的需求构成了一个最强的政治联盟的纽带,这些承载自然面积的范围就是自然供给中所说的多样性。来自不同种族的人所给出的建议将受到谴责,这种谴责是对不同种族的人们追求伟大的共同目标的破坏,也是对各种族的人们和睦相处的破坏。

思想的追随与利益的密切联系是成比例的,它存在于同一政府统治下的社会的全部领域。这些领域有助于促进繁荣流通的多种渠道及其他部分。根据这种比例关系,由于地区之间的差别,几乎不受恐惧、焦虑等因素的干扰。这是一个与其适宜性同等重要的事实,并且难以想象特殊情况。所有趋向于在国家事务中以增加工业和财富总量而建立重要、永久性秩序的事情最终让其各个部分均受益。在信任这一伟大真理方面,可以默认为每个地区所有机构和安排要保证确认公共秩序以及国家资源的扩充都符合安全。

但是也存在有助于强化这一理念更具体的注意事项,即鼓励制造业的发展对联盟的所有部分都有好处。如果北部和中部各州是形成这些理念的主要场所,通过创造生产需求,其足以直接使更多的南部地区获益;其中一些地区与其他州有共同之处,其他地区或有由其独享,或有与其他地方相比更丰富或质量更好的物资。这些物资生产活动,尤其是指木材、亚麻布、大麻、棉花、羊毛、生丝、靛蓝染料、铁、铅、皮草、皮革、皮毛以及煤炭的生产。在这些物资中,棉花及靛蓝染料为南部各州独有,迄今为止铅及煤炭同样如此。这里的亚麻和大麻种植可能比北部各州生长得更为茂盛。弗吉尼亚州的羊毛据说比任何其他州的质量都要好,原因可能是弗吉尼亚州的照射条件在所有产羊毛的同一纬度上的欧洲国家中最好。南部的气候条件也更适合蚕丝生产。

大面积种植棉花或许很难实现,但是根据先前国内独资工厂建立的文章来看,对其他人来说,一定的鼓励和情感上的宣泄将会产生与之类似工厂的建立。

2.3.3 Passage Ⅲ

答案解析

23. The main purpose of Passage 1 is to _____.

A. provide information about plans to reform the federal system

B. highlight inconsistent government principles across multiple states

C. introduce plans for a new kind of government that differs greatly from the current one

D. question a proposal to consolidate in a single federal system

答案:D

解析:考查主旨大意,根据 Line 18:The first interesting question is how far the states can be consolidated into one entire government on free principles. 选项 A:文章并没有 provide information about plans principles。选项 B:作者讨论了 a federal plan,而不是 government。选项 C:作者介绍了 a plan to reform and strengthen the government,而不是一个与现在完全不同的 government。

24. Which statement about the federal government most accurately reflects the point of view of the author of Passage 1?

A. The current form of government has been in place for too long and increased consolidation is long overdue.

B. The proposed changes would bring about more negative consequences than maintaining the current form of government would.

C. A well-functioning confederation is impossible because independent states will never agree on policies.

D. The uniform system of laws proposed by a federal government will help unite the country as one nation.

答案:B

解析:考查文章细节。根据:Line 7:Whether such a change can ever be effected in any manner; whether it can be effected without convulsions and civil wars; whether such a change will not totally destroy the liberties of this country—time only can determine,可知改革可能带来很多不确定性和内乱,甚至破坏国家的人民自由,再根据最后一段,一个政府和立法无法同时满足各个不同州的实际情况。

选项 A:根据 Line 15:We find, therefore, members of congress urging alterations in the federal system almost as soon as it was adopted. 议会成员急于寻找改变,每当人们刚适应一种体系时。

选项 C:根据 Line 12:The confederation was formed when great confidence was placed in the voluntary exertions of individuals, and of the respective states; and the framers of it, to guard against usurpation, so limited and checked the powers. 联邦政府形成之初,各个州各自发挥其行政职能,并运行良好。

选项 D:根据 Line 40:United States contain about a million of square miles, and in half a century will, probably, contain ten millions of people. 与作者态度相反。

25. Which idea is presented in Passage 2 but NOT in Passage 1?

A. The proposed form of federal government will inevitably result in tyranny.

B. The happiness and liberty of the people should be the priority of any form of government.

C. The country is too large and has too many people for a federal government to rule effectively.

D. It is better for states to govern themselves due to their differences in customs.

答案:A

解析:根据 Line 60:To promote the happiness of the people it is necessary that there should be local laws; and it is necessary that those laws should be made by the representatives of those who are immediately subject to the want of them. 作者讨论了 tyranny,而第一篇文章没有。选项 C:文章第一、二段和最后一段提及美国国土面积。选项 D:同上,均提到各自习俗不同。

26. In explaining their ideas on federal government, both authors make use of which kind of evidence?

A. Historical records   B. Expert testimony
C. Hypothetical scenarios   D. Personal anecdotes

答案:C

解析:根据 Line 7:Whether such a change can ever be effected in any manner; whether it can be effected without convulsions and civil wars; whether such a change will not totally destroy the liberties of this country—time only can determine. 和 Line 47：This is precisely the principle which has hitherto preserved our freedom. 均假设情景。选项 A：在文章一中未使用历史记录。选项 B：文章一与大多数学者观点反其道而行。选项 D：文章一、二均未提及个人事迹。

27. Both passages argue that individual states _____.

   A. would not benefit from following the same set of laws
   B. are becoming too unwieldy due to lack of one unifying government
   C. run the risk of engaging in multiple civil wars over time
   D. duplicate functions and should be eventually consolidated

答案：A

解析：考查文章细节。根据文章一 line 35：Independent of the opinions of many great authors, that a free elective government cannot be extended over large territories, a few reflections must evince, that one government and general legislation alone, never can extend equal benefits to all parts of the United States：Different laws, customs, and opinions exist in the different states, which by a uniform system of laws would be unreasonably invaded. 和文章二 line 73：The idea of an uncompounded republic, on an average, one thousand miles in length, and eight hundred in breadth, and containing six millions of inhabitants all reduced to the same standard of morals, or habits, and of laws, is in itself an absurdity, and contrary to the whole experience of mankind. 均表明强化中央集权不能受益民众。选项 B：态度与作者相反。选项 C：在第二篇文章中未提及内战。选项 D：提倡各州的法律与作者态度相反。

28. It can reasonably be inferred from Passage 1 that the author is _____.

   A. skeptical that consolidating the government can occur peacefully
   B. curious about reforming the federal system of government
   C. concerned that increasing the independence of states will weaken local governments
   D. doubtful that the majority of people will vote for new government legislation

答案：A

解析：选项 A：文章一表述了作者对强化中央实权的质疑，正确。选项 B：作者不是好奇，而是怀疑其可行性。选项 C：根据 line 35：Independent of the opinions of many great authors, that a free elective government cannot be extended over large territories, a few reflections must evince, that one government and general legislation alone, never can extend equal benefits to all parts of the United States：Different laws, customs, and opinions exist in the different states, which by a uniform system of laws would be unreasonably invaded. 表述与作者态度相反。选项 D：文中未提及。

29. Which choice provides the best evidence for the answer to the previous question?

   A. lines 1~3("Our ... presents")   B. lines 3~5("The ... people")
   C. lines 5~7("Instead ... government") D. lines 7~11("Whether ... determine")

答案：D

根据：line 7~11：Whether such a change can ever be effected in any manner; whether it can be effected without convulsions and civil wars; whether such a change will not totally destroy the liberties of this country—time only can determine. 表述了作者对政策施行过程中可能会遭遇的各种阻力,表明了其否定态度。

选项 A:对政府改革的简要介绍。选项 B:改革目的。选项 C:改革模式。

30. In line 40, "invaded" most nearly means _____.
   A. infringed   B. usurped   C. trespassed   D. permeated
   答案:A
   解析:根据 invaded 定位到 line 40: The United States contain about a million of square miles, and in half a century will, probably, contain ten millions of people. 根据句意,可猜测统一法律体系不合理地运用于各个州,加之作者态度相反,与选项 A 最接近。选项 B 表示"夺取",选项 C 表示"侵入",选项 D 表示"渗透",均与之不符合。

31. By referring to the potential government as "a despotism" (line 48), the author of Passage 2 implies that the proposal is _____.
   A. extreme and dangerous   B. unwise but possible
   C. troublesome and uncertain   D. hazardous but inevitable
   答案:A
   解析:定位到文章相应处可知,作者举了一个极端的例子,并假设了后果,即一个帝国的可能发展,退化为一个独裁政权,A 选项与之呼应。选项 B:possible 与作者态度无关。选项 C:uncertain 并不是作者所要讨论的。选项 D:inevitable 不可避免的,答非所问。

32. How would the author of Passage 2 most likely respond to the authors ideas about consolidation of power in lines 33～42 of Passage 1?
   A. With disapproval, because they contradict his argument.
   B. With approval, because they help support his argument.
   C. With caution, because while the authors agree on some points, they do not agree on all.
   D. With support, because they bring up a new idea about the debate.
   答案:B
   解析:在第一、二篇文章中,两位作者态度相同,未论述了集权的不利。选项 A:与作者态度相反。选项 C:caution 并非作者态度。选项 D:并未带来新观念,而是与之相反。

33. Which choice provides the best evidence for the answer to the previous question?
   A. lines 53～56 ("Large ... misery")   B. lines 56～57 ("In ... parts")
   C. lines 63～66 ("To ... them")   D. lines 69～71 ("The ... states")
   答案:B
   解析:一个立法原则不能适应所有地区,恰是问题的回答。选项 A 是对政策的一个预测。选项 C 表示如何提升民主幸福度,答非所问。选项 D 表示讨论了地方法和宪法的一个关系,不是所问所答。

译文

第 1 篇文章摘自一位称为"联邦农夫"的作者所写的公开信。第 2 篇文章摘自阿格里巴(詹姆斯·温思罗普的笔名)所写的公开信。温思罗普曾参与反联邦运动。两篇文章的写作时间均为 1787 年。

文章1

我们的目标一直是改革我们的联邦系统并巩固我们的政府,但一个新的目标现在出现了。现在提出的政府计划是审时度势,并将完全改变我们作为一个自然人状态的计划。(这个计划)很明显是为了将我们变成一个由联邦政府领导的、统一的政府,而非十三个(相对独立的)邦联。这样一种改变是在任何情况下都有效的吗?要是没有动乱或内战,它能起效果吗?它会彻底摧毁这个国家的自由吗?

邦联制度建立的时候,(这个国家建设)对个人以及相应的州政府的遵从怀有极大的自信。制定这一(制度)框架的人出于防范篡权而对权利加以限制和制衡。因此我们发现,议会成员在联邦系统被采纳之初就极力主张要有所改变。第一个很有意思的问题是这些州在没有任何原则管束的情况下能统一多久呢?人们的最大幸福必须是每一个务实的政治家最大的追求,而且他的每一步都会照着这一目标前进。如果我们是以一个人民群体出现的,而在同一个政府之下我们不能够享受到同等的快乐和好处,那么州政府的结合就不能实现。

而说到联邦政府这一计划,我不认为它有什么好处:如果缺乏强制有效的权利机制保证(其政策的推行)力度,我们就不能将国家主权作为有关政府作用等问题的答案。同时,在一个有各州代表的议会里,(要维持议会正常运行)就必须要保证各种权利集中在一些人手里,(而这种集权是)极为不合理的。人们的最大幸福必须是每一个务实的政治家在最多50年内让人口达到千万。

文章2

让我们现在来想想(这个新系统)能在多大程度上保证人民的快乐和自由?在这方面最有才干的写手们认为,没有一个大规模的帝国能够通过共和党人的准则来进行管理,除非是由享有完全内部管理权的、由各州构成的邦联制,要不然政府就会沦为专制统治。这的确是到目前为止让我们保有自由的准则。以其他方式来管理一个大国的例子还未曾见到。集权的大帝国可能的确会以其显赫让远方的对手目眩,但(只要)近距离看看就会发现它(不过是)金玉其外,败絮其中。原因显而易见。同样的立法准则并不适用于大国内的每一部分。那些并非是由人民制定的法律,让人们觉得很不方便,也并不适合人民群众的日常生活。也就是在这样的暴政下,西班牙人曾殖民的那些省份饱受折磨。如果我们以统一立法来管理整个帝国的话,我们也会有同样的问题,而这将会是我们的不幸和堕落。为了增进人们的幸福,有地方法律是很有必要的。而由那些与该事务直接相关的代表们来制定这些法律同样非常必要。

一套法律要同时适合佐治亚州和马萨诸塞州是不可能的。因此,他们必须为自己(的州)立法。而议会(通过的这套)法律无论何时都是美国的最高法律,凌驾于各州的宪法之上。所以,这个新系统无视各州的不同情况,(强行)将各州合并为一个大的整体。将一个约1000英里长、800英里宽,包含600万居民的合众国简化成一套(统一的)道德标准、习惯和法律体,本身就是一个荒谬的想法,也是与人类经验相违背的。因此,这个与各州政府相联系的新系统,应该立刻被否决。

2.4 New SAT Official Guide Test 1 解析

2.4.1 Passage I

答案解析

1. Which choice best describes what happens in the passage?

A. One character argues with another character who intrudes on her home.

B. One character receives a surprising request from another character.

C. One character reminisces about choices she has made over the years.

D. One character criticizes another character for pursuing an unexpected course of action.

答案：B

解析：我们来看这篇文章的首尾句：

Akira came directly, breaking all tradition.

"I mean to have him."

通过阅读全文的段首句我们知道，这篇文章主要是在说 Akira 突然前去 Naomi 家向她妈妈提出迎娶 Naomi 的事。因此选项 B 中的 receive a surprising request 正好对应这一突发的请求。错误选项 A、C、D 中均缺乏对于全文主要内容的提及。

2. Which choice best describes the developmental pattern of the passage?

A. A careful analysis of a traditional practice.

B. A detailed depiction of a meaningful encounter.

C. A definitive response to a series of questions.

D. A cheerful recounting of an amusing anecdote.

答案：B

解析：读完原文我们知道文章在说 Akira 上门求亲，而这一过程是严肃的，显然与选项 D 中的 cheerful、amusing、anecdote 等词语不符合。而原文第一句就说到 Akira broke all tradition，因此与选项 A "对于一项传统的解析"也不符合。同时，Chie 在文中并没有给出一个 definitive response，而 Akira 也说 "If you don't wish to contact me, I'll reapproach you in two weeks' time. Until then, good night"（Line 74），因此可以排除选项 A、C、D。文中的确有不少细节化的描写，而 encounter 也是对该事件的高度描述，因此可以选到答案 B。

3. As used in line 1 and line 65, "directly" most nearly means _____.

A. frankly   B. confidently

C. without mediation   D. with precision

答案：C

解析：回到原文：

Akira came directly, breaking all tradition.

I ask directly because the use of a go-between takes much time.

从第一段中我们知道第一句中的 tradition 指的是请 Akira 的父母去 go-between,与第二句中的 go-between 刚好对应。而 go-between 是 takes much time,那么与之相反的 came directly、ask directly 就是为了避免 takes much time,因此对应选项 C。做这道题时应注意 directly 在这里是与 takes much time,即时间相对应的。

4. Which reaction does Akira most fear from Chie?
   A. She will consider his proposal inappropriate.
   B. She will mistake his earnestness for immaturity.
   C. She will consider his unscheduled visit an imposition.
   D. She will underestimate the sincerity of his emotions.

答案:A

解析:Akira 和 Chie 的互动集中在文章中后段,我们可以通过题干中的 fear 定位,看到文中第 57 行"Akira blushed."这句话表达的含义与 fear 有相似之处,因此我们仔细看之后 Akira 的话:

"We have an understanding. Please don't judge my candidacy by the unseemliness of this proposal. I ask directly because the use of a go-between takes much time."

毛脚女婿上门最担心、最害怕的是什么?当然是丈母娘对自己不满意啊。这篇文章中的主人公都是日本人,而东方文化一脉相承,因此我们可以做出这样的大胆推测,上文中的这个句子也印证了我们的猜测。因此我们可以排除选项 B(文中并没有写到 Akira 担忧的原因是自己的不成熟)和选项 D(同选项 B)。那么可能会对哪里不满意呢?我们在文中开头就看到说 Akira 是打破传统的,与这句话中的 go-between 相呼应。Unseemliness(不得体)与选项 A 中的 inappropriate 相对应,因此选 A。选项 C 是迷惑选项,但只要回到上文中这个句子,就能找到排除这个选项的理由。

5. Which choice provides the best evidence for the answer to the previous question?
   A. Line 33 ("His voice ... refined")   B. Lines 49~51 ("You ... mind")
   C. Lines 63~64 ("Please ... proposal") D. Lines 71~72 ("Eager ... face")

答案:C

解析:从上题我们可知,Akira 感到害怕的原因是担心自己求婚被丈母娘拒绝,而证据就是选项 C。选项 A "His voice was soft, refined. He straightened and stole a deferential peek at her face."是对表情、动作的描述,完全没有牵涉到害怕的内容,因此排除。选项 B "You know how children speak so earnestly, so hurriedly, so endearingly about things that have no importance in an adult's mind?"是 Chie 的心理描写,我们不能推断 Akira 害怕的就是 Chie 的这种心态,因此同样排除。选项 D "Eager to make his point, he'd been looking her full in the face."中的 eager 一词与 fear 显然不是一个意思,所以排除。

6. In the passage, Akira addresses Chie with _____.
   A. affection but not genuine love
   B. objectivity but not complete impartiality
   C. amusement but not mocking disparagement
   D. respect but not utter deference

答案:D

解析:这道题在题干中虽然没有明显主旨题的标志,但是 Akira 对于 Chie 的态度是从全文后半部分的对话中体现出来的,因此这道题考察的是对全文后半部分的一个概括总结。我们直接从 Chie 见到 Akira 的部分看首句。

Line 31:"Madame," said Akira,"forgive my disruption, but I come with a matter of urgency."

Line 35:In the dim light his eyes hone with sincerity.

Line 57:Akira blushed.

Line 71:Eager to make his point, he'd been looking her full in the face.

Line 77:He bowed and left.

从上述句子我们可以看出 Akira 对于 Chie 是尊敬的(sincerity;bowed),所以选项 D 中的 respect 正好对应,而从第一句话我们可以看出,尽管唐突,但 Akira 仍坚持登门求亲。此文中的 Lines 69~70,Lines 74~76 两处都表明男主准备不折不挠地死缠烂打,所以并非完全彻底地服从,这整个行为就表现他并非对 Chie 是 utter deference,因此选 D。其余选项在文中都没有找到直接证据。

7. The main purpose of the first paragraph is to _____.
   A. describe a culture　　　　　　B. criticize a tradition
   C. question a suggestion　　　　D. analyze a reaction

答案:D

解析:这是一道段落主旨题,因此我们来看看第一段的首尾句。

• Akira came directly, breaking all tradition.

• Had he followed form—had he asked his mother to speak to his father to approach a go-between—would Chie have been more receptive?

很显然,第一句话说出了 Akira 的行为,而后一句则指出"如果他不是这么做的话……",因此是在解析 Akira 的行为。选项 C 是迷惑选项,注意 question 一词有质问的含义,而文中的 had he(即 if he had …)和 would 则表达了一种不确定性,因此可以排除该选项。而选项 A 没有将重点放在 Akira 的行为上。所以选择答案 D。

8. As used in line 2,"form" most nearly means _____.
   A. appearance　　　　　　　　B. custom
   C. structure　　　　　　　　　D. nature

答案:B

解析:回到原文:Had he followed form—had he asked his mother to speak to his father to approach a go-between—would Chie have been more receptive?

显然,破折号中的内容就是解释主句中的 form 的,那么破折号中的内容又说了些什么呢? 这句话说到 form 就是请他的父母做一个中间人撮合一下,明显可以排除选项 A 和 D。我们再看到在这一句话之前,"Akira came directly, breaking all tradition."句中的 tradition 一词是选项 B 的近义词,那么我们就可以选到答案 B。

9. Why does Akira say his meeting with Chie is "a matter of urgency" (line 32)?
   A. He fears that his own parents will disapprove of Naomi.
   B. He worries that Naomi will reject him and marry someone else.
   C. He has been offered an attractive job in another country.
   D. He knows that Chie is unaware of his feelings for Naomi.

答案:C

解析:我们回到第32行前后文定位关键词matter of urgency,可以看到这件紧急的事在第41行出现:

Line 41:I've an opportunity to go to America, as dentist for Seattle's Japanese community. 因此可以选到答案C。

10. Which choice provides the best evidence for the answer to the previous question?

A. Line 39 ("I don't ... you")
B. Line 39~42 ("Normally ... community")
C. Line 58~59 ("Depending ... Japan")
D. Line 72~73 ("I see ... you")

答案:B

解析:从上一题可知,Akira的紧急事件在第39~42行出现,因此选B。选项A的句子只是一个谦辞,因此排除。选项C和选项D距离上题中的a matter of urgency太远,一般不做考虑。

译文

这篇文章来自于莉迪亚·港谷于1999年出版的《美之奇异性》。小说背景设置在1920年的日本。智惠和她女儿奈绪美是贵族富士家族的成员。

明这么直接地登门拜访了,此举破坏了所有的传统。是这样吗?如果他遵从祖制,先去跟他母亲提,再让母亲跟父亲商量,再由父亲出面找一个媒人。这样智惠是不是接受起来会更好一些呢?

他是一个冬天的晚上贪夜而来的。当他敲门的时候,正好冷雨声声打在百叶窗外面的阳台上,所以一开始智惠将他的动静当成了风。女仆却知道是有访客。智惠听见了女仆细碎的脚步声,听见她打开了门发出"吱呀"一声。接着女仆将一张名片拿到了客厅交给了智惠。

一开始智惠并不想去见这个客人,智惠待得非常舒服,不大想动。她正在客厅和女儿奈绪美一起读书。她们正坐在一张矮桌子旁,桌子下面是烧得旺旺的炭火盆,桌子被一床厚厚的被子罩着。她们的腿都在被子里,十分暖和。

"这种天气,这么晚了,会是谁呢?"智惠一边问女仆,一边将名片从女仆的托盘里拿起来。

"筱田明。神户牙科大学。"智惠边看边读。

奈绪美明显熟悉这个名字,智惠听见她轻轻地吸了一口气。

"我觉得你应该去见他。"奈绪美说。

明在房子的入口处等待着,他大概20岁出头的年纪,高瘦身材,穿着学生常穿的黑色军装风格制服,看起来有些严肃。当他弯腰鞠躬的时候,他的两只手笔直地垂在身体两边,一只手拿着顶黑帽子,另一只手拿着把黄色的油纸伞。智惠的目光穿过明,看向屋外被雨淋得透湿、闪着微光的石阶,明的影子印在石阶上,看起来黑乎乎的像有两个人。

"夫人,"明说,"非常抱歉打扰到您了。我是为了一件紧急的事情而来的。"

他的声音礼貌而轻柔,在他直起身的时候,他悄悄恭敬地看了一眼智惠的脸。

在微光下,他的眼中散发着真诚的光芒,智惠发现自己已经开始喜欢上这个年轻人了。

"快进来吧,这个天气的夜晚糟透了。我想你的事情不急在这一时半会儿吧。"

"夫人,我真的不愿意打扰您。要是平常,我会以一种合适得多的方式拜访您。但是我等不及了,我得到了一份在美国的工作:西雅图一个日本社区当一名牙医。"

"那恭喜了,"智惠有些好笑地回答,"这无疑是一个很好的机会。但是这事儿跟我有什么关系呢?"

即使之前注意到奈绪美看到名片时那种无法呼吸的异常反应,智惠还是完全没想到发生了什么事。明在说这段话的时候,像是在很正式地发表一个演讲。这使智惠突然对这个年轻人萌生了母性的关怀,觉得很有趣。他像一个孩子,急切真诚地讲述一件事情,并且对这件事投注了很多的感情。但是事实上,这件事在大人看来并没有什么大不了的,智惠也完全把他当成了一个孩子。

智惠也是这样看待自己的女儿奈绪美的。虽然奈绪美已经18岁了,一直在学艺术,正需要缔结一段好婚姻,但智惠从来没想急着给奈绪美找个丈夫。

明突然脸红了。

"这就要看您是怎么回答了,夫人,我有可能留在日本的。我来是向奈绪美求婚的。"

智惠一下子感受到了夜的潮湿。

"奈绪美知道你的……意图吗?"

"我们心意相通的。请不要因为我用这种不得体的方式提出求婚,而质疑我是否是个合适的候选人。我选择这种直接上门的方式实在是因为找媒人太费时间了。但是不管我用什么方式,最终都是要父母准许的。如果您同意我的求婚,我就变成了奈绪美的入赘女婿,我们会留在富士家族。如果您不同意,我就只能去美国了,我得在美国打拼出一片天地,让我的新娘能有个家。"

明急切地想剖白自己的心意,在说话的时候直勾勾地盯着智惠。突然,他的声音又变柔和了。"我吓到您了吧,夫人。真是非常抱歉。我不能再占用您的时间了。我的地址名片上有。如果您不想再跟我联系,我两周后再来拜访您。到那之前,我不会再麻烦您。晚安。"

他又鞠了一躬,以一种与生俱来的优雅悄然离去,像只偷到了鱼的猫儿,没有给智惠带来任何困扰。

"妈妈?"智惠听见女儿在后面低低地叫,她转向了楼梯:"他已经对你求过婚了吗?"

奈绪美黑黑的眼睛和浓密的眉毛给了智惠一些力量。也许他的想法荒谬透顶。

"你在哪儿认识这小子的?你能想象吗?他认为他就这样轻易地跟富士家族的继承人结婚,然后带她到美国去!"

智惠等着奈绪美赞同的大笑。

奈绪美没有说话,她站在那里整整一分钟,直直地看向智惠的眼睛。最终,她开口了:"我是在我的文学交流会上认识他的。"

接着奈绪美转身往屋内走去,然后又停住了。

"妈妈。"

"嗯?"

"我已经决定嫁给他了。"

2.4.2 Passage II

答案解析

11. The authors most likely use the examples in lines 1~9 of the passage ("Every ... showers") to highlight the _____.
    A. regularity with which people shop for gifts
    B. recent increase in the amount of money spent on gifts
    C. anxiety gift shopping causes for consumers
    D. number of special occasions involving gift-giving

答案：A

解析：既然已经是全文首句了，那么很显然我们要到这个例子后面去找总结句：

Line 9：This frequent experience of gift-giving can engender ambivalent feelings in gift givers.

句中的 this frequent experience 显然就是例子的高度概括，对应选项 A 中的 regularity，因此选 A。选项 B 中的 recent increase 在例子中并没有提到，且与 frequent 一词的含义有出入。选项 C 中的 anxiety 对应的是 ambivalent，是该总结句后要引入的内容，因此排除。选项 D 强调的是 number，而并非总结句中强调的 frequent，因此同样是迷惑选项。

12. In line 10, the word "ambivalent" most nearly means _____.
    A. unrealistic   B. conflicted
    C. apprehensive   D. supportive

答案：B

解析：回到原文：This frequent experience of gift-giving can engender ambivalent feelings in gift-givers.

这句话显然是一个总起句，因此我们到之后的句子中看具体的例子是怎么阐述的，就可以相对应得到 ambivalent 的含义。后面一句句子写道：

Many relish the opportunity to buy presents because gift-giving offers a powerful means to build stronger bonds with one's closest peers. At the same time, many dread the thought of buying gifts; they worry that their purchases will disappoint rather than delight the intended recipients.

也就是说，买礼物者一方面希望自己的礼物能够让自己与对方建立起亲密关系，另一方面却又担心自己的礼物会让对方失望，是一种矛盾的情绪，因此我们很容易就能选出答案 B。

13. The authors indicate that people value gift-giving because they feel it _____.
    A. functions as a form of self-expression
    B. is an inexpensive way to show appreciation
    C. requires the gift-recipient to reciprocate
    D. can serve to strengthen a relationship

答案：D

解析：从之后一题我们知道该题的答案在第 10 行：

Line 10：Many relish the opportunity to buy presents because gift-giving offers a powerful means to build stronger bonds with one's closest peers. 句中 build bond 则与选项 D 中的 strengthen a relationship 对应，因此选 D。

14. Which choice provides the best evidence for the answer to the previous question?
    A. Lines 10~13 ("Many ... peers")
    B. Lines 22~23 ("People ... own")
    C. Lines 31~32 ("Research ... perspectives")
    D. Lines 44~47 ("Although ... unfounded")

答案：A

解析：选项 A 句中的 relish 与题干中的 value 对应，因此正确。选项 B 说的是人们对于礼物的选择，与 value gift-giving 无关，因此排除。选项 C 说的是人们对于礼物选择过程中遇到的困难，也与 value gift-giving 无关，同样排除。选出 D 说的是对于一个理论的否定，同样与 value gift-giving 无关，因此排除。

15. The "social psychologists" mentioned in paragraph 2（lines 17~34）would likely describe the "deadweight loss" phenomenon as _____.
    A. predictable   B. questionable
    C. disturbing   D. unprecedented

答案：A

解析：我们通过题干中的 deadweight loss 和 social psychologist 进行定位：

Line 28：This "deadweight loss" suggests that gift-givers are not very good at predicting what gifts others will appreciate. That in itself is not surprising to social psychologists. 句中的 not surprising 与选项 A 中的 predictable 含义相同，因此选 A。

16. The passage indicates that the assumption made by gift-givers in lines 41~44 may be _____.
    A. insincere   B. unreasonable   C. incorrect   D. substantiated

答案：C

解析：见下题。

17. Which choice provides the best evidence for the answer to the previous question?
    A. Lines 53~55 ("Perhaps ... consideration")
    B. Lines 55~60 ("According ... relationship")
    C. Lines 63~65 ("As ... consideration")
    D. Lines 75~78 ("In ... relations")

答案：C

解析：第一题问的是对于送礼物者心态的推断是怎样的，因此我们先来看下面的具体句子：选项 A 和选项 D 是对于送礼物者为什么会有这样的 assumption 的解释，而非对于该 assumption 本身的评价，因此排除。选项 B 关注的是人们为什么会送礼物给他人，与上题所问内容不符，因此排除。选项 C 说收礼物者并不认为礼物大小代表心意大小，与送礼物者的 assumption 正好相反，是对该 assumption 的侧面评价，因此选 C。

得出第 17 题的答案后，我们回到第 16 题，看第 63 行：

Line 63：As for gift-recipients, they may not construe smaller and larger gifts as representing smaller and larger signals of thoughtfulness and consideration. 这一收礼物者的心态显然与送礼物者的预期是相反的,侧面印证了送礼者在挑选礼物时对于收礼物者的 assumption 是错误的。因此选 C。

18. As it is used in line 54, "convey" most nearly means _____.
    A. transport   B. counteract   C. exchange   D. communicate
    答案:D

    解析:回到原文:Perhaps givers believe that bigger (i. e., more expensive) gifts convey stronger signals of thoughtfulness and consideration. 这道题就可以根据词根词缀法来解。首先,con 来自拉丁语中的 com,是一个表示共同、强调的词缀,而 vey 来自于 via,是表示路、移动的词缀,因此这个词应该有"传递、传送"的含义,而选项中有这个含义的只有选项 A 和选项 D。我们将两个选项代入原文就会发现 transport signal 与文中的语境不符,并不是传输物理信号,而是传递交流信号,因此可以选到正确答案 D。

19. The authors refer to work by Camerer and others (line 56) in order to _____.
    A. offer an explanation   B. introduce an argument
    C. question a motive   D. support a conclusion
    答案:A

    解析:我们回到原文,可以看到在 Camerer 的研究之前有明显的总起句:

Line 53：Perhaps givers believe that bigger (i. e., more expensive) gifts convey stronger signals of thoughtfulness and consideration. 句中的 signal 一词与 Camerer 描述句中的 signal 一词正好对应,说明 Camerer 这句话是为该总起句而服务的,因此我们可以排除选项 B 和选项 C。而总起句中的 perhaps 说明这并不是一个结论,因此排除选项 D,选到答案 A。

20. The graph following the passage offers evidence that gift-givers base their predictions of how much a gift will be appreciated on _____.
    A. the appreciation level of the gift-recipients
    B. the monetary value of the gift
    C. their own desires for the gifts they purchase
    D. their relationship with the gift-recipients
    答案:B

    解析:既然题干中问的是 gift-givers 对于礼物被 appreciated 的预期,我们就只要关注图表中对于 giver 的描述即可。而观察图表,我们发现 giver 的 mean appreciation(纵轴)是根据礼物价钱正向相关的,也就是说,礼物越贵,他们所预期的 appreciation 就越高。因此,他们的 prediction 是基于礼物价值的,即选项 B 中的 monetary value。

21. The authors would likely attribute the differences in gift-giver and recipient mean appreciation as represented in the graph to _____.
    A. an inability to shift perspective
    B. an increasingly materialistic culture
    C. a growing opposition to gift-giving
    D. a misunderstanding of intentions
    答案:A

解析：这就是一道典型的图文关系题，意在定位这种对于礼物 appreciation 不匹配的原因。我们根据题干中的 differences、gift-giver 和 recipient 进行定位，去找同时出现这三个关键词的句子：

Line 70：Yet, despite the extensive experience that people have as both givers and receivers, they often struggle to transfer information gained from one role (e. g., as a giver) and apply it in another, complementary role (e. g., as a receiver). 句中的 struggle to transfer information ... and apply it in another, complementary role 对应选项 A 中的 inability to shift perspective，因此选 A。选项 D 是干扰选项，其中的 intention 解释为意图，与原文中说的 perspective（理解、认知）是不一样的，因此排除。

译文

这篇文章来自弗朗西斯·福林和加布里埃尔·亚当斯的《金钱买不到爱：礼物价值和感激程度的不对称》，版权归埃尔斯维尔公司所有。

每一天，都有数百万购物大军浩浩荡荡地全力杀向商店——既有网上商店也有传统商店，他们疯狂地搜寻自己觉得最完美的礼物。去年光是12月这一个月，美国人就在零售商店里面花了超过300亿美金。除了购买节日礼物之外，大多数人们在一年中间也在不停地购买各种其他礼物，如结婚礼物、生日礼物、周年纪念礼物、毕业礼物和婴儿受洗礼物。如此频繁地送出礼物会在送礼者的心中产生矛盾的感情。有些人会享受这个去购买礼物的机会，因为送礼这个过程会让收受双方之间产生更强的联系，从而和自己亲近同辈更加亲近，有些人非常害怕购买礼物，因为他们害怕自己送出的礼物对方不喜欢，反而会让对方失望。

人类学家将送礼这个过程形容为一种积极的社会现象，它承担着各种政治上的、宗教上的、心理上的功能。经济学家们却从一个不那么讨人喜欢的角度看这个现象。伍德福格尔（1993）说，送礼这件事情代表着资源的浪费。因为送礼的那方买的礼物往往是收礼者自己不会选择购买的东西，或者至少不会花那么多钱去购买（这一现象被称之为"圣诞节的全损失"），就是说，送礼者可能会花上100美元去买一件礼物，但是如果收礼者自己权衡的话，他只会花80美元去买。这种"全损失"显示了送礼者一般不擅长猜到什么样的礼物对方会喜欢。这种现象本身对于社会心理学家来说并不陌生。研究显示人们很难真正考虑别人的想法——这种洞察力会受到自我主义、相似性投射和多样归因错误的影响。

一个有趣的现象是，送礼者们自身也有很多作为收礼者的经验感受，但是他们每次出去买礼物的时候，仍然会费尽脑筋，最后超支购买。在最近的研究中，我们对于这种超支的问题提出了一个独特的心理学解释：送礼者往往会将礼物的价值和收礼者感激的程度联系起来（买的礼物越贵重，收礼者就会越加感动）。这种将礼物价值和感动程度连接起来的想法对于送礼者来说是直觉的反应，但是事实上，这种假设是没有根据的。我们认为收礼者不倾向于送礼者期望的那样，将他们的感受和礼物的贵重程度联系起来。

为什么送礼者会假定礼物价值和收礼者的感激程度紧密联系呢？大概送礼者们都相信礼物越大（就是越贵），就越能显现他们在选购礼物时的细致和体贴入微。根据卡梅尔（1988）和其他一些研究，送礼这种行为代表着一种象征性的仪式，送礼者往往会尝试在这种行为中发出积极的信号，使收礼者感受到他们正面积极的态度，感到他们愿意给这段关系更多的投资。如此一来，为了让收礼者感受到更加强烈的正面信号，送礼者可能会愿意花更多的钱在买礼物这件事上。但是对于收礼者来说，他们可能并不会将礼物的大小和对方的体贴细致程度联系起来。

送礼者和收礼者没法理解对方的立场这件事情看起来很让人迷惑,因为人们几乎每天都这两种角色中转换,有时候,甚至一天里面就要经历几次转换。但是不管作为送礼者和收礼者的经验有多么丰富,人们还是很难将扮演一种角色(比如送礼者)得到的经验应用到扮演另一种角色(比如收礼者)中。从理论上来说,人们没法运用自身经验和偏好来指导自己在交换关系中得到更有效的结果。在现实层面上来说,人们每年花费大笔钱在购买礼物上,但是从来没有学会用自己的洞察力去标定送礼的花销。

2.4.3 Passage Ⅲ

答案解析

22. The authors use the word "backbone" in lines 3 and 39 to indicate that _____.
A. only very long chains of DNA can be taken from an organism with a spinal column
B. the main structure of a chain in a DNA molecule is composed of repeating units
C. a chain in a DNA molecule consists entirely of phosphate groups or of sugars
D. nitrogenous bases form the main structural unit of DNA

答案:B

解析:我们回到原文找到第一次出现 backbone 一词的地方:
Line 2:The molecule is a very long chain, the backbone of which consists of a regular alternation of sugar and phosphate groups. 这句话描述了 backbone 最大的 main structure,即 regular alternation of sugar and phosphate groups。换言之,就是 backbone 的结构是 repeating units(选项 B)。而这个 backbone 又是 DNA 中的,因此选项 B 与其信息完全对应。

23. A student claims that nitrogenous bases pair randomly with one another. Which of the following statements in the passage contradicts the student's claim?
A. Lines 5~6 ("To each ... types")
B. Lines 9~10 ("So far ... irregular")
C. Lines 23~25 ("The bases ... other")
D. Lines 27~29 ("One member ... chains")

答案:D

解析:这是一道单独的循证题,要找的是与该学生相反的观点证据,即不 random,而是 regular。因此我们带着这种预设去看四个选项:选项 A 说的是 nitrogenous base 的四种类型,而非配对信息,答非所问,因此排除。选项 B 中的 irregular 与 student 的观点并不冲突,因此排除。选项 C 是干扰选项,说的是 two chains 之间是怎样联系的,对应的是前一句中的 hydrogen bonds,也就是说,这个选项说的是 base 之间是怎样 hydrogen-bonded 的,而不是 focus 是否在 pair randomly 或 regularly 上,因此排除。选项 D 说的正是 nitrogenous bases 的配对信息,且通过 one member of a pair must be... and the other... in order to... 可以得出这种配对并非是 random 的,因此正确。

24. In the second paragraph (lines 12~19), what do the authors claim to be a feature

of biological interest?

  A. The chemical formula of DNA   B. The common fiber axis

  C. The X-ray evidence   D. DNA consisting of two chains

答案:D

解析:我们回到原文,用 feature 一词进行定位:

 Line 12:The first feature of our structure which is of biological interest is that it consists not of one chain, but of two.

 很明显,句中 consists not of one chain, but of two 对应选项 D 的内容,因此选 D。

25. The authors' main purpose of including the information about X-ray evidence and density is to _____.

  A. establish that DNA is the molecule that carries the genetic information

  B. present an alternate hypothesis about the composition of a nucleotide

  C. provide support for the authors' claim about the number of chains in a molecule of DNA

  D. confirm the relationship between the density of DNA and the known chemical formula of DNA

答案:C

解析:我们根据 X-ray 和 density 进行定位:

 Line 18:However, the density, taken with the X-ray evidence, suggests very strongly that there are two. 句中的 two 明显是一个指代,因此我们回看上一句:

 Line 15:It has often been assumed that since there was only one chain in the chemical formula there would only be one in the structural unit. 从这句话中我们得出,第一个句子是在反驳第二个句子的观点,认为在 structural unit 中有两个 chains。因此第一句话是提出了一个相反的观点,对应选项 B 中的 alternate hypothesis,但选项 B 中的 composition of nucleotide 在句子中没有出现。因此,选项 B 是一个非常具有迷惑性的干扰选项。

 既然看完了上句没有得出答案,我们再回到该段落的首句:

 Line 12:The first feature of our structure which is of biological interest is that it consists not of one chain, but of two. 从这句话中,我们可知作者是持与 X-ray 证据相同的态度的,因此对应选项 C 中的 provide support for the author's claim。

26. Based on the passage, the authors' statement "If a pair consisted of two purines, for example, there would not be room for it" (lines 29~30) implies that a pair _____.

  A. of purines would be larger than the space between a sugar and a phosphate group

  B. of purines would be larger than a pair consisting of a purine and a pyrimidine

  C. of pyrimidines would be larger than a pair of purines

  D. consisting of a purine and a pyrimidine would be larger than a pair of pyrimidines

答案:B

解析:我们回到原文:

 Line 29:If a pair consisted of two purines, for example, there would not be room for it. 这句话是对一个论点的论据支撑,因此我们回到上文去找该论点:

 Line 25:The important point is that only certain pairs of bases will fit into the structure. One member of a pair must be a purine and the other a pyrimidine in order to bridge between the two chains. 从这两句话中我们可以得出，purine 和 pyrimidine 就像是两个子集，共同构成了 a pair 这一合集，如果两个 purines 就会没有足够空间、超出合计范围的话，意味着就比原先的两个子集要大，因此对应选项 B。

27. The authors' use of the words "exact," "specific," and "complement" in lines 47~49 in the final paragraph functions mainly to _____.

    A. confirm that the nucleotide sequences are known for most molecules of DNA

    B. counter the claim that the sequences of bases along a chain can occur in any order

    C. support the claim that the phosphate-sugar backbone of the authors' model is completely regular

    D. emphasize how one chain of DNA may serve as a template to be copied during DNA replication

答案：D

解析：首先我们观察这三个词，会发现其中两个都有"特定的"之意，那么我们带着这种预设回到原文：

Line 47：If the actual order of the bases on one of the pair of chains were given，one could write down the exact order of the bases on the other one，because of the specific pairing. Thus one chain is，as it were，the complement of the other…这段话说明了 bases 的 order 是特定的、有规律可循的。那为什么要提到这一信息呢？我们往下看到其总结句：

Line 49：… and it is this feature which suggests how the deoxyribonucleic acid molecule might duplicate itself. 句中的 duplicate 对应选项 D 中的 be copied，因此选 D。

28. Based on the table and passage, which choice gives the correct percentages of the purines in yeast DNA?

    A. 17.1% and 18.7%   B. 17.1% and 32.9%

    C. 18.7% and 31.3%   D. 31.3% and 32.9%

答案：C

解析：我们根据图表中的 adenine、guanine、cytosine 和 thymine 进行定位：

Line 6：Two of the possible bases—adenine and guanine—are purines，and the other two—thymine and cytosine—are pyrimidines. 因此，我们只要到表中找 yeast 对应的 adenine 和 guanine 数据即可，可以选到答案 C。

29. Do the data in the table support the authors' proposed pairing of bases in DNA?

    A. Yes, because for each given organism, the percentage of adenine is closest to the percentage of thymine, and the percentage of guanine is closest to the percentage of cytosine.

    B. Yes, because for each given organism, the percentage of adenine is closest to the percentage of guanine, and the percentage of cytosine is closest to the percentage of thymine.

    C. No, because for each given organism, the percentage of adenine is closest to the percentage of thymine, and the percentage of guanine is closest to the percentage of cytosine.

D. No, because for each given organism, the percentage of adenine is closest to the percentage of guanine, and the percentage of cytosine is closest to the percentage of thymine.

答案：A

解析：我们根据题干中的 pair 和图表中的 adenine、guanine、cytosine 和 thymine 进行定位：

Line 32: If this is true, the conditions for forming hydrogen bonds are more restrictive, and the only pairs of bases possible are: adenine with thymine, and guanine with cytosine. Adenine, for example, can occur on either chain; but when it does, its partner on the other chain must always be thymine. 而图表中 adenine/thymine 以及 guanine/cytosine 之间的百分比的确非常接近，因此选 A。

30. According to the table, which of the following pairs of base percentages in sea urchin DNA provides evidence in support of the answer to the previous question?

    A. 17.3% and 17.7%　　　　　　B. 17.3% and 32.1%

    C. 17.3% and 32.8%　　　　　　D. 17.7% and 32.8%

答案：A

解析：从上一题我们可知，应该选择数值相近的一组数字，因此选 A。

31. Based on the table, is the percentage of adenine in each organism's DNA the same or does it vary, and which statement made by the authors is most consistent with that data?

    A. The same; "Two of ... pyrimidines" (lines 6~8)

    B. The same; "The important ... structure" (lines 25~26)

    C. It varies; "Adenine ... thymine" (lines 36~38)

    D. It varies; "It follows ... information" (lines 41~45)

答案：D

解析：这道题是图表题和循证题的结合。我们首先观察数字，发现 adenine 在每个生物体中占比是不同的，因此排除选项 A 和选项 B。第二步我们通过行数回看原文：选项 C 说的是 adenine 必须和 thymine 在一起，并没有说 adenine 在 DNA 中占比的情况。选项 D 中的 many different permutations are possible 正好对应 vary，因此正确。

译文

这篇文章来自 FD·沃特森和 F·H·C·克里克于1953年发表的《脱氧核糖核酸结构的遗传学含义》。版权归自然出版集团所有。沃特森和克里克使用了罗萨琳·德·富兰克林和 RG·高斯灵的 X 光 DNA 结晶图表、额尔文·查格尔富关于 DNA 基本构成的数据作为证据，推论出了 DNA 的结构。

DNA 的化学结构现在已经颇为完善了。这个分子是个很长的链条，其主干由糖和磷酸基规律地交替组成。每份糖中附着一个可能有四种不同类型的含氮碱基。其中可能的两种是嘌呤——腺嘌呤和鸟嘌呤，另外两种是嘧啶类，分别为胸腺嘧啶和胞嘧啶。就我们现在所知，围绕着长链的基团序列是无规律的。单体单元由磷酸盐、糖和基团组成，被称作核苷酸。

DNA结构的第一个生物显著特征就是它不是由一条长链组成的,而是两条。这两条长链交缠在纤维轴上。过去我们曾认为在化学式里只能有一条链,所以结构单元里也只能有一条链。但是,从X光照射的密度提供的证据来看,应该有两条长链。

另一个生物学上的重要特征是这两条链交缠在一起的方式。这项工作由氢键来完成。两个基团成对结合在一起,一条链上的一个基团和另一条链上的一个基团由氢键连接。重要的一点是这个结构只有特定的一对基团才能够形成。这对基团必须一个是嘌呤,一个是嘧啶,才能在这两条链中架起桥梁,如果这一对都是嘌呤组成,那么空间是不够容纳的。

我们认为两个基团必须以最可能结合的形式来呈现。如果这一点成立的话,氢键形成的条件就非常苛刻了,可能只有两个基团的结合能够完成:腺嘌呤和腺嘧啶,鸟嘌呤和胞嘧啶。举例说明,腺嘌呤可以出现在一条链上,但是当这条链出现了腺嘌呤时,另一条链上必须是腺嘧啶才可以完成配对。

我们模型中的碳酸糖骨架是完全有序的,但是一对基团中的任意序列都可以融入这个结构中。在一个长分子中会有很多种不同的序列组合,所以看起来每个基团的精准排序就成了遗传基因的密码。如果一条链上一对基团中的一个已知,那么我们就能根据配对规则,将另一条链上基团的顺序完整写出来。这就是为什么一条链是另一条链的补足。这样的特性也暗示了DNA分子有可能进行自我复制。

2.4.4 Passage Ⅳ

答案解析

32. The main purpose of the passage is to _____.
A. emphasize the value of a tradition
B. stress the urgency of an issue
C. highlight the severity of social divisions
D. question the feasibility of an undertaking

答案:B

解析:我们先一起来看全文首尾句和每段首句:

• Close at hand is a bridge over the River Thames, an admirable vantage ground for us to make a survey.

• There they go, our brothers who have been educated at public schools and universities, mounting those steps, passing in and out of those doors, ascending those pulpits, preaching, teaching, administering justice, practising medicine, transacting business, making money. It is a solemn sight always—a procession, like a caravanserai crossing a desert...

• Where in short is it leading us, the procession of the sons of educated men?

第一句中说到"我们"现在处于一个make a survey的有利时机。而第二句中的our brothers与第三句中的the procession of the sons of educated men则很明显指的是同一群人,因此可以判断出第一句中的survey就是最后一句中提到的"他们要将我们带去哪里"的问题。由此可知,作者写该文的目的在于抛出一个紧急的问题,即女性在当时的时代大背景下到底应该如何自处,而非强调传统价值、社会分工或承诺的可行性。原文中的 Lines 8~11,"Now we are pressed for time. Now we are here to consider facts; now we must fix our eyes upon the procession—the procession of the sons of educated men."第一句话以及第二句话中的两个 now 都能体现紧迫性。因此选 B。

33. The central claim of the passage is that _____.

A. educated women face a decision about how to engage with existing institutions.

B. women can have positions of influence in English society only if they give up some of their traditional roles.

C. the male monopoly on power in English society has had grave and continuing effects.

D. the entry of educated women into positions of power traditionally held by men will transform those positions.

答案:A

解析:我们同样通过阅读首尾句来对应答案:

• Close at hand is a bridge over the River Thames, an admirable vantage ground for us to make a survey.

• There they go, our brothers who have been educated at public schools and universities, mounting those steps, passing in and out of those doors, ascending those pulpits, preaching, teaching, administering justice, practising medicine, transacting business,making money. It is a solemn sight always—a procession, like a caravanserai crossing a desert…

此外,文中的 Lines 53~57,Lines 77~83 均能体现出"面对决定"这个信息,所以选 A。

34. Woolf uses the word "we" throughout the passage mainly to _____.

A. reflect the growing friendliness among a group of people

B. advance the need for candor among a group of people

C. establish a sense of solidarity among a group of people

D. reinforce the need for respect among a group of people

答案:C

解析:题干考查的是使用第一人称"we"所达成的效果。

Lines 19~24:This passage is adapted from Virginia Woolf, *Three Guineas*. © 1938 by Harcourt, Inc. Here, Woolf considers the situation of women in English society.

But now, for the past twenty years or so, it is no longer a sight merely, a photograph, or fresco scrawled upon the walls of time, at which we can look with merely an esthetic appreciation. For there, trapesing along at the tail end of the procession, we go ourselves.

从原文中,不难发现"we"指代的是全体女性,而 Woolf 呼吁女性要"we go ourselves"。回到选项,选项 A 的"growing friendliness",选项 B 的"need for candor"以及选项 D 的"need for respect"并没有在原文有特定的体现,而选项 C 的"solidarity"(团结)则凸显了 Woolf 所提出的"we go ourselves",所以在本文中,使用"we"这一人称,能够让女性们感到自己属于一个团体,要为共同的目标而努力。

35. According to the passage, Woolf chooses the setting of the bridge because it _____.

A. is conducive to a mood of fanciful reflection

B. provides a good view of the procession of the sons of educated men

C. is within sight of historic episodes to which she alludes

D. is symbolic of the legacy of past and present sons of educated men

答案：B

解析：我们首先根据题干中的 bridge 进行定位：

Line 1：Close at hand is a bridge over the River Thames, an admirable vantage ground for us to make a survey … It is a place to stand on by the hour, dreaming. But not now. Now we are pressed for time. Now we are here to consider facts; now we must fix our eyes upon the procession—the procession of the sons of educated men.

句中的 consider facts 与选项 A 中的 fanciful reflection 不符，因此排除。选项 C 中的 historic episodes 在这段话中并没有提及。选项 D 中的 legacy 也在该段落中没有提到。而选项 B 中的 provide a good view 与句中的 fix our eyes 相对应，后半句内容更是完全一样，因此选 B。

36. Woolf indicates that the procession she describes in the passage _____.

A. has come to have more practical influence in recent years

B. has become a celebrated feature of English public life

C. includes all of the richest and most powerful men in England

D. has become less exclusionary in its membership in recent years

答案：D

解析：见下题。

37. Which choice provides the best evidence for the answer to the previous question?

A. Lines 12～17 ("There ... money")   B. Lines 17～19 ("It ... desert")

C. Lines 23～24 ("For ... ourselves")   D. Lines 30～34 ("We ... pulpit")

答案：C

解析：第 36 题问的是文中 Woolf 对于 procession 的阐述，因此我们带着问题看第 37 题的选项：选项 A 说的是男人们在社会上从事的职业，选项 B 同样是对这种 procession 的描述，而非 Woolf 对 procession 的 indication，因此选项 A 和选项 B 都可以排除。选项 C 中提到了 procession，还说到了 we (educated women) go by ourselves，信息符合。选项 D 是对于女性未来可能会做的工作的展望，并没有提到 procession，因此排除。所以就可以选到答案 C。

我们来看选项 C 的句子：

Line 23：For there, trapesing along at the tail end of the procession, we go ourselves.

也就是说女性也开始加入这支本身只有男性能参与的队伍了，对应到第 36 题的选项 D 中的 become less exclusionary in its membership，因此选 D。

38. Woolf characterizes the questions in lines 53～57 ("For we ... men") as both _____.

A. controversial and threatening　　B. weighty and unanswerable
C. momentous and pressing　　D. provocative and mysterious

答案:C

解析: 见下题。

39. Which choice provides the best evidence for the answer to the previous question?

A. Lines 46～47 ("We ... questions")　　B. Lines 48～49 ("And ... them")
C. Line 57 ("The moment ... short")　　D. Line 62 ("That ... Madam")

答案:B

解析: 我们先来看第53行的句子说了些什么:

Line 53:For we have to ask ourselves, here and now, do we wish to join that procession, or don't we? On what terms shall we join that procession? Above all, where is it leading us, the procession of educated men?

第38题问的是对这一句子的概括,因此我们带着问题来看第39题的选项:选项A告诉我们现在是时候让女性问问自己这些问题了,但没有提出这些问题的特性,因此排除。选项B用一个同位语从句点出了question的特点,因此是与第38题有关联的,可以保留。选项C说的问题的时间很短,也并不是直接说问题本身,因此排除。选项D的这句话完全没有提及问题,因此同样排除,这样我们就能选出正确答案B。

那么选项B的句子说的是什么呢?

Line 49:The questions that we have to ask and to answer about that procession during this moment of transition are so important that they may well change the lives of all men and women for ever. 句中的 moment 体现出 pressing,而 so important 则对应选项中的 momentous,因此可以选到答案C。

40. Which choice most closely captures the meaning of the figurative "sixpence" referred to in lines 70 and 71?

A. Tolerance　　B. Knowledge　　C. Opportunity　　D. Perspective

答案:C

解析: 回到原文:It was thus that they won us the right to our brand-new sixpence. It falls to us now to go on thinking; how are we to spend that sixpence? 从这句话中解析得出,sixpence应该是女性之前未曾享有过的(brand-new),而且是之后要仔细思考该如何好好运用的。而全文说的正是女性现在有了、之前未曾有过的走向社会的权利和机会,因此选C。

41. The range of places and occasions listed in lines 72～76 ("Let us ... funerals") mainly serves to emphasize how _____.

A. novel the challenge faced by women is

B. pervasive the need for critical reflection is

C. complex the political and social issues of the day are

D. enjoyable the career possibilities for women are

答案;B

解析: 原文中的这个句子列举了一系列地点和场合,作者运用了多次 let us think,可以明显看出 think 是作者想要强调的,与选项 B 中的 critical reflection 对应。选项 A 中的 challenge 并没有在这句话中提到,选项 C 中的 political and social issues 也无从说起,选项 D 中的 enjoyable 更是毫无证据,因此选 B。

译文

这篇文章来自弗吉尼亚·伍尔夫的《三个基尼金币》,此书于 1938 年发行,版权归属哈尔库特公司。在这里,伍尔夫对英国社会的女性现状做了思考。

手边就是一座桥,这座桥横跨在泰晤士河之上,给我们提供了绝佳的地点来进行一番调查。泰晤士河静静地在下面流淌,装载着木材和几乎满溢出来的玉米的船只来来往往。桥的一边是城市的穹顶和尖顶,另一边是西敏寺和国会大厦。在这里,我们可以静静地站上几小时来欣赏景致,来做梦。但是现在不行,现在我们时间紧迫。我们到这儿是来思考的,我们必须牢牢盯住眼前的这队行进的队伍——由有教养者的儿子们组成的队伍。

他们来了,我们的兄弟们,他们在公立学校和大学中接受教育,一步步地爬上阶梯,走上各式各样的岗位。他们登上讲台布道,他们登上讲台授课,他们以正义之名行使职权,他们行医济世,他们经商挣钱。每次见到这样的队伍,总是给人一种肃穆之感,就像沙漠中缓缓行进的商队一般。但是近 20 年来,这已经不只是一个景观了,不再是我们纯粹从审美的意义上来欣赏的涂鸦在时间之墙上的一张照片或一幅壁画。但是这儿不一样,因为在这儿,我们将要加入这支队伍的尾部。这么久以来,我们一直从书中看着社会的盛会,过惯了从窗帘的后面望着男人们早上 9 点 30 分离开家去办公室,下午 6 点 30 分回来这样的生活,但是现在,我们不用再被动接受了。我们也可以离开家,走上那些台阶,进出那些大门,我们也可以挣钱、执行法律等。或许再过一两个世纪,我们这些现在正用手中的笔摇旗呐喊的女人,也可以走上讲台进行布道。那时候没有人胆敢提出异议,我们也能成为那些先贤的代言人,这难道不是一个庄严的想法吗?谁知道呢?也许再过一些时候,我们还能穿上那种军装制服腰悬佩剑,胸前点缀着金色蕾丝,再戴上那种古老家族的煤斗,只要这煤斗没有用白色的马毛装饰过。看,您笑了——确实,那些作为囚禁牢笼的私人宅邸所投下的心灵阴影,让我描述的这种着装看起来有些古怪,而我们自己确实也穿了这种禁锢的服装太久了。但是我们到这儿来不是为了开怀大笑或者讨论男人、女人的时尚。我们来到这桥上是为了来问自己一些问题,一些非常重要的问题,并且我们必须马上回答出这些问题。在这个转变的时期,关于那只行进的队伍,我们必须提出和回答的问题是如此重要,它很可能永远地改变所有男人、女人的命运。此时此刻的问题是:我们是否希望加入这个队伍,还是说不希望?我们加入队伍的条件是什么?最关键的是,这支队伍会将我们指向何方?做决定的瞬间是短暂的,但是这个决定可能会持续五年,十年,或者也可能只持续几个月。你会反对,你说你没有时间,你得挣扎求存,你得付房租,你得管理市场。但是女士,这些理由都不成立。你从你自身的经验和一些佐证都能知道女人们总能在干活的时候进行思考,而不是正儿八经的在封闭的修道院的绿色台灯下。她们在烧菜的时候思考,在哄孩子睡觉的时候也思考。正因为此她们给我们赢得了那枚崭新的六便士。于是我们又有了新的问题去思考:我们将如何使用这枚六便士?让我们继续思考下去吧。让我们在办公室里思考,在公交车上思考,让我们在人群里围观国王加冕或者市长上台时思考;让我们在下议院的旁听席中思考,让我们在法庭上思考,让我们在参加洗礼、婚礼、葬礼的时候,永远都不要停止思考——在这些所谓的文明中我们自己身处何处?这些仪式到底是什么？为什么我们一定要参加它们？这些职业的意义何在？为什么我们从中能挣钱？简言之，这支队伍，这支由男人们组成的队伍，到底会将我们带到哪里？

2.4.5　Passage V

答案解析

42. In lines 9~17, the author of Passage 1 mentions several companies primarily to _____.
  A. note the technological advances that make space mining possible
  B. provide evidence of the growing interest in space mining
  C. emphasize the large profits to be made from space mining
  D. highlight the diverse ways to carry out space mining operations

答案：B

解析：文章1的作者列举了很多公司，例如"Planetary Resources of Washington""Deep Space Industries of Virginia"和"Golden Spike of Colorado"，主要目的是支持他的观点：很多对太空开发感兴趣的公司，正在将太空开发变成现实。

43. The author of Passage 1 indicates that space mining could have which positive effect?
  A. It could yield materials important to Earth's economy.
  B. It could raise the value of some precious metals on Earth.
  C. It could create unanticipated technological innovations.
  D. It could change scientists' understanding of space resources.

答案：A

解析：文章1的作者明确提到，太空开发的一个巨大好处是可以获得地球上的稀缺金属和要素，例如金、铂等。这些稀缺金属对于经济发展是重要的。所以答案选 A。

44. Which choice provides the best evidence for the answer to the previous question?
  A. Lines 18~22 ("Within … lanthanum")
  B. Lines 24~28 ("They … projects")
  C. Line 29~30 ("In this … commodity")
  D. Lines 41~44 ("Companies … machinery")

答案：A

解析：见下题。

45. As used in line 19, "demands" most nearly means _____.
  A. offers　　　B. claims　　　C. inquiries　　　D. desires

答案：D

解析：原文中讲述到太空开发能够满足人们对于稀缺金属的需求（meet earthly demands for precious metals），因此这里的 demands 是需求、欲望的意思，所以第 45 题的答案选择 D，第 44 题的答案选择 A。

46. What function does the discussion of water in lines 35~40 serve in Passage 1?

A. It continues an extended comparison that begins in the previous paragraph.

B. It provides an unexpected answer to a question raised in the previous paragraph.

C. It offers hypothetical examples supporting a claim made in the previous paragraph.

D. It examines possible outcomes of a proposal put forth in the previous paragraph.

答案：C

解析：文章第 17 行提到从太空中开采出的水资源是特别有价值的。Line 20~23 通过叙述太空水资源可以怎样被有效利用(for drinking or as a radiation shield)来"支持太空水资源有价值"这一观点。

47. The central claim of Passage 2 is that space mining has positive potential but _____.

A. it will end up encouraging humanity's reckless treatment of the environment

B. its effect should be thoughtfully considered before it becomes a reality

C. such potential may not include replenishing key resources that are disappearing on Earth

D. experts disagree about the commercial viability of the discoveries it could yield

答案：B

解析：作者在文章 2 中反复提到：太空开发应该三思而后行(But before the miners start firing up their rockets, we should pause for thought.)，所以答案选择 B。

48. As used in line 68, "hold" most nearly means _____.

A. maintain   B. grip   C. restrain   D. withstand

答案：A

解析：作者先是提到反对太空开发的环境顾虑，但是面对着太空开发的经济回报时，那些环境顾虑就很难再起作用(hard to hold)，答案选择 A。

49. Which statement best describes the relationship between the passages?

A. Passage 2 refutes the central claim advanced in Passage 1

B. Passage 2 illustrates the phenomenon described in more general terms in Passage 1.

C. Passage 2 argues against the practicality of the proposals put forth in Passage 1.

D. Passage 2 expresses reservations about developments discussed in Passage 1.

答案：D

解析：文章 1 的作者积极支持太空开发，并且列举了太空开发所能带来的各种经济回报；文章 2 的作者虽然承认太空开发的好处，但是仍然表达出"三思而后行"的顾虑。所以答案选择 D。

50. The author of Passage 2 would most likely respond to the discussion of the future of space mining in lines 11~16, Passage 1, by claiming that such a future

A. is inconsistent with the sustainable use of space resources.

B. will be difficult to bring about in the absence of regulations

C. cannot be attained without technologies that do not yet exist.

D. seems certain to affect Earth's economy in a negative way.

答案：B

解析：在文章1的第11～16行中，作者表达出太空开发的各种好处；文章2的作者则认为，在没有形成规章制度的情况下，太空开发会引起各种分歧。

51. Which choice provides the best evidence for the answer to the previous question?
    A. Lines 34～35 ("Some ... pristine")
    B. Lines 42～43 ("The resources ... Earth")
    C. Lines 47～48 ("One ... avoided")
    D. Lines 49～50 ("Without ... insecure")

答案：D

解析：见第50题解释。

52. Which point about the resources that will be highly valued in space is implicit in Passage 1 and explicit in Passage 2?
    A. They may be different resources from those that are valuable on Earth.
    B. They will be valuable only if they can be harvested cheaply.
    C. They are likely to be primarily precious metals and rare earth elements.
    D. They may increase in value as those same resources become rare on Earth.

答案：A

解析：文章1和文章2都表达出太空中珍贵资源不同于地球上珍贵资源的观点。文章2在第42～43行明确提到：太空轨道中的珍贵资源不同于地球上的珍贵资源，但是文章1没有这样的观点。并且文章1没有这么直接，只是间接提到太空中的水资源，甚至比地球上的稀缺金属还珍贵。

译文

第一篇文章改编自麦克·斯勒扎克于2013年发表在《新科学家》上的《太空开采：下一波的淘金热？》，第二篇文章来自于2013年发表在《新科学家》的编辑文章《驯服最后的边界》。

文章1

跟着钱走，最后你会发现你来到了太空。这就是有史以来首届太空采矿论坛所传递出来的信息。

这届论坛由澳大利亚太空工程研究中心召开，在悉尼举行。它聚集了包括采矿公司、机器人专家、月球研究科学家、政府相关部门的所有力量，力求将太空采矿变为现实。

这次论坛是紧随着2012年横空出世的两家私人星际采矿公司的脚步召开的。华盛顿行星资源公司说他们会在两年内将第一部探矿望远镜投放市场；弗吉尼亚的深空工业打算在2020年就能从小行星采集回第一批金属矿石。除了这两家之外，2012年还有一家科罗拉多的金色尖峰公司，准备给人们提供月球旅行的服务，这其中就包括了潜在的月球开矿者。

在未来几十年中，这些公司也许就能满足地球上对于像铂金和金子这样的贵金属的需求，也能满足一些稀有金属的需求，比如制作个人电子产品所必需的稀有金属钇和镧。但是就像改变了美国西部的第一批淘金者一样，这些太空采矿的先行者们不满足于仅让自己富起来，他们有着远大的理想，要建立完全不受地球限制的太空经济体，在这个经济体中，从月球和小行星采得的材料都会再次用于与太空相关的各种项目中。

在这个情境下，从其他外太空而来的各种资源中，水资源可能会成为最抢手的商品。来自纽约的蜜蜂机械机器人公司的克里斯·扎克尼说："在沙漠中什么更加贵重？一公斤金子还是一公斤水?""金子一点用都没有,而水能让你活下去。"

从月球极地而来的冰块可以运给空间站的宇航员们,他们可以喝掉这些水,或者将之用于防辐射的盾牌。而将水分子分离成氧和氢的时候会产生宇宙飞船所需的燃料,所以有充足水资源的小行星可以被用作太阳系的太空加油站。

有些公司还着眼于月球和小行星上的铁元素、硅元素和铝元素,这些元素可以被用在3D打印机内来制作备用零件和器械。还有公司提出可以将太空尘变成水泥以作为飞船降落时的垫板、庇护所和马路。

文章 2

去外太空遨游的动力已经从以探索为目的变为如今的经济驱使了。去年一整年,各种各样致力于将星际间的珍宝带到地球的提案层出不穷。毫无疑问,这些项目将会使一些亿万富翁更加富有,而且我们大家都能从中获利:太空中极为丰富的矿物质和从中可能衍生出来的各种新技术会使我们的生活更加充实。

但是在这些太空矿工们迫不及待地要发射他们的火箭之前,我们先暂停一下,好好想想。最初猛地一看,太空能源开采貌似避免了所有有可能的环境问题:小行星上(很有可能!)没有生命,因此也不会破坏栖息地。但是这样的开采会给地球和太空带来什么样的后果,值得我们仔细地考虑一下。

这其中的一点就是原则问题。有些人会说,太空是一片"壮阔的荒芜之地",但是我们并没有权利去那里予取予夺,就像我们地球上的两极地带一样,这些地方应该保持它们的远古以来本来的样子。另一些人会提出,将矛头对准宇宙的丰富储藏来满足我们自身,而不是致力于找出一种可持续发展的路子,这样不可行。

历史已经证明了这些关于环境的忧虑很难被真正实施,再说要说服大众这样荒芜的环境值得保留可能本身就不是容易的事。不管怎么说,太空有自己的广袤无垠,但是能够真正登上太空的人比踏上南极洲冰川大陆的还要少。

新兴的外太空经济也是需要被考虑的因素之一。在行星轨道上特别珍贵的资源可能和在地球上的完全不一样。怎样对这些资源进行管理,这一点还没有人提到过,更不用说随之而来的一系列法律和规范的架构,温和点说,这些全都只是零零散散的想法,不成系统。

外太空的开采者就像他们在地球上的同类一样,总是不想去思考这些问题。上周在澳大利亚悉尼举行的太空开采论坛上,有一位发言者甚至在结束自己的发言时,恳请人们别谈管制问题。但是事实上,太空开采者们如果能就以盈利为目的的太空探索达成一个广泛的协议,他们从中是能够获利非凡的。如果没有这样的共识,那么声明会被质疑,投资会有风险,收益也没有保障。我们就此要搭建的这个管理框架,从长远来看绝对是有利的。

2.5　New SAT Official Guide Test 2 解析

2.5.1　Passage Ⅰ

答案解析

1. Which choice best summarizes the passage?

A. A character describes his dislike for his new job and considers the reasons why.

B. Two characters employed in the same office become increasingly competitive.

C. A young man regrets privately a choice that he defends publicly.

D. A new employee experiences optimism, then frustration, and finally despair.

答案：A

解析：我们回看原文首尾句：

• No man likes to acknowledge that he has made a mistake in the choice of his profession, and every man, worthy of the name, will row long against wind and tide before he allows himself to cry out, "I am baffled!" and submits to be floated passively back to land.

• Antipathy is the only word which can express the feeling Edward Crimsworth had for me—a feeling, in a great measure, involuntary, and which was liable to be excited by every, the most trifling movement, look, or word of mine.

• I had received my first quarter's wages, and was returning to my lodgings, possessed heart and soul with the pleasant feeling that the master who had paid me grudged every penny of that hard-earned pittance—(I had long ceased to regard Mr. Crimsworth as my brother—he was a hard, grinding master; he wished to be an inexorable tyrant: that was all).

• ... As I approached my lodgings, I turned from a general view of my affairs to the particular speculation as to whether my fire would be out; looking towards the window of my sitting-room, I saw no cheering red gleam.

这些句子中反复出现的关键词是反感、不快，如 antipathy、no cheering、inexorable tyrant，这些词都表现出主人公强烈的不满，对应选项 A 中的 dislike, 而全文首句就点出了主人公不满意的对象：made a mistake in the choice of his profession, 对应选项 A 中的 new job。因此选 A。

2. The main purpose of the opening sentence of the passage is to

A. establish the narrator's perspective on a controversy.

B. provide context useful in understanding the narrator's emotional state.

C. offer a symbolic representation of Edward Crimsworth's plight.

D. contrast the narrator's good intentions with his malicious conduct.

答案：B

解析：我们先来看全文首句：No man likes to acknowledge that he has made a mistake in the choice of his profession, and every man, worthy of the name, will row long against wind and tide before he allows himself to cry out, "I am baffled!" and submits to be floated passively back to land. 这句话说到没有人会轻易承认自己在职业选择上犯下的错误，而就算是错了，也会要求自己为之奋斗到精疲力竭的那一刻。很显然，这是作者在为下文做一个总起的铺垫。那么下面具体说了什么呢？

Line 6：From the first week of my residence in X—I felt my occupation irksome. 也就是说，主人公自己在职业道路的选择上犯错误了，而 irksome 正是一种 emotional state, 对应选项 B 中的内容，因此选 B。

3. During the course of the first paragraph, the narrator's focus shifts from _____.
A. recollection of past confidence to acknowledgment of present self-doubt.
B. reflection on his expectations of life as a tradesman to his desire for another job.
C. generalization about job dissatisfaction to the specifics of his own situation.
D. evaluation of factors making him unhappy to identification of alternatives.

答案：C

解析：像这样的写作手法题，我们就要找到一些明显的逻辑词或总起总结句，这些逻辑词可能是表达心情的或转折、递进、并列等。这些关键词一般会出现在段首句和段尾句：

• No man likes to acknowledge that he has made a mistake in the choice of his profession, and every man, worthy of the name, will row long against wind and tide before he allows himself to cry out, "I am baffled!" and submits to be floated passively back to land.

• But this was not all; the antipathy which had sprung up between myself and my employer striking deeper root and spreading denser shade daily, excluded me from every glimpse of the sunshine of life; and I began to feel like a plant growing in humid darkness out of the slimy walls of a well.

很显然，第一句是一句总起句，表达自己对职业的不满，对应选项 C 中的 generalization about job dissatisfaction；而第二句则说出了具体不满的原因——the antipathy which had sprung up between myself and my employer, 指出是与上司之间的嫌隙，对应选项 C 中的 specifics of his own situation, 因此选 C。

4. The references to "shade" and "darkness" at the end of the first paragraph mainly have which effect?
A. They evoke the narrator's sense of dismay.
B. They reflect the narrator's sinister thoughts.
C. They capture the narrator's fear of confinement.
D. They reveal the narrator's longing for rest.

答案：A

解析：我们一起来看第一段最后一句：But this was not all; the antipathy which had sprung up between myself and my employer striking deeper root and spreading denser shade daily, excluded me from every glimpse of the sunshine of life; and I began to feel like a plant growing in humid darkness out of the slimy walls of a well.

很明显，这一句话是对第一段的总结，而第一段的基调从 antipathy 一词中就可以看出，是对于工作的反感，对应选项 A 中的 sense of dismay，而 shade（阴影）、darkness（黑暗）则是主人公具体 dismay 的形象化表现，因此选 A。

5. The passage indicates that Edward Crimsworth's behavior was mainly caused by his _____.

　　A. impatience with the narrator's high spirits

　　B. scorn of the narrator's humble background

　　C. indignation at the narrator's rash actions

　　D. jealousy of the narrator's apparent superiority

答案：D

我们根据 Edward Crimsworth 进行定位，第一次出现这个名字是在第二段第一行，但这句话是对 EC 的印象描述，因此我们继续往下看：

Line 38：My southern accent annoyed him; the degree of education evinced in my language irritated him; my punctuality, industry, and accuracy, fixed his dislike, and gave it the high flavour and poignant relish of envy; he feared that I too should one day make a successful tradesman.

主人公的口音、教育背景、谈吐气质对应选项 D 中的 apparent superiority，深深激怒（annoyed）了 EC，让 EC 有对主人公也会成为一名优秀销售的惧怕，EC 心生不满。而句中的 envy 也对应选项 D 中的 jealousy，因此选 D。

6. The passage indicates that when the narrator began working for Edward Crimsworth, he viewed Crimsworth as a _____.

　　A. harmless rival　　　　　　B. sympathetic ally

　　C. perceptive judge　　　　　D. demanding mentor

答案：B

解析：见下题。

7. Which choice provides the best evidence for the answer to the previous question?

　　A. Lines 28~31 ("the antipathy ... life")

　　B. Lines 38~40 ("My southern ... irritated him")

　　C. Lines 54~56 ("Day ... slumber")

　　D. Lines 61~62 ("I had ... brother")

答案：D

解析：第 6 题问的是主人公一开始对 EC 的态度看法，有了这个问题预设，我们一起来看第 7 题的选项：选项 A 说的是与 EC 之间的不快，并没有提到时间，因此排除；选项 B 说的是主人公相较于 EC 的优势，与态度无关，因此排除；选项 C 说的是 EC 造成主人公不满的行为，也与态度无关，同样排除；选项 D 中用到了过去完成时，说到自己以前将 EC 视作兄长，是一种对 EC 的态度，因此可以选到答案 D。

我们一起来看选项 D 中的句子：Line 61：I had long ceased to regard Mr. Crimsworth as my brother. 很显然，句中的 brother 是一个褒义的词汇，而第 6 题的选项中只有选项 B 的 ally 有兄弟间的情谊，因此选 B。

8. At the end of the second paragraph, the comparisons of abstract qualities to a lynx and a snake mainly have the effect of _____.

A. contrasting two hypothetical courses of action
B. conveying the ferocity of a resolution
C. suggesting the likelihood of an altercation
D. illustrating the nature of an adversarial relationship

答案：D

解析：我们根据 lynx 和 snake 进行定位：

Line 51：... and prowling and prying as was Edward's malignity, it could never baffle the lynx-eyes of these, my natural sentinels. Day by day did his malice watch my tact, hoping it would sleep, and prepared to steal snake-like on its slumber; but tact, if it be genuine, never sleeps.

很显然，句中的两种动物对应的是第一行中 EC 本性中 prowl 和 pry 的特性，而 prowl 和 pry 的对象则是 my natural sentinel，因此可以看出一种对抗的关系，对应选项 D 中的 adversarial relationship。选项 A 中的 contrast 无中生有，选项 B 中的 resolution 也没有提到，选项 C 中的 altercation 与 prowl 和 pry 的特征不符合，因此选 D。

9. The passage indicates that, after a long day of work, the narrator sometimes found his living quarters to be _____.
    A. treacherous   B. dreary   C. predictable   D. intolerable

答案：B

解析：见下题。

10. Which choice provides the best evidence for the answer to the previous question?
    A. Lines 17～21 ("I should ... scenes")
    B. Lines 21～23 ("I should ... lodgings")
    C. Lines 64～67 ("Thoughts ... phrases")
    D. Lines 68～74 ("I walked ... gleam")

答案：D

解析：第 9 题问的是作者对于 living quarters 的态度，我们先来看第 10 题的选项：选项 A 和选项 C 说的都不是有关于 living quarters 的内容，因此排除；选项 B 中说到了 lodging，但对于 lodging 的描述金镶玉 small bedroom，是客观描述，而非主观的态度，因此排除；选项 D 中 saw no cheering red gleam 明显是一种对于 lodging 的心理状态描述，因此选 D。

我们一起来看这个句子：

Line 68：I walked fast, for it was a cold, frosty night in January; as I approached my lodgings, I turned from a general view of my affairs to the particular speculation as to whether my fire would be out; looking towards the window of my sitting-room, I saw no cheering red gleam.

句中的 whether my fire would be out 和 saw no cheering red gleam 都是非常消极的表述，对应第 9 题选项 B 中的 dreary，因此选 B。

译文

文章节选自夏洛蒂·勃朗特的著作《教授》，此书于 1857 年出版。

没有人喜欢承认自己在选择职业时做出了错误的决定。凡是人——只要无愧于人这一名号,当顶着风浪划行于人生汪洋之时,总会坚持很久,直到不得不无奈地大声疾呼:"唉!我无能为力了!"然后听凭自己的船飘飘摇摇地被推到岸上。从我住到 X 的第一个礼拜开始,我就对工作产生了反感。我负责誊写、翻译商务信函,工作本身枯燥单调。但要只是这样,我早就学会忍受这种令人生厌的工作了;我不是个没耐性的人,且心中渴望自力更生,渴望向自己和他人证明我成为商人的决心可以实现。我应该默默忍受自己最佳才能的凋零和破败;我也不会喃喃自语,说我渴望自由,甚至内心也不留一丝对自由的向往;我应该忍住每一声叹息,防止内心透过叹息暗示封闭、烟雾弥漫、单调、毫无喜悦的环境,暗示对更自由、更自然的风光的向往;我会在金太太租给我的小卧室里挂上"责任"和"坚持"的画像,做我家中的守护神,以防我的挚爱、我内心最珍视的想象力,那柔弱又强大的力量软硬兼施地把我与责任和坚持分离。但我的反感并不止于此。我和老板对彼此的厌恶与日俱增,把我生命中一丝一缕的阳光都压榨殆尽;我开始感觉自己好像一株生长在阴湿井壁上的植物,终日不见阳光。

老板爱德华·克里姆斯沃斯对我的感情只能用厌恶来形容。这种厌恶很大程度上是不由自主的。我的每一个最细微的动作、神态或一句话也可能引发他的厌恶。我的南方口音让他反感,我谈吐流露出的受教育程度让他反感,还有我从不迟到、刻苦勤奋、办事毫无瑕疵,更加剧了他对我的反感,甚至让这反感中夹杂了尖刻的嫉妒。他担心有一天我也会成为一名事业有成的商人。要是我有哪一点比他差,他还不会对我恨得如此彻底,但他知道的事我都知道,更糟的是,他认为我拥有他所没有的精神财富且对此讳莫如深。要是我曾经陷入可笑或难堪的境地,可能他还会对我保有一点点仁慈。但慎重的处事风格、机敏的反应和良好的观察力一直以来守护着我:爱德华潜伏窥视的行踪和刺探还是逃不过我天生的机敏。每一天他的恶毒都对我的机敏虎视眈眈,希望趁机敏疏忽大意之时,像蛇一样伺机而动。但真正的机敏永不休眠。

我拿到了自己头三个月的工资,此刻正走回住处。想到老板对我辛苦挣来的一分一厘都给得不情不愿,我身心充满欢喜(我早已不把他看作是我的弟兄,对我而言,他冷酷无情、令人难以忍受,他只想成为一个不折不扣的暴君,仅此而已)。有一些强烈的想法反复萦绕在我脑海。有两个声音在说话,一个说:"威廉,你的生活简直难以忍受。"另一个说:"你能做点什么改变现状吗?"正值一月,夜晚寒意逼人,我快步行走着。快到家门口的时候,我脑子里已经不再想工作处境方面的事了,我关心的只是屋子壁炉中的火是不是灭了。我朝客厅窗口看了眼——的确,没有一丝令人欢喜的暖光。

2.5.2 Passage II

答案解析

11. The main purpose of the passage is to _____.
A. consider an ethical dilemma posed by cost-benefit analysis
B. describe a psychology study of ethical economic behavior
C. argue that the free market prohibits ethical economics
D. examine ways of evaluating the ethics of economics

答案:D

解析：我们首先来看全文首尾句：

- Recent debates about the economy have rediscovered the question, "is that right?", where "right" means more than just profits or efficiency.
- Some argue that because the free markets allow for personal choice, they are already ethical. Others have accepted the ethical critique and embraced corporate social responsibility.
- There are different views on where ethics should apply when someone makes an economic decision.
- Instead of judging consequences, Aristotle said ethics was about having the right character—displaying virtues like courage and honesty.
- There is yet another approach: instead of rooting ethics in character or the consequences of actions, we can focus on our actions themselves.
- Many moral dilemmas arise when these three versions pull in different directions but clashes are not inevitable.
- Whenever we feel queasy about "perfect" competitive markets, the problem is often rooted in a phony conception of people.
- These human quirks mean we can never make purely "rational" decisions.
- Ethical economics would then emerge from one of the least likely places: economists themselves.

总结这些关键句中重复出现的词语或意群，我们不难发现以下这些关键词：debate (different views、dilemmas)、ethics (ethical economics)、approach (decision) 等，因此我们大致可以推断这篇文章说的是对于经济行为中的伦理问题的正反两面评估，对应选项 D 中的 evaluating，而上述这些关键词在选项 D 中也最大限度地出现了，因此选 D。

12. In the passage, the author anticipates which of the following objections to criticizing the ethics of free markets?

A. Smith's association of free markets with ethical behavior still applies today.

B. Free markets are the best way to generate high profits, so ethics are a secondary consideration.

C. Free markets are ethical because they are made possible by devalued currency.

D. Free markets are ethical because they enable individuals to make choices.

答案：D

解析：见下题。

13. Which choice provides the best evidence for the answer to the previous question?

A. Lines 4~5 ("Some ... ethical")

B. Lines 7~10 ("But ... about")

C. Lines 21~22 ("Smith ... outcome")

D. Lines 52~54 ("When ... way")

答案：A

解析：第12题问的是作者预想下列选项中，哪个选项是抨击自由市场伦理的反对意见，即下列哪个选项是赞同自由市场伦理的。我们先来看第13题的选项：选项 A 说自由市场本就是ethical的,与第12题中的所问切合,因此保留;选项B是一个总体性的观点,并没有对哪一方的偏向,因此排除;选项C和选项D则没有提到ethics,因此同样排除。

我们来看选项A中的这个句子:Some argue that because the free markets allow for personal choice, they are already ethical. 这句话中的 allow for personal choice 对应第12题选项D中的 enable individuals to make choices,因此第12题选D,第13题选A。

14. As used in line 6, "embraced" most nearly means _____.
　　A. lovingly held　　　　　　　　B. readily adopted
　　C. eagerly hugged　　　　　　　D. reluctantly used
　　答案:B
　　解析:我们回到原文:

Line 5:Others have accepted the ethical critique and embraced corporate social responsibility. 很显然这是一个并列句,那么 embraced 应与前半句中的 accepted 是同义词,与选项B中的 adopted 对应,因此选B。

15. The main purpose of the fifth paragraph (lines 45~56) is to _____.
　　A. develop a counterargument to the claim that greed is good
　　B. provide support for the idea that ethics is about character
　　C. describe a third approach to defining ethical economics
　　D. illustrate that one's actions are a result of one's character
　　答案:C
　　解析:我们来看第五段的第一句:There is yet another approach: instead of rooting ethics in character or the consequences of actions, we can focus on our actions themselves. 很显然,这句话是一个转折,引出下文对于 ethics 的另一种 approach,而这种 approach 是基于我们行为本身的。因此对应选项C中的 describe a third approach。

16. As used in line 58, "clashes" most nearly means _____.
　　A. conflicts　　　B. mismatches　　　C. collisions　　　D. brawls
　　答案:A
　　解析:我们回到原文:

Line 57:Many moral dilemmas arise when these three versions pull in different directions but clashes are not inevitable. 这句话中的 clashes 与前半句中的 many moral dilemmas arise 是转折的关系,前面说很多退退两难的处境出现了,其中的 arise 对应后半句中的 not inevitable(非必要的),因此 clashes 就应该对应 dilemmas,表达冲突的意思,因此选A。

17. Which choice best supports the author's claim that there is common ground shared by the different approaches to ethics described in the passage?
　　A. Lines 11~12 ("There ... decision")
　　B. Lines 47~50 ("From ... advertisements")
　　C. Lines 59~64 ("Take ... market")
　　D. Lines 75~77 ("We ... facts")
　　答案:C
　　解析:这是一道单一循证题,问的是支持不同 approaches 共同点的证据,我们直接看选项:选项 A 是一个总论点,说的是 different views,与问题无关,因此排除;选项 B 说的仅仅是一个 perspective 中的观点,不具备共同点的信息,因此排除;选项 C 以 fair trade coffee 为例,论证了稳重过的三个 approaches 是有 common ground 的,句中的 might have good consequences、be virtuous 和 be the right way to act in a flawed market 正对应三种 approaches,因此选 C;选项 D 说的是人们的行为,与 different approaches 无关,因此排除。

18. The main idea of the final paragraph is that _____.

　　A. human quirks make it difficult to predict people's ethical decisions accurately

　　B. people universally react with disgust when faced with economic injustice

　　C. understanding human psychology may help to define ethics in economics

　　D. economists themselves will be responsible for reforming the free market

答案:C

解析:我们来看最后一段的第一句:These human quirks mean we can never make purely "rational" decisions. 句中说人们的 quirks 让我们没法做出真正理性的选择,与选项 A 中的 predict 不符合,因此选项 A 排除。但这句话没有透露更多的信息,因此我们看第二句:A new wave of behavioral economists, aided by neuroscientists, is trying to understand our psychology, both alone and in groups, so they can anticipate our decisions in the marketplace more accurately. 很显然,这句话中说经济学家们正在试图从心理学的角度来预测人们在市场中的行为,而这正是选项 C 的同义改写,因此选 C。

19. Data in the graph about per-pound coffee profits in Tanzania most strongly support which of the following statements?

　　A. Fair trade coffee consistently earned greater profits than regular coffee earned.

　　B. The profits earned from regular coffee did not fluctuate.

　　C. Fair trade coffee profits increased between 2004 and 2006.

　　D. Fair trade and regular coffee were earning equal profits by 2008.

答案:A

解析:图表中的数据显示:2000~2008 年期间,Tanzania 生产的公平贸易咖啡利润约是每磅 1.3 美元,大于普通咖啡利润(每磅是 20~60 美分),因此选 A。

20. Data in the graph indicate that the greatest difference between per-pound profits from fair trade coffee and those from regular coffee occurred during which period?

　　A. 2000 to 2002　　　　　　　　B. 2002 to 2004

　　C. 2004 to 2005　　　　　　　　D. 2006 to 2008

答案:B

解析:图表数据显示,2002~2004 年期间每磅公平贸易咖啡与普通咖啡的利润差为 1 美元,是其中差值最大的,因此选 B。

21. Data in the graph provide most direct support for which idea in the passage?

　　A. Acting on empathy can be counterproductive.

　　B. Ethical economics is defined by character.

　　C. Ethical economics is still possible.

　　D. People fear losses more than they hope for gains.

答案:C

解析： 在第 59～61 行，文章将公平贸易咖啡定义为"coffee that is sold with a certification that indicates the farmers and worker who produced it were paid a fair wage"被贴上了认证标签的咖啡，这种认证标签可以表明生产咖啡的农民和工人都获得了公平工资。通过这种定义可以看出，购买公平贸易咖啡实际上是一种道德选择。图表中数据表明公平贸易咖啡比普通咖啡价格高，说明道德经济仍然是大家的一种选择，因此选 C。

译文

文章改编自 Lain King 的著作《经济能有道德吗？》，此书于 2013 年由前景出版社出版。

最近有关经济学的讨论又提出了议题："这么做对吗？"只是这里的"对"指的不是利润或效率。

一部分人表示自由市场给了人们个人选择的空间，因此经济市场已然是道德的。另一部分人赞同道德批评，拥护企业社会责任。但不论是要将任何市场结果贴上"不道德"的标签，还是鄙视那些给道德加价码的经济学家，在此之前，我们需要明确我们所谈论的道德到底是什么。

一个人做经济判断的时候，该如何表现出道德，对此有诸多不同观点。"现代经济学之父"亚当·斯密是一位道德哲学家，他认为道德的基石是同情心（我们今天所说的同理心）。但在《国富论》一书中，斯密的一项重要观点是依凭同理心做事可能对生产有害无益——他发现人往往在不顾同理心、以自利的方式进行往来时变得富有。斯密依据结果论证自私行为的合理。不论是设计者用成本效益分析来论证新修铁路线的价值，还是人们为获得更高收入进行进修学习，或是购物者的买一赠一，采用的都是同样的方式：对某人产生同理心，努力使该人尽可能富有——只不过，他们同理心的对象是未来的自己。

与结果评判论不同，亚里士多德认为道德是正确的品格，即表现出诸如勇气、诚实的美德。某人因其品格优良被擢升为企业领导即是实践这一观点的表现。但要传授这种思想难度很大，比如对一家一直在亏钱的公司你应当多大程度上表示忠诚呢？如果你表现出的忠诚过少，你无疑是崇尚"贪婪即美德"的企业侵袭者，忠诚过多，你又是在没有生产价值的资本上浪费钱。亚里士多德认为过多或过少之间存在一个恰好的中间值，而找到这个中间值与优秀的判断力密不可分。但如果道德就是品格，哪些品格特性算是道德的呢？

还有一种观点与道德品格论和行为结果论都不同，它在行为中关注道德。据此就有了正确与错误的行为之分——我们应该买公平贸易的商品，不能在广告中说谎。伦理于是变成了诫命清单，上面列出了"应当"与"不应当"的事宜。财政官员拒绝实行货币贬值，因为他们曾做出许诺不这么做，他们就是在践行这种道德准则。依照这种观点，即使实行贬值可以让大家生活更富足，这么做也是不好的。

当上述三种看法导致不同结果时，会出现诸多道德困境。不过冲突并非不可避免。拿公平交易的咖啡来说（所谓公平交易的咖啡，是指售卖的咖啡有证书标明种植的农民和生产工人在待遇上都受到公平对待），购买这种商品可以带来好结果，符合美德，是一个不完美市场中的正确行为。像这样的交集暗示，即使对道德体现方式有不同见解，道德经济学仍是可能的。

我们对"永不失灵"的竞争市场感到不安，是因为我们对人有一种错误的看法。古典经济学将人视为完全理性且自利的客体——这其实是个笑话。这个模型由哲学家约翰·斯图亚特·密尔率先提出。但如今大多数人（包括经济学家在内）都承认"经济人"的概念是虚构的。人类行为上流行跟风，恐惧失去的心理远胜于期盼得到，且我们的大脑很难考虑到所有相关事实。

这些人类特性意味着我们根本无法做出完全"理性"的决定。在神经科学家的理论支持下,新一拨的行为经济学家正力图理解人类个体与人在群体中的心理特点,从而更准确地预测人们在经济行为中的决定。心理学也有助于解释为何我们对经济不公深恶痛绝,同时愿意接受普适的道德规范。这意味着这门关于人类行为的新兴科学可能会影响我们对道德的理解。到那时,道德经济学可能会从看似最不可能的地方——经济学家——冒出来。

2.5.3 Passage Ⅲ

答案解析

22. The author of Passage 1 indicates which of the following about the use of screen-based technologies?

A. It should be thoroughly studied.
B. It makes the brain increasingly rigid.
C. It has some positive effects.
D. It should be widely encouraged.

答案:C

解析:见下题。

23. Which choice provides the best evidence for the answer to the previous question?

A. Lines 3~4 ("Certain ... Net")
B. Lines 23~25 ("But ... smarter")
C. Lines 25~29 ("In a ... ability")
D. Lines 29~31 ("She ... others")

答案:A

解析:第22题问的是作者对screen-based technologies的态度,我们来看第23题的选项:选项A中说对于电脑和网络的使用增强了我们的cognitive skills,符合第22题所问,因此保留;选项B说的是这种科技的坏处,同样是态度,也符合第22题所问,因此同样暂时保留;选项C说的是一种研究方法,答非所问,因此排除;选项D说的是实验结论,且是针对every medium,而非单指screen-based technologies的,因此同样可以排除。

在选项A和选项B中,我们可以这样判断。因为全文都在说screen-based technologies,因此,第22题其实是一道全文主旨题,我们可以根据全文首尾句进行判断。

• The mental consequences of our online info-crunching are not universally bad.

• We're exercising the neural circuits devoted to skimming and multitasking while ignoring those used for reading and thinking deeply.

从这两句话中我们可以明显看出作者对于这种科技的偏好:not universally bad,对于skimming、multitasking、reading和thinking deeply的作用等,这些都说明这种科技的优势,因此选项B与全文基调不符合,选到答案A。

回到第22题,既然说的是这种科技的优势,那么就可以对应选项C中的positive effects,因此选C。

24. The author of Passage 1 indicates that becoming adept at using the Internet can _____.

  A. make people complacent about their health

  B. undermine the ability to think deeply

  C. increase people's social contacts

  D. improve people's self-confidence

答案：B

解析：我们根据 the Internet 进行定位，又因为第 25 题的答案在第 40 行，因此范围缩小：

Line 31：Our growing use of the Net and other screen-based technologies, she wrote, has led to the "widespread and sophisticated development of visual-spatial skills." But those gains go hand in hand with a weakening of our capacity for the kind of "deep processing" that underpins "mindful knowledge acquisition, inductive analysis, critical thinking, imagination, and reflection."

  But 后的转折是上述句子的重点，也就是对于 deep processing 的 weakening，对应选项 B 中的 undermine the ability to think deeply，因此选 B。

25. As used in line 40, "plastic" most nearly means _____.

  A. creative B. artificial C. malleable D. sculptural

答案：C

解析：我们回到原文：

Line 39：We know that the human brain is highly plastic; neurons and synapses change as circumstances change. 根据分号后对于 plastic 的补充说明，我们可以推断出 plastic 在这里有适应性强的意思，也就是选项 C "malleable"（可锻造的）。

26. The author of Passage 2 refers to the novel War and Peace primarily to suggest that Woody Allen _____.

  A. did not like Tolstoy's writing style

  B. could not comprehend the novel by speed-reading it

  C. had become quite skilled at multitasking

  D. regretted having read such a long novel

答案：B

解析：我们根据 War and Peace 和 Woody Allen 进行定位：

Line 62：Speed-reading programs have long claimed to do just that, but the verdict was rendered by Woody Allen after he read Leo Tolstoy's famously long novel War and Peace in one sitting: "It was about Russia."

  句中的 just that 指的是前文中的 basic information-processing capacities，而 but 引导的转折则说明 Woody Allen 并没有这种能力，因此对应选项 B 中的 could not comprehend。

27. According to the author of Passage 2, what do novelists and scientists have in common?

  A. They take risks when they pursue knowledge.

  B. They are eager to improve their minds.

  C. They are curious about other subjects.

D. They become absorbed in their own fields.

答案:D

解析:我们根据 novelists 和 scientists 进行定位,第 79 行文章 2 的作者提到:小说家和科学家都会通过沉浸在自己领域的方式提高他们的专业能力"immers[ing] themselves in their fields"。换句话说:小说家和科学家的共同点是都会沉浸在自己领域当中,因此选 D。

28. The analogy in the final sentence of Passage 2 has primarily which effect?

A. It uses ornate language to illustrate a difficult concept.

B. It employs humor to soften a severe opinion of human behavior.

C. It alludes to the past to evoke a nostalgic response.

D. It criticizes the view of a particular group.

答案:D

解析:我们回到原文最后一句:As with ancient peoples who believed that eating fierce animals made them fierce, they assume that watching quick cuts in rock videos turns your mental life into quick cuts or that reading bullet points and online postings turns your thoughts into bullet points and online postings. 很显然,这个类比之前一定会有总起句:

Line 81:The effects of consuming electronic media are likely to be far more limited than the panic implies.

这句话告诉我们,consuming electronic media 的危害远没有我们想象的大,之后就做了一个 analogy,用浅显的方式喻示人们对于 consuming electronic media 想法的荒谬,因此对应选项 D。

29. The main purpose of each passage is to _____.

A. compare brain function in those who play games on the Internet and those who browse on it

B. report on the problem-solving skills of individuals with varying levels of Internet experience

C. take a position on increasing financial support for studies related to technology and intelligence

D. make an argument about the effects of electronic media use on the brain

答案:D

解析:很显然,这道题考察的是两个 passage 的核心主旨,因此我们根据首尾句来做题。

Passage Ⅰ:

• The mental consequences of our online info-crunching are not universally bad.

• We're exercising the neural circuits devoted to skimming and multitasking while ignoring those used for reading and thinking deeply.

Passage Ⅱ:

• Critics of new media sometimes use science itself to press their case, citing research that shows how "experience can change the brain." But cognitive neuroscientists roll their eyes at such talk.(显然第一句是有让步意味的,因此我们要接着把后面的转折句看完整。)

• As with ancient peoples who believed that eating fierce animals made them fierce, they assume that watching quick cuts in rock videos turns your mental life into quick cuts or that reading bullet points and online postings turns your thoughts into bullet points and online postings.

根据首尾句中划出的关键词我们不难发现，这两篇文章都是在讨论新媒体对人们的影响，因此对应选项 D 中的 effects。

30. Which choice best describes the relationship between the two passages?

A. Passage 2 relates first-hand experiences that contrast with the clinical approach in Passage 1.

B. Passage 2 critiques the conclusions drawn from the research discussed in Passage 1.

C. Passage 2 takes a high-level view of a result that Passage 1 examines in depth.

D. Passage 2 predicts the negative reactions that the findings discussed in Passage 1 might produce.

答案：B

解析：我们首先来看 Passage Ⅰ 中的段首句和全文尾句：

• The mental consequences of our online info-crunching are not universally bad.

• It's likely that Web browsing also strengthens brain functions related to fast-paced problem solving, particularly when it requires spotting patterns in a welter of data.

• But it would be a serious mistake to look narrowly at such benefits and conclude that the Web is making us smarter.

• We know that the human brain is highly plastic; neurons and synapses change as circumstances change.

• We're exercising the neural circuits devoted to skimming and multitasking while ignoring those used for reading and thinking deeply.

总结下来，我们会发现有些关键词频繁出现：mental consequences/human brain/neural circuits、online info-crunching/web browsing、not ... bad/strengthens brain functions/a mistake to look narrowly at such benefits/exercising the neural circuit。以此我们可以推断作者认为电子设备的使用对于人脑是有利的，持支持的态度。我们再来看 Passage Ⅱ：

• Critics of new media sometimes use science itself to press their case, citing research that shows how "experience can change the brain."

• Experience does not revamp the basic information-processing capacities of the brain.

• Moreover, the effects of experience are highly specific to the experiences themselves.

• The effects of consuming electronic media are likely to be far more limited than the panic implies.

• As with ancient peoples who believed that eating fierce animals made them fierce, they assume that watching quick cuts in rock videos turns your mental life into quick cuts or that reading bullet points and online postings turns your thoughts into bullet points and online postings.

在 Passage Ⅱ 中重复出现的关键词有：critics/does not revamp、experience/effects of experience/effects of consuming electronic media、highly specific/far more limited。可以看出，作者对电子设备的使用是持保留，甚至是负面态度的，认为其对人们的好处有限，与

Passage Ⅰ中的观点是相冲突的,因此对应选项 B 中的 critiques。

31. On which of the following points would the authors of both passages most likely agree?

A. Computer-savvy children tend to demonstrate better hand-eye coordination than do their parents.

B. Those who criticize consumers of electronic media tend to overreact in their criticism.

C. Improved visual-spatial skills do not generalize to improved skills in other areas.

D. Internet users are unlikely to prefer reading onscreen text to reading actual books.

答案:C

解析:我们结合第 30 题的段首句和全文尾句中总结出的关键词就会发现,既然要选两个作者的共识,就不能有明显的对于电子设备使用的褒贬。因此可以排除选项 A 和选项 B,而选项 D 是明显的常识性错误,因此可以选到答案 C。

32. Which choice provides the best evidence that the author of Passage 2 would agree to some extent with the claim attributed to Michael Merzenich in lines 41～43, Passage 1?

A. Lines 51～53 ("Critics ... brain")

B. Lines 54～56 ("Yes ... changes")

C. Lines 57～59 ("But ... experience")

D. Lines 83～84 ("Media ... consumes")

答案:B

解析:我们首先回到原文:When we adapt to a new cultural phenomenon, including the use of a new medium, we end up with a different brain, says Michael Merzenich, a pioneer of the field of neuroplasticity. 这句话的关键词在于 new、different 这两个反复出现的词,因此这是我们选择的关键。选项 A、C、D 中并没有提到这些关键词,只有选项 B 中的 change 能够与以上关键词对应,因此选 B。

译文

文章 1 节选自 Nicholas Carr 的著作《网络粉碎注意力,重写大脑》,2010 年由康泰纳仕出版。文章 2 来自 Steven Pinker 的著作《思考与大众传媒》,2010 年由纽约时报公司出版。

文章 1

我们上网处理大量信息带来的心智影响并不都是负面的。我们在使用计算机和网络时,某些认知技能会得以增强。这些技能往往包含一些更为基础的心智功能,比如手眼协调、反射性反应和视觉信息的处理。在有关视频游戏的研究中,常被提及的一项研究反映的是一群年轻人连续 10 天玩打斗游戏后,他们在各种图像和任务之间切换视觉焦点的速度有了明显的提升。

浏览网页也很可能有助于大脑增强快速解决问题的能力,尤其当需要从大量杂乱无章的资料中识别出模式时。英国一项针对女性上网搜索医药信息的研究表明,至少在一些情况下,有经验的网络用户可以在几秒钟之内评估网页的可信度和可能具有的价值。我们网上浏览信息的经验越多,大脑处理问题的熟练度会越局限。

但是,如果我们只是片面地关注这类益处,从而得出结论认为网页会让我们变得更聪明,那就大错特错了。著名的发展心理学专家帕特里夏·格林菲尔德在2009年年初的《科学》上发表了一篇文章,对逾40篇探讨不同类型的媒体对智力和学习能力的影响的研究进行了综述,她总结说:"每一种媒体都会有助于发展一些认知技能,其代价是抑制另一些技能的发展。"她在文章中写到,我们对网络及其他视频技术加大使用,将有助于促进"视觉空间技能更广泛、更复杂的发展",但这些发展同时会削弱我们"深度加工"的能力,这种能力是进行"有意识的知识获取、归纳分析、批判性思考、想象和深思熟虑"的基础。

我们都知道,人的大脑可塑性很强,神经元和突触更会随环境改变而变化。神经易变领域的先行者迈克尔·默策尼希表示,当我们适应了一种新的文化现象,包括使用新媒体,我们的大脑会变得不同。这意味即使是不用电脑的时候,我们的网络习惯仍会对大脑细胞的工作产生影响。我们在不断锻炼专门用来进行略读、多任务处理的神经回路,而忽视了那些用于阅读或深入思考的神经回路。

文章 2

新媒体的批判者有时会用科学来竭力推行他们的主张,引述"经验如何改变大脑"的研究成果。但认知神经学家对这种言辞往往不屑。的确,每当我们掌握一种知识或技能时,我们大脑的线路会发生改变,这与信息存储在胰腺中肯定不同,但神经的可塑性并不意味着大脑是一团由经验铸形的黏土。

经验并不能翻新大脑基本的信息处理能力。快速阅读项目曾一度被认为可以做到改进大脑的信息处理能力,但这一判断通过美国导演伍迪·艾伦的经验被推翻了,艾伦在不长的等餐时间阅读托尔斯泰的长篇巨著《战争与和平》,最后对书的内容只说了一句:"这本书讲的是俄罗斯的事。"真正的多任务处理也已经被证实是不可靠的传言(myth),人们得出这样的结论并非通过实验研究,而只是经常看到在高低起伏的车道上前行的越野车司机还同时用手机谈生意。

另外,经历得到效果仅限于这个特定的经历。如果你训练他人做一件事(识别形状、解数独、找出隐藏的文字),他们可以在这项任务上做得更好,但在其他方面几乎没有长进。音乐不能帮你提高数学成绩,练习拉丁语动词词形变化无法使你变得更有逻辑,训练大脑的游戏也不会帮你变得更聪明。成功人士不会在大脑里储备其他知识的体验,他们只专注于自己的领域。小说作者阅读大量小说,科学家阅读大量的科学作品。

消费电子媒体造成的影响并没有恐慌暗示的那么大。媒体批判者认同大脑吸收什么内容,就会呈现什么样的特点,这等同于"你吃什么,就是什么人"。正如远古时期的人认为吃猛兽的肉会让他们变得勇猛,这些批判者相信观看摇滚视频的快速片段会让你的精神生活变成快速片段,而阅读要点和网络帖子会让你的思想变成要点和网络帖子。

2.5.4 Passage IV

答案解析

33. The central problem that Stanton describes in the passage is that women have been _____.

A. denied equal educational opportunities, which has kept them from reaching their potential

B. prevented from exerting their positive influence on men, which has led to societal breakdown

C. prevented from voting, which has resulted in poor candidates winning important elections

D. blocked by men from serving as legislators, which has allowed the creation of unjust laws

答案:B

解析:我们来看全文首尾句:

• I urge a sixteenth amendment, because "manhood suffrage," or a man's government, is civil, religious, and social disorganization.

• The male element has held high carnival thus far;

• People object to the demands of those whom they choose to call the strong-minded, because they say "the right of suffrage will make the women masculine."

• We ask woman's enfranchisement, as the first step toward the recognition of that essential element in government that can only secure the health, strength, and prosperity of the nation.

• Here that great conservator of woman's love, if permitted to assert itself, as it naturally would in freedom against oppression, violence, and war, would hold all these destructive forces in check, for woman knows the cost of life better than man does, and not with her consent would one drop of blood ever be shed, one life sacrificed in vain.

在这些关键句中重复出现的语义有:manhood/social disorganization/male element … held high/masculine、suffrage/women's enfranchisement/woman's love,也就可以推断在这种阻碍里,男性起了很大的作用。而出现"man"类似词语的只有选项B和选项D,选项B中的 societal breakdown 对应第一句关键句中的 social disorganization,因此选B。

34. Stanton uses the phrase "high carnival" (line 15) mainly to emphasize what she sees as the _____.

A. utter domination of women by men B. freewheeling spirit of the age

C. scandalous decline in moral values D. growing power of women in society

答案:A

解析:我们回到原文:The male element has held high carnival thus far; it has fairly run riot from the beginning, overpowering the feminine element everywhere, crushing out all the diviner qualities in human nature, until we know but little of true manhood and womanhood, of the latter comparatively nothing, for it has scarce been recognized as a power until within the last century. 显然,分号之后的内容就是对 high carnival 的解释,而句中的 overpowering the feminine element、crushing out、power 等词都显示着男性对于女性的控制,因此对应选项 A。

35. Stanton claims that which of the following was a relatively recent historical development?

A. The control of society by men.

B. The spread of war and injustice.

C. The domination of domestic life by men.

D. The acknowledgment of women's true character.

答案：D

解析：见下题。

36. Which choice provides the best evidence for the answer to the previous question?

A. Lines 3~7 ("The male ... death")

B. Lines 15~22 ("The male ... century")

C. Lines 22~25 ("Society ... home")

D. Lines 48~52 ("[M]an ... repression")

答案：B

解析：第 35 题问的是 relatively recent historical development，我们在第 36 题的选项中应该出现这个关键词：选项 A、C、D 均没有提到近代的发展，只有选项 B 中的 until within last century 提到了，因此选 B。那么我们来看选项 B：The male element has held high carnival thus far; it has fairly run riot from the beginning, overpowering the feminine element everywhere, crushing out all the diviner qualities in human nature, until we know but little of true manhood and womanhood, of the latter comparatively nothing, for it has scarce been recognized as a power until within the last century. 其中 womanhood 与第 35 题选项 D 中的 women's true character 相对应，而 know 则与选项 D 中的 acknowledgement 相对应，因此第 35 题选 D。

37. As used in line 24, "rule" most nearly refers to _____.

A. a general guideline B. a controlling force

C. an established habit D. a procedural method

答案：B

解析：我们回到原文：Society is but the reflection of man himself, untempered by woman's thought; the hard iron rule we feel alike in the church, the state, and the home. 句中的 rule 在这里对应前一句汇总的 the reflection of man himself 和 untempered by woman's thought，因此有 control 的意思，对应选项 B。

38. It can reasonably be inferred that "the strong-minded" (line 32) was a term generally intended to _____.

A. praise women who fight for their long-denied rights

B. identify women who demonstrate intellectual skill

C. criticize women who enter male-dominated professions

D. condemn women who agitate for the vote for their sex

答案：D

解析：我们回到原文：People object to the demands of those whom they choose to call the strong-minded, because they say "the right of suffrage will make the women masculine. 很显然，句中的 people 对于 women 的态度是非常负面的，从 make woman masculine 就可以看出。因此，the strong-minded 在这里不可能是一个褒义的词，可以直接排除选项 A 和选项 B。但选项 D 中的 enter male-dominated professions 在句子中并没有提到，也可以排除。选项 D 中的 agitate for the vote 对应句中的 suffrage，因此选到答案 D。

39. As used in line 36, "best" most nearly means _____.

A. superior   B. excellent   C. genuine   D. rarest

答案：C

解析：我们回到原文：Though disfranchised, we have few women in the best sense; we have simply so many reflections, varieties, and dilutions of the masculine gender. 很显然，分号后面的内容是对 women in the best sense 的具体说明，而 dilution of the masculine gender 意味着 few women 真正明白自己的定位，因此对应选项 C。

40. Stanton contends that the situation she describes in the passage has become so dire that even men have begun to _____.

A. lament the problems they have created

B. join the call for woman suffrage

C. consider women their social equals

D. ask women how to improve civic life

答案：A

解析：见下题。

41. Which choice provides the best evidence for the answer to the previous question?

A. Lines 25～30 ("No one ... matters")

B. Lines 53～55 ("And now ... life")

C. Lines 56～60 ("The need ... action")

D. Lines 61～64 ("We ask ... nation")

答案：B

解析：第 40 题问的是男士对女性社会地位现状的表现行为，主题题干中的 even 一词，表明男士的行为是与他们原先行为有转折的，带着这个预设我们来看第 41 题的选项：选项 A、C、D 均未体现出这种 even 的让步转折关系，因此排除，选到答案 B。我们来看原文：And now man himself stands appalled at the results of his own excesses, and mourns in bitterness that falsehood, selfishness, and violence are the law of life.

句中的 stands appalled 对应选项 A 中的 lament，而 the results of his own excesses 则对应选项 A 中的 the problems they have created，因此第 40 题选 A。

42. The sixth paragraph (lines 67～78) is primarily concerned with establishing a contrast between _____.

A. men and women

B. the spiritual world and the material world

C. bad men and good men

D. men and masculine traits

答案：D

解析：我们来看第六段的段首句：In speaking of the masculine element, I do not wish to be understood to say that all men are hard, selfish, and brutal, for many of the most beautiful spirits the world has known have been clothed with manhood; but I refer to those characteristics, though often marked in woman, that distinguish what is called the stronger sex. 显然，句中比较的是 hard, selfish, and brutal 与 those characteristics ... that distinguish what is called the stronger sex，是男士习性的对比，因此选 D。

译文

这篇文章改编自伊丽莎白·凯迪斯坦顿于 1869 年在华盛顿女权大会上的演讲。

我呼吁建立宪法第 16 条修正案，因为"男性选举权"，换言之男性的统治，造成了政府、宗教或社会领域的破坏。男性力量是一种破坏性的力量，男性强硬自私，好大喜功，热爱战争和暴力、征服和掠取，给世俗世界和道德世界带来不和与混乱、疾病与死亡。看看历史书上那些血腥与残暴的记录吧！千百年来，人类经受了各种奴役、屠杀和牺牲，在盘问与监禁、痛苦与迫害、暗无天日的法规与令人悲观的教义中苦苦挣扎，众生不见仁慈的降临，而其心灵对爱与希望的渴望已如死灰！

迄今为止，男性力量就一直是人类狂欢与崇拜的对象；从最初它就蔓延滋长，不论在何地都压迫着女性力量，摧残着人类天性中所有神圣的品质，最终使我们对真正的男性力量、女性力量所知甚少，对真正的女性力量了解得则更少，直到最近一个世纪女性力量才开始被认可为一种力量。社会只是男人意志的体现，女性的情感思想对其毫无影响。这坚硬的铁律，我们在教堂、一国乃至一家中都深有体会。只要我们记得男性仅代表完整性别中的半数人群，他们对事物的见解也只是半数群体的见解，但他们完全主宰人间的一切大小事务，我们就不必对一切的混乱和分崩离析的状况感到讶异了。

人们反对一些女性的要求，称这些女性是意志坚强者，因为人们认为"选举权会让女性变得男性化"，而女性男性化恰是我们今天所面临的阻力。尽管我们被剥夺了选举权，我们之中却极少有女性可以称之为真正意义上的女性。我们有的只是男性的种种投射、各种表现或男性特征的弱化表现。女性特有的强大天赋因其对男性的依附受到压制和忽视，只要女性靠男性养活的局面一天不改变，女性就会努力取悦她的供养者，调整自身适应男性的状况。为了获得一定的社会地位，女性必须尽可能接近男性的特质，反映他的思想和观点、美德和动机、偏见和恶习。她必须尊重男性制定的法律规定，尽管这些法律规定会剥夺她所有不可剥夺的权利，而且还与上帝赋予女性的更高准则相违背。

……男性通过施加直接而积极的影响将女性塑造为符合其想法的对象，而女性虽不反抗，会采用间接的手段控制男性，所以在多数情况下，会发展出一些特征，而这些特征不管是在女性自身还是在男性身上都需要被压制。如今，男性对自己暴行的后果感到恐惧，并哀叹谎言、自私和暴力成为了生活的法则。此时此刻我们需要的不是土地、金矿、铁路或硬币，而是女性的新福音——歌颂纯洁、美德、道德和真正的宗教，将人类提升至思想与行动的更高境界。

我们呼吁给予女性公民权，把这当作是承认人类管理需要女性力量的第一步，这种认可带来的只会是对一国健康、力量和繁荣的保障。我们在提升女性到其真正的位置方面做出的任何努力，都会有助于人类迎来和平与完美的崭新日子。

关于男性力量的言论，我不希望被理解为所有男人都是强硬、自私、残暴的，因为世界上有过的许多最为美好的灵魂是带有男性特质的。我所说的那些特质（虽然它们也会在女性身上有体现）只是男性区别于大家所称的更强大的性别。比如，喜欢对地球、海洋、大自然的其他各种元素、财富和力量进行掠取与征服——这些推动人类文明的力量当被用于人对人的征服或为实现个人雄心致国家于不顾的做法时，就会成为毁灭性的力量。

如果女性——女性之爱的伟大守护者——被允许坚持她自身的想法,只要这想法可以不受压迫、暴力、战争的侵扰,就会抑制所有破坏性的力量。因为相比男性,女性对生命的代价体会更深,只要不征得女性同意,就不会白流一滴血,不会枉死一人。

2.5.5 Passage V

答案解析

43. The first paragraph serves mainly to _____.
A. explain how a scientific device is used
B. note a common misconception about an event
C. describe a natural phenomenon and address its importance
D. present a recent study and summarize its findings

答案:C

解析:我们来看第一段的段首句:Some of the largest ocean waves in the world are nearly impossible to see.

这句话明显描述了一个现象,对应选项 C 中的 a natural phenomenon,因此选 C。

44. As used in line 19,"capture" is closest in meaning to _____.
A. control   B. record   C. secure   D. absorb

答案:B

解析:我们回到原文:"If we want to have more and more accurate climate models, we have to be able to capture processes such as this," Peacock says. 句中的 this 是指代前文的内容,因此我们往上看一句:Most models fail to take internal waves into account. 从这句话中,我们可以看出 capture 就是 take... into account 的近义词,也就是把 interval waves 记入考虑范围,因此可以对应选项 B。

45. According to Peacock, the ability to monitor internal waves is significant primarily because _____.
A. it will allow scientists to verify the maximum height of such waves
B. it will allow researchers to shift their focus to improving the quality of satellite images
C. the study of wave patterns will enable regions to predict and prevent coastal damage
D. the study of such waves will inform the development of key scientific models

答案:D

解析:见下题。

46. Which choice provides the best evidence for the answer to the previous question?
A. Lines 1~2 ("Some... see")
B. Lines 4~6 ("they... equipment")
C. Lines 17~19 ("If... this")
D. Lines 24~26 ("Internal... high")

答案：C

解析：第45题问的是internal waves重要性的体现在哪里，带着这个问题我们来看第46题的选项：选项A和选项B描述的是internal waves的特性，因此排除；选项C说要有更精确的climate models的前提就是要能够capture（internal wave的）processes，提到重要性，因此保留；选项D描述的同样是internal waves的特征，也可以排除。我们来看选项C的这个句子："If we want to have more and more accurate climate models, we have to be able to capture processes such as this," Peacock says. 其中climate models对应选项中的scientific models, 因此第45题选D。

47. As used in line 65, "devise" most nearly means _____.
  A. create   B. solve   C. imagine   D. begin

答案：A

解析：我们回到原文：The researchers were also able to devise a mathematical model that describes the movement and formation of these waves. 题干中的devise并没有选项B、C、D中的含义，且create更符合原文的上下文，因此选A。

48. Based on information in the passage, it can reasonably be inferred that all internal waves _____.
  A. reach approximately the same height even though the locations and depths of continental shelves vary
  B. may be caused by similar factors but are influenced by the distinct topographies of different regions
  C. can be traced to inconsistencies in the tidal patterns of deep ocean water located near islands
  D. are generated by the movement of dense water over a relatively flat section of the ocean floor

答案：B

解析：见下题。

49. Which choice provides the best evidence for the answer to the previous question?
  A. Lines 29~31 ("Although ... formed")
  B. Lines 56~58 ("As the ... it")
  C. Lines 61~64 ("As these ... shelf")
  D. Lines 67~70 ("Whereas ... world")

答案：D

解析：第48题问的是所有internal waves的特点，带着这个问题我们来看第49题的选项：选项A说的是scientists的反应，与第48题题目无关，因此排除；选项B说的是一个distinct double-ridge shape的underwater topography的形成过程，与题干中的all internal waves有冲突，因此排除；选项C是对选项B中内容的补充，同样排除；选项D中in other places around world与题干中的all internal waves相对应，因此是正确答案。我们来看选项D的这个句子：Whereas the model is specific to the Luzon Strait, it can still help researchers understand how internal waves are generated in other places around the world. 这句话中的model指代的是前文的内容，因此我们往前看一句：The researchers were also able to devise a mathematical model that describes the movement and formation of these waves. 其中 the model 是对应 distinct topographies 的,但能帮助人们理解 other places around the world,对应第 48 题选项 B 中的 different regions,因此第 48 题选 B。

50. In the graph, which isotherm displays an increase in depth below the surface during the period 19:12 to 20:24?

A. 9 ℃　　　　B. 10 ℃　　　　C. 11 ℃　　　　D. 13 ℃

答案:D

解析:在 19:12 到 20:24 之间,图表显示从 20 米提高到 40 米,等温线提高 13 ℃,因此选 D。

51. Which concept is supported by the passage and by the information in the graph?

A. Internal waves cause water of varying salinity to mix.

B. Internal waves push denser water above layers of less dense water.

C. Internal waves push bands of cold water above bands of warmer water.

D. Internal waves do not rise to break the ocean's surface.

答案:D

解析:文章第 2~4 行,作者提到内部波浪从不突破海平面,而是在水下运动(move underwater, undetectable without the use of satellite imagery or sophisticated monitoring equipment). 图表中也能看到内部波浪的等温线从没有到达海洋表面(深度没有到达 0),因此选 D。

52. How does the graph support the author's point that internal waves affect ocean water dynamics?

A. It demonstrates that wave movement forces warmer water down to depths that typically are colder.

B. It reveals the degree to which an internal wave affects the density of deep layers of cold water.

C. It illustrates the change in surface temperature that takes place during an isolated series of deep waves.

D. It shows that multiple waves rising near the surface of the ocean disrupt the flow of normal tides.

答案:A

解析:文章第 5~6 行,作者提到内部波浪可以将热量带到海洋底部,把海洋底部的冷水带到海洋表面(transfer heat to ocean depths and bring up cold water from below)。图表确实印证了这一点,例如:在 13:12 时,10 ℃、11 ℃、13 ℃ 的等温线都延伸到底部原本温度更低的地方,说明内部波浪将热量带到了海洋底部,因此选 A。

译文

这篇文章改编自 Geoffrey Giller 的著作《悠久的神秘,500 米高的海底波浪是如何形成的?》,2014 年由科学美国人出版。

有一些巨浪人眼几乎是无法看到的。这些被称作"内波"(internalwave)的海浪与其他巨浪不同,它们并不发生在海洋表层,而是在水下流动,只有通过卫星图或精密的检测设备才能观测到。尽管难以被观察到，内波是海洋动力学的重要组成部分，它们将热量传递到海洋深处，并将深处的冷流往海面方向推。内波的高度可以十分惊人——有些可以和摩天大楼比肩。

麻省理工学院的研究人员汤姆·皮科克表示，由于内波在海水的融合构成及热量传导方面的作用，理解内波对全球气候建模至关重要。大多数气候模型都没有将内波考虑在内。"如果我们想建立更加精确的气候模型，我们必须对这种过程进行记录。"皮科克说道。

皮科克和他的同事正试图这么去做。他们将针对吕宋海峡（分隔中国台湾和菲律宾）的内浪研究发表在《地球物理学研究快报》11月刊上。这一地区的内浪排名全球前列，可以高达500米。"这一高度和纽约新建成的自由塔一样。"皮科克说。

虽然科学家们早就了解中国南海及之外区域的内波现象，他们对内波的形成原理并不完全清楚。因此，皮科克及来自麻省理工和伍兹霍尔海洋研究所的研究团队协同法国科技研究中心一起致力于此，他们采用了称为科里奥利平台（Coriolis Platform）的巨型设备。科里奥利平台是直径为15米的旋转平台，可以以不同的转速旋转并模拟地球自转。平台含四壁，因此科学家可以在其中注水，从而对不同的海洋场景进行准确的大规模场景模拟。

皮科克及其团队用碳纤维树脂搭设了吕宋海峡（包括其周边岛屿与洋底地形）的等比例缩小模型。接着在平台中注入不同盐度的水（底部的水密度大则盐度大，上部密度和盐度偏小）来复制在吕宋海峡发现的不同密度的水。溶液中添加了小颗粒，这些小颗粒能用水底的灯光照亮，来监测液体流动的情况。最后，他们用两个大柱塞泵模拟海浪，观测内波的形成方式。

实验发现，吕宋海峡的水下地形，即其特殊的双脊形状，是产生水下海浪的原因。当海浪起伏、水流经过该海域时，密度大、温度偏低的水越过山脊被推入上层温度较高、密度较大的水流中。这一运动形成了暖流紧跟寒流的波动，从而形成了内波。当内波逐渐向陆地移动，海浪越来越高，直至最后撞上大陆架而停止——这一过程与海面波浪在离岸越近、高度越高是基本一致的。

研究人员还创设了数学模型来解释这些内波的运动和形成。尽管这一数学模型针对的是吕宋海峡的情况，模型仍能有助于研究人员理解世界其他地方的内波是如何形成的。最后，这些信息可以融入到全球气候模型中，提高气候模型的准确性。"很明显，在这些全球气候模型的背景下，内波对推动海洋循环方面是有影响的。"皮科克说。

2.6 New SAT Official Guide Test 3 解析

2.6.1 Passage Ⅰ

答案解析

1. Which choice best summarizes the passage?

A. A woman weighs the positive and negative aspects of accepting a new job.

B. A woman does not correct a stranger who mistakes her for someone else.

C. A woman impersonates someone else to seek revenge on an acquaintance.

D. A woman takes an immediate dislike to her new employer.

答案：B

解析：对于小说类文章或段落过多的文章，其逻辑关系并非特别突出。因此，段首句的阅读可能并不能够有效地突出文章的有效信息。然而，如果阅读全文，那么将会花费大量的时间，在做题的时间分配上就显得捉襟见肘了。针对这种情况，我们有两种应对技巧：其一，如果该小说中有长段的、集中出现的对话，那么这些对话以及对话前后对人物神态和表情的描写是很能突出人物关系的。而小说类文章的大部分主旨题考察的就是人物关系。其二，如果该小说内对话过多、过散或没有对话，我们就将这类题型放到最后做。在其他有行数提示的题目做完，对文章的大致内容已经有了了解之后再来答题。这篇文章中的对话还是非常明显的，我们来看原文：

• "You must be Miss Hope, the governess I've come to meet," said the apparition, in a tone that admitted of very little argument.

"Very well, if I must I must," said Lady Carlotta to herself with dangerous meekness.

"I am Mrs. Quabarl," continued the lady; "and where, pray, is your luggage?"

"It's gone astray," said the alleged governess, falling in with the excellent rule of life that the absent are always to blame; the luggage had, in point of fact, behaved with perfect correctitude. "I've just telegraphed about it," she added, with a nearer approach to truth.

"How provoking," said Mrs. Quabarl; "these railway companies are so careless. However, my maid can lend you things for the night," and she led the way to her car.

这是文中集中出现的一段对话，从黑体部分我们可以看出，Lady Carlotta 被误认为是 Miss Hope 了，其中 if I must I must、alleged、correctitude 都能提示这一错误，但 Lady Carlotta 并没有说破，因此对应选项 B 中的 does not correct a stranger。

2. In line 2, "turn" most nearly means _____.

A. slight movement   B. change in rotation
C. short walk   D. course correction

答案：C

解析：我们回到原文：Lady Carlotta stepped out on to the platform of the small wayside station and took a turn or two up and down its uninteresting length, to kill time till the train should be pleased to proceed on its way. 从这句话中我们可以看出，女主人公 took a turn 的目的是为了 kill time，因此选项 C 是最为恰当的。

3. The passage most clearly implies that other people regarded Lady Carlotta as _____.

A. outspoken   B. tactful
C. ambitious   D. unfriendly

答案：A

解析：见下题。

4. Which choice provides the best evidence for the answer to the previous question?
A. Lines 10～14 ("Certain ... business")
B. Lines 22～23 ("It is ... lady")

C. Lines 23~26 ("On this ... her")

D. Lines 30~32 ("She ... train")

答案：A

解析：第 3 题问的是人们印象中的 Lady Carlotta，因此第 4 题的答案中应该包含他人的想法，我们来看第 4 题的选项：选项 A 中的 of her acquaintances 说到了熟人对她的评价，同时，undesirability of interfering 是对性格的描述，因此保留。选项 B、C 和 D 并没有他人对 Lady Carlotta 的看法和对她性格的直接描述，因此排除。我们来看选项 A 中的这个句子：Certain of her acquaintances were wont to give her plentiful admonition as to the undesirability of interfering on behalf of a distressed animal, such interference being "none of her business." 这句话说 her acquaintances 一直责怪她爱管闲事，因此选项 B、C、D 就都可以排除了，第 3 题选到答案 A。

5. The description of how Lady Carlotta "put the doctrine of non-interference into practice" (lines 14~15) mainly serves to _____.

A. foreshadow her capacity for deception

B. illustrate the subtle cruelty in her nature

C. provide a humorous insight into her character

D. explain a surprising change in her behavior

答案：C

解析：我们来看原文的这个句子：Only once had she put the doctrine of non-interference into practice, when one of its most eloquent exponents had been besieged for nearly three hours in a small and extremely uncomfortable may-tree by an angry boar-pig, while Lady Carlotta, on the other side of the fence, had proceeded with the water-colour sketch she was engaged on, and refused to interfere between the boar and his prisoner.

这句话是对于 Lady Carlotta 唯一一次不管闲事的具体描写。既然只有一次不管闲事，那么说明她平时是很热心的，因此可以直接排除选项 A 和选项 B。又因为这个例子中说她不管闲事的对象是教导她 the doctrine of non-interference into practice 的 most eloquent exponent，说明她仍然是坚持"管闲事"的，因此选项 D 也可以排除，选到选项 C。如果要找总起句，也能对应到答案：Certain of her acquaintances were wont to give her plentiful admonition as to the undesirability of interfering on behalf of a distressed animal, such interference being "none of her business."总起句说她的熟人们总是批评她爱管闲事，因此这个例子是对她性格的具体描绘，对应选项 C。

6. In line 55, "charge" most nearly means _____.

A. responsibility   B. attack   C. fee   D. expense

答案：A

解析：我们回到原文：

During the drive to the Quabarl mansion Lady Carlotta was impressively introduced to the nature of the charge that had been thrust upon her; she learned that Claude and Wilfrid were delicate, sensitive young people, that Irene had the artistic temperament highly developed, and that Viola was something or other else of a mould equally commonplace among children of that class and type in the twentieth century. 显然分号后的内容是对

charge 的具体阐述,而这些孩子是她之后做 governor 的对象。因此 charge 在这里解释为责任,对应选项 A。

7. The narrator indicates that Claude, Wilfrid, Irene and Viola are _____.
   A. similar to many of their peers
   B. unusually creative and intelligent
   C. hostile to the idea of a governess
   D. more educated than others of their age

答案:A

解析:我们根据题干中的名字进行定位,看到原文第 56 行:… she learned that Claude and Wilfrid were delicate, sensitive young people, that Irene had the artistic temperament highly developed, and that Viola was something or other else of a mould equally commonplace among children of that class and type in the twentieth century.

这句话中的 delicate、artistic、highly developed、mould 等词都说明这三个孩子天分极高,因此可以排除选项 A 和选项 C,而选项 D 中的 educated 并没有提到,Claude、Wilfrid 和 Irene 也没有与其他孩子的比较,因此选 A。

8. The narrator implies that Mrs. Quabarl favors a form of education that emphasizes _____.
   A. traditional values   B. active engagement
   C. artistic experimentation   D. factual retention

答案:B

解析:我们根据 a form of education 进行定位,看到原文第 62 行:"I wish them not only to be TAUGHT," said Mrs. Quabarl, "but INTERESTED in what they learn. In their history lessons, for instance, you must try to make them feel that they are being introduced to the life-stories of men and women who really lived, not merely committing a mass of names and dates to memory." 既然是 interested,那么就可以对应选项 B 中的 engagement,因此选 B。

9. As presented in the passage, Mrs. Quabarl is best described as _____.
   A. superficially kind but actually selfish.
   B. outwardly imposing but easily defied.
   C. socially successful but irrationally bitter.
   D. naturally generous but frequently imprudent.

答案:B

解析:见下题。

10. Which choice provides the best evidence for the answer to the previous question?
    A. Lines 49~50 ("How … careless")
    B. Lines 62~68 ("I wish … memory")
    C. Lines 70~73 ("I shall … Russian")
    D. Lines 77~82 ("She was … apologetic")

答案:D

解析:第 9 题问的是 Mrs. Quabarl 被描述为怎样的性格,因此第 10 题的选项中应该出现对其性格的描述,我们来看第 10 题的选项:选项 A 是其对女主人公说的话,并不是其性格的最直接描述,因此排除;选项 B 是其对女主人公提出的要求,虽然能够显示她的部分性格,但仍然不够直接,因此排除;选项 C 根本不是 Mrs. Quabarl 所说的话,因此直接排除;选项 D 中说 Mrs. Quabarl 是一个……的 individual,是对其人物特性的直接描述,与第 9 题题干中的 is best described 对应,因此选 D。

我们来看选项 D 的这个句子:She was one of those imperfectly self-assured individuals who are magnificent and autocratic as long as they are not seriously opposed. The least show of unexpected resistance goes a long way towards rendering them cowed and apologetic. 其中,self-assured 和 autocratic 对应第 9 题选项 B 中的 imposing;而 as long as they are not seriously opposed 和 the least show of ... resistance ... cowed and apologetic 对应选项 B 中的 easily defied,因此第一题选 B。

译文

这篇短文来自萨基于 1911 年发表的短篇小说《夏兹-迈特鲁姆教学法》。

卡罗塔夫人走到月台上,这是个路边不起眼的小车站。为了打发时间,使得等待这列任性的火车再度开动好过一点,卡罗塔夫人在这个无甚趣味的展台里来回踱步。离火车轨道不远处,她看到一匹马挣扎着朝这边走来。这匹马拉着沉重无比的货物,一步一挣扎,马车夫却毫无同情心,对待马的态度极其恶劣,就好像他跟这马有多大的仇似的,丝毫没觉得自己其实靠这匹马为生。这一幕被卡罗塔夫人看到后,她立刻拔腿就朝铁轨那边走了过去,洋洋洒洒地就着这匹马的惨状教训了车夫一通。卡罗塔夫人经常会为可怜的动物出头,这种行为很多熟悉卡罗塔夫人的人都知道,他们还经常会给出酸溜溜的评语,说她"这根本不关你的事,何必多此一举"。而只有一次,卡罗塔夫人真的遵循了这种"高高挂起"的价值观。那次的事情发生在一个对于卡罗塔夫人的行为微词最多的熟人身上,她被一只愤怒的野猪追赶,进而以一种极其不舒服的姿势被困在一棵小小五月树上近三个小时。卡罗塔夫人此时就在围栏的另一边,目睹了整个过程,然后悠然地继续自己的水彩风景画,不干预野猪和它的猎物之间的任何事情。被困的这位夫人最终获救了。卡罗塔夫人那时可是冒着失去这位夫人友谊的风险做出了不干预的决定。这次的情况就不一样了,为了干预这匹马,卡罗塔夫人将错过了火车。这列火车在整个旅程中都表现得极其不耐烦,所以刚刚逮到一点机会,就立刻把卡罗塔夫人甩下了,冒着烟从她身边呼啸而过。卡罗塔夫人对此表现得很淡定,显示出一种理性的满不在乎:她的朋友和家人们早就习惯了她的行李比她先到。卡罗塔夫人接着给自己接站的朋友发了封语焉不详的电报,完全没提任何原因,只说自己会"乘另一趟车到达"。就在她原地思考自己的下一步应该怎么办的时候,一个气场强大的夫人过来找卡罗塔夫人说话了,她的眼光上上下下地对卡罗塔夫人打量了一番,仿佛她脑子里已经对卡罗塔夫人的衣着打扮列了一份清单。

"我来这儿是找我的家庭女教师的,就是你吧,侯普小姐?"来人说道,她的嗓音里是不容置疑的权威。

"你说我是,我就是啰。"卡罗塔夫人自言自语,谦和的态度隐藏着一种危险的因素。

"我是卡巴里夫人,"这位夫人继续说道:"上帝啊,你的行李去哪里了?""行李不见了。"这位"家庭女教师"回答说。我们都知道世上有个最好用的不成文规矩,那就是凡事都可以往不在场的身上"栽赃",卡罗塔夫人正在使用此计。但是其实她的行李恰好是最守规矩的,正在沿着既定路线不偏不倚地执行。

"我刚刚打电报就是说这行李的事情。""家庭女教师"接着说,这下离真相又进一步。

"多么让人气愤,"卡巴里夫人说:"这些铁道公司永远这么不小心。但是你不用担心,我让我的女佣今晚借你些东西过夜。"接着她开始带路,领卡罗塔夫人去她的车那里。

在开车往卡巴里宅邸的途中,卡罗塔夫人对于她接下来要完成的任务有了一个详尽的了解:克罗德和威尔弗雷德是非常敏感娇弱的年轻人,艾雷娜有极强的艺术感,艺术家脾气也不小,而维奥拉有一副20世纪那个阶层那种类型的孩子们都具有的性格。

"我希望他们不仅仅是被灌输式教育,"卡巴里夫人说,"我希望他们能对他们所学的东西真正产生兴趣。比如说历史课,你得尽力让他们感觉到他们是在经历真实发生的事情,这些男男女女都是活生生的人,有活生生的故事,而不是只是将一大堆名字和日期塞进他们的记忆里。当然了,还有法语,我希望你每星期在吃饭的时候都有几天要说法语。"

"我一周会说四天法语,剩下的三天说俄语。"

"俄语?我亲爱的侯普小姐,我家没人说俄语,也没人听得懂俄语。"

"啊,那至少我不会难为情了。"卡罗塔夫人冷冷地说。

此时,卡巴里夫人用时髦点的表达,如同当头一棒,完全失去了主导的地位。她是那种只要没人挑战她的权威,就能在表面上维持出一幅高高在上的贵族范儿的人。这种人自视甚高,但是一旦有人对她露出一点点意料之外的抵抗,她就原形毕露,变得唯唯诺诺起来。这个新来的女教师对她刚刚买的昂贵座驾没有表现出一点点大开眼界的羡艳,甚至不经意间还提起刚刚上市的车有这样或那样的卓越性能,于是,卡巴里夫人费了好大劲才端在身上的贵妇派头无影无踪了。她感觉自己就像是在征战年代的将军,目睹自己最引以为豪的战象在战场上被弹弓手和标枪手赶出去了那样沮丧。

2.6.2 Passage II

答案解析

11. What function does the third paragraph (lines 20~34) serve in the passage as a whole?

A. It acknowledges that a practice favored by the author of the passage has some limitations.

B. It illustrates with detail the arguments made in the first two paragraphs of the passage.

C. It gives an overview of a problem that has not been sufficiently addressed by the experts mentioned in the passage.

D. It advocates for abandoning a practice for which the passage as a whole provides mostly favorable data.

答案:A

解析:我们来看第三段的段首句:And yet public transportation, in many minds, is the opposite of glamour—a squalid last resort for those with one too many impaired driving charges, too poor to afford insurance, or too decrepit to get behind the wheel of a car. 这句

话中的 yet 表明这一段是对之前段落的转折,因此排除选项 B 和选项 D(没有提到前两段)。而选项 C 中的 experts 在第一、二段的段首句中均未出现,因此也可以排除,选到答案 A。

12. Which choice does the author explicitly cite as an advantage of automobile travel in North America?

  A. Environmental impact   B. Convenience
  C. Speed   D. Cost

答案:C

解析:见下题。

13. Which choice provides the best evidence for the answer to the previous question?

  A. Lines 5~9 ("In ... automobile")   B. Lines 20~24 ("And ... car")
  C. Lines 24~26 ("In ... experience")   D. Lines 32~34 ("Hopping ... quickly")

答案:D

解析:第 12 题问的是在北美开车的好处,我们来看第 13 题的选项:选项 A 没有提到 automobile travel,因此排除;选项 B 说的是公共交通的缺点,且没有提到北美,因此排除;选项 C 说的是一句非常笼统的概括,没有具体的 advantages,因此排除;选项 D 说到坐车能让你很快到达目的地,的确是 automobile 的优势,因此是正确答案。

我们来看这个句子:Hopping in a car almost always gets you to your destination more quickly. 显然,more quickly 对应第 12 题选项 C 中的 speed,因此第 12 题选 C。

14. The central idea of the fourth paragraph (lines 35~57) is that _____.

  A. European countries excel at public transportation
  B. some public transportation systems are superior to travel by private automobile
  C. Americans should mimic foreign public transportation systems when possible
  D. much international public transportation is engineered for passengers to work while on board

答案:B

解析:见下题。

15. Which choice provides the best evidence for the answer to the previous question?

  A. Line 35 ("It ... this")   B. Lines 35~37 ("Done ... automobile")
  C. Lines 37~40 ("In ... sound")   D. Lines 44~48 ("From ... cities")

答案:B

解析:第 14 题问的是第四段的中心含义,而我们知道段落主旨一般会出现在段落的前两句或最后一句。因此我们来看第 15 题的选项:选项 A 并没有什么实际含义,选项 C 和选项 D 不在前二后一的关键句位置上,因此都可以直接排除,选到答案 B。我们来看选项 B 中的这个句子:Done right, public transport can be faster, more comfortable, and cheaper than the private automobile. 很显然,这句话是选项 B 的同义改写,因此第 14 题选 B。

16. As used in line 58, "credit" most nearly means _____.

  A. endow   B. attribute   C. believe   D. honor

答案:C

解析:我们回到原文:If you credit the demographers, this transit trend has legs. 这是一句总起句,之后具体说到了 the "Millennial". baby boomers 等,因此说的是 demographers

的具体理论。所以 credit 在这里是相信的意思,对应选项 C。

17. As used in line 61,"favor" most nearly means _____.

A. indulge　　　B. prefer　　　C. resemble　　　D. serve

答案:B

解析:我们回到原文:The "Millenials," who reached adulthood around the turn of the century and now outnumber baby boomers, tend to favor cities over suburbs, and are far more willing than their parents to ride buses and subways. 很显然,favor 在这里与之后的 more willing ... to 是并列的同义词,因此选到答案 B。

18. Which choice best supports the conclusion that public transportation is compatible with the use of personal electronic devices?

A. Lines 59~63 ("The ... subways")

B. Lines 63~67 ("Part ... annoyances")

C. Lines 68~70 ("Even ... ago")

D. Lines 77~81 ("Already ... homes")

答案:B

解析:我们直接来看选项:选项 A、C、D 均没有说到个人电子设备的使用,因此排除。选项 B 中的 get serious texting done when you're not driving 对应题干中的 compatible,因此是正确答案。

19. Which choice is supported by the data in the first figure?

A. The number of students using public transportation is greater than the number of retirees using public transportation.

B. The number of employed people using public transportation and the number of unemployed people using public transportation is roughly the same.

C. People employed outside the home are less likely to use public transportation than are homemakers.

D. Unemployed people use public transportation less often than do people employed outside the home.

答案:A

解析:图表 1 显示:公共交通使用者当中,有 10.7% 是学生,6.7% 是退休人员。显然,学生比退休人员多。

20. Taken together, the two figures suggest that most people who use public transportation _____.

A. are employed outside the home and take public transportation to work

B. are employed outside the home but take public transportation primarily in order to run errands

C. use public transportation during the week but use their private cars on weekends

D. use public transportation only until they are able to afford to buy a car

答案:A

解析:图表 1 显示:公共交通乘客中的 72% 在家庭之外的地方工作;图表 2 显示:公共交通行程中有 59.1% 是为了工作。由此可见,大部分乘坐公共交通的人是为了去工作地点上班。

译文

这段文章来自塔拉斯·格雷斯克于 2012 年出版的著作《公共交通出行者：将我们自己和我们的城市从汽车中拯救出来》。

我们这个星球有 6 亿辆车，这个数字还在不停地增长中。与此同时，我们的人口达到了 70 亿，这就意味着大部分人还得依靠类似于公交车、渡船、火车和地铁这一类的交通工具出行。换言之，当我们需要去上班、上学，或者去市场买东西的时候，我们还得做公共交通出行者：不管是否是自愿选择还是必要手段，我们仍然依赖公共交通工具，而不是私家车。

在纽约、东京和伦敦，有一半的人口没有私家车。同时，在亚洲和非洲这两个人口最密集的大洲，乘坐公共交通工具是大多数人出行的方式。通常的一天中，地铁的运量就能达到 1.55 亿人次，这个数字是全世界的飞机运量加起来总和的 34 倍，并且公共交通运输这个产业年估值达到了 4280 亿元。可见，在内燃机引擎问世一个半世纪后，私家车仍然是绝对的少数派。

在很多人的观念里，公共交通出行听起来还是一点都不炫酷，他们觉得公共交通是藏污纳垢的圣地，这里面有那些多次酒后驾车被抓的人，有太穷了买不起保险的人，还有那些太笨拙永远没法学会开车的人。在北美的大多数地方，这样的想法确实有道理：乘坐公共交通出行确实是让人沮丧的经历。有时候你得花上很长的时间在街角等一辆摇摇晃晃、蹒跚而来的公交车，这车上永远人满为患，而你能挤上去就已经是莫大的幸运了；还有的时候你得在地铁站里拖着沉重的行李箱上上下下换乘，只为了能按时赶到机场。凡是有过这些体验的人们都知道，这片大陆上的公共交通管理系统有很大的问题：永远资金不足，永远保养不到位，永远毫无计划地运行。确实是，如果有可能的话，谁不想自己开车呢？跳上私家车风驰电掣永远比乘坐公共交通要先到达目的地。

但是其实事情不总是这样的，没错，就是这个意思：公共交通可以比私家车更快捷、更舒适、更便宜。在上海，德国造的磁悬浮火车以 266 英里的时速轻盈地滑过铁轨，用 1/3 音速的速度将人们送达机场。法国的一些城镇，电力驱动的街车配备着橡胶轮胎，它们滑过安在窄窄的街道鹅卵石中间的单轨，几乎没有任何声音。从西班牙到瑞典，你可以选择乘坐那种有着无线网络信号的新型高速火车，这种火车和城市的地铁系统无缝连接，人们可以在旅行的时候毫无障碍地办公，准备当天的会议资料。先进的公共交通工具连接起了过去看来远隔重洋的两个首都。在拉丁美洲国家、中国、印度，忙碌的人们会乘坐快速公交，这种公交运行起来像地铁系统，有专用的车道，它们往往能在大堵车的时候将各种小车和越野车甩得远远的，任由私家车在那里从黎明堵到天黑。还有些城市已经将它们的街道改造成了自行车道，将自行车出行纳入到大众交通的一种，这无疑是在公共健康、公共安全、公共居住环境等方面迈出的巨大步伐。

如果你相信统计学家，那么你会发现这种公共交通出行的趋势会长久地发展下去。这源于被称之为"千禧代"的人们，他们在世纪之交刚好成年，而现在，他们已经取代了出生于二战晚期到 20 世纪 60 年代早期的这一代，成为新的中坚力量。比起乡村，他们更喜欢城市；并且和父辈相比，他们完全不抗拒乘坐公共交通出行。这其中一部分归功于诸如 iPad、MP3 播放器、Kindle 阅读器、智能手机这些现代发明，你在公共交通里可以疯狂地想发多少信息就发多少信息，这点在开车的时候可做不到，而且当你戴上耳塞，你基本就与外界绝缘了，可以免去一切社交上的烦恼。目前我国青少年人口的数量是历史之最，但是只有 1000

万人有驾照(上一代的青少年中有 1200 万人有驾照)。上一代人可能确实是在《反斗小宝贝》那样的城郊环境中长大,但是当他们退休后,他们中有相当大一部分人都更喜欢在老牌的城市和精致的城镇中生活,在这些地方他们可以自由地选择步行或者骑自行车出行。其实不止年轻人,老年人们也更愿意使用公交。到 2025 年时,将会有 6400 万美国人超过 65 岁。如果你现在去华盛顿特区、亚特兰大和丹佛的老社区看看,你就会发现,那些跟轻轨、地铁站离得近的老社区的价格比一栋典型的城郊别墅贵得多。我们从欧洲和亚洲城市发展的经验来看,如果我们能将公交车、地铁、火车系统发展得舒适便捷、快速安全,选择公共交通而非私家车出行的人数将会非常惊人。

2.6.3 Passage Ⅲ

答案解析

21. Which choice best reflects the overall sequence of events in the passage?

A. An experiment is proposed but proves unworkable; a less ambitious experiment is attempted, and it yields data that give rise to a new set of questions.

B. A new discovery leads to reconsideration of a theory; a classic study is adapted, and the results are summarized.

C. An anomaly is observed and simulated experimentally; the results are compared with previous findings, and a novel hypothesis is proposed.

D. An unexpected finding arises during the early phase of a study; the study is modified in response to this finding, and the results are interpreted and evaluated.

答案:D

解析:像这类全文顺序题我们可以在完成其他题目之后来答,能够有效节省时间。在这道题里,我们要着重关注文中表示时间的词,如 at first、at last 等。我们看到原文第 23 行:At first it seemed unnatural—ground birds don't like the ground?

其中 unnatural 对应选项 C 和选项 D 中的 anomaly 和 an unexpected finding,而之后的一句:o he brought in some hay bales for the Chukars to perch on and then left his son in charge of feeding and data collection while he went away on a short work trip. 则说明他调整了自己的实验,对应选项 D 中的 modified。

22. As used in line 7,"challenged" most nearly means _____.

A. dared
B. required
C. disputed with
D. competed with

答案:A

解析:观察选项可以发现,选项 C 和选项 D 是类似的意思,而原文中并没有"冲突"的含义,因此排除。而 challenge 一词本身没有 require 的含义,因此选 A。

23. Which statement best captures Ken Dial's central assumption in setting up his research?

A. The acquisition of flight in young birds sheds light on the acquisition of flight in their evolutionary ancestors.

B. The tendency of certain young birds to jump erratically is a somewhat recent evolved behavior.

C. Young birds in a controlled research setting are less likely than birds in the wild to require perches when at rest.

D. Ground-dwelling and tree-climbing predecessors to birds evolved in parallel.

答案：A

解析：见下题。

24. Which choice provides the best evidence for the answer to the previous question?

A. Lines 1～4 ("At field ... parents")

B. Lines 6～11 ("So when ... fly")

C. Lines 16～19 ("When ... measured")

D. Lines 23～24 ("At first ... the ground")

答案：B

解析：第23题问的是Ken Dial研究的核心假设，我们来看第24题的选项：选项A描述了Ken Dial看到的一个现象，并非其核心假设，因此排除；选项B说他建立了一个模型来come up with new data，说到了之前的两种理论，因此保留；选项C说的是他向别人展示他的model，与假设无关，可以排除；选项D说的同样是他观察到的现象，不涉及理论，排除。

我们来看选项B中的句子：So when a group of graduate students challenged him to come up with new data on the age-old ground-up-tree-down debate, he designed a project to see what clues might lie in how baby game birds learned to fly. 这句话中说他的project是为了得到ground-up-tree-down debate的最新数据，而这个debate在引言中是被解释过的：Scientists have long debated how the ancestors of birds evolved the ability to fly. 这说明，这两种理论都是基于鸟类祖先的飞行的，对应第23题中的选项A。

25. In the second paragraph (lines 7～17), the incident involving the local rancher mainly serves to _____.

A. reveal Ken Dial's motivation for undertaking his project

B. underscore certain differences between laboratory and field research

C. show how an unanticipated piece of information influenced Ken Dial's research

D. introduce a key contributor to the tree-down theory

答案：C

解析：文章第16～23行，当一名农民观察Ken Dial的实验时，对于Chukars生活在地面这一点有怀疑"incredulous"，于是建议Dial要提供一些道具给幼鸟爬行"something to climb on"。这一条"key piece of advice"（第14行）重要建议使得Dial在他的实验中增添了一些干草，所以选C。

26. After Ken Dial had his "'aha' moment" (line 41), he _____.

A. tried to train the birds to fly to their perches

B. studied videos to determine why the birds no longer hopped

C. observed how the birds dealt with gradually steeper inclines

D. consulted with other researchers who had studied Chukar Partridges

答案：C

解析：我们回到原文，发现在那之后描写 Ken Dial 行动的句子是之后一段的段首句：Working together with Terry (who has since gone on to study animal locomotion)，Ken came up with a series of ingenious experiments，filming the birds as they raced up textured ramps tilted at increasing angles. 只有选项 B 和选项 C 提到了 video 和 observe，因此保留。但选项 B 中的 determine 和 why the birds no longer hopped 均信息错误，因此排除。而选项 C 中的 gradually stepper inclines 则对应这句话中的 ramps tilted at increasing angles，因此选 C。

27. The passage identifies which of the following as a factor that facilitated the baby Chukars' traction on steep ramps?
    A. The speed with which they climbed.
    B. The position of their flapping wings.
    C. The alternation of wing and foot movement.
    D. Their continual hopping motions.

答案：B

解析：我们根据 traction 进行定位，看到第 54 行：In Formula One racing, spoilers are the big aerodynamic fins that push the cars downward as they speed along, increasing traction and handling. The birds were doing the very same thing with their wings to help them scramble up otherwise impossible slopes. 句中的 wings 对应选项 B 中的 flapping wings，因此选 B。

28. As used in line 61, "document" most nearly means _____.
    A. portray   B. record   C. publish   D. process

答案：B

解析：我们回到原文：Ken called the technique WAIR, for wing-assisted incline running, and went on to document it in a wide range of species. 分析上下文可知，document 在这里解释为记录、拍摄，因此选 B。

29. What can reasonably be inferred about gliding animals from the passage?
    A. Their young tend to hop along beside their parents instead of flying beside them.
    B. Their method of locomotion is similar to that of ground birds.
    C. They use the ground for feeding more often than for perching.
    D. They do not use a flapping stroke to aid in climbing slopes.

答案：D

解析：见下题。

30. Which choice provides the best evidence for the answer to the previous question?
    A. Lines 4~6 ("They jumped ... air")
    B. Lines 28~29 ("They really ... traveling")
    C. Lines 57~59 ("The birds ... slopes")
    D. Lines 72~74 ("something ... theory")

答案：D

解析：第 29 题的是 gliding animals 的特性，我们来看第 30 题的选项：选项 A、B 和 C 描述的是 ground birds 的特性，答非所问；选项 D 中提到了 gliding animals，因此是正确答案。我们来看选项 D 中的这个句子：With one fell swoop, the Dials came up with a viable origin for the flapping flight stroke of birds（something gliding animals don't do and thus a shortcoming of the tree-down theory）…这句话说 gliding animals 不会有 flapping flight，因此对应第 29 题的选项 D。

译文

下面这篇短文来自索尔·汉森于 2011 年发表的《羽毛》。科学家们为鸟儿的祖先是如何进化出飞翔的功能这个议题争论了很久。有一种"由地而上"的理论认为它们原本生活在地面上，能跑得特别快，通过跳跃和快速扇动前肢来捕获猎物；还有一种"由树而下"的理论认为它们擅于爬树，常常在树枝间跳跃和滑翔。

肯·戴尔在世界各地都注意到，很多种类的幼鸟会跟在自己父母后面摇摇晃晃地在地面跑，这种鸟类包括野鸡、鹌鹑、鸠等。肯形容它们"跳起来就像蹦高的爆米花一样"，扇动着自己还没有完全成形的小翅膀，努力向空中蹿高。一直以来，关于鸟儿们是如何进化出飞行功能的理论中，有两派"由地而上"和"由树而下"一直争论不休，一次，一群研究生们就这个争论再次向肯提出挑战，让他拿出些新数据来证明一下，到底哪派理论比较靠谱，于是，肯设计了一个新的实验项目，想找出些禽类的幼鸟究竟如何学会飞行的新证据。

肯最终确定石鸡作为研究对象。这些实验用的鸟儿都由蒙塔纳当地一个农场主提供，也正是多亏了他给出的一个关键建议，才使得肯最终在这次实验中有所斩获。有一次这位牛仔路过实验室，想看看实验进展得如何。肯于是带他参观了一下他设计的干净明亮的实验室，并且向他大致解释了鸟儿的第一次跳跃和第一次飞行将被如何测量。这位地道的牛仔露出了非常之疑惑的表情，用极具特色的语言表达了他的意见："你把这些鸟搁在地上干吗？他们特别不喜欢在地上，你得给他们备点东西，他们好往上爬！"这建议一开始的时候听起来挺让人疑惑的——禽类怎么会不喜欢在地上呢？它们整天就是满地跑。但是当肯仔细回想的时候，他意识到在野外观察到的所有这类鸟都比较喜欢栖息在架子上啊，低树枝上啊，或者其他比较高的地方，这样他们能避开猎食者。它们仅仅只是在喂食和移动的时候才待在地面上。于是，肯采取了牛仔的建议，在实验室里放置了一些干草堆之类，以供石鸡们攀爬用。在肯外出进行短途出差的时候，肯的儿子担当起了喂食和搜集相关数据的工作。

年轻的泰瑞·戴尔那时候还是个孩子，连青少年都算不上，当他父亲回来的时候，泰瑞看上去一派愁眉苦脸。"我问儿子实验室的情况如何，"肯后来回忆当时的情景时说，"儿子说，'糟透了，这些鸟都在作弊！'"原来，本该用翅膀飞上栖息地的幼鸟们，实际都是用腿上去的。泰瑞看见了好多次，这些幼鸟完全是用腿冲上干草堆的，边跑边扇翅膀。听见这话，肯立即冲到实验室观察，那一刻他恍然大悟。他后来告诉我："这些鸟儿们将翅膀和腿配合着使用。"这一个发现打开了无数可能性的大门。

肯后来和泰瑞（泰瑞的兴趣从那时开始发展，后来学了动物运动学）一起工作，设计出了一系列精巧的实验，比如他们手工制作了不同角度的斜坡，当鸟儿们冲上这些斜坡的时候，用摄像机将这个过程拍下来。当斜坡的倾斜角度变大的时候，这些石鸡开始更多地使用翅膀，但是它们使用翅膀的方式和飞翔的鸟儿不大一样。石鸡们扇动翅膀的时候，它们更多是向下、向后的方向扇动，利用这股力帮助爪子更牢靠地抓住斜坡。"就像一辆赛车后面的导流板一样。"肯解释说，用了一个非常恰当的类比。在一号方程式赛车中，导流板是那种巨大的空气动力尾翅,用于在赛车加速时增加车身向下的压力,同时增加牵引力和控制力。这些鸟儿将翅膀用作导流板,来帮助自己爬上不可能爬上的斜坡。

肯将这种借助翅膀冲上斜坡的技术称之为 WAIR,并且观察记录了更多种类的鸟类使用这种技术。这种技术不只让幼鸟在刚出生的几周内就能爬上陡峭的平面,也给了成鸟除飞行外另一种更加节能省力的选择。比如石鸡,成鸟经常会用到这种技术来帮助自己爬上比 90° 更加陡峭的斜坡,它们可以冲上墙壁到达房顶。

就革命性意义的层面上来说,WAIR 有惊人的解释能力。戴尔父子一下子就找到了鸟类扑翔动作的一个有力的来源(有些滑翔的鸟类不会这样做,这是"由树而下"理论的一个缺点),和未完全成形的翅膀在空气动力学中的一个作用(这是"由地而上"理论的一个主要缺点)。

2.6.4 Passage IV

答案解析

31. As used in line 21, "common" most nearly means _____.
A. average B. shared C. coarse D. similar
答案:B
解析:我们回到原文:It seems to us incontestable that our common happiness, above all that of women, requires that they never aspire to the exercise of political rights and functions. 这句话中的 above all that of women 很明显将女性群体与作者所在的男性群体割裂开来了,因此 common 在这里解释为共同的,对应选项 B。

32. It can be inferred that the authors of Passage 1 believe that running a household and raising children _____.
A. are rewarding for men as well as for women
B. yield less value for society than do the roles performed by men
C. entail very few activities that are difficult or unpleasant
D. require skills similar to those needed to run a country or a business
答案:C
解析:见下题。

33. Which choice provides the best evidence for the answer to the previous question?
A. Lines 4~6 ("they are ... representation")
B. Lines 13~17 ("If the ... sanction")
C. Lines 25~30 ("Is it ... home")
D. Lines 30~35 ("And ... manner")
答案:C
解析:第 32 题问的是作者对于女性做家务和带孩子的看法,我们来看第 33 题的选项:选项 A 并没有提到做家务或者带孩子,因此排除。选项 B 和选项 D 提到的是社会对于女性的看法,同样无关,排除。选项 C 中的 duties of motherhood 与题干中所问对应,因此是正确的答案。我们来看选项 C 中的句子:Is it not apparent, that their delicate constitutions,

their peaceful inclinations, and the many duties of motherhood, set them apart from strenuous habits and onerous duties, and summon them to gentle occupations and the cares of the home? 这个句子中,作者认为女性的 duties of motherhood 将它们从 strenuous habits 和 onerous duties 中解放出来,对应第32题的选项 C。

34. According to the author of Passage 2, in order for society to progress, women must _____.

  A. enjoy personal happiness and financial security

  B. follow all currently prescribed social rules

  C. replace men as figures of power and authority

  D. receive an education comparable to that of men

答案:D

解析:我们根据题干中的 progress 进行定位,看到原文第一行:Contending for the rights of woman, my main argument is built on this simple principle, that if she be not prepared by education to become the companion of man, she will stop the progress of knowledge and virtue. 很显然,这句话的关键词是 education,对应选项 D。

35. As used in line 50,"reason" most nearly means _____.

  A. motive B. sanity C. intellect D. explanation

答案:C

解析:我们回到原文:And how can woman be expected to co-operate unless she know why she ought to be virtuous? unless freedom strengthen her reason till she comprehend her duty, and see in what manner it is connected with her real good? 句中的 reason 对应的是之后的 comprehend her duty 和 see in what manner it is connected with her real goal,因此 reason 在这里解释为智慧、智商,对应选项 C。

36. In Passage 2, the author claims that freedoms granted by society's leaders have _____.

  A. privileged one gender over the other

  B. resulted in a general reduction in individual virtue

  C. caused arguments about the nature of happiness

  D. ensured equality for all people

答案:A

解析:见下题。

37. Which choice provides the best evidence for the answer to the previous question?

  A. Lines 41~45 ("Contending ... virtue")

  B. Lines 45~47 ("truth ... practice")

  C. Lines 65~66 ("If so ... rest")

  D. Lines 72~75 ("Consider ... happiness")

答案:D

解析:第36题问的是作者认为自由的效用是什么,我们带着问题来看第37题的选项:选项 A 和选项 B 完全没有提到题干中的关键词 freedom,因此排除。选项 C 提出了一个问题,显然也不是我们的答案。选项 D 中出现了关键词 freedom,因此是正确答案。

我们来看选项 D 中的这个句子：Consider—I address you as a legislator—whether, when men contend for their freedom, and to be allowed to judge for themselves respecting their own happiness, it be not inconsistent and unjust to subjugate women, even though you firmly believe that you are acting in the manner best calculated to promote their happiness? 这句话说得是男性将自己对 happiness 的理解强加于女性身上，并且标榜这是他们赋予女性的 freedom，其中 subjugate 对应第 36 题选项中的 privileged，因此第 36 题选A。选项 C 是一个迷惑选项。虽然 happiness 的确是这句话中的关键词，但这句话并没有说这种 freedom 引起了人们对于 happiness 本质的讨论，因此排除。

38. In lines 34~36, the author of Passage 2 refers to a statement made in Passage 1 in order to _____.

   A. call into question the qualifications of the authors of Passage 1 regarding gender issues

   B. dispute the assertion made about women in the first sentence of Passage 1

   C. develop her argument by highlighting what she sees as flawed reasoning in Passage 1

   D. validate the concluding declarations made by the authors of Passage 1 about gender roles

答案：C

解析：文章 1 的作者认为应该将妇女排除在政治活动之外(第 61~65 行)。Wollstonecraft 认为，如果讨论男性的抽象权力，那他们就应该讨论妇女的抽象权力(第 66~69 行)。Wollstonecraft 通过强调文章 1 作者的推理漏洞来展开自己的辩论。

39. Which best describes the overall relationship between Passage 1 and Passage 2?

   A. Passage 2 strongly challenges the point of view in Passage 1.

   B. Passage 2 draws alternative conclusions from the evidence presented in Passage 1.

   C. Passage 2 elaborates on the proposal presented in Passage 1.

   D. Passage 2 restates in different terms the argument presented in Passage 1.

答案：A

解析：由上一题可知，第二篇文章的作者是在反驳第一篇文章作者观点，因此选项 B、C 和 D 就可以直接排除，选到答案 A。

40. The authors of both passages would most likely agree with which of the following statements about women in the eighteenth century?

   A. Their natural preferences were the same as those of men.

   B. They needed a good education to be successful in society.

   C. They were just as happy in life as men were.

   D. They generally enjoyed fewer rights than men did.

答案：D

解析：由上两题可知，Passage Ⅰ 的作者明显是贬低女性权利的，因此可以直接排除选项 A 和选项 B，而 Passage Ⅱ 的作者又是认为社会应该改变对女性的态度的，因此可以排除选项 C，选到正确答案 D。

41. How would the authors of Passage 1 most likely respond to the points made in the final paragraph of Passage 2?

A. Women are not naturally suited for the exercise of civil and political rights.
B. Men and women possess similar degrees of reasoning ability.
C. Women do not need to remain confined to their traditional family duties.
D. The principles of natural law should not be invoked when considering gender roles.

答案：A

解析：我们已经明确知道 Passage Ⅰ 作者的观点了，认为男女本就是不平等的，女性应该在家安心做家庭主妇，因此可以直接排除选项 B 和选项 C。而 Passage Ⅱ 最后一段说到的关键词就是 civil and political rights，因此对应选项 A。

译文

第一篇短文来自泰利兰德于1791年发表的《公众教导报告》，第二篇短文来自玛丽·乌斯科莱福特于1972年发表的《妇女权利辩护》。泰利兰德是一名法国外交官，《公众教导报告》主要是他为了全民教育做的报告。乌斯克莱福特是一名英国小说家、时政作家，她所撰写的辩护主要是为了回应泰利兰德。

文章1

我们注意到，以下这些政治现象在抽象原则上明显是无法解释的：一半人类被另一半彻底地排除在所有政府事务之外；她们在自己生长于斯的土地上享受不到任何本地人的法律权利；她们是产权所有者，但是没有代理权，也没有直接的影响力。但是在另外一个层面上来说，这些看似不合理的现象就都迎刃而解了：我们要考虑的是大多数人类的幸福，所以才形成了这样的社会制度。所有与这个原则背道而驰的都是错误的，所有接近这个原则的才是真理。所以，如果妇女被排除在社会雇佣体系之外是为了全人类大多数的利益考虑，那么这就成为了全社会必须强制认知和认同的律法。

超出这个律法之外的所有企图和尝试将是对我们最重大使命的倒行逆施；对于妇女本身来说，改变她们生而被命运赋予的职责也绝对对她们自己无益。

这一点是毫无争议的，我们全人类大多数人的福祉，在妇女的福祉之上。这就决定了她们不应该去争取行使政治权利和功能。妇女们真正的福祉和使命在哪儿呢？很简单，我们应该从自然赋予她们的特性中去寻找。她们的蒲柳弱质，她们倾向和平、宁静的本质，还有她们作为母亲要做的所有工作，难道不是已经将她们从事的职业摆明了吗？她们应该做一些温和文雅的工作，将重心放在家庭，而不应该染指紧张热烈并且繁重的事务。并且，我们整个社会之所以能井然有序地和谐分工运行，是因为我们遵循了伟大的守恒原则，这个原则符合大自然本身的运行规律。当大自然将男性和女性塑造成了明显不同功能的个体时，这两种个体应该从事不同的工作这一点就已经不言自明了。上述这些已经足够说明我的观点了。我们不需要再到处去找各式各样的说辞，那些对此问题都不适用。我们也不要让我们的生活伴侣成为对手。而你们，你们要坚信我们的结合是坚不可摧的，无论面对何种利诱或者对手。你们要谨记的一点是，为了全人类大多数人的福祉，你们必须这样做。

文章2

在为女性争取权利这个论题上，我的立论基于这样一个简单的原则：如果女性没有得到同等的教育使她们能和男性平起平坐，那么她们会阻碍美德和学识的发展。要知道，真理必须放之四海而皆准，若非如此，其对通常行为便无任何影响。从这一层面上来看，除非她们明白为什么这样做就是贤良淑德的，除非她们被给予了充分的自由，有足够的智慧自己去寻找答案,去理解她所承担的义务,去明白这样做对她们自身真正的好处在哪里,要不然怎么能期待得到女性的配合。很简单,如果一个孩子要理解爱国主义的真意所在,那么他们的母亲必须是一个爱国者;对于人类的热爱并且由此发展出的一系列美德,只能建立在深刻了解人类的道德和权利的基础上。但是我们现阶段的女性教育和处境,完全排除了她们自己去做任何调查研究的可能性……

现在,先生,我请你冷静地不带偏见地看看这些现象——只要细心观察,就会发现真理之光在其中闪现——"一半人类被另一半彻底地排除在所有政府事务之外,这个政治现象在抽象原则上是无法解释的"。你如果承认这个事实,那么你将宪法章程置于何处?如果我们能将男性的抽象权利加以讨论和阐释,那么就公平性的推理来说,女性也不会放弃她们应得的权利。虽然不同政见者的声音在这个国家盛行,被你用来作为压迫女性的立论根据,但是女性在这场被剥夺政治权利的考验之前不会退缩。

我请你从一个立法者的角度仔细考虑一下,当男性争取到自由的时候,他们被赋予了尊重自己、追求幸福的权利,他们能够为自己决定什么对他们来说是幸福的。那么,虽然你真心认为你的所作所为是为了女性考虑,难道剥夺女性的同等权利不是前后矛盾和不公平的吗?女性也和男性一样有理智的天赋,在这个问题上,谁赋予了男性作为唯一法官的权利呢?

在这个逻辑下,各种不同程度的暴君都会如此为己辩护,他们可能是一个弱小的国王,也可以是一个家庭中失去权威的父亲;他们会尽一切手段将道义碾碎,还坚称他们的篡位是为了能发挥自己更大的作用,为人们谋得更大的福祉。当你在强迫女性放弃她们生而具有的政治权利,将她们囚禁在家庭生活中、在黑暗中苦苦摸索的时候,你难道不也是在行这种暴君篡位者之事吗?

2.6.5　Passage V

答案解析

42. How do the words "can" "may" and "could" in the third paragraph (lines 19~41) help establish the tone of the paragraph?

A. They create an optimistic tone that makes clear the authors are hopeful about the effects of their research on colony collapse disorder.

B. They create a dubious tone that makes clear the authors do not have confidence in the usefulness of the research described.

C. They create a tentative tone that makes clear the authors suspect but do not know that their hypothesis is correct.

D. They create a critical tone that makes clear the authors are skeptical of claims that pyrethrums are inherent in mono-crops.

答案:C

解析:首先观察这三个词,会发现它们都带有"可能"的意思,因此是不确定的语气,可以直接排除选项 A。而其中 can 相对而言又有其事实性的一面,因此选项 D 也可以排除。我们接着看这三个词出现的这一段段首句:We suspect that the bees of commercial bee colonies which are fed mono-crops are nutritionally deficient. 显然,作者是提出这一假设的人之一,之后才针对这一假设做了实验,对应选项 C 中的 suspect 和 hypothesis,因此选 C。

43. In line 42, the authors state that a certain hypothesis "can best be tested by a trial." Based on the passage, which of the following is a hypothesis the authors suggest be tested in a trial?

A. Honeybees that are exposed to both pyrethrums and mites are likely to develop a secondary infection by a virus, a bacterium, or a fungus.

B. Beekeepers who feed their honeybee colonies a diet of a single crop need to increase the use of insecticides to prevent mite infestations.

C. A honeybee diet that includes pyrethrums results in honeybee colonies that are more resistant to mite infestations.

D. Humans are more susceptible to varroa mites as a result of consuming nutritionally deficient food crops.

答案: C

解析: 见下题。

44. Which choice provides the best evidence for the answer to the previous question?

A. Lines 3～5 ("These mites ... viruses")

B. Lines 16～18 ("In fact ... cream")

C. Lines 19～21 ("We suspect ... deficient")

D. Lines 24～28 ("Without ... bees")

答案: D

解析: 第 43 题问的是哪个假说最适合被实验验证,我们带着这个问题来看第 44 题的选项:选项 A 说的是一个现象,并没有说到关键词 hypothesis 或 trial,因此排除。选项 B 说的是一个理论,同样排除。选项 C 中的 suspect 一词与 hypothesis 对应,因此保留。而选项 D 则是选项 C 这一假说之下的一个具体分支,我们看到第 43 题选项中都是提到了具体的生物名词,因此选项 C 就显得过于笼统,可以排除选项 C,保留正确答案 D。

我们一起来看这个句子:Without, at least, intermittent feeding on the pyrethrum producing plants, bee colonies are susceptible to mite infestations which can become fatal either directly or due to a secondary infection of immunocompromised or nutritionally deficient bees. 这句话说如果没有 pyrethrum,那么 bee colonies 就会容易受到 mite infestations 的威胁。换言之,有了 pyrethrum,bee colonies 就能够对 mite infestations 更 resistant,对应第 43 题的选项 C。

45. The passage most strongly suggests that beekeepers' attempts to fight mite infestations with commercially produced insecticides have what unintentional effect?

A. They increase certain mite populations.

B. They kill some beneficial forms of bacteria.

C. They destroy bees' primary food source.

D. They further harm the health of some bees.

答案: D

解析: 见下题。

46. Which choice provides the best evidence for the answer to the previous question?

A. Lines 1~2 ("Honey bees ... mites")

B. Lines 6~7 ("Little ... control")

C. Lines 31~35 ("In addition ... infestation")

D. Lines 47~50 ("Mites ... control colonies")

答案：C

解析：第 45 题问的是养蜂人用灭虫剂有什么意想不到的结果，因此第 46 题的答案中应该起码包含 unintentional effect，我们来看第 46 题的选项：

选项 A 和选项 B 完全没有提到灭虫剂或 effect，因此排除。选项 C 说蜜蜂会被 further weakened，的确是 effects，而且是与养蜂人的目的相违背的，符合 unintentional 的标准，因此保留。选项 D 没有提到养蜂人的行为，因此排除。

我们来看选项 C 中的这个句子：In addition, immunocompromised or nutritionally deficient bees may be further weakened when commercially produced insecticides are introduced into their hives by bee keepers in an effort to fight mite infestation. 其中 bees may be furthered weakened 可以对应第 45 题选项 D 中的 further harm the health of some bees，因此第 45 题选 D。

47. As used in line 35, "postulate" most nearly means to _____.

A. make an unfounded assumption

B. put forth an idea or claim

C. question a belief or theory

D. conclude based on firm evidence

答案：B

解析：我们回到原文：We further postulate that the proper dosage necessary to prevent mite infestation may be better left to the bees ... 在这句之后，就出现了第四段的段首句：This hypothesis can best be tested by a trial ... 因此这里的 postulate 就是 hypothesis 的意思，对应选项 B。

48. The main purpose of the fourth paragraph (lines 42~50) is to _____.

A. summarize the results of an experiment that confirmed the authors' hypothesis about the role of clover in the diets of wild-type honeybees

B. propose an experiment to investigate how different diets affect commercial honeybee colonies' susceptibility to mite infestations

C. provide a comparative nutritional analysis of the honey produced by the experimental colonies and by the control colonies

D. predict the most likely outcome of an unfinished experiment summarized in the third paragraph (lines 19~41)

答案：B

解析：我们来看第四段段首句：This hypothesis can best be tested by a trial wherein a small number of commercial honey bee colonies are offered a number of pyrethrum producing plants, as well as a typical bee food source such as clover, while controls are offered only the clover. 这句话说 this hypothesis（第三段）能够被一个实验所验证，并具体描

述了这个实验,因此对应选项 B。

49. An unstated assumption made by the authors about clover is that the plants _____.

 A. do not produce pyrethrums

 B. are members of the Chrysanthemum genus

 C. are usually located near wild-type honeybee colonies

 D. will not be a good food source for honeybees in the control colonies

答案:A

解析:我们根据题干中的 clover 进行定位,看到原文第四段的第一句话:This hypothesis can best be tested by a trial wherein a small number of commercial honey bee colonies are offered a number of pyrethrum producing plants,as well as a typical bee food source such as clover,while controls are offered only the clover.

这句话说 clover 是两个对照组所共有的,也就是说 clover 不是变量,而这个假说研究的就是 pyrethrums。换言之,就是 clover 与 pyrethrums 没有关系,对应选项 A。

50. Based on data in the table, in what percent of colonies with colony collapse disorder were the honeybees infected by all four pathogens?

 A. 0 percent B. 77 percent C. 83 percent D. 100 percent

答案:B

解析:表格显示:在右蜂群崩溃综合征的蜂群中,有 77% 的比例被四种病原体感染。

51. Based on data in the table, which of the four pathogens infected the highest percentage of honeybee colonies without colony collapse disorder?

 A. IAPV B. KBV C. Nosema apis D. Nosema ceranae

答案:D

解析:表格显示:在没有蜂群崩溃综合征的蜂群中,有 81% 的比例被 Nosema ceranae 感染。

52. Do the data in the table provide support for the authors' claim that infection with varroa mites increases a honeybee's susceptibility to secondary infections?

 A. Yes,because the data provide evidence that infection with a pathogen caused the colonies to undergo colony collapse disorder.

 B. Yes,because for each pathogen, the percent of colonies infected is greater for colonies with colony collapse disorder than for colonies without colony collapse disorder.

 C. No,because the data do not provide evidence about bacteria as a cause of colony collapse disorder.

 D. No,because the data do not indicate whether the honeybees had been infected with mites.

答案:D

解析:表格显示了感染病原体的蜂群比例,但是没有任何有关蜂群被螨虫感染的信息。因为没有这些信息,所以也不能得出相关结论。

译文

这篇文章来自于理查德·夏普和丽萨·海顿于 2009 年发表在埃尔斯维尔的科学论文

《蜂群崩坏症候群有可能由蜜蜂食物中菊属类摄入不足而引起》。蜂群崩坏症候群通常表现为成年工蜂大量失踪。

蜜蜂是一种名叫大型致命寄生螨虫的宿主,该螨虫叫作瓦螨(也被称为蜂螨)。瓦螨以蜜蜂的血液为食,它们可以直接置蜜蜂于死地,或者会增加蜜蜂对于二级感染源如真菌、细菌或者各种病毒的易感性,从而致死。怎样才能让蜜蜂建立起对于这种螨虫的天然防护?我们所知甚少。

菊属类植物包含着例如红花除虫菊、白花除虫菊等同系植物。这种植物能产生强有力的杀虫剂,从而起到除螨的作用。这种天然的除虫剂叫作菊酯。这种菊酯在生物学中也被称为除虫菊酯,目前菊酯的合成类似物被叫作拟除虫菊酯。事实上,人体的螨虫感染病疥螨(也叫疥疮)就是用一种热带菊酯霜来治疗的。

我们现在怀疑,人工养殖的蜂群被喂养时食物比较单一,所以营养不均衡,有些营养不良。具体来说,我们假定问题的源头在它们的食物构成中,菊酯以及菊酯类属植物的摄入不足,这部分食物是抵御螨虫侵袭的关键。如果蜂群的食物构成完全没有能产生菊酯的植物,那么蜂群就会因为螨虫侵袭变得抵抗力低下,从而引发各种二级感染,产生致命后果。这种二级感染可能是由一种或者多种病原体引起的各种真菌、细菌和病毒感染。此时,如果养蜂人试图用人工合成的杀虫剂来救急杀螨的话,会让那些已经抵抗力低下或者营养不良的蜜蜂更加虚弱。我们进一步假定,用来预防螨虫的正确菊酯摄入量应该让蜂群自己来决定可能效果更好。蜂群应该根据自己已经摄入的菊酯量来决定它们还需要多少。否则,一旦过度摄入,可能反而会产生毒素。

这个假设可以由一个实验来证明。我们将实验蜂群分为两小拨:一拨在给它们喂养典型的蜜蜂食物比如三叶草的同时,加入能产生菊酯的植物;另一拨只喂养三叶草,然后将蜂螨放入两个蜂巢中,密切记录两个蜂群不同的反应。

事实上,这样的实验最好也能在野生蜂群身上实施。野生蜂群和人工养殖的蜂群有基因上的不同,这些不同可能会使蜜蜂对菊属类植物的偏好产生影响。

2.7　New SAT Official Guide Test 4 解析

2.7.1　Passage Ⅰ

答案解析

1. Over the course of the passage, the narrator's attitude shifts from _____.

A. fear about the expedition to excitement about it

B. doubt about his abilities to confidence in them

C. uncertainty of his motives to recognition of them

D. disdain for the North Pole to appreciation of it

答案:C

解析:见下题。

2. Which choice provides the best evidence for the answer to the previous question?

A. Lines 10～12 ("For ... moment")　　B. Lines 21～25 ("Yet ... will")
C. Lines 42～44 ("And ... stand on")　　D. Lines 56～57 ("What ... myself")

答案：D

解析：第1题问的是全文中作者心态的变化，因此第2题的选项中一定会有转变的元素，我们来看第2题的选项：选项A并没有提到转变，因此排除；选项B中的converted一词对应转变，可以保留；选项C是一句假设，选项D是作者的自白，也都没有转变的元素，因此就可以选到答案C。我们来看选项C中的这个句子：Yet in freely willing this enterprise, in choosing this moment and no other when the south wind will carry me exactly northward at a velocity of eight knots, I have converted the machinery of my fate into the servant of my will. 句中的转变指的是从fate到will，一个是听天由命，另一个是主观意愿，因此对应第1题选项C中的uncertainty和recognition。

3. As used in lines 1～2, "not readily verifiable" most nearly means _____.
　　A. unable to be authenticated　　B. likely to be contradicted
　　C. without empirical support　　D. not completely understood

答案：D

解析：我们回到原文：My emotions are complicated and not readily verifiable. 显然这句话中的not readily verifiable是与complicated同义的，在这里解释为选项D中的not completely understood。选项B是迷惑答案，因为在之后一句提到了pleasure and pain，容易给人contradiction的错觉。但要注意的是pleasure and pain是在句中修饰yearning的，而在之后一句中作者写道yearning是do not understand，因此仍然选择答案D。

4. The sentence in lines 10～13 ("For years ... other") mainly serves to _____.
　　A. expose a side of the narrator that he prefers to keep hidden
　　B. demonstrate that the narrator thinks in a methodical and scientific manner
　　C. show that the narrator feels himself to be influenced by powerful and independent forces
　　D. emphasize the length of time during which the narrator has prepared for his expedition

答案：C

解析：我们来看这个句子：For years, for a lifetime, the machinery of my destiny has worked in secret to prepare for this moment ...这个句子说作者觉得自己的命运一直在暗中为现在这个时刻做准备，因此可以排除选项B，而更多的信息则需要我们在前文中去找这句话的总起句：... that my motives in this undertaking are not entirely clear. 因此我们就可以推断出第一句中的this moment对应的是this undertaking，而this undertaking的动机又是不明确的，对应第一句中的has worked in secret。所以第一句话是指作者觉得自己受到一种内心力量的指引，对应选项C。

5. The narrator indicates that many previous explorers seeking the North Pole have _____.
　　A. perished in the attempt
　　B. made surprising discoveries
　　C. failed to determine its exact location

D. had different motivations than his own

答案：A

解析：见下题。

6. Which choice provides the best evidence for the answer to the previous question?
   A. Lines 20～21 ("Nobody ... died")
   B. Lines 25～27 ("All ... out")
   C. Lines 31～34 ("The ... newspaper")
   D. Lines 51～53 ("Behind ... bedsteads")

答案：A

解析：第 5 题问的是之前的北极探险者的结局，我们来看第 6 题的选项：选项 A 直接就对应结局，因此可以直接选到正确答案。我们来看这个句子：Nobody has succeeded in this thing, and many have died. 句中的 perished 对应选项中的 died，因此第 5 题同样选 A。

7. Which choice best describes the narrator's view of his expedition to the North Pole?
   A. Immoral but inevitable.
   B. Absurd but necessary.
   C. Socially beneficial but misunderstood.
   D. Scientifically important but hazardous.

答案：B

解析：读完全文首尾句我们发现，全文尾句就是作者对于此次考察的态度：Fundamentally I am a dangerous madman, and what I do is both a challenge to my egotism and a surrender to it. 可以看出作者认为这次考察是必要的，因此只有选项 A 和选项 B 对应。而第一段的段尾句说道：In short, it is the same unthinking lust for knowledge that drove our First Parents out of the garden. 作者将这次考察说成是 lust for knowledge，起码没有贬低的意思，因此选项 A 中的 immoral 是不正确的。而 unthinking 则对应选项 B 中的 absurd，由此可以选到正确答案 B。

8. The question the narrator asks in lines 30～31 ("Will it ... railway") most nearly implies that _____.
   A. balloons will never replace other modes of transportation
   B. the North Pole is farther away than the cities usually reached by train
   C. people often travel from one city to another without considering the implications
   D. reaching the North Pole has no foreseeable benefit to humanity

答案：D

解析：我们首先来看这个句子：Will it carry you from Gothenburg to Malmö like a railway？显然，由这句话不能推断出选项 A 和选项 C，因此可以保留选项 B 和选项 D。而在这句话之前还有一个并列句：Can you eat it？这两句话对应的总起句是之前两句：Who wants the North Pole！What good is it！从这两句话我们就可以推断出作者其实是在用是否 edible 和 railway 的例子说明去 North Pole 没什么用处，对应选项 D。

9. As used in line 49,"take the slightest interest in" most nearly means _____.
   A. accept responsibility for
   B. possess little regard for
   C. pay no attention to
   D. have curiosity about

答案：D

解析：我们回到原文：No one but a Swedish madman could take the slightest interest in it. 句中的 a Swedish madman 指的就是作者本人,而作者显然是对去北极有兴趣的,因此可以直接排除其他答案,选到答案 D。

10. As used in line 50, "bearing" most nearly means _____.
A. carrying   B. affecting   C. yielding   D. enduring

答案:A

解析:我们回到原文:The wind is still from the south, bearing us steadily northward at the speed of a trotting dog. 既然是往北极走,那么 bearing 在这里就只能解释为带领,对应选项 A 中的 carrying。

译文

这篇文章节选自 MacDonald Harris 著的《气球师》,2011 年由 The Estate of Donald Heiney 出版。1897 年夏天,故事的叙述者——一位虚构的瑞典科学家踏上氢气球飞往北极。

我的感情很复杂,一时难以理解。我感到一种巨大的渴望,同是快乐和痛苦。我非常确定这个渴望是极致完美的,但是我难以名状,因为我不理解这个渴望想要的是什么。第一次,在我内心生出了一小时前我对医生所说的真相:我做这件事情的目的并不明确。这么多年来,一辈子的时光,我的命运秘密运作,为此刻做好准备;它的发条精确地朝着此时此地移动,慢慢从生我养我的土地上升起,我被无助地载往一个荒无人烟、不宜居住、最多也只能算是冷漠的地方。那个地方布满了探险者的尸骨和船只的残骸、冰冻的物资供应储藏点、冻伤的手指潦草写下的信息以及肉眼无法看到的坟墓。从未有人成功过,有许多人因此而死。但自愿做这件事,选了这一刻,南风以八节的速度把我吹向北方,我已经把自己的命运换成了我意志的仆人。这些我都理解,像我理解这一切得以运作的每个技术细节一样。我不理解的是我为何会想要去那个特定的地方。谁会想要去北极?北极有什么用?能吃吗?能像火车一样把你从哥德堡带到马尔默吗?丹麦大臣在讲台上说,参与极地探险对灵魂的永久健康有益。这大约是我从报纸上读到的信息。这句话也不知该怎么理解,但其中暗示了极地难以到达,甚至不可能到达,但必须被追寻,因为人注定要追求和了解所有事情,尽管这些事情并不一定会给他带来快乐。简而言之,正是这种对知识不假思索的渴求导致亚当、夏娃被逐出了伊甸园。

假设你打算不顾一切去寻找那个每个人都急切想要踏上的美妙之地!你会发现什么?什么也没有。这个地方和围着它绵延好几百英里毫无特色的荒地一模一样。它是一个抽象之地,一个类似数学的虚构之物。只有像我一样的瑞典疯子才会对它有那么一点兴趣。我就在这儿。仍然是南风,以狗跑的速度稳稳地带着我们一路向北。我们身后,也许永远,是人类城市,里面充满茶杯和铜质床架。我在按照自己的意志前行,加入白令及可怜的富兰克林、冻僵的德隆及他手下的鬼魂。我现在明白了,我将要知道的东西不是稍纵即逝的数学点,而是我自己。医生说得对,尽管我讨厌他。从根本上说,我是一个危险的疯子,我做的事情既是自我的挑战也是自我的屈从。

2.7.2 Passage Ⅱ

答案解析

11. Which choice best summarizes the first paragraph of the passage (lines 1~35)?

A. The 2010 census demonstrated a sizable growth in the number of middle-class families moving into inner cities.

B. The 2010 census is not a reliable instrument for measuring population trends in American cities.

C. Population growth and demographic inversion are distinct phenomena, and demographic inversion is evident in many American cities.

D. Population growth in American cities has been increasing since roughly 2000, while suburban populations have decreased.

答案：C

解析：我们先来看第一段的首句：We are not witnessing the abandonment of the suburbs, or a movement of millions of people back to the city all at once. 通过这句话我们可以排除选项 A（并没有提到 inner city）和选项 D（suburban populations have decreased）。而这句话显然还没有说完，说明之后一句才是重点，我们来看第二句：The 2010 census certainly did not turn up evidence of a middle-class stampede to the nation's cities. 这句话只是说普查数据没有反驳中层阶级向城市迁移的证据，并没有说其数据不可信，因此选项 B 也是错误的，保留选项 C。

12. According to the passage, members of which group moved away from central-city areas in large numbers in the early 2000s?

A. The unemployed B. Immigrants
C. Young professionals D. African Americans

答案：D

解析：我们根据选项和题干中的 central-city area 进行定位，看到第 13 行：A closer look at the results shows that the most powerful demographic events of the past decade were the movement of African Americans out of central cities（180,000 of them in Chicago alone）and the settlement of immigrant groups in suburbs, often ones many miles distant from downtown. 因此可以直接对应到选项 D。

13. In line 34, "flat" is closest in meaning to _____.

A. static B. deflated
C. featureless D. obscure

答案：A

解析：我们回到原文：... it can occur in cities that are growing, those whose numbers are flat, and even in those undergoing a modest decline in size. 这句话中 flat 与之前的 growing 和之后的 modest decline 一样，都是修饰 numbers 的。既然有了上升和下降，那么 flat 显然就解释为平稳的、静止的，对应选项 A。

14. According to the passage, which choice best describes the current financial situation in many major American cities?

   A. Expected tax increases due to demand for public works.

   B. Economic hardship due to promises made in past years.

   C. Greater overall prosperity due to an increased inner-city tax base.

   D. Insufficient revenues due to a decrease in manufacturing.

答案:B

解析:见下题。

15. Which choice provides the best evidence for the answer to the previous question?

   A. Lines 36~39 ("America's ... decades")

   B. Lines 43~44 ("How ... not know")

   C. Lines 44~46 ("What ... now")

   D. Lines 48~51 ("The truth ... end")

答案:A

解析:第14题问的是如今大部分美国大城市的金融问题,我们来看第15题的选项:选项A中的fiscal problem与第14题的关键词对应,因此保留;选项B说的是解决这个问题的方法,选项C说的是这个问题的影响,都没有说到底是什么问题,因此排除;选项D完全没有提到美国的主要城市,因此同样排除,选到答案A。我们来看选项A中的这个句子:America's major cities face enormous fiscal problems, many of them the result of public pension obligations they incurred in the more prosperous years of the past two decades. 这句话中的public pension obligations they incurred ... of the past two decades对应第14题选项B中的promises made in past years,因此选B。

16. The passage implies that American cities in 1974 _____.

   A. were witnessing the flight of minority populations to the suburbs

   B. had begun to lose their manufacturing sectors

   C. had a traditional four-zone structure

   D. were already experiencing demographic inversion

答案:C

解析:见下题。

17. Which choice provides the best evidence for the answer to the previous question?

   A. Lines 54~57 ("Much ... Ernest W. Burgess")

   B. Lines 58~59 ("It was ... settlement")

   C. Lines 66~71 ("Virtually ... continuum")

   D. Lines 72~75 ("As ... home")

答案:C

解析:第16题问的是美国城市在1974年的情况,我们来看第17题的选项:选项A提到1925年的情况,因此排除;选项B没有提到过任何年代信息,同样排除;选项C描述的是一个城市的规划情况,而在这一句话之前提到了1975年这一关键词,因此保留;选项D是对这一规划和现象的补充说明,因此同样排除,选到正确答案C。我们一起来看选项C中的这个句子:Virtually every city in the country had a downtown,where the commercial life of the metropolis was conducted; it had a factory district just beyond; it had districts of working-class residences just beyond that; 70 and it had residential suburbs for the wealthy and the upper middle class at the far end of the continuum. 这句话中说到了几乎每一个城市都会有一个 downtown、factory district、districts of working-class residences 和 residential suburbs for the wealthy and the upper middle class,对应第 16 题选项 C 中的 four-zone structure,因此第 16 题选 C。

18. As used in line 68,"conducted" is closest in meaning to _____.
A. carried out　　B. supervised　　C. regulated　　D. inhibited

答案:A

解析:我们回到原文:Virtually every city in the country had a downtown, where the commercial life of the metropolis was conducted … 在这句话中 conducted 对应的是 commercial life,而 commercial life 又对应 downtown。Downtown 显然是进行 commercial life 的地方,而非抑制商业活动的地方,因此可以排除选项 B、C、D,选到正确答案 A。

19. The author of the passage would most likely consider the information in chart 1 to be _____.

A. excellent evidence for the arguments made in the passage

B. possibly accurate but too crude to be truly informative

C. compelling but lacking in historical information

D. representative of a perspective with which the author disagrees

答案:B

解析:我们先来图表 1 的信息,发现这是 2010 年美国人口普查的数据。因此我们根据 2010 census 进行定位,看到作者对此次人口普查的态度:The 2010 census certainly did not turn up evidence of a middle-class stampede to the nation's cities. 这句话说明图表中的信息部分支持作者的观点,因此可以排除选项 D。But when it comes to measuring demographic inversion, raw census numbers are an ineffective blunt instrument. 但之后的这句话则说明该数据还不够细致,其中的 ineffective 对应选项 B 中的 too crude to be truly informative,因此可以选到答案 B。

20. According to chart 2, the years 2000~2010 were characterized by _____.

A. less growth in metropolitan areas of all sizes than had taken place in the 1990s

B. more growth in small metropolitan areas than in large metropolitan areas

C. a significant decline in the population of small metropolitan areas compared to the 1980s

D. roughly equal growth in large metropolitan areas and non-metropolitan areas

答案:A

解析:我们在图表 2 中重点关注 2000~2010 年的信息,发现无论在什么规模的城市,白色的柱状条都比灰色的要短,因此对应选项 A。

21. Chart 2 suggests which of the following about population change in the 1990s?

A. Large numbers of people moved from suburban areas to urban areas in the 1990s.

B. Growth rates fell in smaller metropolitan areas in the 1990s.

C. Large numbers of people moved from metropolitan areas to non-metropolitan areas in the 1990s.

D. The US population as a whole grew more in the 1990s than in the 1980s.

答案:D

解析:我们关注图表2中1990年的信息,通过排除法发现选项A、B、C都与图表中的信息不符合,因此选到答案D。而将1980～1990年这10年间的三条黑色柱状条相加,也的确比1990～2000年这10年间的三条灰色柱状条相加的数值小,因此选项D正确。

译文

这篇文章节选自Alan Ehrenhalt的著作《美国城市的大反转和未来》,2013年由Vintage出版。Ehrenhalt是一个城市学家,是研究城市和城市发展的学者。人口反转的现象描述了都市圈生活模式的重新安排。

我们并没有看到人们离开郊区,或百万人一起回到城市。2010年的人口统计的确表明中产阶级蜂拥进入城市。消息是混杂的:有些东海岸的大城市人口有所增加,却是少量逐步增加。中西部的大城市包括芝加哥,人口有很大流失。整个十年,总人口数量增加的城市都在南部和西南部。但是,若要测量人口反转,粗糙的人口统计数字是无效迟钝的工具。更仔细地看结果,就会发现过去十年中最大的人口事件是非裔美国人离开中心城市(仅芝加哥就有18万人)和移民在郊区定居,通常离市中心很远。这十年初吸引富裕居民的城市中心地区在2007～2009年的萧条时期维持住了人口数量。根据布鲁斯金学会2011年的研究,这些地区并没有郊区那么严重的失业率。在萧条年份,移居新的城市公寓的年轻职业人士并不多,因为几乎没有新建多少住房,但我们也没理由认为房产泡沫破裂之前的主流人口趋势不会在泡沫结束后恢复。需要记住的是,人口反转并不能代表人口增加;它可以出现在人口增加、人口不变甚至人口稍稍减少的城市。

美国的大城市都遇到巨大的财政问题。许多问题都是这些城市在过去繁荣的二十年中招来的公共津贴责任所导致的。有些城市,芝加哥尤其突出,根本没有足够的税收去支持如此级别的公共服务,而大多数城市公民却觉得享受这些服务理所当然。我也不知道这些城市该怎么去解决这个问题。我只知道如果财政危机会把富裕的职业人士逼出中心城市,那这事儿早就应该发生了,但没有证据表明有过此事。

事实上,我们现在生活在这样的时刻,20世纪后半叶富裕人群大量外迁的特点已经不复存在了。我们需要调整对城市、郊区以及由此引起的城市流动性的理解。

不管是否意识到,我们对都市定居过程的看法可以追溯到芝加哥大学社会学家Ernest W. Burgess在1925年发表的一篇文章。Burgess定义了城市和郊区的四个区域:一个中央商务区;一个商务区之外的制造业地区;一个供工业和移民工人居住的地区;最后在外面包围的是以家庭为单位的居住地区。

Burgess对1925年的美国城市描述是对的;他对1974年美国城市的描述也是对的。我们国家几乎每个城市都有一个商业中心,城市的商业活动在那里展开;有一个工厂地区在商业中心外围;再外面还有工人阶级居住地区;最外面是富裕家庭和中上层阶级居住的郊区。随着一个家庭经济水平的提高,这个家庭会慢慢从拥挤的工人居住地向外迁徙到空间更大的公寓,最后搬到郊区的房屋中。

但过去十年,在不少地方,这个模型已经无法描述现实了。商业中心仍然有,但旁边不再有工厂地区,几乎看不到工厂。这些城市内部地区,其居民当年被 Burgess 描述为居住在"贫穷恶化和疾病无处不在的地区",越来越多地成为在商业中心工作的富裕人群的活动区域。正如许多优秀的美国新居民不会定居在内部而是慢慢积累资源往外跑,这些富人从第一天就住在郊区。

2.7.3　Passage Ⅲ

答案解析

22. The primary purpose of the passage is to _____.
A. present the background of a medical breakthrough
B. evaluate the research that led to a scientific discovery
C. summarize the findings of a long-term research project
D. explain the development of a branch of scientific study

答案:A

解析:我们来看段首句和全文尾句:

• When scientists first learned how to edit the genomes of animals, they began to imagine all the ways they could use this new power.

• Many of the proteins that our cells crank out naturally make for good medicine.

• Throughout the 1980s and '90s, studies provided proof of principle, as scientists created transgenic mice, sheep, goats, pigs, cattle, and rabbits that did in fact make therapeutic compounds in their milk.

• To create its special herd of goats, GTC used microinjection, the same technique that produced GloFish and AquAdvantage salmon.

• Over the course of a year, the "milking parlors" on GTC's 300-acre farm in Massachusetts can collect more than a kilogram of medicine from a single animal.

观察以上这些关键句中的画线部分,我们发现全文是按照时间顺序进行写作的,在这一研究的每一阶段都用了同等笔墨进行阐述,因此对应选项 A 中的 background,第一句中的 new power 则对应选项 A 中的 a medical breakthrough,因此选 A。

23. The author's attitude toward pharming is best described as one of _____.
A. apprehension　　B. ambivalence　　C. appreciation　　D. astonishment

答案:C

解析:我们根据题干中的 pharming 进行定位,看到原文第 9 行:Welcome to the world of "pharming," in which simple genetic tweaks turn animals into living pharmaceutical factories. 句中说仅是小小的基因转变就能大量生产医药,是一件好事。而这句话之前作者还用到了 dream 来描述这件事,再次表现了作者欣赏的态度。以及第 70 行,"human medicine"都能看出作者正向的态度,因此选 C。

24. As used in line 20, "expert" most nearly means _____.
A. knowledgeable　　B. professional　　C. capable　　D. trained

答案:C

解析：我们回到原文：Dairy animals, on the other hand, are expert protein producers, their udders swollen with milk. 这句话中的 on the other hand 表明句中的 expert 一定与前一句转折句中的某词对应，因此我们来看前一句：The trouble is that it's difficult and expensive to make these compounds on an industrial scale, and as a result, patients can face shortages of the medicines they need. 这句话说问题在于很难大规模生产。结合第一句，我们可以推断出，dairy animals 能够大规模生产这些 compounds，因此对应选项 C。

25. What does the author suggest about the transgenic studies done in the 1980s and 1990s?

　　A. They were limited by the expensive nature of animal research.

　　B. They were not expected to yield products ready for human use.

　　C. They were completed when an anticoagulant compound was identified.

　　D. They focused only on the molecular properties of cows, goats, and sheep.

答案：B

解析：见下题。

26. Which choice provides the best evidence for the answer to the previous question?

　　A. Lines 16~19 ("The trouble ... need")

　　B. Lines 25~29 ("If they ... milk")

　　C. Lines 35~36 ("At first ... true")

　　D. Lines 37~40 ("That all ... clots")

答案：C

解析：第 25 题问的是 1980~1990 年期间 transgenic studies 的信息，因此我们带着问题来看第 26 题的选项：选项 A 和选项 B 说的都是在 1980 年之前发生的事，因此排除；选项 C 描述的是这一研究最初的形式，可以保留；而选项 D 说的则是 ATryn 的出现改变了这一切，并将重点放在了介绍什么是 ATryn 上，因此并不是最佳答案。所以我们来看选项 C 中的这个句子：At first, this work was merely gee-whiz, scientific geekery, lab-bound thought experiments come true. 这句话的意思是一开始这项研究只不过是实验室里的产物，对应第 25 题选项 B 中的 not expected ... for human use，因此第 25 题选 B，第 26 题选 C。

27. According to the passage, which of the following is true of antithrombin?

　　A. It reduces compounds that lead to blood clots.

　　B. It stems from a genetic mutation that is rare in humans.

　　C. It is a sequence of DNA known as a promoter.

　　D. It occurs naturally in goats' mammary glands.

答案：A

解析：见下题。

28. Which choice provides the best evidence for the answer to the previous question?

　　A. Lines 12~16 ("Many ... more")

　　B. Lines 42~44 ("It acts ... bloodstream")

　　C. Lines 44~46 ("But as ... antithrombin")

　　D. Lines 62~65 ("The researchers ... production")

答案：B

解析: 第 27 题问的是有关于 antithrombin 的信息,我们来看第 28 题的选项:选项 A 完全没有提到这个关键词,因此排除;选项 B 中的 it 指的就是 ATryn,而 ATryn 就是一种 antithrombin,这句话描述了其功能,因此保留;选项 C 说的是美国人的生理情况,因此不是最佳答案;选项 D 同样没有提到 antithrombin,排除。因此我们来看选项 B 中的这个句子:It acts as a molecular bouncer, sidling up to clot-forming compounds and escorting them out of the bloodstream. 这句话说 antithrombin 的作用是去除血管中的结状物,句中的 sidling up 和 escorting them out 对应第 27 题选项 A 中的 reduce,而句中的 clot-forming compounds 则对应选项 A 中的 blood clots,因此第 27 题选 A,第 28 题选 B。

29. Which of the following does the author suggest about the "female goats" mentioned in line 59?

　　A. They secreted antithrombin in their milk after giving birth.

　　B. Some of their kids were not born with the antithrombin gene.

　　C. They were the first animals to receive microinjections.

　　D. Their cells already contained genes usually found in humans.

答案: B

解析: 我们直接根据题干中的行数和关键词 female goats 进行定位,看到原文第 59 行: Then they implanted the eggs in the wombs of female goats. 通过这句话我们可以排除选项 A 和选项 D,更多信息则需要我们继续往下看:When the kids were born, some of them proved to be transgenic, the human gene nestled safely in their cells. 很显然,上两句话中都没有提到这是 the first animals to receive microinjections,因此可以排除选项 C。而这句话中的 some of them 则可以对应选项 B 中的 some of their kids,因此选到正确答案 B。

30. The most likely purpose of the parenthetical information in lines 63~64 is to _____.

　　A. illustrate an abstract concept　　B. describe a new hypothesis

　　C. clarify a claim　　D. define a term

答案: D

解析: 我们直接看到原文第 63 行的这个句子:The researchers paired the antithrombin gene with a promoter (which is a sequence of DNA that controls gene activity) that is normally active in the goat's mammary glands during milk production. 显然,括号内的内容是一个定语从句,用于解释什么是 a promoter,而 promoter 并不是一个 abstract concept,也不是一个 new hypothesis,更不是一个 claim,而是一个名词。因此可以选到答案 D。

31. The phrase "liquid gold" (line 71) most directly suggests that _____.

　　A. GTC has invested a great deal of money in the microinjection technique

　　B. GTC's milking parlors have significantly increased milk production

　　C. transgenic goats will soon be a valuable asset for dairy farmers

　　D. ATryn has proved to be a financially beneficial product for GTC

答案: D

解析: 我们直接看到原文第 71 行:Et voilà—human medicine! And, for GTC, liquid gold. 首先,liquid gold 说明这是稀有的、高回报的,因此可以直接通过选项 A 中的 invested 排除该选项。而这句话中拥有 liquid gold 的对象是 GTC,并不是选项 C 中的 dairy farmers,因此同样排除。我们继续往下看:ATryn hit the market in 2006…既然是 hit the market,就

意味着第一句中的 liquid gold 指的是其金钱上的高回报，而并非 milk 的产量，因此可以选到正确答案 D。

译文

这篇文章改编自 Emily Anthes 的著作《科学怪人的猫》，2013 年由 Emily Anthes 出版。

科学家首次学会如何改变动物基因组的时候，就开始想象它的各种用途。最要紧的肯定不是创造颜色鲜艳、小巧精致的猫。大多数研究者想象的是远比此重要的运用，他们希望能够创造出救人性命的转基因动物。有一家公司就正朝着这个梦想前行。欢迎来到"药耕"的世界，在此世界中简单的基因修改就能使动物变成制药工厂。

人类体内细胞天然产出的许多蛋白质都是上好的药物。我们自身的酶、荷尔蒙、凝固因子以及抗体常被用来治疗癌症、肥胖症、自身免疫性疾病等。麻烦的是，工业化大量制造这些化合物非常困难且价格昂贵，所以病人不得不面临医药短缺。另一方面，产奶动物是职业蛋白质生产者，它们饱满的乳房充满了乳汁。所以，20 世纪 80 年代创造了首只转基因动物——老鼠，然后是其他动物，给了科学家一个这样的想法：如果科学家把人类产生抗体或酶的基因注入奶牛、山羊或者绵羊，会发生什么？如果他们把基因放在正确的位置，使用分子开关控制，也许制造出的动物，其奶汁会包含有治愈作用的人类蛋白质，然后医生就可以一桶一桶地装药了。

20 世纪八九十年代，许多研究证明此原理可行，这期间科学家们制造了转基因老鼠、转基因绵羊、转基因山羊、转基因猪、转基因牛和转基因兔子。这些动物分泌的奶汁的确包含有疗效的化合物。最初，这个工作虽然是一种科学热情，是实验室内的思想实验，但这一切都随着 ATryn 的到来而发生改变。ATryn 是麻省的生物制药公司 GTC 的药物产品，是一种抗凝血酶，能够清理威胁生命的血块。这种化合物由肝制造，保证我们体内处于无血块的状态。它的作用就像一个分子保镖，靠近形成血块的化合物，然后把这些化合物送出血流。但是，2000 个美国人中就有一个因为基因突变而缺乏抗凝血酶。这些病人易患血栓，而且尤其容易发生在腿部和肺部，因此在手术和分娩的时候更容易遭受致命的并发症。补充抗凝血酶能减低风险，所以 GTC 决定用转基因山羊制造这种化合物。

为了制造特种山羊，GTC 使用微注射（荧光鱼和三文鱼就是用此技术制造出来的）。这个公司的科学家把人类体内生产抗凝血酶的基因直接注入山羊的受精卵。然后，他们把受精卵植入母山羊的子宫。等到生出小羊，其中一些是转基因的，那人类的基因就安全地进入了它们的细胞。研究者给每个抗凝血酶基因配上了一个启动子（控制基因活动的一块 DNA）。当山羊产奶时，启动子通常在乳房腺体活动。当转基因山羊分泌奶汁时，启动子启动"转基因"，山羊的乳房便会充满含有抗凝血酶的乳汁。剩下的事儿就是收集乳汁，提取并纯化蛋白质。欢呼吧——这是人类的药品！对 GTC 来说，这是液态黄金。ATryn 在 2006 年上市，是全球首个转基因动物药品。一年的时间，GTC 在麻省 300 公顷的"产奶场"从一个动物身上能够收集超过 1 千克的药。

2.7.4 Passage IV

答案解析

32. In Passage 1, Burke indicates that a contract between a person and society differs from other contracts mainly in its _____.
    A. brevity and prominence B. complexity and rigidity
    C. precision and usefulness D. seriousness and permanence

答案：D

解析：我们通过题干中的 differ 和 other contracts 去定位，看到原文第 17 行：Subordinate contracts for objects of mere occasional interest may be dissolved at pleasure——but the state ought not to be considered as nothing better than a partnership agreement in a trade of pepper and coffee, calico or tobacco, or some other such low concern, to be taken up for a little temporary interest, and to be dissolved by the fancy of the parties. 这句话中的 ought not to be considered as … some other such low concern 对应选项 D 中的 seriousness，而 not … a little temporary interest 则对应选项 D 中的 permanence，因此选到答案 D。

33. As used in line 4, "state" most nearly refers to a _____.
    A. style of living B. position in life
    C. temporary condition D. political entity

答案：D

解析：我们回到原文：… we have consecrated the state, that no man should approach to look into its defects or corruptions but with due caution …我们已经知道这篇文章说的是公民与政府之间的社会契约论，因此 state 在这里对应的就是政府，选到答案 D。

34. As used in line 22, "low" most nearly means _____.
    A. petty B. weak C. inadequate D. depleted

答案：A

解析：我们回到原文：… but the state ought not to be considered as nothing better than a partnership agreement in a trade of pepper and coffee, calico or tobacco, or some other such low concern, to be taken up for a little temporary interest, and to be dissolved by the fancy of the parties. 句中的 low concern 对应的就是 a trade of pepper and coffee, calico or tobacco，指的是相对不重要的。而选项 B、C、D 的含义就不够切合文义了，而选项 A 中的 petty 就是不重要的意思，因此可以选到选项 A。

35. It can most reasonably be inferred from Passage 2 that Paine views historical precedents as _____.
    A. generally helpful to those who want to change society
    B. surprisingly difficult for many people to comprehend
    C. frequently responsible for human progress
    D. largely irrelevant to current political decisions

答案:D

解析:我们可以根据题干中的 historical precedents 进行定位,看到原文第一句:Every age and generation must be as free to act for itself, in all cases, as the ages and generations which preceded it. 句中的 be as free to act for it self 对应选项 D 中的 irrelevant,因此选 D。

36. How would Paine most likely respond to Burke's statement in lines 30~34, Passage 1 ("As the ... born")?

　　A. He would assert that the notion of a partnership across generations is less plausible to people of his era than it was to people in the past.

　　B. He would argue that there are no politically meaningful links between the dead, the living, and the unborn.

　　C. He would question the possibility that significant changes to a political system could be accomplished within a single generation.

　　D. He would point out that we cannot know what judgments the dead would make about contemporary issues.

答案:B

解析:见下题。

37. Which choice provides the best evidence for the answer to the previous question?

　　A. Lines 41~43 ("Every ... it")

　　B. Lines 43~45 ("The vanity ... tyrannies")

　　C. Lines 56~58 ("It is ... accommodated")

　　D. Lines 67~72 ("What ... time")

答案:D

解析:第 36 题问的是 Passage Ⅱ 对于"As the ends of such a partnership cannot be obtained in many generations, it becomes a partnership not only between those who are living, but between those who are living, those who are dead, and those who are to be born...."的看法。这其实是循证题和对比题的结合,而通过阅读原文的首尾句,我们可知 Passage Ⅱ 对 Passage Ⅰ 中的观点是不认可的,因此可以直接把第 36 题中的选项 A、C、D 排除。而这句话中的强调点是 partnership,因此我们带着这种预设来看第 37 题的选项:选项 A、B 和 C 都没有对于 partnership 的描述,排除。选项 D 说这种 partnership 是没有意义的,是对 partnership 的评价,因此是正确答案。我们来看选项 D 中的这个句子:What possible obligation, then, can exist between them; what rule or principle can be laid down, that two nonentities, the one out of existence, and the other not in, and who never can meet in this world, that the one should control the other to the end of time? ...句中的 obligation ... between them 对应选项 B 中的 politically meaningful links,而句中的 the one out of existence、the other not in 和 who never can meet in this world 则对应选项 B 中的 the dead 和 the unborn,因此第 36 题选 B,第 37 题选 D。

38. Which choice best describes how Burke would most likely have reacted to Paine's remarks in the final paragraph of Passage 2?

　　A. With approval, because adapting to new events may enhance existing partnerships.

　　B. With resignation, because changing circumstances are an inevitable aspect of life.

C. With skepticism, because Paine does not substantiate his claim with examples of governments changed for the better.

D. With disapproval, because changing conditions are insufficient justification for changing the form of government.

答案：D

解析：见下题。

39. Which choice provides the best evidence for the answer to the previous question?

A. Lines 1~4 ("To avoid ... state")

B. Lines 7~9 ("he should ... solicitude")

C. Lines 27~29 ("It is ... perfection")

D. Lines 34~38 ("The municipal ... community")

答案：D

解析：这一题同样是循证题和对比题的结合，因此结合两位作者的态度，我们可以直接把第 38 题中的选项 A 和选项 B 排除。我们来看第 39 题的选项：选项 A 和选项 B 并没有对 Paine 论点的直接反驳，因此排除。选项 C 是对这一 partnership 的描述，与观点的联系不大，同样排除。选项 D 中的 not morally at liberty 与 Paine 的观点是明显相悖的，因此是正确答案。我们来看选项 D 中的这个句子：The municipal corporations of that universal kingdom are not morally at liberty at their pleasure, and on their speculations of a contingent improvement, wholly to separate and tear asunder the bands of their subordinate community...句中的 not ... at liberty at their pleasure 对应第 38 题选项 D 中的 disapproval 和 insufficient justification。因此第 38 题和第 39 题都选 D。

40. Which choice best states the relationship between the two passages?

A. Passage 2 challenges the primary argument of Passage 1.

B. Passage 2 advocates an alternative approach to a problem discussed in Passage 1.

C. Passage 2 provides further evidence to support an idea introduced in Passage 1.

D. Passage 2 exemplifies an attitude promoted in Passage 1.

答案：A

解析：我们通过阅读原文首尾句，可知两篇文章的观点是相悖的，因此选项 B、C 和 D 可以直接排除，选到正确答案 A。

41. The main purpose of both passages is to _____.

A. suggest a way to resolve a particular political struggle

B. discuss the relationship between people and their government

C. evaluate the consequences of rapid political change

D. describe the duties that governments have to their citizens

答案：B

解析：我们来阅读两篇文章的首句：Passage Ⅰ—To avoid ... the evils of inconstancy and versatility, ten thousand times worse than those of obstinacy and the blindest prejudice, we have consecrated the state, that no man should approach to look into its defects or corruptions but with due caution ... Passage Ⅱ—Every age and generation must be as free to act for itself, in all cases, as the ages and generations which preceded it. 这两句中重复

出现的关键词 inconstancy/versatility 对应 be as free to act for itself，同时这两篇文章明显是在探讨政府，因此对应选项 B 中的 relationship between people and their government。

译文

文章 1 节选自 Edmund Burke 在 1790 年出版的《反思法国大革命》，文章 2 节选自托马斯潘恩在 1791 年出版的《人权》。

文章 1

为了避免变化多端带来的灾难——这种灾难比顽固和偏见造成的恶果要严重万倍，我们把政府神圣化，阻止任何人鲁莽地对待它的缺陷或腐败；人民没有任何机会通过颠覆的方式发起改革，只能如看待父亲的伤口一般看待政府的缺漏，满怀虔诚地敬畏和揪心地挂念。通过明智的偏好，我们被教导要带着恐惧审视国家的一些孩子。这些孩子几乎是以迅雷不及掩耳之势要将自己年迈的祖国父亲撕成碎片，将他放入一伙巫师的釜里，期望巫师的毒草和诅咒可以更新父亲的血肉，让父亲得以重生。

社会事实上是一部契约。为那些无足轻重之物订立的次等契约可以因个人喜好而被解除，然而社会契约不能等同于与胡椒、咖啡、棉布或烟草商的合作协议，或者其他类似低下的合约——这些合同可以为了一点点暂时性的利益或某方的冲动就被废弃。社会契约应该得到人们满怀崇敬的对待，因为它不是顺从于粗野动物的随时会灰飞烟灭的事宜而达成的合作，而是一项包含了一切科学艺术德性和完美的契约。这一契约关系历经数代人都无法达其目的，所以它并非仅是生者之间的协议，也是在世的、过世的以及尚未降生的人们之间的约定……普天之下的政权机构在道德方面并非随性自由，也不能因为考虑可能的改善，就将其下属社区撕为碎片，让社会契约消失于非社会的、不文明的、分裂而混乱的基础原则中。

文章 2

无论怎样，每代人与前辈一样，都应该有行动的自由。那种死了还想管着别人的虚荣及傲慢是最可笑、最粗野的暴政。

人不能拥有人；一代人同样也不能拥有下一代人。1688 年的人民和议会，或者任何其他时期的人民和议会，都无权处置现今的人，也不能用任何形式约束或控制现今的人；同样，现今的人民和议会也无权处置、约束或控制百年、千年以后的人。

每代人都能也必须能处理那个时代方方面面的要求。活人应该受到关照，而非死人。人死后，权利和欲望也随之消散；既然不再参与当今世界的事物，死去的人也就没有权利任命政府官员，也没有权利控制政府如何组织或运作。

那些死去的人和还未到来的人相距甚远，远到活人无法想象的地步。那么，这些人之间怎么可能会存在责任或义务？两个不存在的个体，一个离去，一个未及，两者之间能有什么规矩和原则？他们永远不能在这个世界相遇，而其中一方要管着另一方到时间的尽头？……

世界一直在变，人的观念也随之改变。既然政府是为了活人，而非死人，那么只有活人才有权利参与政府。在一个年代被认为是对的和方便的东西，在另一个年代可能就是错的和不方便的东西。既然如此，谁才是决策者，活人还是死人？

194

2.7.5 Passage Ⅴ

答案解析

42. The main purpose of the passage is to _____.
A. describe periods in Earth's recent geologic history
B. explain the methods scientists use in radiocarbon analysis
C. describe evidence linking the volcano Samalas to the Little Ice Age
D. explain how volcanic glass forms during volcanic eruptions

答案:C

解析:我们来看全文段首句和尾句:

• About 750 years ago, a powerful volcano erupted somewhere on Earth, kicking off a centuries-long cold snap known as the Little Ice Age.

• That a powerful volcano erupted somewhere in the world, sometime in the Middle Ages, is written in polar ice cores in the form of layers of sulfate deposits and tiny shards of volcanic glass.

• Volcanologist Franck Lavigne and colleagues now think they've identified the volcano in question...

• The team also performed radiocarbon analyses on carbonized tree trunks and branches buried within the pyroclastic deposits to confirm the date of the eruption...

• It's not a total surprise that an Indonesian volcano might be the source of the eruption, Miller says.

• Another possible candidate—both in terms of timing and geographical location—is Ecuador's Quilotoa, estimated to have last erupted between 1147 and 1320 C. E.

• That, they suggest, further strengthens the case that Samalas was responsible for the medieval "year without summer" in 1258 C. E.

文中重复出现的关键词有:volcano、the Little Ice Age、identified (radiocarbon analyses)、the source of the eruption(possible candidate),因此基本上可以推断出这篇文章是说探究火山喷发与 the Little Ice Age 之间的联系,因此选到答案 C。

43. Over the course of the passage, the focus shifts from _____.
A. a criticism of a scientific model to a new theory
B. a description of a recorded event to its likely cause
C. the use of ice core samples to a new method of measuring sulfates
D. the use of radiocarbon dating to an examination of volcanic glass

答案:B

解析:见下题。

44. Which choice provides the best evidence for the answer to the previous question?
A. Lines 17~25 ("In 2012...1455 C. E.")
B. Lines 43~46 ("The researchers...atop the volcano")

C. Lines 46~48 ("They examined ... material")

D. Lines 55~60 ("The team ... 13th century")

答案：A

解析：第43题问的是全文的行文顺序，文章最开始第一句就说，Little Ice Age 是一个 "centuries-long cold snap"，可能是由火山爆发引起的，到了第17~25行，解释了科学家如何使用放射性碳分析，来确定 Little Ice Age 是何时开始以及火山爆发时如何导致空气变冷的，因此第43题选B，第44题选A。

45. The author uses the phrase "is written in" (line 6) most likely to _____.

A. demonstrate the concept of the hands-on nature of the work done by scientists

B. highlight the fact that scientists often write about their discoveries

C. underscore the sense of importance that scientists have regarding their work

D. reinforce the idea that the evidence is there and can be interpreted by scientists

答案：D

解析：我们回到原文，看到这句话之后的总结句：These cores suggest that the amount of sulfur the mystery volcano. 句中的 suggest 对应选项 D 中的 can be interpreted，因此可以选到正确答案 D。

46. Where does the author indicate the medieval volcanic eruption most probably was located?

A. Near the equator, in Indonesia.　　B. In the Arctic region.

C. In the Antarctic region.　　D. Near the equator, in Ecuador.

答案：A

解析：见下题。

47. Which choice provides the best evidence for the answer to the previous question?

A. Lines 1~3 ("About 750 ... Ice Age")

B. Lines 26~28 ("Such a ... the cooling")

C. Lines 49~54 ("The volume ... the Holocene")

D. Lines 61~64 ("It's not ... climate impacts")

答案：D

解析：第46题问的是 medieval volcanic eruption 的位置，我们来看第47题的选项：选项A、B和C中没有位置信息，因此排除，选到答案D。我们来看选项D中的这个句子：It's not a total surprise that an Indonesian volcano might be the source of the eruption, Miller says. "An equatorial eruption is more consistent with the apparent climate impacts."因此我们能很快根据句中的 Indonesian 和 equatorial 选到第46题中的选项 A。

48. As used in line 68, the phrase "Another possible candidate" implies that _____.

A. powerful volcanic eruptions occur frequently

B. the effects of volcanic eruptions can last for centuries

C. scientists know of other volcanoes that erupted during the Middle Ages

D. other volcanoes have calderas that are very large

答案：C

解析：显然，句中的 another possible candidate 之前一定有与其对应的内容，我们看到原文第 61 行：It's not a total surprise that an Indonesian volcano might be the source of the eruption, Miller says. 因此可以选到答案 C。

49. Which choice best supports the claim that Quilotoa was not responsible for the Little Ice Age?

　　A. Lines 3~4 ("Identifying ... tricky")
　　B. Lines 26~28 ("Such a ... cooling")
　　C. Lines 43~46 ("The researchers ... atop the volcano")
　　D. Lines 71~75 ("But ... closer match")

答案： D

解析： 题目问的是支持 Quilotoa 的证据，我们直接来看选项，发现只有选项 D 中的句子提到了 Quilotoa，因此选 D。

50. According to the data in the figure, the greatest below-average temperature variation occurred around what year?

　　A. 1200 CE　　B. 1375 CE　　C. 1675 CE　　D. 1750 CE

答案： C

解析： 我们去图表中找最低点，直接可以对应到答案 C。

51. The passage and the figure are in agreement that the onset of the Little Ice Age began _____.

　　A. around 1150 CE　　　　B. just before 1300 CE
　　C. just before 1500 CE　　D. around 1650 CE

答案： B

解析： 原文告诉我们 the Little Ice Age 的特点是温度下降，因此选到答案 B。

52. What statement is best supported by the data presented in the figure?

　　A. The greatest cooling during the Little Ice Age occurred hundreds of years after the temperature peaks of the Medieval Warm Period.

　　B. The sharp decline in temperature supports the hypothesis of an equatorial volcanic eruption in the Middle Ages.

　　C. Pyroclastic flows from volcanic eruptions continued for hundreds of years after the eruptions had ended.

　　D. Radiocarbon analysis is the best tool scientists have to determine the temperature variations after volcanic eruptions.

答案： A

解析： 我们直接观察选项发现，只有选项 A 是符合图表中规律的，因此选 A。

译文

这篇文章改编自 Carolyn Gramling 的著作《寻找神秘中世纪大爆发的来源》，2013 年由美国科学进步协会出版。

大约 750 年前，在地球某处，一个强大的火山喷发引起了长达一个世纪的冰冷期，这就是家喻户晓的冰河世纪。寻找这座火山实属不易。

极地冰心中的硫酸盐沉淀物层以及微小的火山玻璃碎片中的记录表明，在中世纪某个时候，世界某处发生了强大的火山喷发。这些冰心表明神秘火山喷出的硫黄上升到平流层，其数量之大，使得此次喷发成为全新世（从一万年前到现今的地质时代）最强的气候波动喷发。平流层的硫黄形成的雾霾反射太阳能，造成降温。

2012年，由地质化学家Gifford Miller领导的科学家团队对巴芬岛和冰岛冰盖下的植物残骸做放射性碳年份检测，再加上冰和沉淀物核心的数据，确定了冰冷夏季与冰川增长是在公元1275年和公元1300年间突然发生的（然后在公元1430~1455年间增强）。这加强了神秘火山喷发和小冰河世纪开启的联系。如此突发的启动表明，一个巨大火山爆发喷出硫黄到平流层，开启了制冷。接下来，其他火山异常巨大和频繁的喷发，外加海冰和海洋回馈在大气层中悬浮颗粒被移除很久以后还持续存在，把降温期延续到了18世纪。

火山学家Franck Lavigne和同事们认为他们已经找到了那座神秘火山——印度尼西亚的沙马拉火山。他们注意到，历史记录可以作为一种证据。根据Babad Lombok（Javanese棕榈叶上有关岛屿的记录），沙马拉在13世纪末之前剧烈喷发，摧毁了周围的村落（包括Lombok那时的首府Pamatan），其中的灰尘、大量快速移动的热岩以及喷出的气体统称为火山灰流。

然后，研究者们开始在火山顶部重新构建巨大的800米深的喷火山口（盆地状的火山坑）。他们估计火山的山腰上会有130块岩层凸出，暴露出一排排浮岩——固化成石的灰尘以及其火山灰流材料。沉淀下来的灰尘数量，以及估计有海拔43千米高的喷发烟幕使得这次喷发级别至少是7级（火山喷发指数的范围是0~8级）——这是全新世已知的最大火山喷发。

这个科学团队还对深埋在火山灰流下的碳化树干及树枝做了放射性碳分析，用以确定喷发的日期。他们的结论是，火山喷发不可能在公元1257年之前发生，并且肯定发生在13世纪。

米勒说印度尼西亚的火山会成为喷发的源头并不令人感到惊讶。"赤道处的喷发与明显的环境影响更一致。"不仅如此，他还说，硫黄既出现在北极冰盖，也出现在南极冰盖，这个"强烈一致"支持了喷发源于赤道的观点。

另一个可能的候选火山——既考虑到时机也考虑到地理位置——是厄瓜多尔的基洛多阿火山，估计最后一次喷发在公元1147~1320年之间。但是当Lavigne的团队检测这个火山的玻璃碎片时，他们发现这些玻璃碎片与极地冰心中玻璃的化学组成并不匹配。相比之下，沙马拉火山玻璃更匹配极地冰心的玻璃。因此，他们认为这愈加证实沙马拉才应该为公元1258年，中世纪"没有夏天的那一年"。

第 2 部分　New SAT 语法

第 3 章　New SAT 语法考点总览

3.1　标点符号

3.1.1　核心知识点

3.1.1.1　分号

分号(Semicolon)：a punctuation mark；used chiefly in a coordinating function between major sentence elements（as independent clauses of a compound sentence）。也就是说,分号主要是在句子间起连接作用的,而逗号是不可以连接两个完整的句子的。从功能上来说,分号的功能几乎等同于句号,可以连接两个独立、完整的句子,只不过句号后面跟大写,分号后面跟小写罢了。

例题　Living independently and demonstrating an intense work ethic; the Harvey Girls became known as a transformative force in the American West, inspiring books, documentaries, and even a musical.

A. NO CHANGE　　　B. ethic：　　　C. ethic, and　　　D. ethic,

解析：根据分号用法规则,分号连接的是两个完整的句子,那么原文中的"Living ... ethic"没有谓语动词,只是一个词组,用分号连接前后错误,所以选项 A 错误。选项 C 中"逗号＋and"的作用在功能上相当于"分号",那么同样错误原因也是不对的,冒号的作用主要为解释说明、举例或引用,这里都从句意角度来说不符合,因此选项 B 也是错误的。只有逗号可以连接一个悬垂结构和主句,正确答案为 D。

3.1.1.2　冒号

冒号(Colon)：a punctuation mark；used chiefly to direct attention to matter (as a list, explanation, quotation, or amplification) that follows. 冒号起解释说明的作用。冒号前面一定是完整句子,冒号后面的结构要和被解释的内容保持结构一致。

例题　It took me by surprise, then, when my favorite exhibit at the museum was one of it's tiniest: the Thorne Miniature Rooms.

  A. NO CHANGE B. its tiniest; C. its tiniest: D. it's tiniest,

解析:"it's"是"it is"的缩写,意思是"它是",后面可以接形容词或者名词,"its"的意思是"它的",后面可以接名词。根据题目中"one of"的用法,应该用"its"。根据语意,"the Thorne Miniature Rooms"是在说明"the tiniest"具体为哪一个,符合冒号解释说明的用法,是最常见的考点。

3.1.1.3 破折号

破折号(Dash):a punctuation mark; used to mark divisions within a sentence: in pairs (parenthetical dashes, instead of parentheses or pairs of commas); or singly (perhaps instead of a colon). They may also indicate an abrupt stop or interruption, in reporting direct speech. 单个破折号起解释说明的作用,破折号任意一边是完整的句子;破折号成对出现,破折号里面是插入语,去除插入语后依旧是完整的句子。

例题 1 Chicano art began as an outgrowth of the more general Chicano Civil Rights Movement; a sociopolitical initiative that began in the 1960s to promote social progress and change for Mexican-Americans.

  A. NO CHANGE   B. Movement, which was:
  C. Movement—   D. Movement

解析:这道题目中," sociopolitical initiative that began in the 1960s to promote social progress and change for Mexican-Americans"部分不是一个完整句子,缺少谓语动词,所以选项 A 错误。选项 B 的"was"后应直接接表语,不需要用冒号。根据句意,"Movement"之后的内容在具体解释 Chicano Civil Rights Movement 的含义,符合破折号解释说明的功能,所以这道题应该选 C。

例题 2 Because she maintains an objective tone for most of the book, the final chapter of Translated Woman offers a personal reflection on Behar's struggle to define her own cultural identity, influenced by Latin America, her birthplace— and the United States.

  A. NO CHANGE   B. Latin America—her birthplace—
  C. Latin America—her birthplace   D. Latin America; her birthplace,

解析:题目中的"her birthplace"和"the United States"两部分皆不是完整句子,所以选项 D 中的分号错误。选项 C 中的"her birthplace"与"the United States"通过 and 进行了连接,接在"Latin America"之后,根据句意与常识,"the United States"不属于"Latin America",并且"birthplace"与"the United States"不构成语义上的平行关系。成对的破折号与成对的逗号在语法功能上是一致的,但是不能混用。根据句意,"her birthplace"是对"Latin America"的解释说明,符合破折号的插入语使用,所以选择 B。

3.1.1.4 逗号

逗号(Comma):is a punctuation mark; is used in many contexts and languages, mainly for separating parts of a sentence such as clauses, and items in lists, particularly when there are three or more items listed.

1. 逗号不能连接两个独立、完整的句子

例题 In a polar covalent bond, the two bonding electrons are shared unequally, in an ionic bond: both electrons are completely transferred to the more electronegative atom.

A. NO CHANGE
B. unequally; in the latter,
C. unequally, in the latter
D. unequally in the latter

解析：在这道题中，in an ionic bond 本身作为介词短语，放在句子结尾处，与前面的整句句子不需要用逗号隔开，并且后半句"both electrons are completely transferred to the more electronegative atom"与 in the bond 之间也不构成解释关系，不需要用冒号，所以选项 A 错误。后半句"both electrons are completely transferred to the more electronegative atom"中的主语是 electrons，谓语是 are transferred，是一个独立、完整的句子，不能用逗号连接，也不能不用手段连接，所以选项 C 和选项 D 错误。分号可以连接两个独立、完整的句子，所以答案选择 B。

2. 平性原则

（1）两者平行

A and B：语法功能相同、平行并列的词或词组，用 and 连接，如 man and woman；sing and dance 等。

Adj 1，Adj 2：形容词平行，可以直接用逗号，也可以用 and 连接，如 a beautiful, elegant lady 或者也可以是 a beautiful and elegant lady。

句子 1，and 句子 2：连接各自语法结构完整的句子，其他连词有 for，and，nor，but，or，yet，so 等。

例题 1 In order to provide useful information to consumers, DTC tests need to be both accurate and reliable.

A. NO CHANGE   B. be reliable   C. to be reliable   D. need reliability

解析：这道题考察形容词的两者平行，在"both ... and ..."的结构中，所用单词的词性必须一致，"accurate"直接用了形容词的形式，所以"reliable"也应该直接用形容词的形式，答案选择 A。

例题 2 At that time, chopsticks—which were then called "Zhu"—were used for cooking rather than to eat.

A. NO CHANGE
B. the purpose of eating
C. when one eat
D. eating

解析：这道题中的"rather ... than"结构也是平行结构的一种特殊应用，"rather"之前的"cooking"意味着之后所接的词也得是 doing 结构，所以答案选择 D。

例题 3 This lower third attaches to the stomach—a hollow, muscular organ—which then digests food both by crushing it mechanically and secretes digestive enzymes and other fluids that break down starches and proteins.

A. NO CHANGE   B. to secrete   C. will secrete   D. by secreting

解析：这道题依旧考察"both ... and ..."的结构，"both"后所接为"by crushing"结构，所以"and"之后也应该为"doing"结构，所以选"by secreting"，选项 D。

（2）三者平行

A，B(,) and C：语法功能相同、平行并列的词或词组，用 and 连接，and 之前的逗号可有可无。

句子1;句子2;(and) 句子3:句子的三者平行需要用分号连接。

例题 1 Johnson's <u>persistence knowledge and a happy accident</u> paved the way for his success as an independent inventor.

 A. NO CHANGE

 B. persistence knowledge, and a happy accident

 C. persistence, knowledge, and a happy accident

 D. persistence, knowledge, and a happy accident,

解析:这道题目中"persistence""knowledge"和"a happy accident"为平行的三个名词,所以符合"Noun1, Noun 2, and Noun 2"的结构,选项 C 正确。选项 D 的错误在于前面三者作为主语,与后面的谓语动词"paved"之间不需要用逗号隔开。

例题 2 It is a quantitative discipline built on probability, statistics, and research <u>methods, a method of causal reasoning based on developing and testing hypotheses, and</u> a tool to promote and protect the health of public.

 A. NO CHANGE

 B. methods; a method of causal reasoning based on developing and testing hypotheses; and

 C. methods, a method of causal reasoning based on developing and testing hypotheses; and

 D. methods; a method of causal reasoning based on developing and testing hypotheses, and

解析:这道题目除了考察标点之外,还考察了省略结构,还原原句本身是三个句子:"It is a quantitative discipline built on probability, statistics, and research methods.""(It is) a method of causal reasoning based on developing and testing hypotheses."以及"(It is) a tool to promote and protect the health of public."因为是句子之间的平行关系,所以应该用分号连接,所以答案选择 B。

3. 状语与逗号

当 when、while 引导的时间状语从句和 although 引导的让步状语从句位于主句之前,与主句之间用逗号隔开。

从句位于句中或位于主句之后,一般不加逗号。

例题 1 <u>Because</u> she maintains an objective tone for most of the book, the final chapter of Translated Woman offers a personal reflection on Behar's struggle to define her own cultural identity, influenced by Latin America—her birthplace—and the United States.

 A. NO CHANGE B. When C. If D. Although

解析:此题中的"she maintains an objective tone for most of the book"是整个句子的从句部分,所以与主句"the final chapter of Translated Woman offers a personal reflection on Behar's struggle to define her own cultural identity, influenced by Latin America—her birthplace—and the United States"之间用了逗号连接。根据从句中提到的"maintains an objective tone"与主句中的"offers a personal reflection"这两个词中的"objective"与"personal",可以看出主句与从句之间是转折关系,所以答案选择 D。

例题 2 Since they are based in the hospital hospitalists can also check-up on each patient multiple times a day, and they can coordinate care from specialists and ancillary departments such as the physical and occupational therapy, social services and nursing care management.

  A. NO CHANGE   B. hospital,   C. hospital；   D. hospital：

解析：这道题是"they are based in the hospital"在"Since"的引领下作为原因状语从句，放在主句之前，主句与从句之间应该用逗号隔开，所以答案选择 B。

4. 插入语与逗号

成对出现的逗号与成对出现的破折号一样，逗号中间的也是插入语。注意，不能和省略了 which 或 that 的限定性定语从句之间发生混淆。如：

The book, I think, is interesting.

这一句中，I think 作为插入语，用成对的逗号隔开。原句可改为 I think the book is interesting.

The book I read is interesting.

这一句中，省略了 which 或 that，原句应为 The book (which/that) I read is interesting. 即限制性定语从句和先行词之间不加逗号。

同位语与逗号的考察也遵循上述原则，所以这里合并在一起讲解。

例题 1 The person chosen for this task, digital artist, Eldar Zakirov painted the cats in the style traditionally used by portrait artists, in so doing presenting the cats as noble individuals worthy of respect.

  A. NO CHANGE   B. task, digital artist, Eldar Zakirov,

  C. task digital artist Eldar Zakirov,   D. task, digital artist Eldar Zakirov,

解析：在这题中，主语是"The person chosen for this task"，谓语动词是"painted"，插入语部分是 digital artist Eldar Zakirov，进一步解释说明了"The person"到底是谁，所以应该用成对逗号隔开，所以答案选择 D。

例题 2 The man she married Leo Tolstoy was one of the world's greatest writers.

  A. NO CHANGE   B. married Leo Tolstoy, was

  C. married, Leo Tolstoy was   D. married, Leo Tolstoy, was

解析：这道题目中，"Leo Tolstoy"是"the man"具体的名字，作为其同位语，应该用成对逗号与句子其他成分隔开，所以答案选择 D。

5. 非谓语与逗号

(1) 动词不定式与逗号

形式 1：S①V②O③, doing（注意：doing 的发出者是整句句子的主语）。

形式 2：SVO doing（注意：doing 的发出者是前面修饰的名词）。

例题 In addition to working on the frontlines of the Union Army from 1863 to 1865, Walker was also a Union spy. Who relayed Confederate secrets across enemy lines while

---

① 表示 Subject，主语的意思，以下同。

② 表示 Verb，谓语动词的意思，以下同。

③ 表示 Object，宾语的意思，以下同。

treating civilians in the South.

  A. NO CHANGE   B. spy, Walker relayed

  C. spy, relaying   D. spy. Relaying

  解析：这道题目中，"relayed"修饰对象是"Walker"，呈主动关系，所以在使用非谓语的情况下应该为 doing 结构。选项 A 的错误在于 who 引导从句，不能单独以句子的形式出现。选项 B 的错误在于"Walker"出现后，"relayed"作为谓语动词，前后构成了两个句子，但逗号不能连接两个句子。选项 D 的错误在于 doing 结构不是一个完整句子，不能单独成句。所以答案选择 C，"relaying"修饰的是整个句子的主语"Walker"。

  （2）过去分词与逗号

  形式1：S, done..., VO（注意：done 与主句没有因果关系，加逗号）。

  如：Another, made of glass, looks like our old house.

  形式2：S done VO（注意：done 与主句有因果关系，不加逗号）。

  如：Coins created during WWII reflected the changes during the war.

  例题 Dotted with pin-sized knobs, another visitor noticed my fascination with a tiny writing desk and its drawers.

  A. NO CHANGE

  B. Another visitor, dotted with pin-sized knobs, noticed my fascination with a tiny writing desk and its drawers.

  C. Another visitor dotted with pin-sized knobs noticed my fascination with a tiny writing desk and its drawers.

  D. Another visitor noticed my fascination with a tiny writing desk and its drawers, dotted with pin-sized knobs

  解析：选项 A 中分词成分放在句首作为悬挂结构变成了"visitor"被"dotted with pin-sized knobs"，主被动出现错误；其次，这里"dotted with pin-sized knobs"应该是修饰的 drawers。选项 B 中"dotted with pin-sized knobs"也修饰了"Another visitor"，同样的道理，选项 C 的错误也是如此。又因为"dotted with pin-sized knobs"与"drawer"之间不存在因果关系，可以用逗号隔开，所以答案选择 D。

  6. 定语从句与逗号

  限定性定语从句与主句之间不用逗号隔开，表示从句对先行词起到限定对象的作用，关系紧密；非限定性定语从句与主句之间用逗号隔开，表示从句对先行词（有可能是整个句子）起到补充说明的作用，关系不紧密。

  例题 Last year, one of our school's exchange students was Ligia Antolinez, who came from Bucaramanga, Colombia.

  A. NO CHANGE   B. Antolinez; who

  C. Antolinez. Who   D. Antolinez—who

  解析：这道题是由 who 引导的定语从句修饰"Ligia Antolinez"，选项 B 的错误在于主句和从句之间不能用分号连接，从句需依附主句出现，不是一个独立的句子。选项 C 的错误同选项 B，主句与从句之间不能用句号连接。因为"who came from Bucaramanga, Colombia"与主句的信息之间为互相补充的关系，是非限定性定语从句，用逗号与主句隔开，所以选项 A 正确，选项 D 错误。

7. 不加逗号的情况

注意 1：oneself 与主语之间不加逗号。

注意 2：SVO 结构之间不能只有一个逗号。

注意 3：固定搭配不能加逗号。

注意 4：that 前面不能加逗号。

注意 5：介词词组和形容词修饰名词时不能加逗号。

3.1.1.5 其他标点

1. 括号

括号（Parentheses）：a punctuation mark; contain material that serves to clarify (in the manner of a gloss) or is aside from the main point. 括号主要起补充说明的作用，括号里的内容主要是对前面提到的信息的补充，或者是前面提到信息的例外。通常括号与前面的修饰对象之间不用逗号隔开。

例题　At the beginning of the 1930s, San Francisco along with the rest of the country was reeling from the effects of the Great Depression.

A. NO CHANGE

B. San Francisco, along with the rest of the country

C. San Francisco,（along with the rest of the country），

D. San Francisco（along with the rest of the country）

解析：选项 B 中的"along with the rest of the country"是介词短语，与"San Francisco"之间不需要用逗号隔开，错误。选项 C 中的括号与逗号不能共存，错误。选项 A 是根据上下文的语境，上下文主要想对"San Francisco"进行描述，所以"along with the rest of the country"应该作为补充信息出现，错误。这道题除了可以使用选项 D 的这种方法外，还可以使用成对逗号或者成对破折号，"along with the rest of the country"作为插入语的方法。

2. 引号

引号（Quotation Mark）：punctuation marks; used in pairs in various writing systems to set off direct speech, a quotation, or a phrase. 引号主要起引用或特殊含义的作用，在 SAT 中的考察频率偏低。但为了知识体系的完整性，这里简单进行说明。特别注意一点，句末句号、逗号等标点与引号同时使用，需写在引号里面。如：

"A name with a story behind it," he said at last, "which were circumstances otherwise I would be pleased to hear. But I would like to speak to you, Smith, about your son."

3.1.2　例题分析

例题 1&2　But Jason(1) Box, an associate professor of geology at Ohio State believes that another factor added to the early (2) thaw; the "dark snow" problem. （OG 第一套第 15、16 题）

(1) A. NO CHANGE

B. Box an associate professor of geology at Ohio State,

C. Box, an associate professor of geology at Ohio State,

D. Box, an associate professor of geology, at Ohio State

(2) A. NO CHANGE

B. thaw; and it was

C. thaw:

D. thaw; being

答案：(1) C；(2) C

解析：(1) 考点 4。an associate professor of geology at Ohio State 是对 Jason Box 这个人身份的介绍，应该跟在主语 Jason Box 后面，作为同位语，前后都需要添加逗号，而 believe 则是作为这整个句子的谓语动词。

(2) 考点 1。the dark show problem 解释说明了前面的 another factor added to the early thaw，因此根据上述逻辑关系，两者之间应该用冒号连接，以引出这另外一个因素具体是什么。如果用选项 A 或选项 B 中的分号则表示 problem 与 factor 之间是相互关联的两件事，不符合原文语意。选项 D 中的 being 表示"正在……"的意思，与原文语意不符。

例题 3 A recent study by two professors at the University of California, Santa Cruz, Chris Wilmers and James Estes, suggests, that kelp forests protected by sea otters can absorb as much as twelve times the amount of carbon dioxide from the atmosphere as those where sea urchins are allowed to devour the kelp.（OG 第二套第 27 题）

A. NO CHANGE
B. suggests—that
C. suggests, "that"
D. suggests that

答案：D

解析：考点四。suggest 为这个句子中的谓语动词，该句由 that…引导了宾语从句，谓语与宾语之间不需要任何标点符号。选项 A、选项 C 中的","和选项 B 的"—"多余。因此只有选项 D 正确。

例题 4 Proponents of organic food, of course, are quick to add that there are numerous other reasons to buy organic food, such as, a desire to protect the environment from potentially damaging pesticides or a preference for the taste of organically grown foods.（OG 第四套第 22 题）

A. NO CHANGE
B. food such as:
C. food such as,
D. food, such as

答案：D

解析：考点四。在举例说明的结构中，such as 前需要逗号与前面的句子进行分隔。但是在 such as 的后面不需要任何的标点符号。因此选项 A、B、C 都为错误选项。选项 D 为正确答案。

3.1.3 更多练习

(1) The tallest species of palm tree on the island, Tahina spectabilis, reaches heights of over 60 feet.（可汗 *An Unusual Island* 第 7 题）

A. NO CHANGE
B. island Tahina spectabilis,
C. island, Tahina spectabilis
D. island Tahina spectabilis

(2) According to a survey analysis, veterans returning to the University of Illinois had one "predominating request": an efficient course of study to prepare for a job. (可汗 *GI Bill: A Real American Hero* 第 6 题)

  A. NO CHANGE
  B. one,"predominating request":
  C. one,"predominating request";
  D. one "predominating request";

(3) The Founding Father spent the last years of his life not in government but instead pursuing one of his most treasured missions, it was creating the University of Virginia. (可汗 *Thomas Jefferson, Academic Visionary* 第 1 题)

  A. NO CHANGE
  B. missions. The creation of
  C. missions, he created
  D. missions: the creation of

(4) As of 2014, twenty-five states and five Canadian provinces have confirmed cases of WNS; the affected region now reaches as far west as the Missouri-Kansas border. (可汗 *The Battle Against White-Nose Syndrome* 第 2 题)

  A. NO CHANGE
  B. WNS, the affected region now reaches,
  C. WNS: the affected region now reaches,
  D. WNS, the affected region, now reaches

(5) This excessive activity results in the depletion of vital fat stores leading to life-threatening emaciation. (可汗 *The Battle Against White-Nose Syndrome* 第 5 题)

  A. NO CHANGE   B. stores;
  C. stores-   D. stores,

(6) While it is unlikely that affected species will recover quickly (due to their slow reproductive rates bats have one offspring, or pup, annually). Several resistance to the destructive powers of WNS. (可汗 *The Battle Against White-Nose Syndrome* 第 9 题)

  A. NO CHANGE   B. annually); and several
  C. annually), several   D. annually) and several

(7) Their work in Bangladesh involves removing toxins, from the drinking water, primarily through water purification. (可汗 *Chemists for Clean Water* 第 3 题)

  A. NO CHANGE
  B. Bangladesh, involves removing toxins, from the drinking water
  C. Bangladesh, involves removing toxins from the drinking water,
  D. Bangladesh involves removing toxins from the drinking water,

(8) While some volunteers are concerned citizens who want to assist with public education campaigns. Others hold actual chemistry training. (可汗 *Chemists for Clean Water* 第 7 题)

  A. NO CHANGE

B. campaigns, others hold

C. campaigns; others hold

D. campaigns, others holding

(9) Statements without predictive power are static because, they cannot be disproved, we cannot move forwards. （可汗 *False or False*：*The Question of Falsifiability* 第 9 题）

    A. NO CHANGE   B. static：because

    C. static because—   D. static, because,

(10) Disappointed that Venezuela did not have its own orchestra—Abreu wanted to educate children about classical music on the national level. （可汗 *El Sistema*：*Venezuela's Revolutionary Music Education* 第 2 题）

    A. NO CHANGE   B. orchestra, Abreu

    C. orchestra；Abreu   D. orchestra：Abreu

解析：(1) A。考点 4。Tahina spectabilis 作为插入部分，前后都需要用逗号进行分隔，具体解释了前面出现的 the tallest species of palm tree on the island。

(2) A。考点 2。one "predominating request" 中间无须出现任何标点符号打破原有的连贯，request 后 an efficient course of study to prepare for a job 作为对前者的解释说明，前后两者之间用冒号引出说明。

(3) D。考点 2。选项 A 和 C 中，逗号错误地连接了两个句子。the creation of the University of Virginia 是作为 one of his most treasured missions 的解释说明，两者之间应该用冒号进行连接。

(4) A。考点 1。"twenty-five states and five Canadian provinces have confirmed cases of WNS"和"the affected region now reaches as far west as the Missouri-Kansas border."是结构上各自独立的两个句子，并且内容上相互存在关联。根据上述情况，连接两个独立的句子，应该用分号，所以答案选择 A。

(5) D。考点 4。句中"... the depletion of vital fat stores, leading to life-threatening emaciation."也就等同于 "... the depletion of vital fat stores, which leads to life-threatening emaciation."，这里的 leading to...作为非谓语成分，应该与主句之间用逗号隔开，stores 后面逗号不能省略或换作其他标点符号。

(6) C。考点 4。while 后为从句，"several resistance ..."后面为主句，并且从句位于句首，从句与主句之间需要用逗号连接。

(7) D。考点 4。在 remove ... from ...这个结构中，from 前面不需要任何标点符号，所以选项 A 和选项 B 错误。Their work in Bangladesh 是该句的主语，involve 是谓语。主谓之间不需要任何标点符号，因此 C 错误。

(8) B。考点 4。while 后跟从句部分，others 引导主句部分，从句与主句之间用逗号连接。

(9) B。考点 3。选项 A，逗号错误地连接了两个句子"they cannot be disproved"和"we cannot move forwards"。选项 B 中冒号引出后面解释说明的内容。because 引导原因状语从句，"we ..."为主句。从句与主句之间用逗号连接。

(10) B。考点 4。句首 disappointed 是-ed 形式的过去分词做非谓语用法，Abreu 作为整个句子动作的发出者，也是"Abreu wanted to educate children about classical music

on the national level."这个句子的主语,Abreu 前面应该用逗号与之前的非谓语结构分隔开。

3.2 词汇

3.2.1 核心知识点

考点介绍

词汇题的考评形式主要分为两种,即近义词与形似词。New SAT 语法部分通常要求学生具备这两类情况,即近义词与形似词的辨析能力。学生在理解词义的基础上,更需要结合原文的句意语境,将单词还原到句子中,并掌握该词如何在句中正确恰当使用的方法。

核心考点

考点 1,近义词的词义辨析。

考点 2,使用可数名词,涉及一个单、复数的问题。在 SAT 语法中常见的考点有:名词与相应名词间数的一致 。

考点 3,词性辨析。

3.2.2 例题分析

例题 1 Given these solutions as well as the many health benefits of the food, the advantages of Greek yogurt <u>outdo</u> the potential drawbacks of its production. (OG 第一套第 1 题)

A. NO CHANGE B. defeat C. outperform D. outweigh

答案:D

解析:考点 1。本题考查近义词辨析,因此要把四个选项代入文中,结合语意,意思最贴切的一项就是正确答案,选项 B 表示"击败、战胜",选项 C 表示"胜过、做得好",选项 D 表示"比……有价值、超过",outweigh 多用于表达利大于弊,而原文中的 outdo 多用于人做某事超过其他人。因此将选项 D 代入,原文可翻译成:希腊酸奶优点是大于它的产品的潜在缺点。

例题 2 Also, because it is more concentrated, Greek yogurt contains slightly more protein per serving, thereby helping people stay <u>satiated</u> for longer periods of time. (OG 第一套第 10 题)

A. NO CHANGE B. fulfilled C. complacent D. sufficient

答案:A

解析:考点 1。本题考查近义词的词义辨析。只有原文中的 satiate 可以表达希腊酸奶在长时间满足饥饿。选项 B fulfill 是指在精神上的满足,不能形容满足人的饥饿状态;选项 C 表示"自满、得意";选项 D 表示"足够、充足";原文意思是希腊酸奶帮助人们在更长时间段的饥饿中保持饱腹感。

例题 3 In recent years, public libraries in the United States have experienced reducing in their operating funds due to cuts imposed at the federal, state, and local government levels. （OG 第二套第 1 题）

    A. NO CHANGE   B. reductions   C. deducting   D. deducts

答案：B

解析：考点 3。本题考查词性辨析。三个选项都是减少的意思，但根据语法规则，此处需一个名词做 experience 的宾语，因此四个选项中只有选项 B 符合，选项 C 是现在分词，选项 D 是动词。

例题 4 A recent study by two professors at the University of California, Santa Cruz, Chris Wilmers and James Estes, suggests, that kelp forests protected by sea otters can absorb as much as twelve times the amount of carbon dioxide from the atmosphere as those where sea urchins are allowed to devour the kelp. （OG 第二套第 28 题）

    A. NO CHANGE   B. dispatch   C. overindulge on   D. dispose of

答案：A

解析：考点 1。本题考查词义辨析。选项 B 表示"派遣"，选项 C 表示"溺爱"，选项 D 表示"处置、安排"。而原文的意思是被水獭保护的海藻森林可以吸收 12 倍多的来自空气中的二氧化碳，空气中海胆会吞噬海藻。这一题题目与文中第一段"海胆狼吞虎咽地吸收海藻"相互呼应。

3.2.3 更多练习

（1）CWB staff members create and give arsenic testing kits to Bangladeshi locals and work with interpreters to dissipation information and instructions. （可汗 *Chemists for Clean Water* 第 4 题）

    A. NO CHANGE   B. disseminate   C. proliferate   D. propagate

答案：B

解析：disseminate 表示"散布，传播"；proliferate 表示"激增、增殖"；propagate 表示"宣传"。原文 dissipation 是名词，此处是不定式短语，需要从此来完成句子成分；根据原文意思为"传播信息和指令"，可以排除选项 C。disseminate 指传播信息，而 propagate 指传播信念和观点。因此选项 B 最贴切。

（2）What is the difference between science and pseudoscience? According to Karl Popper, one of the most potent philosophers of the twentieth century, it is a matter of falsifiability. （可汗 *False or False: The Question of Falsifiability* 第 1 题）

    A. NO CHANGE   B. pervasive   C. saturating   D. influential

答案：D

解析：原文 potent 指"强大的（武器、论据）"，并不能形容人；只有选项 D influential 表示"有影响力的"，可以形容人，在原文中的意思是：20 世纪有影响力的哲学家。其他选项，saturating 表示"浸透的，湿透的"；pervasive 表示"弥漫的，普遍的"。

（3）A 150-plus wedding party, a business conference, and a family reunion have all plummeted on the hotel grounds in the same weekend. （可汗 *The Business of Hospitality*

第2题)

  A. NO CHANGE   B. submerged   C. lowered   D. descended

答案:D

解析:plummet 表示"(价格)下降";submerge 表示"浸没,掩盖";lower 表示"更低";descend 表示"下降";descend on 表示"蜂拥而至";原文意思是:150-plus 婚礼派对,一个商业会议,一个家庭聚会,使所有人在同一个周末都蜂拥而至。因此选项 D 符合文义。

(4) Women continued to push for expanded job opportunities, entry into professional roles, and greater access to higher education.(可汗 A *"Rosie" Turn on American Labor* 第10题)

  A. NO CHANGE   B. inflated   C. amplified   D. prolonged

答案:A

解析:考点1,词义辨析。根据原文意思:女人持续努力追求拓展的工作机会,去进入职场角色,并寻找更强的获得高等教育的途径。而其他选项,inflate 表示"(空气)膨胀";amplify 表示"(电力,声音,概念)增强"。显然,此处不需要改变。

(5) The basic principle of Mendeleev's periodic order of elements have remained the same, even as it has grown in size.(可汗 *A Work in Progress: The Periodic Table* 第3题)

  A. NO CHANGE   B. principles   C. principals   D. principal

答案:B

解析:考点1和考点2,名词辨析及单复数考查。principle 表示"原则,(行为)准则";principal 表示"最重要的,校长,主角"。原文意思是:Mendeleev 周期规则的元素的基本原则仍然保持一样。依据文义,此处需要 principle 复数。因此,选项 B 正确。

(6) Truman marketed himself as attainable—making himself available to discuss local political issues with the residents of the small towns he visited.(可汗 *Truman's Winning Whistle-Stop Tour* 第9题)

  A. NO CHANGE   B. plausible   C. approachable   D. palatable

答案:C

解析:plausible 表示"(道理)貌似合理的,(语言)花言巧语的";approachable 表示"可接近的,和蔼可亲的";palatable 表示"(味道)可接受的";attainable 表示"(知识,快乐,荣誉)可获得的",而文中的意思是 Truman 把自己当成和蔼可亲的人。选项 C 最符合文义。

(7) Abreu also believed that the opportunity to play music is a basic human right, and he wanted to reinsure that all children had access to it.(可汗 *El Sistema: Venezuela's Revolutionary Music Education* 第2题)

  A. NO CHANGE   B. ensure   C. assure   D. reassure

答案:B

解析:考点1,近义词辨析。reinsure 表示"再保险,分保";ensure 表示"保证,确保",用法是 ensure that 从句;assure 表示"向……保证",用法是 ensure sb. of sth. /that 从句;reassure 表示"使某人安心",用法是 reassure sb. about/that 从句;根据原文句意:Abreu 也相信演奏音乐的机会是一项基本的人权,他想确保所有的孩子都有演奏音乐的权利。结合文义和用法,此处选项 B 最贴切。

(8) It produced a bizarre-looking shoot that resembled a pine tree with each branch

bearing hundreds of bunches of tiny white flowers. To date, only about three dozen of these durable trees are known to exist in the wild.

Which choice is most consistent with the characterization of the trees throughout the paragraph?（可汗 *An Unusual Island* 第 8 题）

  A. NO CHANGE B. plentiful C. intriguing D. beneficial

答案：C

解析：plentiful 表示"丰富的，多的"；intriguing 表示"有趣的，迷人的"；beneficial 表示"有利的，有益的"；根据上文中描述，"It produced a bizarre-looking shoot that resembled a pine tree with each branch bearing hundreds of bunches of tiny white flowers."这些树样子奇特、有趣。因此，选项 C 符合。

（9）Her work reflected this exposition, as she sought to capture what she termed the "natural" art of African Americans through speech song and folklore.（可汗 *Resurrecting Zora* 第五题）

  A. NO CHANGE B. disposition C. deposition D. composition

答案：B

解析：exposition 表示"展示、展览，解释"；disposition 表示"性格，性情"；deposition 表示"沉积物、沉淀物，存款、订金"；composition 表示"作文，曲子，组成"。根据原文意思：她的工作反映了她的性格。因此答案选 B。

（10）Two of the movement's rulers, authors Langston Hughes and Richard Wright, saw Hurston's work as a harmful caricature of African American life and even accused Hurston of creating new stereotypes that were no better than the old.（可汗 *Resurrecting Zora* 第 8 题）

  A. NO CHANGE B. luminaries C. moguls D. tycoons

答案：B

解析：考点 1，近义词的词义辨析。原文中 rulers 表示"统治者，支配者"，而 Langston Hughes and Richard Wright 是两位杰出的作者，luminaries 表示"杰出者"，因此选项 B 正确。其他选项的意思分别是：moguls 表示"有权势者"，tycoons 表示"企业巨头"。

3.3 主谓一致

3.3.1 核心知识点

考点介绍

  主谓一致的原则是指主语和谓语在单复数的形式上保持统一：主语是单数形式，谓语也采取单数形式；主语是复数形式，谓语亦采取复数形式。

核心考点

考点1：S+长串修饰+V①，即有比较复杂的定语，甚至是定语从句，所以需要先分清句子主干。

考点2：N_1 of N_2，谓语取决于 $N_1$②。

考点3：主语为 N_1 和 N_2 的并列，并列主语的谓语应该用复数。

考点4：普通型。主语是单数形式，则谓语也采取单数形式；主语是复数形式，谓语亦采取复数形式。需要注意的是，此类考点通常和时态一起考察。

3.3.2 例题分析

例题1 The article goes on to suggest that the most valuable resources provided by co-working spaces are actually the people whom use them. (OG 第一套第 30 题)

A. NO CHANGE B. whom uses C. who uses D. who use

答案：D

解析：考点1。Whom 引导定语从句，people 在定语从句中充当的是主语成分，因此关系代词便应该是 who，而不是宾格形式 whom，选项 A、B 错误。

定语从句中的谓语动词，遵循主谓一致原则，与主语的 people 进行搭配。people 是集合名词，谓语动词使用复数，并且可以根据 actually 前面的 are 帮助判断，从而进一步确定 people 在这里是复数，因此 use 在句中使用正确，用一般现在时，与整个句子时态保持一致，所以选择 D。

例题2 Like any other health problems, these ailments can increase employee absenteeism, which, in turn, is costly for employers. (OG 第三套第 5 题)

A. NO CHANGE B. are C. is being D. have been

答案：A

解析：考点1。Which 引导非限制性定语从句，先行词为 absenteeism，为单数形式，谓语动词——be 动词也应该是单数形式，选项 B、D 排除。

句子的时态是讲述一种通常的情况，不用现在进行时，使用一般现在时，所以答案选 A。

例题3 Proponents of organic food, of course, are quick to add that their are numerous other reasons to buy organic food, such as, a desire to protect the environment from potentially damaging pesticides or a preference for the taste of organically grown foods. (OG 第四套第 21 题)

A. NO CHANGE B. there are C. there is D. their is

答案：B

解析：考点4。there be 结构中是 there 而不是所有格 their，选项 A、D 错误；主谓一致，

---

① 此处 S 表示主语，V 表示谓语动词。
② 此处 N 表示名词。

there be 的完全倒装句型中主语是 reasons，因此谓语动词应该是 are，而不是 is，所以选项 B 正确。

例题 4 There were a number of steps you can take to determine whether game design is the right field for you and, if it is, to prepare yourself for such a career. （OG 第四套第 34 题）

  A. NO CHANGE   B. has been   C. are   D. was

正确答案：C

解析：考点四。there be 的完全倒装句型中主语是 a number of steps，为复数形式，谓语动词用复数形式，选项 B、D 错误；整句句子的时态为一般现在时，而不是过去时，所以选项 C 正确，选项 A 错误。

3.3.3 更多练习

（1）As a result, the island has been an ideal setting for allopatric speciation, a process in which geographically isolated populations of the same species evolves independently. （可汗 WI 第 1 篇第 4 题）

  A. NO CHANGE   B. evolve   C. is evolving   D. has evolved

（2）At the time, the city was divided into many small, cramped neighborhoods that was disconnected from one another, making transportation difficult. （可汗 WI 第 11 篇第 5 题）

  A. NO CHANGE   B. is   C. has been   D. were

（3）The significance of her contributions to the Chicano art movement were recognized as early as 1981, when Hernandez was commissioned by the Los Angeles Bicentennial Committee to produce a mural in celebration of the city's 200th anniversary. （可汗 WA 第 1 篇第 7 题）

  A. NO CHANGE   B. is   C. was   D. have been

（4）Interestingly, the research is beginning to suggest that humans may play a prominent role in the spread of the fungus, as the distance between infected caves often exceed the typical migratory patterns of bat populations. （可汗 WI 第 5 篇第 7 题）

  A. NO CHANGE   B. exceeds   C. have exceeded   D. are exceeding

（5）However, adapting a novel as beloved as *The Great Gatsby* has proved to be a great challenge. F. Scott Fitzgerald's iconic tale of 1920s excess have been taken on by Hollywood four times: in 1926, 1949, 1974, and 2013. （可汗 WA 第 3 篇第 2 题）

  A. NO CHANGE   B. were   C. are   D. has been

（6）Also worth noting is the fact that demand for skilled water chemists are on the rise. （可汗 WI 第 7 篇第 10 题）

  A. NO CHANGE   B. is   C. were   D. have been

（7）According to many historians, the Antiquities Act have been one of the most important steps taken toward preserving cultural artifacts and sites. The act also, however, posed some serious problems, which should not be forgotten. (可汗 WA 第 4 篇第 2 题)

  A. NO CHANGE   B. are   C. were   D. was

（8）Although the distinction between science and pseudoscience <u>remains</u> controversial, falsifiability has many valuable implications for the scientific method and beyond. (可汗 WI 第 8 篇第 10 题)

  A. NO CHANGE   B. were remaining

  C. have remained   D. remain

（9）Gandhi's principles of nonviolent resistance <u>was</u> the primary influence that helped King build momentum in the American civil rights movement. (可汗 WN 第 8 篇第 2 题)

  A. NO CHANGE   B. were

  C. is   D. DELETE the underlined portion.

（10）This lower third attaches to the stomach—a hollow, muscular organ—which then <u>digest</u> food both by crushing it mechanically and by secreting digestive enzymes and other fluids that break down starches and proteins. (可汗 WN 第 11 篇第 5 题)

  A. NO CHANGE   B. are digesting

  C. were digesting   D. digests

解析：(1) B. 考点 2。谓语取决于 geographically isolated populations，复数形式，排除选项 A、C、D，快速得出答案，整个句子处于现在时，选项 B 正确。

（2）D. 考点 1。That 引导定语从句，先行词 cramped neighborhoods，为复数形式，排除选项 A、B、C，由于整个句子处于过去时，所以选项 D 正确。

（3）A. 考点 2。谓语取决于 cramped neighborhoods，为复数形式，排除选项 B、C，整个句子处于过去时，排除选项 D 现在完成时。

（4）B. 考点 1。谓语取决于 the distance 而不是 infected caves，between the infected caves 为修饰成分，谓语应该是单数形式，选项 A、C、D 排除，整句话处于现在时，选项 B 正确。

（5）D. 考点 2。谓语取决于 F. Scott Fitzgerald's iconic tale，单数形式，排除选项 A、B、C，前一句同时采用现在完成时，选项 D 正确。

（6）B. 考点 1。Demand 为同位语从句中的主语，for skilled water chemists 为修饰成分，选项 A、C、D 排除，整个句子处于现在时，选项 B 正确。

（7）D. 考点 4。主语为 the Antiquities Act，单数形式，选项 A、B、C 排除，后一句为过去时，选项 D 同样是过去式，正确。

（8）A. 考点 1。谓语取决于 the distinction，between science and pseudoscience 为修饰成分，谓语应该是单数形式，排除选项 B、C、D，整个句子处于现在时，选项 A 正确。

（9）B. 考点 2。谓语取决于 Gandhi's principles，为复数形式，选项 A、C、D 排除，快速得出答案，整个句子处于过去时，选项 B 正确。

（10）D. 考点 1。定语从句，先行词为 the stomach 或者 a hollow, muscular organ，都为单数形式，排除选项 A、B、C，整个句子处于现在时，选项 D 正确。

3.4 固定搭配

3.4.1 核心知识点

考点介绍

固定搭配的正确熟练掌握在于日常积累,也在于对真题句意的正确理解。常见的 New SAT 语法考试的固定搭配用法如下:

not only ... but (also) ... neither ... nor ...
either ... or ...
such as ...
so ... that ...
as ... as ...
No sooner ... than ...
comply with ...
serve ... as ...
...

核心考点

考点 1,介词搭配。

在 SAT 中对固定搭配的考察主要是集中在介词的考察上,这是 SAT 考试中的一个重点。一个动词、名词或者形容词到底和什么介词搭配,很多时候都是约定俗成的,这就要求考生们在平时多积累。介词使用不当,很多时候是很难通过语感察觉的,做题技巧也没有多大的作用。

考点 2,动词不定式。

有些动词后面只能接动词不定式在 SAT 中,这些动词主要包括:attempt、claim、refuse、fail、determine 等。注意:下面短语中的 to 是介词,to 后面要接 V-ing 的形式而不是动词不定式。

Look forward to
Object to＝be opposed to
Be used to＝get used to＝be accustomed to＝get accustomed to
In addition to
Amount to
Devote oneself to＝ dedicate oneself to ＝be devoted to ＝be dedicated to
Be averse to
The way (approach, solution, key) to Secret to
Resort to
Be sensitive to

考点 3,固定句式,尤其是特殊句式的考察,如倒装句、强调句等。

3.4.2 例题分析

例题 1 Nutritionists consider Greek yogurt to be a healthy food: it is an excellent source of calcium and protein, serves as a digestive aid, and [8] it contains few calories in its unsweetened low and non-fat forms. （OG 第一套第 7 题）

  A. NO CHANGE   B. as   C. like   D. for

答案：B

解析：考点 1，介词搭配。serve as 表示"担当、充当其作用"，固定搭配用法。从原文句意分析，选项 C、D 意思不妥帖。原文意思是营养家认为作为健康食物的希腊酸奶：它是钙和蛋白质的非常好的来源，起助消化的作用。

例题 2 It was during this time that I read an article <u>into</u> coworking spaces.（OG 第一套第 25 题）

  A. NO CHANGE   B. about   C. upon   D. for

答案：B

解析：考点 1，介词搭配。原文的意思：正是在这段时间，我读了关于公共合作空间的文章。此处选项 B 表示"关于"，选项 C 表示"在上面"，选项 D 表示"为了，对于"。只有选项 B 符合文义。

例题 3 Glass walls and dividers can also be used to replace solid walls as a means <u>through</u> distributing natural light more freely.（OG 第三套第 11 题）

  A. NO CHANGE   B. of

  C. from   D. DELETE the underlined portion

答案：B

解析：考点 1，介词固定搭配。as a means of 固定搭配，"作为……的方法"。其他四个选项没有此搭配的含义。原文意思是玻璃墙和分割器可以被用来代替固体墙，作为一种通过散步自然光线更自由的方式。

3.4.3 更多练习

（1）The main challenge lies <u>with</u> a lack of longitudinal data collected over an extended period of time.（可汗 *The Boreal Chorus Frog: An Exceptional Amphibian*? 第 7 题）

  A. NO CHANGE   B. on   C. at   D. in

答案：B

解析：考点 1，介词固定搭配。with 表示"伴随"，也有"和"的意思；而根据原文意思：主要的挑战在于……显然 with 不合适。在其他选项中，at、in 用于时间和地点介词，只有 on 可以作为时间、地点介词外，还可以用于观点。

（2）Einstein's theory of gravitation was scientific because it made concrete predictions about what we should observe in the future, and therefore could be falsified if inconsistent <u>to</u> these observations.（可汗 *False or False: The Question of Falsifiability* 第 6 题）

  A. NO CHANGE   B. for   C. with   D. by

答案：C

解析：考点1，介词固定搭配。本题考查 inconsistent with "与……不一致" 动词固定搭配。其他选项，for，by，to 都不可以和 inconsistent 搭配。

(3) These duties require an array of interpersonal and planning skills, as well as the ability to juggle multiple assignments. （可汗 *The Business of Hospitality* 第7题）

  A. NO CHANGE   B. in
  C. from   D. DELETE the underlined portion

答案：A

解析：考点1，介词固定搭配。an array of 表示"一系列"，固定搭配，原文意思：这些指责需要一系列人际间的和有计划的技巧。其他选项不能搭配 an array 表示一系列。

(4) He spoke to thousands of voters of a time, but the nature of the whistle stop campaign allowed voters to glimpse a more intimate view of the candidate. （可汗 *Truman's Winning Whistle-Stop Tour* 第7题）

  A. NO CHANGE   B. on the   C. at a   D. of the

答案：C

解析：考点1，介词固定搭配。根据文义：他逐次和数以千计的选举人谈话。at a time 表示"依次，逐次"。其余选项搭配 on the time 没有此用法；of the time 表示"当代的，当时的"，因此正确选项是 C。

(5) As a precaution, he also preserved material evidence—including the microfilm—that verified both his own involvement and the involvement of other underground agents prior from his defection. （可汗 *The Pumpkin Papers* 第7题）

  A. NO CHANGE   B. for   C. To   D. in

答案：C

解析：考点1，介词固定搭配。根据原文意思：作为预防措施，他也持有重要的证据——包括微缩胶卷来证实先于他的背叛之前，他自己的参与和其他秘密代理人的参与。根据原文意思及 prior to 固定搭配，正确答案是 C。

(6) After Rosa Parks famously refused to give up her seat on a public bus, King organized a year-long boycott upon Montgomery buses, which ended with the U. S. Supreme Court ruling that segregation on public buses was unconstitutional. （可汗 *Dr. King's Guiding Light* 第7题）

  A. NO CHANGE   B. with   C. of   D. about

答案：C

解析：考点1，介词搭配。根据原文意思：在 Rosa Parks 公然拒绝在公共汽车上让座后，King 组织了一个长达一年的对 Montgomery buses 的抵制。boycott with，boycott about/upon 意思分别是"和……的联合抵制，关于……的联合抵制"，不符合文义，因此正确答案是 C。

(7) The 'dead' language of Latin lives on in its connections from modern languages, literature, and philosophical traditions. Perhaps its influence can best be summarized by the inversion of a familiar maxim: ex uno, lures (from one, many). （可汗 *The Relevance of Linguae Latinae* 第11题）

  A. NO CHANGE   B. to   C. for   D. in

答案:B

解析:考点1,介词固定搭配。from 表示"从……";for 表示"为了;对于";in 是时间,地点介词。原文中 its connections from modern languages,意思是它的与现代语言的联系;从搭配而言,没有 connections from 表示"和……联系"的搭配。因此,只有选项 B 符合文义。

(8) This safety training will be required of employees traveling to offshore facilities, so she will stand out from other applicants by already being safety certified. (可汗 *A Bridge Between Classes and Careers* 第38题)

  A. NO CHANGE   B. stand down   C. stand up   D. stand alone

答案:A

解析:考点1,介词固定搭配。stand out 表示"突出";stand down 表示"推出,离职";stand up 表示"站起来";stand alone 表示"孤立,独一无二"。根据原文意思:从其他申请者中脱颖而出。因此正确答案是 A。

(9) Just type the phrase into Google and see what turns down. (可汗 *Look It Up!* 第24题)

  A. NO CHANGE   B. in   C. back   D. up

答案:D

解析:考点1,介词固定搭配。首先根据文义:把习语输入到谷歌浏览器去看看出现了什么。turn up 表示"出现";turn in 表示"熟悉,了解";turn back to 表示"返回到,重新提到",没有单独 turn back 用法。只有选项 D 符合文义。

3.5 代词

3.5.1 核心知识点

考点介绍

当我们在 New SAT 语法中看到代词 it,人称代词 they,指示代词 this、that、these、those 时,我们要尤其谨慎地去对待。首先,指代对象。倘若结合原句,我们仍然无法判断这些词的指代对象究竟是什么,那么,下一步,我们需要去做的,便是通过上下文进一步尝试理解,并还原真正明确的指代对象到原句中,或将指代不清的指代词删去。其次,代词用法在句中是否无意义,可删去。在类似的情况下,代词指代的内容往往与上一句的句意产生了重复,那么,语法中避免无谓的重复,该类代词是应该考虑删去而后合并两个句子的。此外,代词以及其形容词性物主代词的正确使用也是 New SAT 中的常见考点。形容词性物主代词分为 my、your、his、her、its、our、your、their,这些词在语句中什么时候用、如何使用,同学们务必熟练正确掌握。

核心考点

考点1,主格、宾格、所有格、反身代词辨析。
考点2,人称一致和指代的精确。

代词属于 SAT 语法最常考的考点之一，遇到考试中出现代词画线，一定要万分注意。代词用以指代前文提到过的名词，以避免重复。用到 this、that、it、they 等代词时，必须有明确的所指。若句意所指的名词概念未明确出现，而直接使用这类代词，就犯了"模糊指代"或"空指代"(vague pronoun)的错误。若句中出现了两个及以上的名词性概念，且在形式上都与所用的指示代词相匹配，则易引起歧义，造成"歧义指代"(ambiguous pronoun)的错误；句中出现两次及以上人称代词时，要注意这些代词间的一致性，包括数的一致和第一、二、三人称间的一致。例如：You don't have so-called freedom, because at times what we do/one does depends on other people. 其中的第二人称(you)转变成了第一(we)或第三(one)人称，这类错误称为 shift of pronoun。

3.5.2 例题分析

例题 1 According to Box, a leading Greenland expert, tundra fires in 2012 from as far away as North America produced great amounts of soot, some of it drifted over Greenland in giant plumes of smoke and then fell as particles onto the ice sheet. Scientists have long known that soot particles facilitate melting by darkening snow and ice, limiting its ability to reflect the Sun's rays.（OG 第一套第 19 题）

  A. NO CHANGE   B. its   C. there   D. their

答案：D

解析：考点 2，人称代词、物主代词、指示代词的精确。此处 ability 前面是一个物主代词，因此可以排除选项 C，而要代替上文中的 snow and ice 两个对象，只能用复数形式物主代词 their。因此选项 D 符合。

例题 2 Because today's students can expect to hold multiple jobs—some of which may not even exist yet—during our lifetime, studying philosophy allows them to be flexible and adaptable.（OG 第一套第 44 题）

  A. NO CHANGE   B. one's   C. his or her   D. their

答案：D

解析：考点 1，物主代词辨析。根据原文意思：因为当今的学生们期待能胜任多样化的工作，其中有些工作甚至还没问世，因此在他们的一生中，学习哲学能帮助他们变得足够变通（从而适应自己心仪的岗位）。文中代词 our 应该代替 students，此处需要第三人称复数物主代词，因此选项 D 正确。

例题 3 Just as travelers taking road trips today may need to take a break for food at a rest area along the highway, settlers traversing the American West by train in the mid-1800s often found themselves in need of refreshment.（OG 第三套第 12 题）

  A. NO CHANGE   B. himself or herself
  C. their selves   D. oneself

答案：A

解析：考点 1，反身代词辨析。根据原文意思：就像时下开车旅行的游客需要在高速公路沿线休息吃饭，19 世纪中叶的移民们在乘坐列车横穿美国西部时也常常有吃点心的需求。此处代替上文中的 setters，第三人称复数，因此 themselves 在此处贴切。

例题 4 While 1-MCP keeps apples tight and crisp for months, it also limits their scent production. (OG 第三套第 26 题)

  A. NO CHANGE   B. there   C. its   D. it's

答案：A

解析：考点 2，指代精确。此处 their 指代上文 apples，apples 是第三人称复数，因此 their 是其对应的代词。上文的意思是：虽然 1-MCP 能使苹果保持数月的紧实爽脆，但他也会遏制苹果的香味。

3.5.3 更多练习

(1) After three years of proceedings, the auditor found USIA liable and suggested it should pay damages of ＄300000—the equivalent of more than ＄30 million today. Instead of rejecting the findings and going to trial before a jury, USIA chose to settle the case. Ultimately, we ended up paying more than double what the auditor recommended to resolve all 119 cases. (可汗 *A Wave of Molasses* 第 7 题)

  A. NO CHANGE   B. one   C. it   D. he

答案：C

解析：考点 1，关系代词辨析。根据上文意思：经过三年的诉讼，审计员发现 USIA 负有法律责任。此处指代上文中的 USIA，应该使用指物的第三人称单数，因此答案是选项 C。

(2) After the judgment, inspections, regulations, and corporate restrictions became commonplace. Furthermore, the trial illustrated the power of citizen action and encouraged people to protect they're interests. (可汗 *A Wave of Molasses* 第 10 题)

  A. NO CHANGE   B. there   C. their   D. it's

答案：C

解析：考点 2，物主代词、人称代词、指示代词的精确指代。根据句意：而且，这次审判彰显了公民行动的力量，并且鼓励人们保护自己的权益。此处，指的是 people 的利益，因此，需要第三人称复数的物主代词，只有选项 C 符合语法和语意要求。

(3) Ethnographers work anywhere from communities in small villages to bustling cities, but its work is always the same: listening to someone else's story. (可汗 *Personal Anthropology* 第 1 题)

  A. NO CHANGE   B. their   C. her   D. my

答案：B

解析：考点 2，物主代词指代精确。根据文义：人种学者在各个地方工作，从小村庄的社区到热闹的城市，但是他们的工作总是同样的。这里的工作指的是人种学者的工作，因此，此处依据句意语法要求，需要一个第三人称复数的物主代词。只有选项 B 符合。

(4) The GI Bill is best known, however, for the education and training assistance they provided veterans. (可汗 *GI Bill: A Real American Hero* 第 2 题)

  A. NO CHANGE   B. it   C. this   D. that

答案：B

解析：考点 1、2，代词，指示代词的精确。This 指代上文，that 指代下文，it 指代单数物，

they 指代复数人或物。根据句意理解,然而 GI Bill 最被大家熟知,因为教育和训练协助,它提供了老战士。此处 it 指代 GI Bill。

(5) Whether they enrolled in technical engineering class or a vocational class on auto-repair, they're overarching objectives were to become employed. (可汗 *GI Bill*: *A Real American Hero* 第 5 题)

  A. CHANGE   B. their   C. there   D. they are

答案:B

解析:考点 1,人称代词、指示代词、物主代词辨析。首先从句式分析,逗号前面的句子是让步状语从句,后面是主句,但主句包含了两个 be 动词 were,因此此处需要被替换,同时排除选项 D。选项 C 缺少 are,构成 there be 句型,因此答案是 B,构成物主代词加名词结构,their 代替从句中的 they。

(6) The critical component of a scientific theory is the element of risk; its value lies in predictive rather than explanatory power. (可汗 *False or False*: *The Question of Falsifiability* 第 4 题)

  A. NO CHANGE   B. their   C. it's   D. they're

答案:A

解析:考点 1,人称代词、物主代词辨析。its 指代第三人称单数,their 指代第三人称复数,此处指代上文中 the critical component,意思是重要元素的价值,因此答案是 A,不需要做改变。

(7) Ballrooms need tables and food; front desk and cleaning staff need to be supervised and require shift assignments; and all of the other hotel guests not affiliated with these large-scale affairs also must have his needs met. (可汗 *The Business of Hospitality* 第 3 题)

  A. NO CHANGE   B. her   C. their   D. its

答案:C

解析:考点 2,物主代词的精确指代。根据原文意思:舞厅需要食物和桌子,前台和清洁工需要被监督并且需要调度安排,同时所有的其他不隶属于这个大规模的事件中的旅店客人也一定需要使他们的需求得到满足。因此,画线部分指代上文中的 ballrooms, front desk and cleaning staff, all of the other hotel guests,此处需要第三人称复数物主代词,因此选项 C 是最佳答案。

(8) By 1945, the number of African American women working for the federal government had more than tripled, and the percentage working in the defense industry was equal to it's proportion of the general population. (可汗 *A "Rosie" Turn on American Labor* 第 8 题)

  A. NO CHANGE   B. their   C. her   D. one's

答案:B

解析:考点 2,物主代词指代精确。根据句意:截至 1945 年,为联邦政府工作的非洲裔美国女性人数已经增长三倍多,其中在国防局工作的非洲裔美国女性的比例等同于她们在全国总人口中的比例。画线部分指代上文的 African American women,此处需要第三人称物主代词复数,因此,只有选项 B 是最佳答案。

(9) Like many scientific breakthroughs, <u>Mendeleev</u> was partially anticipated by the work of other scientists. （可汗 *A Work in Progress: The Periodic Table* 第 5 题）

  A. NO CHANGE   B. Mendeleev's periodic table
  C. this   D. it

答案：B

解析：根据句意：像许多科学突破一样，前人也预先为门捷列夫的元素周期表做了部分铺垫。此题的难点在于 anticipate 的多重词义，如果将其理解为最常见的"期待"一义，则很可能会理解为某人对某人有所期待，从而错选 A，但此处搭配的 partially（部分地）一词暗示着这里的 anticipate 并非预期的意思，毕竟很少会出现部分地期待、预期这一表达，结合紧接着给出的之前科学家对化学周期表做出的贡献事例，我们可以推理出这里的 anticipate 是指"先于某人做某事"，因此此处指代的对象就是被做的事，即 Mendeleev's periodic table。答案是 B。

(10) Over 800000 young Venezuelans have learned music through El Sistema in the 40 years since <u>their</u> inception. （可汗 *El Sistema: Venezuela's Revolutionary Music Education* 第 8 题）

  A. NO CHANGE   B. its   C. his   D. Our

答案：B

解析：考点 2，物主代词精确指代。根据原文句意，能推理出指代 inception（起源）的所属正是状语词组中的 El Sistema，因此需要第三人称单数物主代词，在四个选项中，只有选项 B 符合。

3.6　语境理解

3.6.1　核心知识点

考点介绍

语境理解题，对于大部分考生来说，是比较容易失分的一块。与其说它是语法题，不如说它更类似于阅读题，需要考生结合上下文来判断、理解。语境理解题主要分为三类题型：句子插入/删除题、排序题和最佳内容题。

核心考点

考点 1，句子插入/删除题——主要考察加不加、删不删。

如果定位句和原文关系密切，就不删除或添加。如果偏离主题，就删除或不添加。

错误选项可能是句子偏离主题、删除了帮助理解的信息（supporting detail）或者缺少了特殊含义。

考点 2，排序题。

主要考察一个句子在哪个位置是最合适的，分为两类：加入原文中没有的句子；重排原文中已有的句子，甚至段落。

做这个类型的题目最重要的步骤就是分析被排序的句子，首先观察句首、句尾有没有指代词，如指示代词 this，that，these，those，such，人称代词的主格或宾格如 he，she，they，them，或者其他诸如不定代词 some，any，no，every，all，each，both，much，many，(a) little，(a) few，other(s)，another，either，neither 等。其次观察有没有一些逻辑关系词，如 therefore，however，similarly 等。最后还可以借助被插入句子中的一些特殊词进行判断，如大写的专有名词、时间、地点等。

考点 3，最佳内容题。

主要分成三种类型：细节考察、衔接关系考察和主旨考察。

第一种考察需要学生去找出哪一个选项提供了 specific information。

例如：Which choice provides the most relevant information?

例如：The writer wants a conclusion that conveys how the shortcomings of 1-MCP presented in the passage affect the actions of people in the fruit industry. Which choice best accomplishes this goal?

第二种考察需要学生去确认哪个选项的句子最适合被放在位置。

例如：Which choice provides the most logical and effective transition to the rest of this paragraph?

注意：这个类型的题目和排序题不同。这个题型句子被安排的位置是固定的，选哪一个句子是不确定的。排序题则是，被排序句子是确认的，放在哪个位置不确定。

第三种考察需要学生去回答哪一个选项能最好地引出一段的中心，或者总结全文。

例如：Which of the following sentences, if added here, would most effectively express one of the main ideas of the essay?

例如：Given that all the following statements are true, which one, if added here, would most effectively conclude the paragraph and support information given in the preceding sentence?

不管是哪一种考察，都需要学生具备很强的阅读能力，读题目、回读上下文、读选项、进行选择。

3.6.2 例题分析

例题 1 <u>Though these conservation methods can be costly and time-consuming, they are well worth the effort.</u> Nutritionists consider Greek yogurt to be a healthy food: it is an excellent source of calcium and protein, serves to be a digestive aid, and it contains few calories in its unsweetened low and non-fat forms. Greek yogurt is slightly lower in sugar and carbohydrates than conventional yogurt is. Also, because it is more concentrated, Greek yogurt contains slightly more protein per serving, thereby helping people stay.

The writer is considering deleting the underlined sentence. Should the writer do this? (OG 第一套第 6 题)

A. Yes, because it does not provide a transition from the previous paragraph.

B. Yes, because it fails to support the main argument of the passage as introduced in the first paragraph.

C. No, because it continues the explanation of how acid whey can be disposed of safely.

D. No, because it sets up the argument in the paragraph for the benefits of Greek yogurt.

答案:D

解析:考点 1。这一段包括了几个喝希腊酸奶的好处,来支持这句话说保护方法是"well worth the effort",这句话也照应了文章之前声称"the advantages of Greek yogurt outweigh the potential drawbacks of its production",选项 D 正确,选项 A 错误,选项 B 错误。这一句话并没有再说"acid whey",所以选项 C 错误。

例题 2 [1] Thus, even though I already had all the equipment I needed in my home office, I decided to try using a coworking space in my city. [2] Because I was specifically interested in coworking's reported benefits related to creativity, I chose a facility that offered a bright, open work area where I wouldn't be isolated. [3] Throughout the morning, more people appeared. [4] Periods of quiet, during which everyone worked independently, were broken up occasionally with lively conversation.

The writer wants to add the following sentence to the paragraph.

After filling out a simple registration form and taking a quick tour of the facility, I took a seat at a table and got right to work on my laptop.

The best placement for the sentence is immediately _____. (OG 第一套第 31 题)

A. before sentence 1
B. after sentence 1
C. after sentence 2
D. after sentence 3

答案:C

解析:考点 2。此句话是作者已经填好注册表,开始选工作区域进行工作。此段第一句是作者开始决定要用共事的场所。第二句是作者选择场所,所以一定插入在第二句话之后。而第三句描述的是场所内发生的事:在这个早上,越来越多的人出现了,所以插入在第三句之前。答案选 C。

例题 3 For as long as Harvey Houses served rail travelers through the mid-twentieth century, working there was a steady and lucrative position for women. Living independently and demonstrating an intense work ethic; the Harvey Girls became known as a transformative force in the American <u>West</u>.

The writer is considering revising the underlined portion of the sentence to read: West, inspiring books, documentaries, and even a musical.

Should the writer add this information here? (OG 第三套第 22 题)

A. Yes, because it provides examples of the Harvey Girls' influence.
B. Yes, because it serves as a transitional point in the paragraph.
C. No, because it should be placed earlier in the passage.
D. No, because it contradicts the main claim of the passage.

答案:A

解析:考点 1。前面提到了"the Harvey Girls became known as a transformative force",加入的部分支持了这个观点,体现了 Harvey Girl 的影响,选项 A 正确。这并不是一个转

折,选项 B 错误。也不应该放在文章之前,选项 C 错误。加入部分并没有与文章主要声称矛盾,选项 D 错误。

例题 4 Evidence also undermines the claim that organic food is safer to eat. While researchers have found lower levels of pesticide residue in organic produce than in nonorganic produce, the pesticide residue detected in conventional produce falls within acceptable safety limits. According to such organizations as the US Environmental Protection Agency, the minute amounts of residue falling within such limits have no negative impact on human health.

At this point, the writer wants to further reinforce the paragraph's claim about the safety of nonorganic food. Which choice most effectively accomplishes this goal? (OG 第四套第 20 题)

A. To be labeled organic, a product must meet certain standards determined and monitored by the US Department of Agriculture.

B. Organic food, however, is regulated to eliminate artificial ingredients that include certain types of preservatives, sweeteners, colorings, and flavors.

C. Moreover, consumers who are concerned about ingesting pesticide residue can eliminate much of it by simply washing or peeling produce before eating it.

D. In fact, the Environmental Protection Agency estimates that about one-fifth of the pesticides used worldwide are applied to crops in the United States.

答案:C

解析:考点 3。要加入的部分要符合这句话的主要意思,也就是非有机食品对健康没有坏处。选项 A 说的是要被标注为有机,一个产品所需满足的要求,与非有机食品无关,错误。选项 B 说的是关于有机食品的,与非有机食品无关,错误。选项 C 说非有机食品的农药残留可以通过简单的洗和剥皮来去除,即非有机食品对健康没有坏处,正确。选项 D 说的是环保局估计全球五分之一的杀虫剂都是在美国用的,与非有机食品无关,错误。

例题 5 [1] A basic understanding of computer programming is essential. [2] In fact, many designers initially begin their pursuits as programmers. [3] Consider taking some general computer science courses as well as courses in artificial intelligence and graphics in order to increase your understanding of the technical challenges involved in developing a video game. [4] Courses in psychology and human behavior may help you develop emphatic collaboration skills, while courses in the humanities, such as in literature and film, should give you the background necessary to develop effective narrative structures. [5] A designer also needs careful educational preparation. [6] Finally, because a designer should understand the business aspects of the video game industry, such as budgeting and marketing, you may want to consider taking some business courses. [7] Although demanding and deadline driven, video game design can be a lucrative and rewarding field for people who love gaming and have prepared themselves with the necessary skills and knowledge.

To make this paragraph most logical, sentence 5 should be _____ . (OG 第四套第 44 题)

A. placed where it is now
B. placed before sentence 1

C. placed after sentence 3   D. DELETED from the paragraph

答案：B

解析：考点 2。第五句话说的是一个设计家需要教育。注意这里的 also，不一定是这一段句间的逻辑，也可能是上一段与这一段段间的逻辑。这一段第一句话就说设计家需要会电脑编程，第四句话说也需要心理课和人类行为课，第六句话说成为一个设计家应该要懂一些商业方面的知识。整段都在说一个设计家需要教育，所以第五句话是总起句或者总结句，而 also 限定了它只能是总起句，答案选 B。

3.6.3 更多练习

（1）Many new programs began to emerge in response to the rising demand for job-oriented training and education. For example, a proposal to expand the programs for technical and general education in New York surfaced as early as 1944. The State University of New York (SUNY) was subsequently founded in 1948. Massachusetts' Stonehill College, which has been established in the same year, estimates that veterans comprised up to a third of its first entering class. Some vocational training programs were even created specifically for the benefit of returning veterans. One of the most unique examples in this category is the Culinary Institute of America, founded in 1946 to offer a novel curriculum for learning cooking stuff.

Which choice provides the most effective transition at this point?（可汗 WI 第 3 篇第 9 题）

A. NO CHANGE.

B. Eventually, these numbers would taper off.

C. Nevertheless, the GI Bill had a long-lasting impact on the demographics of higher education.

D. Nor were these figures unique to one college.

（2）In the spirit of his new nation, ending what he termed an "artificial aristocracy", Jefferson introduced the notion of what we now call electives. In lieu of a strictly dictated curriculum, students could select from ten academic disciplines. These disciplines were subject areas that ranged from ancient and modern languages to certain branches of science. (Not one to overlook the slightest detail, Jefferson showcased the ten categories by placing a carefully chosen Roman symbol on each of the ten pavilions.) To support the science components of the university's curriculum, Jefferson has included a botanical garden, an experimental farm, and an observatory.

Which sentence most effectively establishes the main topic of the paragraph?（可汗 WI 第 4 篇第 5 题）

A. Some historians consider Jefferson a better architect than American statesman.

B. In order to further his legacy, Jefferson created an epitaph that many would discuss.

C. As meticulously as he laid out the grounds, Jefferson drafted an inspirational curriculum.

D. Thomas Jefferson's legacy would not be intact if not for the university library.

(3) While it is unlikely that affected species will recover quickly (due to their slow reproductive rates bats have one offspring, or pup, annually), several species of bats have exhibited resistance to the destructive powers of WNS. The Virginia big-eared bat population, for example, has not been significantly affected, which led scientists to an exciting discovery: a naturally occurring yeast on the bats' fur inhibits the growth of the fungus. This disclosure offers a glimmer of hope in the battle against WNS.

The writer wants an optimistic conclusion that emphasizes the importance of bats' recovery by referencing an idea included in the passage's opening paragraph. Which choice best accomplishes this goal?（可汗 WI 第 5 篇第 11 题）

A. This devastating fungal disease could continue to spread, sickening bat populations in states west of Missouri.

B. North American bat populations will continue to exhibit unusual winter behavior and perish due to WNS if scientists cannot find a way to curb its spread.

C. With some bat populations already experiencing 90 percent declines, recovery from this disease will prevent them from extinction.

D. The sooner the bat population can recover from this disease, the greater the ecological and agricultural benefit to all.

(4) In a 1953 lecture at Cambridge University, Popper shared that the concept of falsifiability had first occurred to him more than thirty years earlier, when he was pondering and considering Einstein's theory of gravitation and Freud's psychoanalytical approach. Popper realized that Freud's approach has great "explanatory power," because psychoanalysis can be applied to completely opposite behavior patterns with equal aptness. Although this flexibility might seem valuable, Popper argued that a theory which cannot be proven false—one which can 'adapt' to any critical environment—is not science but pseudoscience. The critical component of a scientific theory is the element of risk; its value lies in predictive rather than explanatory power. Einstein's theory of gravitation was scientific because it made concrete predictions about what we should observe in the future, and therefore could be falsified if inconsistent to these observations.

At this point, the writer is considering adding the following sentence.

Predictive power can be illustrated by examining the work of Albert Einstein, who, though born in Germany, conducted much of his scientific work in the United States after he immigrated in 1933.

Should the writer make this addition here?（可汗 WI 第 8 篇第 5 题）

A. Yes, because it introduces an example of a scientist whose work can be analyzed using Popper's approach.

B. Yes, because it illustrates that other highly regarded scientists agreed with Popper's approach to the scientific method.

C. No, because it digresses from the main topic of the paragraph by introducing unrelated details.

D. No, because it blurs the paragraph's focus on Einstein's theory of gravitation.

(5) He spoke to thousands of voters of a time, but the nature of the whistle stop campaign allowed voters to glimpse a more intimate view of the candidate. By coming to voters' hometowns and speaking directly to them, Truman presented himself as a "man of the people." Truman marketed himself as attainable—making himself available to discuss local political issues with the residents of the small towns he visited.

Which choice provides the best supporting details for claim made in the previous sentence?（可汗 WN 第 1 篇第 8 题）

A. He told jokes, spoke without flourish, and even introduced his family to the onlookers.

B. He traveled in the presidential train car and was able to visit many constituents' hometowns.

C. He spoke to the citizens from the raised platform of his expansive train car.

D. He emphatically enumerated the reasons that his opponent was not the best candidate.

(6) At the beginning of the 1930s, San Francisco along with the rest of the country was reeling from the effects of the Great Depression. Looking for an opportunity to improve San Francisco's economy, the city's politicians were seizing upon the idea of hosting a World's Fair. They reasoned that a platform for global attention and tourism would draw business, and that the construction of the fair would also create jobs. Leland W. Cutler, a local business leader, was appointed president of the committee tasked with seeking funding for the project. Cutler found a funding solution in US President Franklin Delano Roosevelt's Works Progress Administration.

The writer is considering deleting the underlined sentence. Should the writer make this deletion?（可汗 WN 第 4 篇第 5 题）

A. Yes, because the sentence provides information irrelevant to the subject of the essay.

B. Yes, because the sentence distracts from the main purpose of the paragraph.

C. No, because the sentence answers a question raised in the previous paragraph.

D. No, because the sentence highlights the motivations behind the subjects' actions.

(7) Ethnographers work anywhere from communities in small villages to bustling cities, but its work is always the same: listening to someone else's story. A subfield of anthropology, ethnography is the study of people and the cultures in which they live.

At this point, the writer is considering adding the following sentence.

Ruth Behar, a Princeton-educated anthropologist, enjoys the process of listening to and interpreting such stories.

Should the writer make this addition here?（可汗 WN 第 6 篇第 2 题）

A. Yes, because it provides information essential to the passage.

B. Yes, because it introduces the subject of the passage.

C. No, because it provides information contradicted later in the passage.

D. No, because it interrupts the introduction of the passage.

(8) [1] Sophia's marriage to Leo gave her the opportunity to put her abilities as a good reader to use, often advising him on his work throughout the writing process. [2] She served as her husband's copyist (since this was before the advent of the typewriter), writing out multiple copies of his novels by hand. [3] She made suggestions for and edits to his work, many of which were inculcated into the final product. [4] In addition, she served as his manager, publicist, and agent, keeping track of the financial and legal sides of her husband's writing career. [5] She juggled these many roles with grace and skill. [6] If Sophia were alive today, she might have found her calling at a publishing house or literary agency.

To make this paragraph most logical, Sentence 5 should be placed _____. (可汗 WN 第 7 篇第 6 题)

A. where it is now
B. after sentence 1
C. after sentence 2
D. after sentence 3

(9) Chicano art began as an outgrowth of the more general Chicano Civil Rights Movement; a sociopolitical initiative that began in the 1960s to promote social progress and change for Mexican-Americans. Chicano artists sought to mirror the challenges faced by Mexican-Americans, often by challenging the xenophobic stereotypes of Mexican-Americans in American culture. However, since the vast majority of Chicano artists were men, much of the Chicano artwork of the 1960s and early 1970s represented the experiences of Mexican-American men, failing to represent some of the unique struggles faced by their female counterparts.

During her time with "Los Four," Hernandez developed a distinct visual style as she incorporated indigenous images along with figurative portrayals of Hispanic women, often restrained by elements such as vines or thorns. The significance of her contributions to the Chicano art movement were recognized as early as 1981, when Hernandez was commissioned by the Los Angeles Bicentennial Committee to produce a mural in celebration of the city's 200th anniversary.

At this point, the writer wants to provide a transition that effectively links the topics of the second and third paragraphs. Which choice best accomplishes this goal? (可汗 WA 第 1 篇第 6 题)

A. As one of the first prominent US artists to depict the experiences of Mexican-American women, Judith Hernandez played a vital role in the Chicano art movement.

B. All of the members of "Los Four" were college-educated artists who served as activists and educators within the Chicano movement.

C. Hernandez and Alvarez collaborated together on a number of public murals for the United Nations Farm Workers and the Ramona Gardens Housing Project in East Los Angeles.

D. Chicano artists were heavily influenced by artists from the Mexican Mural Movement, particularly Diego Rivera.

(10) To illustrate the importance of contemporary research on cholesterol, its presence in abnormally high concentrations can result in significant health issues. Many researchers believe that certain dietary choices, for example, eating—significant amounts of saturated fats and avoiding unsaturated fats—contribute to high cholesterol levels in the bloodstream. Since cholesterol molecules do not dissolve in water or blood, they are also transported to various parts of the body by lipoproteins, which are constructed from both fats and proteins. When the concentration of LDL cholesterol is high, it may clog an individual's arteries and lead to a variety of medical conditions.

At this point, the writer wants to add details about the specific functions of lipoproteins.

Which choice most effectively accomplishes this goal? （可汗 WA 第5篇第9题）

A. There are many different types of lipoproteins, including very low density lipoproteins, intermediate density lipoproteins, low density lipoproteins, and high density lipoproteins.

B. While the liver is the primary organ of lipoprotein synthesis, research has demonstrated that chylomicrons, a type of lipoprotein, are synthesized in the mucosa of the small intestine.

C. Low density lipoproteins (LDL) carry cholesterol into the bloodstream and various parts of the body, while high density lipoproteins (HDL) remove cholesterol from the bloodstream for disposal.

D. Lipoproteins are classified by density, which can be calculated from the ratio of triacylglycerol/protein concentration and the actual diameter of the molecule.

解析：(1) A。考点3。后面介绍的是一个特定的教育项目，而不是在讲前一句的数字，所以选项 B、D 错误，而前文和后文都没有提到 GI Bill，所以选项 C 也错误。选项 A，前面讲的是一些学校创立了，而后一句的 even 表示"甚至"，还成立了一些专业的培训项目，正确。

(2) C。考点3。这一段主要说的是杰弗逊在大学中设立的课程，要填入表明段落主要内容的句子。选项 A 重点在 architect，但这一段并不是在说杰弗逊作为一个建筑家，错误。选项 B，epitaph 指墓志铭，也是这一段所没有提及的，错误。选项 C 既提到了这一段的重点"curriculum"，也承接了上文的"la[y] out the grounds"，正确。选项 D，大学图书馆也是这一段没有提及的，错误。

(3) D。考点3。读题，重点在于：第一，"optimistic"选择的需要是乐观的；第二，"emphasize the importance of bats' recovery"要强调蝙蝠恢复的重要性；第三，"an idea included in the passage's opening paragraph"要含有文章开头段的信息。尽管选项 A、B、C、D 都含有文章开头段的信息，但只有选项 D 是乐观的。选项 A"devastating""sickening"表示不好的方面，选项 B"perish""if scientists cannot find a way to curb its spread"表示不好的方面，选项 C"decline"表示不好的方面，都错误。

(4) C。考点1。要加入的话描述的是爱因斯坦的介绍，以及 predictive power 可以被说明，这不是文章主要说明的对象，是一个无关紧要的细节，选 C。文章也不是主要在说爱因斯坦的万有引力，选项 D 错误。

(5) A。考点3。前一句话提到 Truman 要作为"man of the people"，所以应该要接地气，而选项 B 中的"presidential train car"以及 C 中的"expansive train car"与此相矛盾,错误。而选项 D,并不是这一方面的内容,而且反映的是 Truman 反面的形象,现在需要的是正面的形象,答案为 A。

(6) D. 考点 1。全文在说旧金山要举办 World's Fair,而这句话说的是举办的好处,选项 D 正确,这一句话并没有与全文不相关,选项 A、B 错误;而前文并没有提出问题,所以选项 C 错误。

(7) D. 考点 1。空格前一句话和后一句话都是在介绍 ethnography 这一概念,而加入的句子是在介绍一个人,与这两句话没有直接关系,所以选项 A、B 错误,这句话并没有与前文矛盾,所以选项 C 错误,选项 D 正确。

(8) A. 考点 2。These 代词表明之前说了 Sophia 的 many roles,如果选择选项 B 或选项 C 或选项 D,但第四句还在讲作为"manager, publicist, and agent",不合适,答案选 A。

(9) A. 考点 3。第三段主要说的就是 Hernandez 这个人,而不是她所在的"Los Four",所以选项 B 错误。也没有提到 Alvarez 或者 Diego Rivera,所以选项 C、D 错误。选项 A 总起第三段,正确。

(10) C. 考点 3。要加的是 lipoproteins 的特定功能,而选项 A 描述的是 lipoproteins 的不同类别,选项 B 描述的是 lipoproteins 的生产,选项 D 描述的是 lipoproteins 的分类,错误。只有选项 C 说 lipoproteins 的功能是从血液中清除胆固醇。

3.7 时态

3.7.1 核心知识点

考点介绍

在 SAT 中,常考的时态主要有四种,分别是一般现在时、一般过去时、现在完成时和过去完成时。一般现在时和现在完成时属于"现在"这个大范围,一般过去时和过去完成时属于"过去"这个大范围,"现在"和"过去"在复合句也就是在主从句或者并列句里不能混搭,除非有明确的时间词来区分时态或者在说客观真理。同时,SAT 是一门很注重平行和一致的考试,所以在时态方面,也要保证句子时态的平行和一致。

核心考点

考点 1,时态基本用法,以及根据上下文所在时态判断。
考点 2,时态与平行结构。
考点 3,时态与主谓一致。
考点 4,时态与非谓语动词。尤其要注意一句话一定有且只有一个谓语动词。

3.7.2 例题分析

例题 1 If it is improperly introduced into the environment, acid-whey runoff <u>can</u>

pollute waterways, depleting the oxygen content of streams and rivers as it decomposes. (OG 第一套第 3 题)

  A. NO CHANGE   B. can pollute waterway's

  C. could have polluted waterways   D. has polluted waterway's

答案:D

解析:考点 1。if 引导的条件状语从句普遍都遵循"主将从现"的语法规则。在该句中,从句 is introduced 为一般现在时,原句 can 在主句中作为情态动词,具有"可能/将来会"的意味,在句中恰当通顺。选项 B 中,waterway's 用了单数名词所有格,表示航道的,但根据句意,没有必要做此类修改。选项 C 中 could have polluted 用了虚拟语气,或者作为对过去的一种推测,与原句 if 从句的现在时不同,时态不符。选项 D 中 has polluted 用完成时态,表示"如处理不当,则已经构成污染",句意不通。且 waterway's 的用法与选项 B 出现了一样的问题。

例题 2   For centuries, cats have guarded this famous museum, ridding it of mice, rats, and other rodents that could damage the art, not to mention <u>scared</u> off visitors. (OG 第三套第 38 题)

  A. NO CHANGE   B. scaring

  C. scare   D. have scared

答案:C

解析:考点 2。Not to mention 前后平行,但要注意画线部分说的是"吓到游客",在句意上与 damage"毁坏艺术"平行,都是"老鼠们可能做的事",而不是与 could damage 平行陈述一个经常发生的事或者是与 ridding 平行表示"猫做的事",又或者是与 have guarded 平行表示"猫做的事"。此题容易错选为其他选项,但要分清平行对象,所以选 C。

例题 3   On the Graduate Record Examination (GRE), for example, students intending to study philosophy in graduate school <u>has scored</u> higher than students in all but four other majors. (OG 第一套第 40 题)

  A. NO CHANGE   B. have scored

  C. scores   D. scoring

答案:B

解析:考点 3、考点 4。此句话主语为 students, intending to study philosophy in graduate school, 现在分词做后置定语, 画线部分为谓语动词, 而不是非谓语动词, 选项 D 错误, 形式为复数形式, 选项 A、C 错误, 选项 B 正确。

例题 4   The centerpiece of the work was dominated by images of native people being oppressed and <u>including</u> an eagle symbolizing the United States. (OG 第四套第 6 题)

  A. NO CHANGE   B. included

  C. includes   D. had included

答案:B

解析:考点 1、考点 3。整句话处于过去时态,选项 C 错误。and 平行结构,画线部分不修饰 native people,所以不与 being oppressed 平行,选项 A 错误。画线部分主语为主句主语 the centerpiece of the work,所以画线部分与 was dominated 平行,不需要使用过去完成式,过去式足够,所以选项 D 错误,选项 B 正确。

3.7.3 更多练习

(1) The State University of New York (SUNY) was subsequently founded in 1948. Massachusetts' Stonehill College, which has been established in the same year, estimates that veterans comprised up to a third of its first entering class. (可汗 WI 第 3 篇第 8 题)

    A. NO CHANGE   B. will be   C. is   D. was

(2) These efforts led to the creation of one of the most famous and enduring icons in American history—an icon who would have an incalculable influence on American labor and society. (可汗 WI 第 10 篇第 2 题)

    A. NO CHANGE   B. will have

    C. is to have   D. would have had

(3) His arduous travels were covering 30000 miles and over 200 train stops, starting in the summer of 1948 and ending that fall before the November 2nd election. He began the tour in Michigan, then moved on to Iowa, Ohio, Missouri, Kansas, and Colorado as the summer progressed. (可汗 WN 第 1 篇第 4 题)

    A. NO CHANGE   B. cover   C. will cover   D. covered

(4) They now operate from 2 p.m. to 6 p.m. six days a week, and the government funding every facet of the program, from the instruments to the teachers. (可汗 WN 第 2 篇第 7 题)

    A. NO CHANGE   B. funded   C. will fund   D. funds

(5) Inside the hollowed interior laid a small package wrapped in wax paper. Within this unassuming package were both developed and undeveloped microfilm images—evidence that produced the final impetus needed for the controversial indictment of suspected Communist spy Alger Hiss. (可汗 WN 第 5 篇第 2 题)

    A. NO CHANGE   B. lying   C. lay   D. lain

(6) In 1950, King was introduced to Gandhi's teachings through a sermon by Mordecai Johnson, who had just returned from a trip to India. After studying Gandhi's achievements, King concludes that Gandhi was the first person in history to use the Christian ethic of love as a "potent instrument for social and collective transformation." (可汗 WN 第 8 篇第 5 题)

    A. NO CHANGE   B. concluded

    C. has concluded   D. was concluding

(7) Should the translation of a poem from one language to another be evaluated primarily on its adherence to the original text? While some consider such adherence to be the gold standard, this approach will overlook the fact that the very act of translation is centered on an act of change. (可汗 WA 第 2 篇第 1 题)

    A. NO CHANGE   B. had overlooked

    C. would have overlooked   D. overlooks

(8) Although the inclusion of hip-hop culture and high-end consumerism in this latest

film surprised some critics and probably some faithful readers of the novel, at least the director made the movie using the tools of his own medium. （可汗 WA 第 3 篇第 9 题）

A. NO CHANGE
B. would make
C. makes
D. will make

（9）Devils Tower, a geologic feature in Wyoming and a sacred site for the Lakota and numerous other Native American tribes, was Roosevelt's first designated monument, and seventeen more have followed before 1909. （可汗 WA 第 4 篇第 4 题）

A. NO CHANGE
B. followed
C. will follow
D. follow

（10）Furthermore, cholesterol is a key component of the central nervous system, where it primarily existed in the myelin sheaths of nerve cells; these sheaths help increase the speed of nerve impulse transmission. （可汗 WA 第 5 篇第 4 题）

A. NO CHANGE
B. was existing
C. had existed
D. exists

解析：（1）D. 考点 1。前一句时态为过去式时态，由于有明确的过去式标志词"in 1948"，画线部分后也有明确的过去式标志词"in the same year"，所以即使此句有 estimates 表示现在时，选项 A、C 错误，答案选 D。

（2）A. 考点 1。由"led"可得知整句话的时态处于过去式，选项 B、C 错误，不需要选项 D 的过去将来完成时；选项 A，站在过去的点预测未来的情况，选择使用过去将来时，正确。

（3）D. 考点 1。由后一句中的"began"可得知这一句话的时态处于过去式，选项 B、C 错误，过去进行时表示过去某个特定的时间点做的事，不需要运用在此情景下，选项 A 错误，选项 D 正确，表示对于过去发生的一件事的陈述。

（4）D. 考点 1、考点 3。由"operate"可得知整句话的时态处于现在式，选项 B、C 错误；and 连接两句完整的句子，后一句如果选 A 则没有谓语动词，选项 D 正确。

（5）C. 考点 1、考点 3。这个句子如果选 B 则没有谓语动词，选项 B 错误。由后一句中的"were"可得知这一句话的时态处于过去式，两个关键动词的过去式、过去分词要记住。第一个，lie-lay-lain，lie 指"说谎"；第二个，lay-laid-laid，lay 指"放"，此处词义为"躺"lie，过去式为 lay，答案选 C。

（6）B. 考点 1。由"was"可得知整句话的时态处于过去时，选项 A、C 错误，过去进行时表示过去某个特定的时间点做的事，不需要运用在此情景下，选项 D 错误，选项 B 正确，表示对于过去发生的一件事的陈述。

（7）D. 考点 1。由"consider"可得知整句话的时态处于现在式，选项 A、B、C 错误，选项 D 正确。

（8）A. 考点 1。由"surprised"可得知整句话的时态处于过去式，选项 C、D 错误；选项 B，过去将来时表示站在过去的点预测未来的情况，不需要，错误。选项 A 正确。

（9）B. 考点 1。由"was"可得知整句话的时态处于过去式，选项 A、C、D 错误，又有明确的时间状语"before 1909"，但这是发生在 first designated monument 之后，不需要用过去完成式，只需要过去式即可，选项 B 正确。

（10）D. 考点 1。由"is"可得知整句话的时态处于现在式，选项 A、B、C 错误，选项 D 正确。

3.8 平行原则

3.8.1 核心知识点

考点介绍

在 New SAT 语法中,平行原则是经常在题目中出现的高频考点。那么什么样的词会在 New SAT 语法考试部分中被作为平行原则来考察大家呢?

这些考点大体分为三类。即
- 并列连接词 and
- 选择连接词 or
- 转折连接词 but

另外,还有一类比较特殊的类型——比较级结构。

核心考点

考点 1,and。

考点 2,or。

考点 3,but。

上述这些考点主要又是以什么样的方式来考察大家呢?

广大考生们务必需要明确平行原则的真谛。我们不妨来看一些例子,大家就明了了。

e. g.　singing and dancing

　　　　pull or push

　　　　tall but fat

大家有没有发现,以上例子中在三类连接词 and、or、but 左右两边单词的词性都是一致的呢? 这便是 New SAT 语法中最经常考察的平行原则的核心方式。

另外,我们再来看一个例句。

(1) The population of China is larger than that of Thailand.

译:中国人口大于泰国人口。

在 than 的比较级结构中,依然遵循一种特殊的平行。简而言之,是比较对象的统一。很多学生会习惯将上述句子误写为下面这个句子:

(2) The population of China is larger than Thailand.

译:中国人口大于泰国。

中文翻译过来听起来的确特别通顺,但是这个句子为什么在英语语法上是有问题的呢? 因为它打破了比较级结构中比较对象的平行一致。应该遵循第(1)句中,"中国人口"和"泰国人口"在做比较,而不是"中国人口"在和"泰国"这个国家在做比较。

3.8.2 例题分析

例题 1 Nutritionists consider Greek yogurt to be a healthy food; it is an excellent source of calcium and protein, serves as a digestive aid, and <u>it contains</u> few calories in its unsweetened low-and non-fat forms. （OG 第一套第 8 题）

    A. NO CHANGE   B. containing

    C. contains   D. will contain

答案：C

解析：考点一。并列连词 and 前后应该遵循平行原则，此处动词应该为 contains 与 and 前面的 serves 时态及单复数保持一致。时态为一般现在时，单复数方面则为单数形式。

例题 2 According to Box, a leading Greenland expert, tundra fires in 2012 from as far away as North America produced great amounts of soot, some of which drifted over Greenland in giant plumes of smoke and then <u>fell</u> as particles onto the ice sheet. （OG 第一套第 18 题）

    A. NO CHANGE   B. fall   C. will fall   D. had fallen

答案：A

解析：考点一。and 左右两边遵循平行原则。这里动词应为 fell 在时态、单复数与 and 前的 drifted 以及 produced 保持一致，做一般过去时。选项 B、C、D 时态均不符。

例题 3 But they suggest that the presence of otters provides a good model of how carbon can be sequestered, <u>or removed</u>; from the atmosphere through the management of animal populations. （OG 第 2 套第 33 题）

    A. NO CHANGE   B. or removed from,

    C. or, removed from,   D. or removed, from

答案：D

解析：考点二。选择连词 or 左右两边遵循平行原则，removed 时态上与 or 前面的 sequestered 保持一致，做一般过去时。sequestered 后跟逗号，那么 removed 后面也要与其保持一致，添加上逗号，形成与后面 from the atmosphere 的合理分隔。

例题 4 The centerpiece of the work was dominated by images of native people being oppressed and <u>including</u> an eagle symbolizing the United States. （OG 第 4 套第 6 题）

    A. NO CHANGE   B. included

    C. includes   D. had included

答案：B

解析：考点一。and 左右两边遵循平行原则，时态上应该与 was dominated 保持一致，做一般过去时。

3.8.3 更多练习

（1）Her work reflected this exposition, as she sought to capture what she termed the "natural" art of African Americans <u>through speech song and folklore</u>. （可汗 *Resurrecting*

Zora 第 6 题)

    A. NO CHANGE

    B. through speech, song, and, folklore

    C. through: speech, song, and folklore

    D. through speech, song, and folklore

(2) The overarching objective of Popper's approach is not to choose the weaker <u>hypothesis and choose</u> the hypothesis which will lead us towards truth. (可汗 *False or False: The Question of Falsifiability* 第 8 题)

A. NO CHANGE	B. hypothesis, and choosing
C. hypothesis that choosing	D. hypothesis but to choose

第 3 部分　New SAT 数学

第 4 章　New SAT 数学全解

在以往 SAT 各科考试中，数学一直是中国学生引以为傲的优势科目。与美国学生相比，中国学生普遍数学知识和计算能力非常扎实，取得 800 分的成绩并不鲜见。然而随着 2016 年 1 月旧 SAT 最后一次考试结束，SAT 考试全面改革。考试形式总体上发生了比较大的变化，比较明显的是计分标准、题目长度和考察知识点。

虽然考试时间增加 10 min，但是总题目数也增加了 4 道，同时易错的填空题增加了 3 道。中国学生普遍数字计算能力较强，所以是否使用计算器相信影响并不是很大，但是考场上分秒必争，如何精简做题步骤，提高做题效率则是备考的关键，那么在最重要的考试内容和题型方面，到底 New SAT 数学做了哪些变化？这些变化对学生备考有什么影响？下面我们会重点介绍。

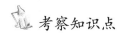考察知识点

1. 新旧 SAT 知识点变化

New SAT 去掉了对于数字或者公式本身的运算考查以及经常让同学们头疼的排列组合题目。然而，新增了一些部分同学没有接触过或者很少使用的知识点，如置信区间、抛物线趋势等。不过同学们不用担心，这部分知识点只需要大家知道并理解概念即可，并不需要去实际计算。

2. 知识点全分布

很多同学看到 College Board 给出的 New SAT 数学知识点分类会感到无从下手，其实 College Board 的分类主要是根据考查学生在数学技能、实际应用以及是否已经具备好进入高等学府学习的知识储备方面来划分的。

第一部分为代数核心，顾名思义是围绕代数相关的知识，主要包括常变量、不等式、一次方程等；

第二部分解决问题和分析数据，主要考查学生在实际生活中运用数学知识和思维解决问题的能力（包括阅读图表），这个部分题目因为会涉及与实际相关的比较复杂的运算，所以只会出现在可以使用计算器的部分；

第三部分通往高等数学，包括对复杂的函数和方程等的考查，检测学生是否有能力进入 STEM（Science，Technology，Engineering and Math）领域进行更深入的学习；

第四部分为附加内容,主要涉及一些额外知识点,这个部分内容是不计入 Subscore 评分的,其中主要包括平面、解析几何以及三角函数和虚数的基础知识内容。

四个部分分别对应考查学生不同方面的能力以及对同一知识点不同层级的掌握。

那么 New SAT 实际上究竟考察哪些知识点呢?

方程、函数、不等式、代数式变化以及比例等能够与实际问题紧密结合的知识点的考查比重较大。不过大家并不需要太过担心,这些知识点中国学生在初、高中基本已经学过,并且题目难度相比初、高中练习题可要简单不少。只不过在题目阅读量增加的前提下,学生必须非常熟练地掌握上面提到的每一个知识点的概念以及相关公式,才能在有限的时间内完成所有题目。

题目分析及策略

New SAT 数学不仅在知识点考查方面更加贴近实际生活应用,包括题目和题型也变得更加接地气。最明显的表现是题目长度大大增加,单词难度加大,长句出现频率增加,这对学生的阅读能力和速度提出了更高的要求。

阅读量增加

New SAT 数学平均每道题的字数增加 10 个字左右,最长的题目有 330 字。与美国学生相比,以前的中国学生赢在数学知识和计算能力上,但中国学生在专业英语词汇量、与实际生活联系、逻辑思维、批判性思维阅读上与美国学生存在很大差距。

所以,在单词方面,学生首先要对数学专业词汇以及常见表达熟练掌握,同时在平常也需要更多积累其他 STEM 相关领域的词汇和背景知识。针对题目中的长句,则需要快速理解题意、辨识出考察的知识点,然后分析句子结构,迅速剥离出与解题相关的数据信息,包括题目最后的问题也会经常出现在长句中,如果句子没有读懂,那么很有可能会减缓做题速度甚至会影响解题切入点。

例题 1 An online store receives customer satisfaction ratings between 0～100, inclusive. In the first 10 ratings the store received, the average (arithmetic mean) of the ratings was 75. What is the least value the store can receive for the 11th rating and still be able to have an average of at least 85 for the first 20 ratings.

题目主要意思是:一家在线商店会收到评分为 0～100 分之间的顾客满意度评价,收到的前 10 个评价的平均得分为 75 分,如果要保证前 20 个评价的平均得分为 85 分,商店收到的第 11 个评价最少为多少分?

大家可以发现题目非常贴近我们的生活,在网购如此发达的中国,相信大家作为买家都给过店家评价吧。

在这道题中,商店需要计算好评率。这类题我们都可以看作"应用题",解答应用题首先需要将题目给出的情境抽象化:

在 0～100 中先按顺序选择 10 个数,它们的平均数为 75,如果再依次选择 10 个数,为了保证这 20 个数的平均数为 85,第 11 个数最少应该是几?

然后再根据我们已经掌握的相关知识点解题即可。

题目的内容和形式更加多样化

与实际生活、工作相结合。

要求：积累与留心更多社会常识与经验。

例题 2 A bank has opend a new branch and, as part of a promotion, the bank branch is offering $1000 certificates of deposit at an interst rate of 4% per year, compounded semiannually. The bank is selling certificates with terms of 1, 2, 3 or 4 years. Which of the following fuctions gives the total amount, A, in dollars, a customer will receive when a certificate with a term of k years is finnally paid.

A. $A = 1000(1+0.04k)$ B. $A = 1000(1+0.08k)$
C. $A = 1000(1.04)k$ D. $A = 1000(1.04)2k$

解读：银行几乎与每个人的生活都息息相关，存款利率与收益具体如何计算则是这道题考察的重点。

例题 3 The cost of using a telephone in a hotel meeting room is $0.20 per minute. Which of the following equations represents the total cost c, in dollars, for h hours of phone use?

A. $c = 0.20(60h)$ B. $c = 0.20h + 60$
C. $c = 60h/0.20$ D. $c = 0.20h/60$

解读：在实际生活中，在酒店除了房间费用，其他费用包括电话、mini-bar 里的食品，甚至网络都是要收取相应费用的。这道题则是需要我们根据题目提供的信息建立酒店会议室电话费的计算公式。

 图表题增加

要求：提高解读和整合数据的能力。

第 5 章　重点知识点精讲

5.1　解线性方程

 知识点总结

含有绝对值的不等式的同解变形原理：

$$|ax+b| < c(c>0) \Leftrightarrow -c < ax+b < c$$
$$|ax+b| \leq c(c>0) \Leftrightarrow -c \leq ax+b \leq c$$
$$|ax+b| > c(c>0) \Leftrightarrow ax+b > c \text{ or } ax+b < -c$$
$$|ax+b| \geq c(c>0) \Leftrightarrow ax+b \geq c \text{ or } ax+b \leq -c$$

例题

1. $4-\dfrac{1}{3}z=-7z+6$

Which of the following is the solution to the equations shown above?

A. $z=\dfrac{3}{10}$　　　　B. $z=-\dfrac{3}{10}$　　　　C. $z=\dfrac{20}{3}$　　　　D. $z=\dfrac{20}{6}$

知识点：解线性方程。

解析：合并同类项化简方程，$\dfrac{20}{3}z=2$，解得 $z=\dfrac{3}{10}$，选 A。

2. $\dfrac{2(4p+1)}{5} \leqslant \dfrac{3+12p}{4}$

Which of the following best describes the solutions to the inequality shown above?

A. $p \leqslant -\dfrac{13}{7}$　　　　B. $p \geqslant -\dfrac{13}{7}$　　　　C. $p \leqslant -\dfrac{1}{4}$　　　　D. $p \geqslant -\dfrac{1}{4}$

知识点：解线性不等式。

解析：不等式两边同时乘以 20，去分母，得 $4 \times 2(4p+1) \leqslant 5 \times (3+12p)$，合并同类项化简可得，$p \geqslant -\dfrac{1}{4}$，选 D。

3. $-4+bx=2x+3(x+1)$

In the equation shown above, b is a constant. For what value of b does the equation have no solutions?

A. 3　　　　B. 4　　　　C. 5　　　　D. 6

知识点：方程无解的含义。

解析：化简方程得 $(b-5)x=7$，当 $b=5$ 时方程无解。

4. If $9<15mx-8<27$, where m is a positive constant, what is the possible range of values of $\dfrac{8}{3}-5mx$?

A. Any value greater than -3 or less than -9

B. Any value greater than -9 and less than -3

C. Any value greater than $-\dfrac{7}{3m}$ or less than $-\dfrac{17}{15m}$

D. Any value greater than $-\dfrac{17}{15m}$ and less than $-\dfrac{7}{3m}$

知识点：解线性不等式；不等式两边同时除以一个负数，不等号要改变。

解析：在不等式 $9<15mx-8<27$ 中构造出 $\dfrac{8}{3}-5mx$，则不等号两边同时除以 -3 可得 $-3>\dfrac{8}{3}-5mx>-9$，整理可得 $-9<\dfrac{8}{3}-5mx<-3$，选 B。

5. If $5<2x+3<11$, what is the possible range of values of $-4x-6$?

A. Any value greater than -10 or less than -22

B. Any value greater than -22 and less than -10

C. Any value greater than 1 and less than 4

D. Any value greater than 4 or less than 1

知识点：解线性不等式；不等式两边同时除以一个负数，不等号要改变。

解析：在不等式 $5<2x+3<11$ 中构造出 $-4x-6$，则不等号两边同时乘以 -2 可得 $-22<-4x-6<-10$，选 B。

6. $4(80+n)=(3k)n$

In the equation shown above, k is a constant. For what value of k are there no solutions to the equation?

知识点：方程无解的含义。

解析：化简方程可得 $(3k-4)n=320$，当 $3k-4=0$ 时方程无解，则 $k=\dfrac{4}{3}$。

7. $4|6+2s|-27\leqslant -3$

Which of the following best describes the solutions to the inequality shown above?

A. $-24\leqslant s\leqslant 0$ B. $-6\leqslant s\leqslant 0$ C. $s\leqslant 0$ or $s\geqslant 3$ D. No solution

知识点：解含有绝对值的不等式。

解析：$4|6+2s|-27\leqslant -3$ 不等式两边同时加上 27，然后除以 4 可得 $|6+2s|\leqslant 6$，去绝对值符号，$-6\leqslant 6+2s\leqslant 6$，解得 $-6\leqslant s\leqslant 0$，选 B。

8. $-2(x+2)=6-ax$

In the equation shown above, a is a constant. Which of the following values of a results in an equation with exactly one solution?

A. -2 B. 2   C. Neither value   D. Both values

知识点：解线性方程。

解析：合并同类项化简方程，$(a-2)x=10$，当 $a=-2$ 时，方程为 $-4x=10$，$x=-\dfrac{5}{2}$，有且只有一个解，选 A。

9. If $153=2(z+z)n$, then what is the value of $2n(2z)-193$?

A. -113 B. -40 C. 40   D. 113

知识点：通过方程构造表达式并求解。

解析：化简方程得 $2zn=153$，两边同时乘以 2，减去 193，得 $2n(2z)-193=113$，选 D。

10. $17+27=-7w$

Given the above equation, what is the value of $10(-21w+1)$?

知识点：通过方程构造表达式并求解。

解析：在方程 $17+27=-7w$ 两边同时乘以 3，加上 1 可得 $-21w+1=133$，所以 $10(-21w+1)=1330$。

5.2 解线性函数

例题

1. Officials project that between 2010 and 2050, the Sub-Saharan African population will drastically change. The model below gives the projection of the population, P, in thousands, with respect to time, t (provided that 2010 is when $t=0$).

$$P = 175 + \frac{11}{2}t$$

What does the 175 mean in the equation?

A. In 2010, the population of Sub-Saharan African was 175 thousand.

B. In 2050, the population of Sub-Saharan African will be 175 thousand.

C. Between 2010 and 2050, the population of Sub-Saharan African will increase by 175 thousand.

D. Between 2010 and 2050, the population of Sub-Saharan African will decrease by 175 thousand.

知识点：线性函数 y 轴交点的含义。

解析：当 $t=0$ 时，$P=175$，表示在 2010 年时，人口数为 175000，选 A。

2. $W = -\frac{1}{2}m + 16$

Henry's water bottle is leaking at a constant rate. The amount of water, W, in ounces, that is left in the water bottle after leaking for m minutes is given by the equation above. What does the $-\frac{1}{2}$ mean in the equation?

A. The water bottle loses 2 ounces of water per minute.

B. The water bottle loses $\frac{1}{2}$ an ounces of water per minute.

C. The water bottle has $\frac{1}{2}$ an ounces of water in it at the start.

D. $\frac{1}{2}$ of the water has leaked from the water bottle in one minute.

知识点：线性函数斜率的含义。

解析：m 每增加 1 分钟，W 减少 $\frac{1}{2}$ 盎司的水，所以选 B。

3. $S = 40000 + 500c$

Caden started a new job selling dental chairs. He earns a base salary plus a commission for every chair he sells. The equation above gives Caden's annual salary, S, in dollars, after selling c dental chairs. Based on the equation above, what is Caden's base salary?

A. $39500   B. $40000   C. $40500   D. $50000

知识点：线性函数 y 轴交点的含义。

解析：当 $c=0$ 时，$S=40000$，表示在没有卖出去椅子的情况下，工资为 40000 美元，这就是基本工资，选 B。

4. Anthropologists have noticed that they can predict the height of a human being based on the length of their femur. The relationship between the person's height, H, in centimeters, and length of the femur, f, in centimeters, can be modeled by the equation below.

$$H = 2.72f + 42.12$$

One anthropologist found the femurs of two different people. One femur measured 22 centimeters and the other femur measured 23 centimeters. What is the difference in their heights?

 A. 1 centimeter   B. 2.72 centimeters

 C. 27.2 centimeters   D. 42.12 centimeters

知识点:线性函数的计算。

解析:$H_1 - H_2 = (2.72f_1 + 42.12) - (2.72f_2 + 42.12) = 2.72$,选 B。

5. $C = 1.5b + 67.5$

The total cost, C, in dollars, to produce b books is given by the equation below. What is the meaning of 1.5 in the equation?

 A. 1.5 books will cost \$67.50 to produce.

 B. It costs an extra \$1.50 for each book produced.

 C. If you produce one book, you total cost will be \$1.50.

 D. There is a flat fee of \$1.50 to produce any number of books.

知识点:线性函数的含义。

解析:每多生产一本书,成本增加 1.5 美元,由此可知 67.5 美元是固定成本,而 1.5 美元是生产每本书的成本,选 B。

6. $P = 0.7c$

A store is having a sale on every item purchased. Irina decides to take advantage of the sale and purchases a sweater. The equation that gives the after-sale price, P, of Irina's sweater with an original cost, c, is shown above. What percent off the original cost did Irina save?

 A. 3%   B. 7%   C. 30%   D. 70%

知识点:线性函数的含义。

解析:折扣价是成本的 70%,则省了成本的 30%,选 C。

7. $T = 1200 - 0.06c$

A print shop copies and prints documents in large volume for its customers. For a particular copy machine, the equation above gives the amount of toner, T, in grams, left after making c copies.

How many grams of toner are used per copy?

grams

知识点:线性函数斜率的含义。

解析:由函数可知,当 c 增加 1 时,T 减少 0.06,即每多复印一份文件,墨粉减少 0.06 克。

8. $16B + 3.5W = 22$

Antoine bikes part of the way on a 22 mile trail and walks the rest of the way. If he spends B hours biking and W hours walking, the trip is modeled by the equation shown above. What is the meaning of the $16B$ in the equation?

 A. Antoine travels a total of $16B$ miles.

 B. Antoine bikes for a total of $16B$ miles.

 C. Antoine bikes for $16B$ miles before starting his walk.

 D. Antoine rides his bike at an average speed of $16B$ mile per hour.

知识点:线性函数的含义。

解析：B 表示骑自行车的时间，$16B$ 则表示在走路之前骑车了 $16B$ 英里，选 C。

9. $C=40(5-s)$

After Hiro's family photo shoot the photographer sells the printed photos by the sheet. Hiro has a \$200 credit from a prior session, and the above equation gives the total credit left, C, in dollars, if he buys s sheets. How many sheets can Hiro purchase with his credit?

  A. 5 sheets   B. 8 sheets   C. 35 sheets   D. 200 sheets

知识点：线性函数的含义。

解析：当 $s=5$ 时，$C=0$，所以 Hiro 能买 5 张，选 A。

10. $C=1.5b+67.5$

The total cost, C, in dollars, to produce b books is given by the equation below. What is the meaning of 1.5 in the equation?

  A. 1.5 books will cost \$67.50 to produce.

  B. It costs an extra \$1.50 for each book produced.

  C. If you produce one book, you total cost will be \$1.50.

  D. There is a flat fee of \$1.50 to produce any number of bool.

知识点：线性函数斜率的含义。

解析：当 b 增加 1 时，C 增加 1.5，即多生产一本书，成本增加 1.5 美元，选 B。

5.3 线性方程应用题

例题

1. A food truck owner has determined that her maximum revenue occurs when she sells 950 sandwiches per month. For every sandwich above or below 950 that she sells, her revenue decreases by \$0.10. Which of the following could be the number of sandwiches sold in a month if the owner's revenue decreased \$45 from the maximum? Round the answer to the nearest whole number.

  A. $s=905$ or $s=995$ B. $s=946$ or $s=955$

  C. $s=500$ or $s=1400$ D. $s=500$ or $s=950$

知识点：线性方程的应用。

解析：多卖或者少卖一个三明治减少 0.1 美元收入，减少 45 美元时多卖或者少卖 450 个，所以卖了 500 或者 1400 个三明治，选 C。

2. From 1980 to 2000, the annual profit of a company was \$625000 less \$25000 times the number of years either before or after 1990. Which of the following equations below could be used to determine in which year, x, the profit was \$550000?

  A. $550-25|x-1990|=625$ B. $625-25|x-1990|=550$

  C. $625+25|x-1990|=550$ D. $625+25|x+1990|=550$

知识点：含义绝对值函数的应用。

解析：年利润由 625000 减去 25000 乘以 1990 年前后的年数，当年份为 x 时，年数为

$|x-1990|$,所以选 B。

3. Sam gives his little sister Lisa a 15 second (sec) head start in their 300 meter (m) race. During the race, Lisa runs at an average speed of 5 m/sec and Sam runs at an average speed of 8 m/sec. Which of the following best approximates the number of seconds that Sam will run before he catches Lisa?

  A. 5   B. 25   C. 40   D. 55

  知识点:线性方程的应用。

  解析:假设 Sam 跑了 x 秒追上 Lisa,则他们跑的路程相等,由此可得方程 $15\times 5+5x=8x$,解得 $x=25$,选 B。

4. A car rental company charges \$34.50 a day plus a tax of 6% to rent an economy size car. Additionally, the company charges a one-time untaxed fee of \$10.50 for each rental. If a customer is charged \$193.98 in total to rent an economy size car for d days, which of the following equations models the situation?

  A. $(34.50+1.06d)+10.50=193.98$ B. $1.06(34.50d+10.50)=193.98$

  C. $1.06(34.50d)+10.50=193.98$ D. $(1.06(34.50)+10.50)d=193.98$

  知识点:线性方程的应用。

  解析:租车费用每天 34.5 美元,加上 6% 的税,还有一次性不加税的 10.5 美元,当租车 d 天,费用为 193.98 美元时,方程为 $1.06(34.50d)+10.50=193.98$,选 C。

5. Sasha has \$2.65 in change in her pocket. The \$2.65 is made up of one quarter plus an equal number of nickels and dimes. How many nickels does Sasha have in her pocket?

  知识点:线性方程的应用。

  解析:假设有 x 枚五分硬币,则由题目可列方程 $25+10x+5x=265$,解得 $x=16$。

6. A piece of wood has a mass of 30 grams (g) and a volume of 40 cubic centimeters (cm³). A second piece of wood has the same density $\left(\dfrac{g}{cm^3}\right)$ and a volume of 240 cm³. What is the mass in grams of the second piece of wood?

  知识点:线性方程的应用。

  解析:假设第二根木头的质量为 x 克,则由题意可列方程 $\dfrac{x}{240}=\dfrac{30}{40}$,解得 $x=180$。

7. Alma and Erika work part time stocking shelves at a grocery store. At 7:00 a.m. on Saturday, Alma begins unpacking boxes at a rate of 1 box every 6 minutes. Erika joins her at 7:45 a.m. and unpacks 1 box every 5 minutes. When finished with this task, a total of 24 boxes have been unpacked since 7:00 a.m. If x represents the number of minutes for which Alma has been working, which of the following equations best models the situation?

  A. $\dfrac{1}{6}x+\dfrac{1}{5}(x-45)=24$ B. $\dfrac{1}{6}x+\dfrac{1}{5}\left(x-\dfrac{3}{4}\right)=24$

  C. $6x+5(x-45)=24$ D. $6x+5\left(x-\dfrac{3}{4}\right)=24$

  知识点:线性方程的应用。

  解析:由题意可知,Alma 6 分钟打开一个包裹,x 分钟打开了 $\dfrac{1}{6}x$ 个,Erika 晚了 45 分钟开始,5 分钟打开一个包裹,$(x-45)$ 分钟打开了 $\frac{1}{5}(x-45)$ 个,两人最后一共打开了 24 个包裹,由此可知,选 A。

8. On January 1st, 2014, approximately 450 thousand buildings in the United States (US) had solar panels. This number increased by a total of about 180 thousand over the next 12 months. Assuming a constant rate of change, approximately how many months after January 1st, 2014 would 900 thousand buildings in the US have solar panels?

知识点:线性方程的应用。

解析:12 个月增长 180 千栋。假设 x 个月之后有 900 千栋建筑使用太阳能电池板,由此可列方程为 $\frac{180}{12}x+450=900$,解得 $x=30$。

9. Erika's times for the 1-mile run decreased consistently throughout her track season. She estimates that her time for the 1-mile run decreased by about 15 seconds (secs) for every 2 weeks of training. If Erika ran a mile in 8 minutes (mins) and 20 secs at the start of the season, and x weeks into her training ran a mile in 7 mins and 5 secs, which of the following equations best models the situation?

A. $500-7.5x=425$
B. $500-15x=425$
C. $500+7.5x=425$
D. $500+15x=425$

知识点:线性方程的应用。

解析:训练两周跑 1 英里的时间减少 15 秒,Erika 刚开始需要 8 分 20 秒,即为 500 秒,经过 x 周的训练,跑步时间减少到 7 分 5 秒,即为 425 秒。由此可列方程为 $500-7.5x=425$,选 A。

10. The gas mileage for a car is 23 miles per gallon when the car travels at 60 miles per hour. The car begins a trip with 13 gallons in its tank, travels at an average speed of 60 miles per hour for h hours, and ends the trip with 10 gallons in its tank. Which of the following equations best models this situation?

A. $13-\frac{23h}{60}=10$
B. $13-\frac{60h}{23}=10$
C. $\frac{13-60h}{23}=10$
D. $\frac{13-23h}{60}=10$

知识点:线性方程的应用。

解析:由题意可知,油箱原有 13 加仑的油,以 60 英里/小时的速度行驶 h 小时,行驶了 $60h$ 英里,1 加仑的油可供汽车行驶 23 英里,最后还剩 10 加仑,可列方程为 $13-\frac{60h}{23}=10$,选 B。

5.4 线性不等式应用题

例题

1. Jennifer wants to spend no more than $300 on school clothes. She spends $75 on

a jacket and wants to buy some shirts that are on sale for $10 each. Which inequality represents the number, s, of shirts Jennifer can buy?

  A. $s<22$ B. $s>30$ C. $s>37$ D. $s<38$

知识点：线性不等式的应用。

解析：由题意可知，买一件75美元的夹克以及s件10美元的衬衫，总共不超过300美元，可列不等式为$75+10s<300$，化简为$s<22$，选A。

2. A small airplane can carry less than 1050 pounds of luggage and mail. Tuesday's load of mail weighs 490 pounds. If each passenger brings 70 pounds of luggage, what is the greatest possible number of passengers that can travel on the airplane on Tuesday?

  A. 7   B. 8   C. 14   D. 15

知识点：线性不等式的应用。

解析：由题意可知，小型飞机能载不超过1050磅的行李箱及邮件，周二的邮件重490磅，如果每位乘客携带70磅的行李箱，最多可以有x位乘客，由此可列不等式为$490+70x<1050$，化简为$x<8$，选A。

3. Christopher has at most $18.50 to spend at a convenience store. He buys one bag of bananas for $1.50 and a bottle of apple juice for $1.55. If gasoline at this store costs $2.35 per gallon, which of the following number of gallons can he buy for his car without exceeding his budget?

  A. 4.23   B. 7.61

  C. 10.82   D. 15.17

知识点：线性不等式的应用。

解析：由题意可知，Christopher有18.5美元，买1袋香蕉花1.5美元，一瓶苹果汁花1.55美元。加1加仑汽油需要2.35美元，假设他加了x加仑，可列不等式为$1.5+1.55+2.35x \leqslant 18.5$，解得$x \leqslant 6.57$，所以选A。

4. An audiologist is testing a patient to determine the softest sound of a specific frequency that the patient reports hearing. She begins with a 10 decibel (dB) sound for trial 1, then increases the volume by 2dB for each trial after that. If the patient can hear all sounds of that frequency that have a volume louder than 26dB, and t represents the trial numbers that the patient can hear, which of the following inequalities best models the situation described above?

  A. $2t+10 \geqslant 26$ B. $2t+10>26$

  C. $2(t-1)+10 \geqslant 26$ D. $2(t-1)+10>26$

知识点：线性不等式的应用。

解析：由题意可知，从10分贝开始，在第一次实验之后每次增加2分贝，经过t次实验后，分贝超过26，由此可列不等式为$2(t-1)+10>26$，选D。

5. A college student has equally weighted exam grades of 71, 83, and 90 on three 100-point exams. The student has one more 100-point exam that counts toward his grade and wants an exam average of at least 84. Which inequality represents the range of scores the student can get to achieve this desired exam average?

  A. $m \geqslant 8$ B. $m \geqslant 79$ C. $m \geqslant 81$ D. $m \geqslant 92$

知识点：线性不等式的应用。

解析：由题意可知，学生在几门满分为 100 分的考试中，分别获得 71、83、90 和 m 分，此时的平均成绩至少为 84 分，由此可列不等式为 $\frac{71+83+90+m}{4} \geqslant 84$，化简可得 $m \geqslant 92$，选 D。

6. Crys began a workout regimen at a local health club. She began her workouts at 45 minutes each, but has since increased the workouts by 5 minutes per week. Her total workout time cannot exceed 2 hours. If Crys has workouts for x weeks until she hits 2 hours, which inequality best models the situation?

    A. $45x+5 \leqslant 120$ B. $45x+5 \geqslant 120$

    C. $45+5(x-1) \leqslant 120$ D. $45+5x \leqslant 120$

知识点：线性不等式的应用。

解析：Crys 第一周锻炼 45 分钟，之后的每周增加 5 分钟，锻炼了 x 周，增加 $5(x-1)$ 分钟，总时间不超过 2 小时，即为 120 分钟，锻炼了 x 周，可列不等式 $45+5(x-1) \leqslant 120$，选 C。

7. Anais donates blood for the first time on May 15th, the 135th day of the year. She may donate again every 56 days. If n is the number of total times which Anais donates this year, which equation best models the situation for ?

    A. $56n+135 \leqslant 365$ B. $56(n-1)+135 \leqslant 365$

    C. $56n-1+135 < 365$ D. $56(n+135) < 365$

知识点：线性不等式的应用。

解析：Anais 在 5 月 15 日第一次献血，也是这一年的第 135 天，之后每 56 天献一次血，一共献血 n 次，由此可列不等式为 $56(n-1)+135 \leqslant 365$，选 B。

8. Joanne and Richard volunteer at a hospital. Joanne volunteers 4 hours more per week than Richard does. In a given week, they do not volunteer for more than a combined total of 16 hours. If x is the number of hours that Richard volunteers, which inequality best models this situation?

    A. $x+4 \leqslant 16$ B. $2x+4 \leqslant 16$

    C. $2x+8 \leqslant 16$ D. $2x-4 \leqslant 16$

知识点：线性不等式的应用。

解析：Joanne 每周比 Richard 多做 4 小时志愿者，在某一周他们一共做了不超过 16 小时，Richard 做 x 小时，则 Joanne 做 $(x+4)$ 小时，可列不等式为 $2x+4 \leqslant 16$，选 B。

9. Mikal has a summer project in which he must complete at least 35 hours of community service at a city park. Each day that he goes to the park, he volunteers for 7 hours. It takes him 1.5 hours to get to the park each way, which also counts toward his community service hours. Which of the following inequalities can be used to find the number of days, d, Mikal must volunteer at the park to complete his summer project?

    A. $7d > 35$ B. $7d \geqslant 35$ C. $7d+3 > 35$ D. $7d+3d \geqslant 35$

知识点：线性不等式的应用。

解析：Mikal 每天志愿工作 7 小时，路上单程需要 1.5 小时，来回一共 3 小时，工作 d 天，至少 35 小时，由此可列不等式为 $7d+3d \geqslant 35$，选 D。

10. An insurance agent sells an insurance policy with an out-of-pocket maximum of

$5000. Out-of-pocket expenses include any deductibles and coinsurance that the client pays beyond the normal monthly premium. The client has a deductible of $250. This means that the client has to pay all of the first $250 of expenses insured by the policy. After that, the client has a 20% coinsurance, meaning the client pays 20% of the insured expenses and the insurance company pays the remainder. Which inequality represents how much the total insured expenses, x, could be if the client has not yet reached the out-of-pocket maximum?

A. $x<26000$　　　　B. $x<25000$　　　　C. $x<24000$　　　　D. $x<23750$

知识点：线性不等式的应用。

解析：根据题意可知，客户需要先支付 250 美元，然后支付剩下费用的 20%，总的现款支付的金额不超过 5000 美元，假设总的保险费用为 x 美元，则可列不等式 $250+0.2(x-250)<5000$，解得 $x<24000$，选 C。

5.5　画线性方程

知识点

1. 直线方程的几种形式

直线方程的形式如表 5.1 所示。

表 5.1　直线方程的形式

名称	方程的形式	已知条件
点斜式	$y-y_1=k(x-x_1)$	(x_1,y_1) 为直线上一定点，k 为斜率
斜截式	$y=kx+b$	k 为斜率，b 是直线在 y 轴上的截距
两点式	$\dfrac{y-y_1}{y_2-y_1}=\dfrac{x-x_1}{x_2-x_1}$（其中 $x_1\neq x_2,y_1\neq y_2$）	$(x_1,y_1),(x_2,y_2)$ 是直线上两定点
截距式	$\dfrac{x}{a}+\dfrac{y}{b}=1$	a 是直线在 x 轴上的非零截距，b 是直线在 y 轴上的非零截距
一般式	$Ax+By+C=0$（其中 A,B 不同时为 0）	$A、B、C$ 为系数

2. 直线斜率与直线的位置关系

两直线平行，斜率相等。

两直线垂直，斜率的乘积为 -1。

例题

1. Which of the following equations represents a line in the xy-plane with an x-intercept at $(-15,0)$ and a y-intercept at $(0,-9)$?

A. $\dfrac{x}{15}+\dfrac{y}{9}=1$ B. $-\dfrac{x}{15}-\dfrac{y}{9}=1$

C. $\dfrac{x}{9}-\dfrac{y}{15}=1$ D. $-\dfrac{x}{9}+\dfrac{y}{15}=1$

知识点：直线方程的截距式。

解析：根据直线方程的截距式可知 a 为 -9，b 为 -15，则方程为 $-\dfrac{x}{15}-\dfrac{y}{9}=1$，选 B。

2. Two lines graphed in the xy-plane have the equations $2x+5y=20$ and $y=kx-3$, where k is a constant. For what value of k will the two lines be perpendicular?

A. $-\dfrac{2}{5}$ B. $\dfrac{2}{5}$ C. $\dfrac{5}{2}$ D. $-\dfrac{5}{2}$

知识点：两垂直直线斜率的关系。

解析：两直线垂直，斜率的乘积为 -1，把第一条直线的一般式方程化为斜截式方程，斜率为 $-\dfrac{2}{5}$，则 $-\dfrac{2}{5}k=-1$，所以 $k=\dfrac{5}{2}$，选 C。

3. Which of the following represents the graph of the equation $3y-7=0$?

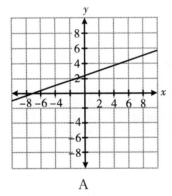

A

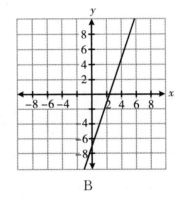

B

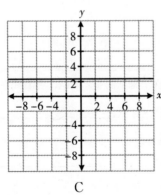

C

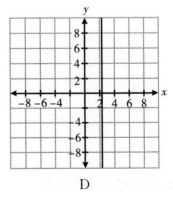

D

知识点：直线方程画图。

解析：化简方程 $3y-7=0$ 得 $y=\dfrac{7}{3}$，选 C。

4. The equations $x+y=3$ and $-5x-5y=-15$ are graphed in the xy-plane. Which of the following must be true of the graphs of the two equations?

A. The slope of the graph of $x+y=3$ is 11 and the slope of the graph of $-5x-5y=-15$ is -1.

B. The graphs of the two equations are perpendicular lines.

C. The y-intercept of the graph of $-5x-5y=-15$ is -15.

D. The graphs of the two equations are the same line.

知识点：直线方程的不同表示。

解析：化简方程$-5x-5y=-15$可得$x+y=3$，由此可知两方程表示同一条直线，选D。

5. If k is a rational constant not equal to 1, which of the following graphs represents the equation $y+5=k(x+y)+5$?

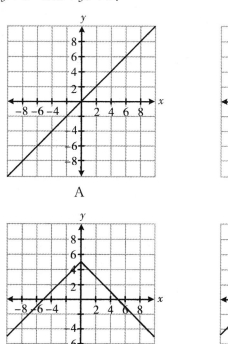

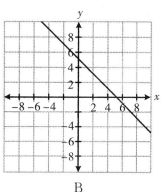

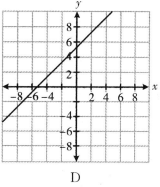

知识点：直线方程的图像。

解析：化简方程$y+5=k(x+y)+5$可得$y=\dfrac{k}{1-k}x$，y轴上的截距为0，则方程$y=\dfrac{k}{1-k}x$过原点，所以选A。

6. What is the equation of the line graphed in the xy-plane that passes through the point $(-4,-5)$ and is parallel to the line whose equation is $3x-4y=-8$?

A. $y=-\dfrac{4}{3}x+10$ B. $y=\dfrac{3}{4}x-2$

C. $y=\dfrac{3}{4}x-8$ D. $y=-\dfrac{4}{3}x-8$

知识点：平行直线斜率的关系。

解析：两直线平行，斜率相等，直线$3x-4y=-8$的斜率为$k=\dfrac{3}{4}$，则另一直线的斜率也

是 $k=\dfrac{3}{4}$，且过点 $(-4,-5)$，所以直线方程为 $y=\dfrac{3}{4}x-2$，选 B。

7. The equation for the gravitational potential energy U of a 1 kilogram object on Earth resting h meters above the ground t seconds after placement is $U=9.8h$ joules. Which of the following is a graph of U versus t for a 1-kilogram object 2 meters above the ground?

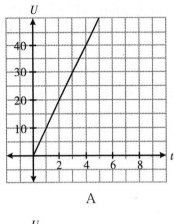

A

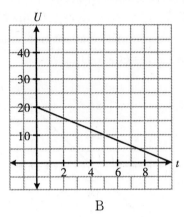

B

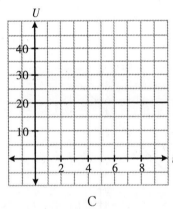

C

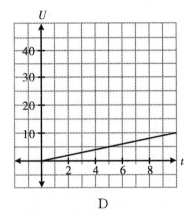

D

知识点：直线方程的图像。

解析：已知 $U=9.8h$，此时 $h=2$，则 $U=19.6$，选 C。

8. The equations below are graphed in the xy-plane. Which equation's graph will have a slope of $\dfrac{7}{8}$ and a y-intercept of 3?

A. $7x+8y=24$ B. $7x-8y=-24$

C. $8x+7y=3$ D. $7x-8y=3$

知识点：直线方程的图像。

解析：y 轴截距为 3 表示直线过点 $(0,3)$，由此排除选项 C、D；由斜率为 $\dfrac{7}{8}$ 可知，选 B。

9. The line represented by the equation $y=\dfrac{1}{12}-x$ is graphed in the xy-plane. Which of the following statements correctly describes the graph of the line?

A. The line is perpendicular to the graph $x+y=1$.

B. The line has a negative slope and a positive y-intercept.
C. The line has a positive slope and a negative y-intercept.
D. The x-intercept is equal to the negative of the y-intercept.

知识点:直线方程的图像。

解析:方程 $y=\frac{1}{12}-x$ 的斜率为 $k=-1$,y 轴截距为 $\frac{1}{12}$,所以选 B。

10. Which of the following represents the graph of the equation $x=-\frac{1}{3}y$?

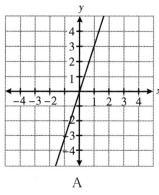

A

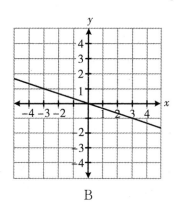

B

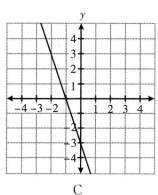

C

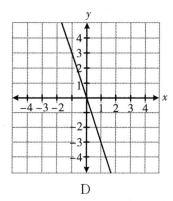

D

知识点:直线方程的图像。

解析:由方程 $x=-\frac{1}{3}y$ 可知直线过原点,当 $y=3$ 时 $x=-1$,直线过点 $(-1,3)$,所以选 D。

5.6 线性函数应用题

例题

1. Gary learned that the value of his car depreciates by 15% per year. Which of the following functions best describes the value of his car the year after the car is worth m dollars?

    A. $f(m)=0.15m$ B. $f(m)=0.85m$

C. $f(m)=1-0.15m$ D. $f(m)=1-0.85m$

知识点：线性函数的应用。

解析：Gary 的车每年贬值 15%，当他的车价值为 m 美元时，第二年的价值为 $f(m)=0.85m$，选 B。

2. Between 2008 and 2012, the revenue obtained from digital music album downloads, r, in millions of dollars, in the United States increased by approximately 132 million dollars per year. In 2010, the digital music revenue in the U.S. was about 872 million dollars. If t represents years since 2008, which of the following best models the situation for?

A. $r(t)=132t$ B. $r(t)=132t+608$
C. $r(t)=132t+872$ D. $r(t)=132t+1136$

知识点：线性函数的应用。

解析：2008~2012 年间数字音乐下载收益为 r 百万美元，每年增加 132 百万美元。2010 年的收益为 872 百万美元，则 2008 年的收益为 608 百万美元，所以函数为 $r(t)=132t+608$，选 B。

3. Mikayla is a waitress who makes a guaranteed $50 per day in addition to tips of 20% of all her customer receipts, t. She works six days per week. Which of the following functions best represents the amount of money that Mikayla makes in one week?

A. $f(t)=50+20t$ B. $f(t)=300+20t$
C. $f(t)=50+0.2t$ D. $f(t)=300+0.2t$

知识点：线性函数的应用。

解析：Mikayla 每天可以拿到 50 美元，一周工作 6 天总共可以拿到 300 美元，加上顾客消费 t 的 20% 小费，则函数为 $f(t)=300+0.2t$，选 D。

4. John's seafood restaurant is trying to estimate its profits. John has found that on average, each meal served costs the restaurant $14.56 and takes in $17.12. John has also found that on average, each beverage served costs the restaurant $1.20 and takes in $5.40. If c customers order a meal, and half of those customers order a beverage, which of the following functions models the restaurant's total profit?

A. $f(c)=17.12c-14.56c+5.40\left(\dfrac{1}{2}c\right)-1.20\left(\dfrac{1}{2}c\right)$

B. $f(c)=17.12c-14.56c+5.40c-1.20c$

C. $f(c)=14.56c-17.12c+1.20c-5.40c$

D. $f(c)=14.56c-17.12c+1.20\left(\dfrac{1}{2}c\right)-5.40\left(\dfrac{1}{2}c\right)$

知识点：线性函数的应用。

解析：John 的海鲜餐厅每一餐的成本为 14.56 美元，售价为 17.12 美元；饮料一份成本为 1.20 美元，售价为 5.40 美元，假设 c 位顾客点餐，一半的顾客，即为 $\dfrac{1}{2}c$ 位顾客点饮料，则关于利润的函数为 $f(c)=17.12c-14.56c+5.40\left(\dfrac{1}{2}c\right)-1.20\left(\dfrac{1}{2}c\right)$，选 A。

5. Maria burns about 600 calories per hour jogging and about 450 calories per hour biking. If Maria spends x hours per day biking, and $\frac{4}{5}$ as much time jogging, which of the following functions best models the amount of calories, C, that Maria burns in one day from jogging and biking?

　　A. $C(x)=840x$　　　　　　　　B. $C(x)=930x$
　　C. $C(x)=960x$　　　　　　　　D. $C(x)=1050x$

知识点：线性函数的应用。

解析：Maria 慢跑每小时消耗 600 卡路里，骑自习车每小时消耗 450 卡路里。Maria 花 x 小时骑车，$\frac{4}{5}x$ 小时慢跑，由此可知，运动消耗的卡路里 C 有关的函数为 $C(x)=450x+\frac{4}{5}\times 600x=930x$，选 B。

6. A roller coaster is currently traveling at a speed of 49 miles per hour (mph). The coaster's speed will increase at a constant rate of 17mph every 2 seconds until the coaster reaches its top speed 5 seconds from now. If $t\leqslant 5$, which function best represents the roller coaster's speed, in miles per hour, t seconds from now?

　　A. $f(t)=49+8.5t$　　　　　　　B. $f(t)=49+17t$
　　C. $f(t)=49+9.8t$　　　　　　　D. $f(t)=49+1.7t$

知识点：线性函数的应用。

解析：过山车现在的速度为 49 英里/小时，每两秒增加 17 英里/小时，直到 5 秒后，当 $t\leqslant 5$ 时，关于速度的函数为 $f(t)=49+\frac{17}{2}t=49+8.5t$，选 A。

7. Sterling silver is an alloy of silver that is 92.5% pure silver. If x grams of sterling silver are mixed with y grams of an 88% silver alloy to produce a 91% silver alloy, which of the following equations correctly relates x and y?

　　A. $0.075x+12y=0$　　　　　　B. $0.015x-0.03y=0$
　　C. $0.925x+0.88y=91$　　　　　D. $0.925x+0.88y=0.91xy$

知识点：线性函数的应用。

解析：标准纯银是一种纯银含量为 92.5% 的合金，如果把 x 克标准纯银跟 y 克含有 88% 的银的合金混合生产纯银含量为 91% 的合金，则 $0.925x+0.88y=0.91(x+y)$，化简可得 $0.015x-0.03y=0$，选 B。

8. Gustav is starting a special sprinting regimen in outdoor track. The regimen suggests sprinting for a certain number of seconds, s, at first. The second time he sprints, he should run 150 more seconds than the first time. For the third time, the regimen suggests sprinting twice the number of seconds as the first time. Finally, the regimen suggests an 80-second sprint. Which of the following functions can be used to find the total number of seconds, t, suggested by the entire sprinting regimen?

　　A. $t=s+230$　　　　　　　　B. $t=2s+230$
　　C. $t=\frac{5}{2}s+230$　　　　　　D. $t=4s+230$

知识点：线性函数的应用。

解析：Gustav 在进行短跑训练，第一次跑 s 秒，第二次多跑 150 秒，即为 $s+150$ 秒，第三次跑的是第一次的两倍，即 $2s$ 秒，最后一次跑 80 秒，总共跑的时间函数为 $t=s+s+150+2x+80=4s+230$，选 D。

9. In 2007, approximately 50% of the world's population lived in rural (defined as non-urban) areas. From 2005 to 2013, the percent of the world's population living in rural areas decreased by about 0.5 percentage points per year. If t represents years since 2005, which of the following equations best models the percent of the world's population living in rural areas, r, from 2005 to 2013?

A. $r-50=-0.5(t-2)$
B. $r-50=-0.5(t-7)$
C. $r-2=-0.5(t-50)$
D. $r-7=-0.5(t-50)$

知识点：线性函数的应用。

解析：2007 年世界人口大约有 50% 住在农村地区，从 2005～2013 年，居住在农村的人口数量每年减少 0.5 个百分点，$r=50-0.5(t-2)$，选 A。

10. The gas tank in Ms. Brown's car holds a total of 15 gallons. At any given time, how many gallons, g, will Ms. Brown have to pump into her car to fill her tank given the fraction of the tank, f, already filled?

A. $g=15f$ B. $g=\dfrac{15}{f}$ C. $g=15-15f$ D. $g=15-\dfrac{15}{f}$

知识点：线性函数的应用。

解析：Brown 女士的油箱能装 15 加仑的油，在任何时间，她要加入油箱的油 g 用邮箱里剩余油占总数的分数 f 表示，则剩余的油为 $15f$，所以 $g=15-15f$，选 C。

5.7 线性不等式组应用题

例题

1. Julia mows lawns in the summer for \$15 per lawn. It costs Julia between \$2 and \$4 to mow 1 lawn. If l represents the number of lawns Julia mows, which graph correctly shades the possible values of Julia's net earnings, d, in dollars?

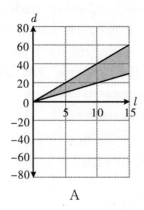

A

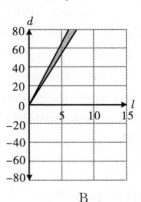

B

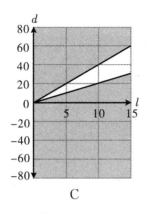
C

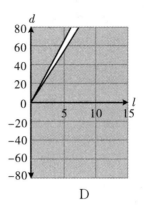
D

知识点：线性不等式组的应用。

解析：Julia 夏天给草坪除草，15 美元一块，她除一块草坪花费 2~4 美元，则她可能的净利润为 $15l-4l \leqslant d \leqslant 15l-2l$，则 $11l \leqslant d \leqslant 13l$，选 B。

2. A barge must carry steel pieces for a construction project such that the total weight of the steel pieces is under 1500000 kilograms (kg). Each steel piece is either a beam, which weighs 363 kg, or a connector plate, which weighs 6 kg. There must be at least 2 connector plates for each beam. If b is the number of beams and c is the number of connector plates, which of the following systems of inequalities must be true?

A. $\begin{cases} 363b+6c<1500000 \\ b \leqslant 2c \end{cases}$ B. $\begin{cases} 363b+6c<1500000 \\ 2b \leqslant c \end{cases}$

C. $\begin{cases} 363b+6c \geqslant 1500000 \\ b \geqslant 2c \end{cases}$ D. $\begin{cases} 363b+6c \geqslant 1500000 \\ 2b>c \end{cases}$

知识点：线性不等式组的应用。

解析：一艘船能运载 1500000 千克以下的钢铁，每块钢铁是重 363 千克的横梁，或者是重 6 千克的连接件。每 1 块横梁至少有 2 块连接件，由此可列不等式组为 $363b+6c<1500000$，选 B。

3. In tennis, a player must win 6 games in order to win a set. However, winning 6 games does not guarantee that the player will win the set. If g is the number of games the player won and s is the number of sets the player won, which of the following inequalities must be true?

A. $s \geqslant 6g$ B. $s \geqslant 6g$ C. $6s \leqslant g$ D. $6s \geqslant g$

知识点：线性不等式组的应用。

解析：在网球比赛中，运动员赢 6 局可以赢 1 盘，但是赢 6 局并不能保证赢 1 盘，则 $\frac{g}{6} \geqslant s$，则 $6s \leqslant g$，选 C。

4. A rancher wants to build a rectangular pen for her animals. She decides that the length, l, of one side of the pen should be at most 60 feet, the width, w, of one side of the pen should be at least 30 feet, and the perimeter of the pen should be at most 200 feet. Which of the following systems of inequalities best models the situation described above?

A. $\begin{cases} l+w \leqslant 200 \\ w \geqslant 30 \\ l \leqslant 60 \end{cases}$ B. $\begin{cases} l+w \geqslant 200 \\ w \leqslant 30 \\ l \geqslant 60 \end{cases}$ C. $\begin{cases} l+w \leqslant 100 \\ w \geqslant 30 \\ l \leqslant 60 \end{cases}$ D. $\begin{cases} 2l+2w \geqslant 200 \\ w \geqslant 30 \\ l \leqslant 60 \end{cases}$

知识点：线性不等式组的应用。

解析：一名农场主想设计一只长方形的笔给她的动物,她决定笔的长最多60英尺,宽至少30英尺,周长最多200英尺,则可列不等式组为 $\begin{cases} l+w \leqslant 100 \\ w \geqslant 30 \\ l \leqslant 60 \end{cases}$,选C。

5. A tennis club is organizing group lessons. The club supplies 40 new balls for each player which cost $1 each. Each player pays $300 for the lessons. The club must pay each instructor $1000 for conducting the lessons, and there must be at least 1 instructor for every 6 players. Which amount of players and instructors meets these requirements and still gives the club a net profit?

    A. 6 players and 2 instructors   B. 10 players and 3 instructors

    C. 13 players and 2 instructors   D. 16 players and 3 instructors

知识点：线性不等式组的应用。

解析：一网球俱乐部组织团课,俱乐部提供40个新网球给每1位运动员,1美元1个,每位运动员付300美元的费用,俱乐部需要给每位教员1000美元。每6位运动员至少需要1名教员,假设有 x 名运动员, y 名教员,由此可列不等式组为 $\begin{cases} 300x - 40x - 1000y \geqslant 0 \\ \dfrac{x}{6} \leqslant y \end{cases}$,则选D。

6. A used car dealer has 20 vehicles, all cars and trucks. He would like to paint and clear coat as many of them as possible with the 260 liters of paint and 300 liters of clear coat that he has. It takes 13.2 liters of paint and 9.5 liters of clear coat for one car. It takes 1.5 times those amounts for one truck. Given the relevant equations graphed at left, which of the following could be the amount of cars and trucks that received paint and clear coat?

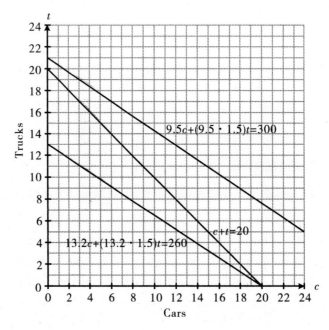

    A. 10 cars and 6 trucks   B. 6 cars and 10 trucks

    C. 14 cars and 11 trucks   D. 11 cars and 14 trucks

知识点：线性不等式组的应用。

解析：一名二手车经销商有小汽车及卡车共20辆,他有260公升油漆以及300公升透明涂层。一辆小汽车需要13.2公升油漆及9.5公升透明涂层,一辆卡车需要小汽车1.5倍的量,由此可得不等式组为 $\begin{cases} c+t \leq 20 \\ 13.2c+(13.2 \cdot 1.5)t \leq 260 \\ 9.5c+(9.5 \cdot 1.5)t \leq 300 \end{cases}$,由图可知,可行区域在三条直线的下方,则只有选项A符合条件。

7. Manoj runs a business at a baseball stadium. This month, with a budget of $17000, Manoj buys p pounds of peanuts at $1.10 per pound and pays his salespeople $200 each. There are s salespeople in total, and it is predicted that each can sell a maximum of 1875 pounds of peanuts this month. Manoj will not buy more peanuts than what he predicts his salespeople can sell. Which of the following systems of inequalities represents this situation?

A. $\begin{cases} \$17000 < \$200s + \dfrac{p}{s} \\ 1875s \leq p \end{cases}$
B. $\begin{cases} \$17000 < \$200s + \$1.10p \\ s \geq 1875 \end{cases}$

C. $\begin{cases} \$17000 \geq \$200s + \dfrac{p}{s} \\ s \leq 1875p \end{cases}$
D. $\begin{cases} \$17000 \geq \$200s + \$1.10p \\ 1875s \geq p \end{cases}$

知识点：线性不等式组的应用。

解析：Manoj的预算为17000美元,买花生 p 磅,每磅1.1美元,付给销售一人200美元,一共有 s 名销售,可以预测每名销售本月最多可以卖1875磅,Manoj的购买量不能超过预测销售能卖的数量,由此可列不等式组为 $\begin{cases} \$17000 \geq \$200 + \$1.10p \\ 1875s \geq p \end{cases}$,选D。

8. A business analyst is deciding the amount of time allotted to each employee for meetings and training. He wants the sum of meeting and training time to be no more than 16 hours per month. Also, there should be at least one training hour for every two meeting hours. Finally, there should be at least 2 meeting hours per month to discuss short-term goals. What is the difference between the maximum and minimum number of monthly training hours that could be allotted to an employee?

A. 10 hours   B. 13 hours   C. 14 hours   D. 16 hours

知识点：线性不等式组的应用。

解析：一名商业分析师在分配给每位员工的会议及培训时间,他希望每个月会议及培训的总时长不超过16小时,同时,每2小时会议至少有1小时培训。最后,每月至少有2小时会议时间讨论短期目标,假设每月有 x 小时会议时间,y 小时培训时间,由此可列不等式组为 $\begin{cases} x+y \leq 16 \\ x \geq 2 \\ \dfrac{x}{2} \leq y \end{cases}$,则 $y_{max}=14, y_{min}=1$,所以差为13小时,选B。

9. Some zoo monkeys are on a diet of fruit and nuts. Fruit has about 13.3 grams (g) of sugar per cup and 1.36g of protein per cup. Nuts have about 4.04g of sugar per cup and

15.56g of protein per cup. Each monkey must get between 70g and 90g of sugar per day and at least 85g of protein per day. Which of the following daily diets fits the monkeys' needs?

A. 0 cups of fruit and 16 cups of nuts

B. 4 cups of fruit and 8 cups of nuts

C. 8 cups of fruit and 4 cups of nuts

D. 16 cups of fruit and 0 cups of nuts

知识点:线性不等式组的应用。

解析:水果每杯有13.3克糖和1.36克蛋白质,每杯坚果有4.04克糖和15.56克蛋白质,每只猴子每天需要70~90克糖和至少85克蛋白质,假设每只猴子每天吃 x 杯水果和 y 杯坚果,由此可列不等式组为 $\begin{cases} 70 \leqslant 13.3x + 4.04y \leqslant 90 \\ 1.36x + 15.56y \geqslant 85 \end{cases}$,所以选 C。

10. A bakery needs to make cakes for Mother's Day, and must prepare by storing ingredients. Each cake is made from 4 cups of batter and $\dfrac{7}{2}$ cups of frosting. The bakery has storage for up to 150 cups of ingredients. The two equations related to these constraints are graphed at left. If the bakery wants no batter leftover, which of the following could be the volume of batter and frosting that they store?

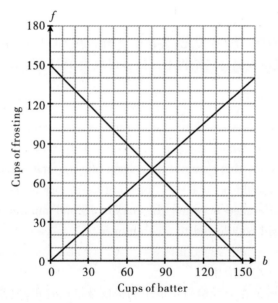

A. 80 cups of batter and 60 cups of frosting

B. 90 cups of batter and 70 cups of frosting

C. 80 cups of batter and 80 cups of frosting

D. 70 cups of batter and 70 cups of frosting

知识点:线性不等式组的应用。

解析:每块蛋糕由4杯面糊和 $\dfrac{7}{2}$ 杯糖霜做成,店里最多有150杯原料,店家想没有面糊剩下,假设有 x 杯面糊和 y 杯白糖,由此可得不等式组为 $\begin{cases} x+y \leqslant 150 \\ \dfrac{x}{4} \leqslant \dfrac{2}{7}y \end{cases}$,则选 D。

5.8 解线性方程组

例题

1. $\begin{cases} -0.2x+by=7.2 \\ 5.6x-0.8y=4 \end{cases}$

Consider the system of equations above. For what value of b will the system have exactly one solution (x,y) with $x=2$? Round the answer to the nearest tenth.

知识点:解线性方程组。

解析:当 $x=2$ 时,$y=9$,则 $b=0.8$。

2. $a\left(\dfrac{y}{2} - \dfrac{3}{2}x + 1\right) = \dfrac{4}{3}y - \dfrac{1}{2}x + \dfrac{5}{6}$ $\dfrac{5}{6}y - \left(\dfrac{5}{6}x + \dfrac{5}{2}\right) = 0$

Consider the system of equations above, where a is a constant. For which value of a is $(x,y)=(4,1)$ a solution?

A. $-\dfrac{34}{27}$ B. $-\dfrac{1}{27}$ C. $\dfrac{34}{9}$ D. None of the above

知识点:解线性方程组。

解析:将 $(x,y)=(4,1)$ 代入第二个方程可知,$(x,y)=(4,1)$ 不是方程的解,则 $(x,y)=(4,1)$ 不是方程组的解,故选 D。

3. $\begin{cases} 5x-2y=6 \\ 10x-4y=c \end{cases}$

Which of the following choices of c will result in a system of linear equations with no solutions?

A. $c=12$ B. c can be any number other than -12

C. c can be any number other than 12 D. c can be any number

知识点:解线性方程组。

解析:化简方程 $10x-4y=c$ 可得 $5x-2y=\dfrac{c}{2}$,只要 $c \neq 12$ 则方程组无解,所以选 C。

4. $\begin{cases} -11y=6(z+1)-13y \\ 4y-24=c(z-1) \end{cases}$

For what value of c does the above system of linear equations in the variables y and z have infinitely many solutions?

知识点:解线性方程组。

解析:化简方程组可得 $\begin{cases} 2y=6z+6 \\ 2y=cz+12-\dfrac{c}{2} \end{cases}$,当 $c=12$ 时,两方程相同,两直线重合,此时方

程组有无数解。

5. $\begin{cases} 2x-1=y \\ 3x-1=y \end{cases}$

Consider the system of equations above. Which of the following statements about this system is true?

A. There is only one (x,y) solution and y is positive.
B. There is only one (x,y) solution and y is negative.
C. There are infinitely many (x,y) solutions.
D. There are no (x,y) solutions.

知识点:解线性方程组。

解析:解方程组为 $3x-1=2x-1$,则 $(x,y)=(0,-1)$,所以选 B。

6. $\begin{cases} 44(j+2k)=12 \\ 22k=-11j+16 \end{cases}$

Consider the system of equations above. How many solutions (j,k) does this system have?

A. 0   B. Exactly 1   C. Exactly 2   D. Infinitely many

知识点:解线性方程组。

解析:化简方程组可得 $\begin{cases} 11(j+2k)=3 \\ 11(j+2k)=16 \end{cases}$,由此可知方程组无解,选 A。

7. $\begin{cases} a(p-q)=1 \\ p=2p-1 \end{cases}$

Consider the system of equations above, where a is a constant. For which value of a is $(p,q)=(1,1)$ a solution?

A. 0   B. 1   C. 2   D. None of the above

知识点:解线性方程组。

解析:由 $a(p-q)=1$ 可知,当 $(p,q)=(1,1)$ 时,方程左边等于 0,等式不能相等,所以选 D。

8. $\begin{cases} 5.2s+0.1r=0 \\ 0.7(r+0.2)+3.2=-3s \end{cases}$

Consider the system of equations above. If (r,s) is the solution to the system, then what is the value of $r+s$? Round the answer to the nearest tenth.

知识点:解线性方程组。

解析:$0.7(r+0.2)+3.2=-3s$ 化简可得 $3s+0.7r=-3.34$,用消元法可求 $s=0.1$,$r=-5.2$,则 $r+s=-5.1$。

9. $\begin{cases} -6.4x=4y+2.1 \\ ky+3.2x=5.8 \end{cases}$

For what value of k does the above system of linear equations in the variables x and y have no solutions?

知识点:解线性方程组。

解析：化简方程组可得 $\begin{cases} 3.2x+2y=-1.05 \\ ky+3.2x=5.8 \end{cases}$，当 $k=2$ 时，方程无解。

10. $\begin{cases} \dfrac{3}{2}x-3y=\dfrac{1}{4} \\ 2x-\dfrac{13}{3}y=\dfrac{1}{9} \end{cases}$

Consider the system of equations above. If (x,y) is the solution to the system, then what is the value of the product of x and y?

A. -1 B. 1 C. $\dfrac{13}{6}$ D. None of the above

知识点：解线性方程组。

解析：将方程 $\dfrac{3}{2}x-3y=\dfrac{1}{4}$ 化简为 $2x-4y=\dfrac{1}{3}$，则方程组解得 $y=\dfrac{2}{3}$，$x=\dfrac{3}{2}$，所以 $xy=1$。

5.9 线性方程组应用题

例题

1. A vegetable stand sells p pumpkins for \$5.00 each and s squashes for \$3.00 each. On Monday, the stand sold 6 more squashes than pumpkins and made a total of \$98.00. Which system of equations can be used to determine the number of pumpkins and squashes sold?

A. $\begin{cases} 3p+5s=98 \\ s=p+6 \end{cases}$
B. $\begin{cases} 3p+5s=98 \\ p=s+6 \end{cases}$
C. $\begin{cases} 5p+3s=98 \\ s=p+6 \end{cases}$
D. $\begin{cases} 5p+3s=98 \\ p=s+6 \end{cases}$

知识点：线性方程组的应用。

解析：p 个南瓜一个 5 美元，s 个西葫芦一个 3 美元，星期一西葫芦比南瓜多卖 6 个，一共卖出 98 美元，由此可知方程组为 $5p+3s=98$，$s=p+6$，选 C。

2. Today, the population of Canyon Falls is 22500 and the population of Swift Creek is 15200. The population of Canyon Falls is decreasing at the rate of 740 people each year while the population of Swift Creek is increasing at the rate of 1500 each year. Assuming these rates continue into the future, in how many years from today will the population of Swift Creek equal twice the population of Canyon Falls?

A. 9 years B. 10 years C. 11 years D. 12 years

知识点：线性方程组的应用。

解析：假设过了 t 年，由题意可列方程为 $2(22500-740t)=15200+1500t$，则 $t=10$，选 B。

3. Jerry has a large car which holds 22 gallons of fuel and get 20 miles per gallon.

Kate has a smaller car which holds 16.5 gallons of fuel and gets 30 miles per gallon. If both cars have a full tank of fuel now and drive the same distance, in how many miles will the remaining fuel in each tank be the same?

  A. 320   B. 325   C. 330   D. 335

  知识点：线性方程组的应用。

  解析：假设 x 英里之后两油箱剩余的燃料相同，由题意可列方程为 $22-\frac{x}{20}=16.5-\frac{x}{30}$，则 $x=330$，选 C。

4. Paulo's economics course requires two papers—one long and one short—throughout the semester. The number of pages, l, in the long paper is one more than two times the number of pages, s, in the short paper. If the total number of pages for both papers is 40, how many pages must be in the long paper?

  知识点：线性方程组的应用。

  解析：由题意可列方程组为 $\begin{cases} l-1=2s \\ l+s=40 \end{cases}$，解方程组得 $\begin{cases} s=13 \\ l=27 \end{cases}$，则长论文有 27 页。

5. For a high school dinner function for teachers and students, the math department bought 6 cases of juice and 1 case of bottled water for a total of $135. The science department bought 4 cases of juice and 2 cases of bottled water for a total of $110. How much did a case of juice cost?

  A. $12.50   B. $15.00   C. $20.00   D. $25.00

  知识点：线性方程组的应用。

  解析：假设一箱果汁 x 美元，一箱水 y 美元，由题意可列方程组为 $\begin{cases} 6x+y=135 \\ 4x+2y=110 \end{cases}$，解方程组得 $\begin{cases} x=20 \\ y=15 \end{cases}$，所以选 C。

6. The length of a rectangular swimming pool is twice the width. If the perimeter is 120 feet, then what is the width in feet?

  知识点：线性方程组的应用。

  解析：假设宽为 x 英尺，则长为 $2x$ 英尺，由此可列方程为 $2(x+2x)=120$，则 $x=20$，宽为 20 英尺。

7. Mikayla is the communications director for a politician and has recommended that a total of 41 talks are given by the politician before election day. She also recommends a total of 9 more formal speeches, s, than informal talks, t. Which of the following systems of equations can be used to find out how many formal speeches versus informal talks she had?

  A. $\begin{cases} t=s+9 \\ s+t=41 \end{cases}$ B. $\begin{cases} t=s+9 \\ s=t-41 \end{cases}$ C. $\begin{cases} s=t+9 \\ s+t=41 \end{cases}$ D. $\begin{cases} t=t+9 \\ s=t-41 \end{cases}$

  知识点：线性方程组的应用。

  解析：一共有 41 个演讲，其中正式演讲 s 个，比 t 个非正式演讲多 9 个，由此可列不等式组为 $s=t+9, s+t=41$，选 C。

8. A charity is planning a raffle to raise money. There are 125 regular tickets and 50

premium tickets. The cost of a premium ticket is 25% more than a regular ticket plus an additional $1.50. The raffle organizers expect to sell all of the tickets, and they want to collect $1950 from the ticket sales. Which of the following systems of equations can be used to determine the price, p, of each premium ticket and the price, r, of each regular ticket?

A. $\begin{cases} 50p+125r=1950 \\ p-1.25r=1.50 \end{cases}$
B. $\begin{cases} 50p+125r=1950 \\ p-1.50r=1.25 \end{cases}$
C. $\begin{cases} 125p+50r=1950 \\ p-1.25r=1.50 \end{cases}$
D. $\begin{cases} 125p+50r=1950 \\ p-1.50r=1.25 \end{cases}$

知识点：线性方程组的应用。

解析：一共有125张常规车票以及50张高价车票，一张高价车票比常规车票贵25%，以及额外的1.50美元，期望销售额为1950美元，由题意可列方程组为$50p+125r=1950$，$p-1.25r=1.50$，选A。

9. Tickets for a concert were $5 for each child and $8 for each adult. At one of the concerts, each adult brought 4 children with them, and 10 children attended without an adult. The total ticket sales were $1730. Which of the following systems of equations can be solved to determine the number of children, c, and adults, a, who attended the concert?

A. $\begin{cases} 5c+8a=1730 \\ 4a+10=c \end{cases}$
B. $\begin{cases} 5c+8a=1730 \\ 4a-10=c \end{cases}$
C. $\begin{cases} 8c+5a=1730 \\ 4a+10=c \end{cases}$
D. $\begin{cases} 8c+5a=1730 \\ 4a-10=c \end{cases}$

知识点：线性方程组的应用。

解析：音乐会儿童票5美元一张，成人票8美元一张，每一位成人带了4名儿童，还有10名儿童没有大人陪同，总售价为1730美元，由题意可列方程组为$5c+8a=1730$，$4a+10=c$，所以选A。

10. The owner of a health food store is developing a new product that consists of peanuts and raisins. Raisins cost $2.50 per pound and peanuts cost $3.50 per pound. The owner wants to create 20 pounds of the product that cost $3.03 per pound. Which of the following systems of equations can be used to determine the number of pounds of peanuts, p, and the number of pounds of raisins, r, that should be combined?

A. $p-r=20, \dfrac{2.50p+3.50r}{20}=3.03$

B. $p+r=20, \dfrac{2.50p+3.50r}{20}=3.03$

C. $p-r=20, 2.50p+3.50r=3.03$

D. $p+r=20, 2.50p+3.50r=3.03$

知识点：线性方程组的应用。

解析：葡萄干2.50美元一磅，花生2.50美元一磅，物主希望生产20磅产品，每磅花费3.03美元，由此可列方程组为$p+r=20$，$\dfrac{2.50p+3.50r}{20}=3.03$，选B。

5.10 解二次方程

 例题

1. $(1-a)+3(1-a)^2=0$

   What are the solutions to the equation above?

   A. $a=1$　　　　　　　　　　　　B. $a=\dfrac{4}{3}$

   C. $a=1$ and $a=\dfrac{4}{3}$　　　　　D. $a=0$ and $a=-\dfrac{1}{3}$

   知识点：解二次方程。

   解析：化简 $(1-a)+3(1-a)^2=0$ 为 $(1-a)(4-3a)=0$，则 $a=1$ and $a=\dfrac{4}{3}$，选 C。

2. $\left(t+\dfrac{8}{3}\right)(t+b)=0$

   In the equation above, b is a constant. If $-\dfrac{8}{3}$ and $\dfrac{13}{3}$ are solutions to the equation, then what is the value of b?

   A. $-\dfrac{13}{3}$　　　B. $-\dfrac{8}{3}$　　　C. $\dfrac{8}{3}$　　　D. $\dfrac{13}{3}$

   知识点：解二次方程。

   解析：由方程 $\left(t+\dfrac{8}{3}\right)(t+b)=0$ 可知，其中一个解为 $-\dfrac{8}{3}$，则另一个解为 $\dfrac{13}{3}$，则 $b=-\dfrac{13}{3}$，选 A。

3. $\left(v+\dfrac{1}{5}\right)^2-9=0$

   What is the sum of the solutions to the equation above?

   A. $-\dfrac{3}{5}$　　　B. $-\dfrac{2}{5}$　　　C. $-\dfrac{1}{5}$　　　D. 0

   知识点：解二次方程。

   解析：解方程 $\left(v+\dfrac{1}{5}\right)^2-9=0$，$\left(v+\dfrac{1}{5}\right)^2=9$，则 $v+\dfrac{1}{5}=\pm 3$，所以 $v=-\dfrac{1}{5}\pm 3$，和为 $-\dfrac{2}{5}$，选 B。

4. $2(x-3)^2-b=0$

   In the equation above, b is a constant. If the equation has the solutions $x=3\pm\sqrt{5}$, what is the value of b?

   知识点：解二次方程。

   解析：解方程 $2(x-3)^2-b=0$ 可得 $x=3\pm\sqrt{\dfrac{b}{2}}$，则 $b=10$。

5. $3x^2+4x-k=0$

In the equation above, k is a constant. For what value of k does the equation have no real solutions?

A. $-\dfrac{4}{3}$ B. $\dfrac{4}{3}$ C. $-\dfrac{5}{3}$ D. $\dfrac{5}{3}$

知识点:解二次方程。

解析:当 $\Delta<0$ 时方程无解,由此可知 $\Delta=4^2-4\times3\times(-k)=16+12k<0$,则 $k<-\dfrac{4}{3}$,所以选 C。

6. $x^2+kx-14=0$

In the equation above, k is a constant. The equation has solutions at 7 and -2. What is the value of k?

A. -9 B. -5 C. 5   D. 9

知识点:解二次方程。

解析:已知方程的解为 7 和 -2,则方程可以写为 $(x-7)(x+2)=0$,则 $k=-5$,故选 B。

7. $at^2+\dfrac{7}{2}t-4=0$

The above equation has solutions at $t=-8$ and $t=1$. What is the value of the constant a?

知识点:解二次方程。

解析:已知方程的解为 -8 和 1,则方程可以写为 $a(t+8)(t-1)=0,a(t^2+7t-8)=0$,所以 $a=\dfrac{1}{2}$。

8. $4+kp=4p^2$

In the equation above, k is a constant. If the sum of the solutions to the equation is 0, what is the value of k?

A. 0   B. 1   C. 2   D. 4

知识点:二次方程解的关系。

解析:二次方程两个解的和为 $x_1+x_2=-\dfrac{b}{a}$,当 $-\dfrac{b}{a}=0$ 时,$-\dfrac{-k}{4}=0$,则 $k=0$,选 A。

9. $16x^2-8x-3=0$

Let $x=q$ and $x=r$ be solutions to the equation shown above, with $q>r$. What is the value of $q-r$?

知识点:解二次方程。

解析:解方程 $16x^2-8x-3=0$ 得 $q=\dfrac{3}{4}$,$r=-\dfrac{1}{4}$,则 $q-r=1$。

10. $(t+1)^2+c=0$

In the equation above, c is a constant.

The equation has solutions at $t=\dfrac{3}{2}$ and $t=-\dfrac{7}{2}$. What is the value of c?

A. $-\dfrac{729}{4}$ B. $-\dfrac{121}{4}$ C. $-\dfrac{25}{4}$ D. -1

知识点:解二次方程。

解析：解方程 $(t+1)^2+c=0$ 得 $t=-1\pm\sqrt{-c}$，则 $-1+\sqrt{-c}=\dfrac{3}{2}$，$c=-\dfrac{25}{4}$，所以选 C。

5.11 表达式的结构

例题

1. $(y^2-32y+256-k)(y^2-32y+256+k)=(y-16)^4-100$

What is the value of k^2 in the above equation?

知识点：表达式的计算。

解析：方程右边的常数项为 65436，左边的常数项为 $(256-k)(256+k)=65536-k^2$，所以 $k^2=100$。

2. $(a^m)^n \cdot a^{mn}$

Which of the following is equivalent to the above expression?

A. $2a^{mn}$ B. a^{2mn} C. $a^{m^2n^2}$ D. a^{m^n+mn}

知识点：指数幂的运算。

解析：$(a^m)^n \cdot a^{mn} = a^{mn} \cdot a^{mn} = a^{2mn}$，选 B。

3. s^3t^3+1

Which of the following is equivalent to the above expression?

A. $(st-1)(s^2t^2+st+1)$

B. $(st-1)((st)^2-st+1)$

C. $(st+1)(s^2t^2+st+1)$

D. $(st+1)((st)^2-st+1)$

知识点：立方和公式。

解析：立方和公式为 $a^3+b^3=(a+b)(a^2-ab+b^2)$，则 $s^3t^3+1=(st)^3+1=(st+1) \cdot ((st)^2-st+1)$，故选 D。

4. If $2^m=x$ and $7^n=y$, then which of the following is equivalent to 784^{mn}?

A. $x^{2m} \cdot y^{4n}$ B. $x^{2n} \cdot y^{4m}$ C. $x^{4m} \cdot y^{2n}$ D. $x^{4n} \cdot y^{2m}$

知识点：指数幂的运算。

解析：$784^{mn}=(2^4 \cdot 7^2)^{mn}=2^{4mn} \cdot 7^{2mn}=(2^m)^{4n} \cdot (7^n)^{2m}=x^{4n} \cdot y^{2m}$，故选 D。

5. If $x^3+b^3=(x+b)(x^2-xb+9)$, what is a possible value of b?

知识点：立方和公式。

解析：立方和公式为 $a^3+b^3=(a+b)(a^2-ab+b^2)$，由此可知 $x^3+b^3=(x+b)(x^2-xb+b^2)=(x+b)(x^2-xb+9)$，则 $b^2=9$，所以 $b=\pm 3$。

6. a^2x-3a^2+2x-6

Which of the following is equivalent to the above expression?

A. $(a^2)(x-3)-2(x+3)$ B. $(ax+3)(a-2)$

C. $(x+3)(a^2-2)$ D. $(x-3)(a^2+2)$

知识点：化简表达式。

解析：$a^2x-3a^2+2x-6=(a^2+2)x-3(a^2+2)=(x-3)(a^2+2)$，选 D。

7. $\dfrac{a+b}{c-d}-\dfrac{a+b}{d-c}$

Which of the following is equivalent to the above expression for $c\neq d$?

A. 0 B. $\dfrac{2b}{c-b}$ C. $\dfrac{2(a+b)}{c-b}$ D. $\dfrac{2a+2b}{2c-2d}$

知识点：化简表达式。

解析：$\dfrac{a+b}{c-d}-\dfrac{a+b}{d-c}=\dfrac{a+b}{c-d}+\dfrac{a+b}{c-d}=\dfrac{2(a+b)}{c-d}$，选 C。

8. $(u+t)^3$

Which of the following is equivalent to the above expression?

A. $u^3+3ut+t^3$
B. $u^3+3ut(u+t)+t^3$
C. $u^3+6ut+t^3$
D. $u^3+6u^2t+6ut^2+t^3$

知识点：多项式的展开。

解析：$(u+t)^3=u^3+3u^2t+3ut^2+t^3=u^3+3ut(u+t)+t^3$，选 B。

9. $\dfrac{x^2-2x-8}{x+3}\cdot\dfrac{x+2}{x+3}$

Which of the following is equivalent to the above expression for $x\neq-3$?

A. $\dfrac{2(x-4)(x+2)}{3(x+3)}$
B. $\dfrac{(x-4)(x+2)^2}{x+3}$
C. $\dfrac{(x-4)(x+2)^2}{x^2+6x+9}$
D. $\dfrac{2(x-4)(x+2)}{x^2+6x+9}$

知识点：化简表达式。

解析：$\dfrac{x^2-2x-8}{x+3}\cdot\dfrac{x+2}{x+3}=\dfrac{(x+2)(x-4)}{x+3}\cdot\dfrac{x+2}{x+3}=\dfrac{(x-4)(x+2)^2}{(x+3)^2}=\dfrac{(x-4)(x+2)^2}{x^2+6x+9}$，选 C。

10. $\left(w-\dfrac{3}{2}\right)\left(w+\dfrac{7}{2}\right)$

Which of the following is equivalent to the above expression?

A. $\dfrac{(w-3)(w+7)}{2}$
B. $\dfrac{(2w+7)(2w-3)}{2}$
C. $\dfrac{(w-3)(w+7)}{4}$
D. $\dfrac{(2w+7)(2w-3)}{4}$

知识点：化简表达式。

解析：$\left(w-\dfrac{3}{2}\right)\left(w+\dfrac{7}{2}\right)=\dfrac{1}{2}(2w-3)\cdot\dfrac{1}{2}(2w+7)=\dfrac{(2w+7)(2w-3)}{4}$，选 D。

5.12 分离变量

 例题

1. $\dfrac{\sin A}{a} = \dfrac{\sin B}{b}$

The Law of Sines, shown above, where A and B represent any two angles of a triangle and a and b represent the lengths of the sides opposite those angles, states that the sines of the angles of a triangle and the lengths of the sides opposite those angles are proportional. Which of the following shows a in terms of $\sin A$, $\sin B$, and b?

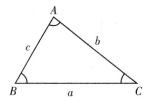

A. $a = b$
B. $a = \dfrac{\sin A}{b \sin B}$
C. $a = \dfrac{b \sin A}{\sin B}$
D. $a = \dfrac{b \sin B}{\sin A}$

知识点：正弦定理。

解析：已知 $\dfrac{\sin A}{a} = \dfrac{\sin B}{b}$，则 $a = \dfrac{b \sin A}{\sin B}$，选 C。

2. $a = \dfrac{5bc}{20} + 10$

Which of the following equations gives b in terms of a and c?

A. $b = \dfrac{4a}{c} - 200$
B. $b = \dfrac{4a - 40}{c}$
C. $b = \dfrac{4a}{c} - 10$
D. $b = \dfrac{4a + 40}{c}$

知识点：分离变量。

解析：已知 $a = \dfrac{5bc}{20} + 10$，则 $4(a-10) = bc$，所以 $b = \dfrac{4a - 40}{c}$，选 B。

3. $T = \sqrt{(\mu g x)^2 + (T_0)^2}$

The equation above gives the tension, T, at a point of the cable of a suspension bridge whose horizontal distance from its lowest point of the cable is x meters, where the cable has a mass to length ratio of μ, and a tension of T_0 at the lowest point. The constant g represents the gravitational acceleration in meters per second. Which of the following equations correctly gives x in terms of T, T_0, and μ?

A. $x = \dfrac{T - T_0}{\mu g}$
B. $x = \dfrac{T - (T_0)^2}{\mu g}$
C. $x = \dfrac{\sqrt{T^2 - (T_0)^2}}{\mu g}$
D. $x = \dfrac{T^2 - (T_0)^2}{\mu g}$

知识点：分离变量。

解析: 已知 $T=\sqrt{(\mu g x)^2+(T_0)^2}$，则 $T^2=(\mu g x)^2+(T_0)^2$，$(\mu g x)^2=T^2-(T_0)^2$，$\mu g x=\sqrt{T^2-(T_0)^2}$，所以 $x=\dfrac{\sqrt{T^2-(T_0)^2}}{\mu g}$，选 C。

4. $L=\pi r\sqrt{h^2+r^2}$

The lateral surface area, L, of a right circular cone with radius, r, and height, h, can be found with the equation above. Which of the following correctly shows the right circular cone's height in terms of its radius, lateral surface area, and π?

A. $h=\sqrt{\dfrac{L^2}{\pi r}+r^2}$ 　　　　　　B. $h=\sqrt{\dfrac{L}{\pi r}+r^2}$

C. $h=\sqrt{\left(\dfrac{L}{\pi r}\right)^2-r^2}$ 　　　　　D. $h=\dfrac{L}{\pi r}-r$

知识点: 分离变量。

解析: 已知 $L=\pi r\sqrt{h^2+r^2}$，则 $\dfrac{L}{\pi r}=\sqrt{h^2+r^2}$，$\left(\dfrac{L}{\pi r}\right)^2=h^2+r^2$，$h^2=\left(\dfrac{L}{\pi r}\right)^2-r^2$，所以 $h=\sqrt{\left(\dfrac{L}{\pi r}\right)^2-r^2}$，选 C。

5. $\dfrac{1}{f}=\dfrac{1}{o}+\dfrac{1}{i}$

By bending incoming light rays through a focal point, a thin lens of focal length f will turn an object that is o units from the lens into an image that is i units from the lens, according to the thin lens equation, shown above. Which of the following correctly shows the object distance in terms of the focal length and the image distance?

A. $o=f-i$ 　　B. $o=fi(i-f)$ 　　C. $o=\dfrac{fi}{i-f}$ 　　D. $o=\dfrac{1}{i-f}$

知识点: 分离变量。

解析: 已知 $\dfrac{1}{f}=\dfrac{1}{o}+\dfrac{1}{i}$，则 $\dfrac{1}{f}=\dfrac{1}{o}+\dfrac{1}{i}=\dfrac{i+o}{oi}$，$f(i+o)=oi$，$o(i-f)$，所以 $o=\dfrac{fi}{i-f}$，选 C。

6. $t=\dfrac{72}{b-d+m}$

The equation above gives the approximate doubling time in years, t, of the population of a country with a b percent annual increase due to births, a d percent annual decrease due to deaths, and a net migration of m percent relative to the initial population over the course of a year. Which of the following equations correctly gives the net migration percent in terms of the doubling time, percent increase from births, and percent increase from deaths over the course of a year?

A. $m=\dfrac{72}{b-d+t}$ 　　B. $m=\dfrac{72}{tb-td}$ 　　C. $m=\dfrac{72}{t}-b+d$ 　　D. $m=\dfrac{72-b+d}{t}$

知识点: 分离变量。

解析: 已知 $t=\dfrac{72}{b-d+m}$，则 $t(b-d+m)=72$，$tm=72-t(b-d)$，所以 $m=\dfrac{72}{t}-b+d$，选 C。

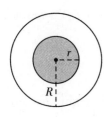

7. The area, A, of the unshaded circular ring shown BELOW can be found with the equation $A=\pi(R^2-r^2)$, where R is the radius of the larger circle, r is the radius of the smaller circle, and π is a constant. Which of the following shows R in terms of A and r?

A. $R=\sqrt{\dfrac{A+r^2}{\pi}}$ 　　　B. $R=\sqrt{\dfrac{A}{\pi}}+r$

C. $R=\sqrt{\dfrac{A}{\pi}-r}$ 　　　D. $R=\sqrt{\dfrac{A}{\pi}+r^2}$

知识点：分离变量。

解析：已知 $A=\pi(R^2-r^2)$，则 $\dfrac{A}{\pi}+r^2=R^2$，所以 $R=\sqrt{\dfrac{A}{\pi}+r^2}$，选 D。

8. $x^2+y^2+z^2=R^2$

Using a 3-dimensional coordinate system, the coordinates of a point, (x,y,z), and the polar coordinate, R, which is the distance of the point from the origin, can be related by the above equation. Which of the following correctly expresses the y-coordinate in terms of the x- and z-coordinates and the distance, R?

A. $y=R-x-z$ 　　　B. $y=\sqrt{R-x-z}$

C. $y=\sqrt{R^2-x^2-z^2}$ 　　　D. $y=\dfrac{R^2-x^2-z^2}{y}$

知识点：分离变量。

解析：已知 $x^2+y^2+z^2=R^2$，则 $y^2=R^2-x^2-z^2$，所以 $y=\sqrt{R^2-x^2-z^2}$，选 C。

9. $E=\dfrac{A-V}{A}$

The formula above gives the extraction ratio, E, of a particular substance by an organ of the body based on the concentration, A, of a substance in the blood entering the organ through the arteries and the concentration, V, of the substance flowing out of the organ through the veins. Which of the following equations correctly gives the concentration entering through the arteries in terms of the extraction ratio and the concentration leaving through the veins?

A. $A=-V(E-1)$ 　　B. $A=V(E-1)$ 　　C. $A=\dfrac{V}{1-E}$ 　　D. $A=\dfrac{V}{E-1}$

知识点：分离变量。

解析：已知 $E=\dfrac{A-V}{A}$，则 $AE=A-V$，$AE=A-V$，$A(1-E)=V$，所以 $A=\dfrac{V}{1-E}$，选 C。

10. $\dfrac{V_1}{T_1}=\dfrac{V_2}{T_2}$

Charles's law, for ideal gases relates the volume, V, and temperature, T, of an ideal gas in its initial (1) and final (2) states. Which of the following shows the initial temperature in terms of the final temperature, the initial volume, and final volume?

A. $T_1=T_2$ 　　B. $T_1=V_1-\dfrac{V_2}{T_2}$ 　　C. $T_1=\dfrac{V_2}{T_2V_1}$ 　　D. $T_1=\dfrac{T_2V_1}{V_2}$

知识点:分离变量。

解析:已知 $\frac{V_1}{T_1} = \frac{V_2}{T_2}$,则 $V_1 T_2 = V_2 T_1$,所以 $T_1 = \frac{T_2 V_1}{V_2}$,选 D。

5.13 函数表示法

例题

1. Consider the graphs of function f and function g shown above. Which of the following could be true?

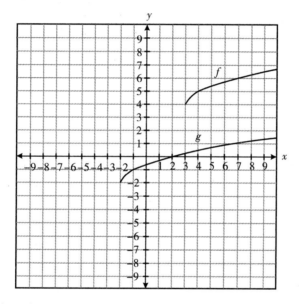

A. $f(x) = g(x+5) + 6$
B. $f(x) = g(x-5) + 6$
C. $g(x) = f(x-5) + 6$
D. $g(x) = f(x+5) + 6$

知识点:函数的移动。

解析:可以看作函数 g 移动变成函数 f,从函数 g 上一点 $(-2,-2)$ 与函数 f 上一点 $(3,4)$ 可以判断出函数 g 向右移动 5 个单位,向上移动 6 个单位,所以 $f(x) = g(x-5) + 6$,选 B。

2. Consider the table shown above. What is the value of $(fg)(3)$?

A. 2　　　　　　　B. 3　　　　　　　C. 6　　　　　　　D. 8

x	$f(x)$	$g(x)$
1	1	1
2	1	3
3	2	6
4	3	10
5	5	15
6	8	21

知识点：复合函数的定义。

解析：$(fg)(3)=f(g(3))=f(6)=8$，选 D。

3. The graph of $y=\sin x$ is shown above. Which of the following is the graph of $y=\sin 3x$?

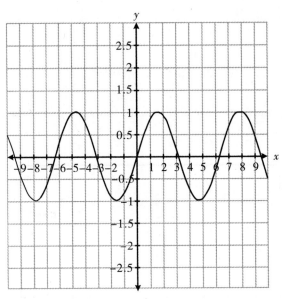

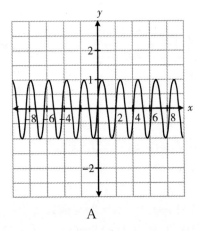

A

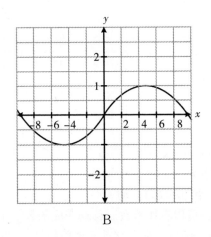

B

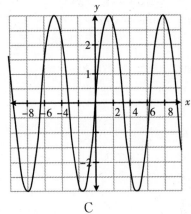

C

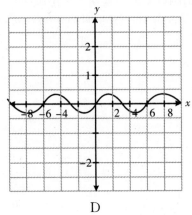

D

知识点：三角函数的图像。

解析：$y=\sin x$ 的周期为 2π，$y=\sin 3x$ 的周期为 $\frac{2\pi}{3}$，所以选 A。

4. The graph of $y=f(x+2)$ is shown above. For which value of x must $f(x)=4$?

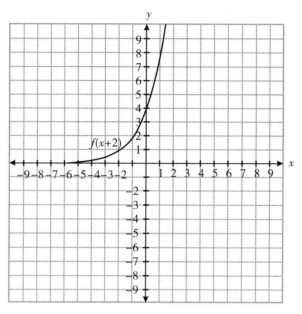

知识点：函数的平移。

解析：从 $y=f(x+2)$ 变为 $y=f(x)$ 只需向右移动 2 个单位，则原点 $(0,4)$ 变为 $(2,4)$，所以 $f(2)=4$。

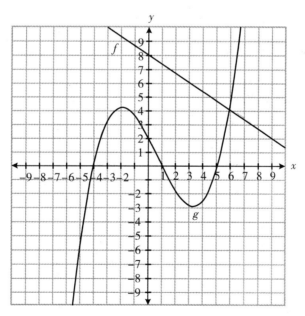

5. $Q(x)=\dfrac{P(2x)}{2}$

Consider the equation shown above, where Q and P are functions. If (x_0, y_0) is a point on the graph $y=Q(x)$, which of the following is a point on the graph of $y=P(x)$?

A. (x_0, y_0) B. $\left(2x_0, \dfrac{y_0}{2}\right)$ C. $\left(\dfrac{x_0}{2}, 2y_0\right)$ D. $(2x_0, 2y_0)$

知识点：函数间的关系。

解析：$Q(x_0) = \dfrac{P(2x_0)}{2} = y_0$，则 $P(2x_0) = 2y_0$，所以点 $(2x_0, 2y_0)$ 在函数 $y = P(x)$ 上，选 D。

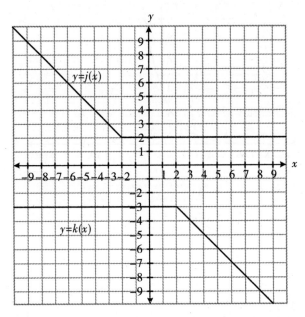

6. The graphs of $y = j(x)$ and $y = k(x)$ are shown above. Which of the following graphs is the graph of $y = j(k(x))$?

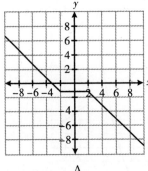

A

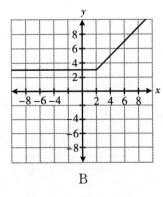

B

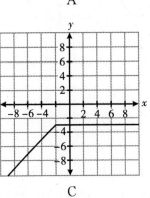

C

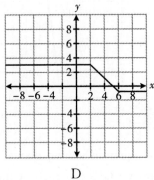

D

知识点：复合函数的定义。

解析：由图可知，在函数 $y=k(x)$ 中，当 $x\in(-\infty,2]$ 时，$k(x)=-3$，则当 $x\in(-\infty,2]$ 时，$j(k(x))=-3$；当 $x\in(-\infty,2)$ 时，$k(x)\in(-\infty,-3)$，则 $j(k(x))\in[3,\infty)$，综上所述，选 B。

7. The graph of $y=f(x)$ can be shifted 3 units in the positive x-direction and 3 units in the positive y-direction to obtain the graph of $y=h(x)$. If $f(x)=4x+10$ and $h(x)=ax+b$, where a and b are real constants, what must be the value of b?

知识点：函数的平移。

解析：$y=f(x)$ 向右移动 3 个单位，向上移动 3 个单位得到函数 $y=h(x)$，则 $y=h(x)=f(x-3)+3$，而 $f(x)=4x+10$，所以 $h(x)=(4(x-3)+10)+3=4x+1$，$b=1$。

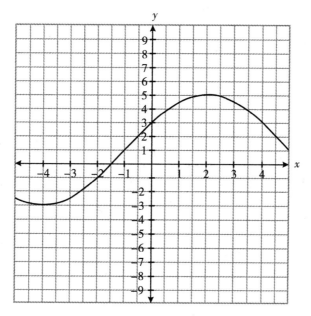

8. The graph of $y=-f(-x)$ is shown above. For which value of x is it true that $f(x)=1$?

知识点：函数的对称。

解析：函数 $y=f(x)$ 根据 y 轴左右对称可得函数 $y=f(-x)$，函数 $y=f(-x)$ 根据 x 轴上下对称可得函数 $y=-f(-x)$，则函数 $y=f(x)$ 上的点 $(x,1)$ 根据 y 轴左右对称可得点 $(-x,1)$，点 $(-x,1)$ 根据 x 轴上下对称可得点 $(-x,-1)$，此点在函数 $y=-f(-x)$ 上，则 $x=2$，所以 $f(2)=1$。

9. The graph of function h is the graph of function g stretched vertically by a factor of 3 and reflected over the y-axis. Which of the following correctly defines function h?

A. $h(x)=-3g(x)$
B. $h(x)=3g(-x)$
C. $h(x)=g(-3x)$
D. $h(x)=-g(3x)$

知识点：函数的对称。

解析：函数 g 竖直方向拉伸 3 倍，可得函数 $3g(x)$，再根据 y 轴对称可得函数 $3g(-x)$，则函数 $h(x)=3g(-x)$，选 B。

10. The functions $f(x)$ and $g(x)$ are graphed in the xy-plane. The graph of $y=f(x)$ is equivalent to the graph of $y=g(x)$ stretched by a factor of 2 in the x-direction. If $g(x)=x \cdot e^x$, which of the following correctly defines $f(x)$?

  A. $f(x)=2x \cdot e^{2x}$ B. $f(x)=2x \cdot e^x$

  C. $f(x)=(x+2) \cdot e^{x+2}$ D. $f(x)=0.5x \cdot e^{0.5x}$

知识点：函数的变换。

解析：函数 $g(x)$ 横向拉伸 2 倍，可得 $g(0.5x)$，则 $f(x)=g(0.5x)=0.5x \cdot e^{0.5x}$，选 D。

5.14 比例与百分比

例题

1. Lea's car travels an average of 30 miles per gallon of gas. If she spent $20.70 on gas for a 172.5 mile trip, what was the approximate cost of gas in dollars per gallon?

  A. $1.45 per gallon   B. $3.40 per gallon

  C. $3.60 per gallon   D. $5.75 per gallon

知识点：平均值的计算。

解析：每加仑汽油可以使汽车行驶 30 英里，Lea 花了 20.70 美元行驶 172.5 英里，则每加仑汽油的平均花费为 20.70÷(172.5÷30)＝3.60 美元/加仑，选 C。

2. A certain high school geometry class is made up of freshmen and sophomores. The ratio of freshmen to sophomores in that class is 3∶4. If there are 12 sophomores in the class, what is the total number of students in the class?

  A. 9   B. 16   C. 21   D. 28

知识点：比例的应用。

解析：九年级与十年级的人数比为 3∶4，十年级有 12 人，则总人数为 12÷4×(3+4)＝21 人，选 C。

3. A marine aquarium has a small tank and a large tank, each containing only red and blue fish. In each tank, the ratio of red fish to blue fish is 3 to 4. The ratio of fish in the large tank to fish in the small tank is 46 to 5. What is the ratio of blue fish in the small tank to red fish in the large tank?

  A. 15∶184   B. 10∶69   C. 69∶10   D. 184∶15

知识点：比例的应用。

解析：假设红鱼有 $3x$ 只，则蓝鱼有 $4x$ 只；假设大鱼缸有 $46y$ 个，则小鱼缸有 $5y$ 个。小鱼缸中蓝鱼与大鱼缸中红鱼的比为 $\dfrac{4x \cdot 5y}{3x \cdot 46y}=\dfrac{10}{69}$，选 B。

4. Two leading brands of paper towels are on sale. Brand A has 6 rolls, each with 56 sheets, for $4.29. Brand B has 8 rolls, each with 48 sheets, for $5.99. Which of the following best describes the relationship between the cost per sheet of the two brands?

A. The two brands cost the same amount per sheet.

B. Brand B costs $0.003 more per sheet than Brand A.

C. Brand A costs $0.003 more per sheet than Brand B.

D. Brand B costs $0.03 more than Brand A.

知识点：比例的应用。

解析：A 品牌每一张的花费为 4.29÷6÷56＝0.0128 美元，B 品牌每一张的花费为 5.99÷8÷48＝0.0156 美元，所以选 B。

5. Zhang Lei spent $20.00 during his last outing at the bowling alley. This included a one time shoe rental fee of $3.50. He spent the rest of the money on bowling a number of games. If it took Zhang Lei 45 minutes to bowl each game and he spent 2 hours and 15 minutes bowling, how much did it cost per game?

   A. $3.00 B. $5.50 C. $6.67 D. $7.34

   知识点：比例的应用。

   解析：2 小时 15 分钟即为 135 分钟，45 分钟玩 1 次游戏，则 135 分钟玩了 3 次，花费为 (20－3.5)÷3＝5.5 美元，选 B。

6. Kavitha and Andrei are truck drivers for the Delightful Delivery Company, which services cities W, T, and Q.

   The distance from city W to city T is 48.5 miles.

   The distance from city T to city Q is 20 miles.

   The distance from city Q to city W is 36 miles.

   If Kavitha's truck and Andrei's truck travel at the same speed, and it takes Andrei 91 minutes to go from city W to city T, about how much time will it take Kavitha to travel from city W to city Q?

   A. 19 minutes B. 38 minutes C. 68 minutes D. 123 minutes

   知识点：比例的应用。

   解析：W 城市到 T 城市 48.5 英里，Andrei 开了 91 分钟，同样的速度 kavitha 从 W 城市开 36 英里到 Q 城市用时 36÷(48.5÷91)＝68 分钟，选 C。

7. Yasemin is using a sugar cookie recipe with a flour to sugar ratio of 11∶6. To make one batch of cookies, 2.75 cups of flour are needed. If Yasemin would like to triple the recipe, which of the following best approximates how much sugar she will need?

   A. 1.5 cups B. 4.5 cups C. 5 cups D. 15 cups

   知识点：比例的应用。

   解析：面粉跟糖的比例为 11∶6，按照食谱需要 2.75 杯面粉，3 倍食谱的量为 8.25 杯面粉，则糖为 8.25÷11×6＝4.5 杯，选 B。

8. A donut company makes cream-filled donuts using $\frac{1}{4}$ cup (c) of dough and $\frac{1}{2}$ tablespoon (tbsp) of cream per donut. The company decides to change their recipe to use 3 times the amount of cream for their "New Triple-Stuffed Donuts!" If the donut company's

new recipe uses the same amount of dough per donut, what is the ratio of dough to cream needed to make 12 triple-stuffed donuts?

  A. 1 c ∶ 3 tbsp   B. 1 c ∶ 6 tbsp   C. 2 c ∶ 3 tbsp   D. 1 c ∶ 2 tbsp

知识点：比例的应用。

解析：原来的食谱是做一个甜甜圈需要 $\frac{1}{4}$ 杯生面团跟 $\frac{1}{2}$ 茶匙的奶油，现在要用3倍的奶油，即为 $\frac{3}{2}$ 茶匙的奶油，跟 $\frac{1}{4}$ 杯生面团做一个，则比例为 $\frac{1}{4} : \frac{3}{2} = 1 : 6$，选 B。

9. The "maximum occupancy" of a room is the total number of people who can be in a room without causing a fire hazard. In a large room, a Fire Safety Code states that the maximum occupancy is 1 person for every 7 square feet (ft^2). A college is hosting a concert in a hall that is 14721 ft^2, and 1000 people are expected to attend. According to the Fire Safety Code, approximately how many more people can attend the concert without causing a fire hazard?

  A. 900 people   B. 1000 people   C. 1100 people   D. 2100 people

知识点：比例的应用。

解析：1个人需要7平方英尺来保障安全，大学的音乐厅有14721平方英尺，则 14721÷7×1=2103 人，预计有1000人参加，所以还能有1100人可以参加，所以选 C。

10. The musical interval between two sounds is called an "octave" if the ratio of the sounds' frequencies is 2 ∶ 1. The following table shows the names of the musical intervals between two sounds based on the ratios of the two sounds' frequencies.

Name of the musical interval	Ratio of two sound frequencies
Major third	4 ∶ 5
Perfect fourth	3 ∶ 4
Perfect fifth	2 ∶ 3
Major sixth	3 ∶ 5

If a sound is played with a frequency of 480 Hz, and a second sound is played with a frequency of 800 Hz, what is the name of the musical interval between the two sounds?

  A. Major third   B. Perfect fourth

  C. Perfect fifth   D. Major sixth

知识点：比例的应用。

解析：480 ∶ 800 = 3 ∶ 5，所以选 D。

5.15　百分数

例题

1. A school has 63% girls and 37% boys. If 23% of the girls wears contacts and 42% of the boys wears contacts, what percent of all students wears contacts?

　　A. 14.5%　　　　B. 15.5%　　　　C. 30.0%　　　　D. 75.0%

知识点：百分数的应用。

解析：一个学校有 63% 的女生和 37% 的男生，23% 的女生戴隐形眼镜，42% 的男生戴隐形眼镜，则学生戴隐形眼镜的百分数为 0.63×0.23+0.37×0.42=0.3003，即为 30%，故选 C。

2. A student answered 86 problems correctly, which was 81.9% of the total number of problems on the test. How many problems did the student answer incorrectly?

　　A. 4　　　　　B. 19　　　　　C. 86　　　　　D. 105

知识点：百分数的应用。

解析：学生答对 86 题，占总数的 81.9%，则总题数为 86÷0.819=105 题，故答错 19 题，选 B。

3. In a college philosophy class during the fall semester, there were 323 students, 42% of whom were male and the rest of whom were female. In the spring semester, the same number of females was in the class as in the fall, but there were only 298 total students in the class. In the spring, what percent of students were female?

　　A. 46%　　　　B. 58%　　　　C. 63%　　　　D. 92%

知识点：百分数的应用。

解析：秋季有 323 名学生，42% 为男性，则 58% 为女性，春季女性人数与秋季相同，但是总共只有 298 名学生，则女性占总数为 323×0.58÷298×100%=63%，故选 C。

4. A chef has a large container of olive oil. In one night, after he used 25 quarts, 35.9% of the oil remained. How many quarts of olive oil remained in the container?

知识点：百分数的应用。

解析：厨师用了 25 夸脱油，剩下 35.9%，则用了 64.1%，所以油总共有 25÷0.641=39 夸脱，还剩下 39×0.359=14 夸脱。

5. Fabrizzio went shopping on Tuesday and decided to purchase a pair of pants that is 15% off the regular price for the rest of the week. If he buys the pants on Tuesday, he will receive an additional 5% off. What percent would Tuesday's sale price be of the original price for the pants?

　　A. 81%　　　　B. 85%　　　　C. 95%　　　　D. 105%

知识点：百分数的应用。

解析：裤子打折 15%，周四买有额外的 5% 折扣，则 (1−15%)×(1−5%)=80.75%，故选 A。

6. On Monday, Harry had 75% as many toys as Teddy did. On Tuesday, after Harry acquired 32 more toys and Teddy acquired 15% more than he had on Monday, Harry had as many toys as Teddy did. How many toys did Harry have on Monday?

知识点：百分数的应用。

解析：假设 Harry 周一有 x 个玩具，则 Teddy 周一有 $\dfrac{x}{0.75}$ 个玩具，Harry 多拿到 32 个玩具，Teddy 多拿到 15% 的玩具，此时两人玩具数量相等，由此可列方程为 $x+32=\dfrac{x}{0.75}(1+15\%)$，$\dfrac{8x}{15}=32$，则 $x=60$。

7. Ivy is downloading a computer program from the Internet. After 8 minutes, the computer program is 35% downloaded. If the computer program continues to download at the current rate, about how much longer will it take for Ivy's computer to finish downloading the program?

  A. 12 minutes   B. 15 minutes   C. 18 minutes   D. 23 minutes

知识点：百分数的应用。

解析：8 分钟下载 35%，则全部下载完需要 $100\% \div 35\% \times 8 \approx 23$ 分钟，故选 D。

8.

Baby name	Denis	Dimitri	Lea	Tanya
Frequency	13	27	125	400

The table above displays the number of babies per million babies born in 1985 with each of 4 names. In 1985, about what percentage of babies were named Lea or Dimitri?

  A. 0.000152%   B. 0.0152%   C. 0.98%   D. 1.52%

知识点：百分数的应用。

解析：每百万新生婴儿中有 27 个叫 Dimitri，125 个叫 Lea，则百分数为 $\dfrac{27+125}{1000000} \times 100\% = 0.0152\%$，选 B。

9. A high school's graduation rate is defined to be the percentage of the senior class that graduates. Last year 406 of Sagamore High School's 452 seniors graduated. This year the school expects the previous year's graduation rate to increase by approximately 2 percentage points. If there are 436 students in this year's senior class, which of the following best approximates the number of seniors that Sagamore High School expects to graduate this year?

  A. 390 students   B. 400 students   C. 410 students   D. 420 students

知识点：百分数的应用。

解析：去年 452 名学生中有 406 名毕业，今年毕业率增加 2%，则 $436 \times \left(\dfrac{406}{452}+2\%\right) \approx 400$，故选 B。

10. In 2013, the population of Nevada and North Carolina were each growing at a rate of approximately 3.3% per year. In addition, the US Census Bureau estimated that the population of Nevada and North Carolina was 2.8 million and 9.8 million people,

respectively. If the population growth rates in each of these states remained the same, approximately how many more people were living in North Carolina compared to Nevada in 2014?

A. 7.0 million　　B. 7.2 million　　C. 9.3 million　　D. 13.0 million

知识点：百分数的应用。

解析：$9.8\times(1+3.3\%)-2.8\times(1+3.3\%)=7.231$，故选 B。

5.16　单位

例题

1. In August 2009, Usain Bolt ran 100 meters in 9.58 seconds (sec), setting the world record at that time. There are approximately 1.094 yards (yd) in a meter. What was Usain Bolt's average speed in yards per second?

A. 9.54　　B. 9.58　　C. 10.44　　D. 11.42

知识点：单位换算。

解析：跑 100 米用时 9.58 秒，1.094 码等于 1 米，则 100 米等于 109.4 码，速度为 $109.4\div 9.58\approx 11.42$ 码/秒，选 D。

2. According to the United States Census Bureau, on September 1, 2014, the population of the United States was increasing by 1 person every 12 seconds. At this rate, by how much would the population of the United States increase in 1 year?

A. 43800　　B. 525600　　C. 2628000　　D. 31536000

知识点：单位换算。

解析：每 12 秒新增 1 人，1 年＝365 天＝31536000 秒，则可以增加 $\dfrac{31536000}{12}=2628000$ 人，选 C。

3. Grace examines two different size bottles of the same laundry detergent. The price for the 100-ounce bottle is $9.99 and the price for the 150-ounce bottle is $12.99. How much money will Grace save per 100 ounces if she purchases the larger bottle?

A. $0.01　　B. $1.33　　C. $2.00　　D. $8.66

知识点：单位换算。

解析：小瓶子 100 盎司的花费为 9.99 美元，大瓶子 100 盎司的花费为 $12.99\div 150\times 100=8.66$ 美元，节省 1.33 美元，故选 B。

4. An ancient Chinese candle clock tells the amount of time that has passed by the amount of wax that has been melted off the candle. Each candle is divided into 12 sections, marked 1 inch (in) apart. It takes 4 hours (hrs) for each candle to completely melt, after which a new candle is lit. If two candles have completely melted and one candle has melted 4 in, how many minutes have passed since the first candle was lit?

A. 480 minutes　　B. 500 minutes　　C. 560 minutes　　D. 600 minutes

知识点：单位换算。

解析：一根蜡烛可以点 4 小时，即为 240 分钟，两根蜡烛烧完，第三根燃了 4 英寸，则为整支蜡烛的 $\frac{1}{3}$，用时 80 分钟，则总时间为 $240 \times 2 + 80 = 560$ 分钟，选 C。

5. Which of the following cities had the largest population density in 2010? (Population density is defined to be the number of people per square mile.)

City	2010 census population	Area (in square miles)
Boston	645149	48.43
Chicago	2695598	227.13
Miami	362470	35.67
Philadelphia	1517550	135.09

A. Boston
B. Chicago
C. Miami
D. Philadelphia

知识点：单位换算。

解析：Boston 的人口密度为 $645149 \div 48.43 = 13321$ 人/平方英里，Chicago 的人口密度为 $2695598 \div 227.13 = 11868$ 人/平方英里，Miami 的人口密度为 $362470 \div 35.67 = 10162$ 人/平方英里，Philadelphia 的人口密度为 $1517550 \div 135.09 = 11234$ 人/平方英里，则 Boston 的人口密度最高，选 A。

6. When traveling in France, Joe purchased gas which cost 1.45 euros per liter. If at the time of the purchase 1 euro was worth $1.35, what was the approximate cost, in dollars, of one gallon of gas?

Note: 1 gallon is approximately 3.785 liters.

A. $0.52
B. $3.52
C. $4.07
D. $7.40

知识点：单位换算。

解析：1 欧元 $=1.35$ 美元，则 1.4 欧元/公升 $= \dfrac{1.45 \times 1.35}{\frac{1}{3.785}} \approx 7.40$ 美元/加仑，故选 D。

7. The apparent brightness of a surface, in "lux", is found by measuring the energy of the light coming from the source and dividing by the area of the surface. Lux are equivalent to candelas per square meter. Abigail is building a new type of television screen and measures the brightness of glare to be 0.0002 kilocandelas per square centimeter. What is the brightness of glare expressed in lux?

A. 0.00002 lux
B. 0.002 lux
C. 20 lux
D. 2000 lux

知识点：单位换算。

解析：0.0002 千坎德拉/平方厘米 $= \dfrac{0.0002 \times 1000}{10^{-4}} = 2000$ lux，故选 D。

8. In 2012, an 11-year-old cheetah set a new record by running 100 meters in 5.95 seconds. During this record-breaking run, at what approximate speed was the cheetah traveling in miles per hour?

Note: There are 1.6 kilometers in 1 mile.

A. 16.81 miles per hour
B. 34.27 miles per hour
C. 37.82 miles per hour
D. 60.50 miles per hour

知识点：单位换算。

解析：跑100米用时5.95秒，则速度为16.807米/秒，16.807 m/s = $\frac{16.807 \div 1.6 \div 1000}{1 \div 3600}$ ≈ 37.82 mi/h，故选C。

9. A generator produces 6.5×10^2 kilojoules per centisecond $\left(\frac{kJ}{cs}\right)$. A watt is equivalent to 1 joule per second $\frac{J}{s}$. What is the measured power of the generator in watts?

A. 6.5×10^7 watts
B. 6.5×10^3 watts
C. 6.5×10^1 watts
D. 6.5×10^5 watts

知识点：单位换算。

解析：$6.5 \times 10^2 \frac{kJ}{cs} = \frac{6.5 \times 10^2 \times 10^3}{10^{-2}} = 6.5 \times 10^7 \frac{J}{s}$，选A。

10. João is looking for an apartment to live in. He finds four available apartments. He then records the monthly rent and the size of each apartment in a table, as seen below. Based on the information in the table, which apartment has the highest cost per square foot?

Apartments	Rent in dollars	Size in square feet
Branton Ave.	$500	400
Dobbs St.	$600	450
St. Claire Rd.	$750	500
Woodwick Dr.	$800	550

A. Branton Ave.
B. Dobbs St.
C. St. Claire Rd.
D. Woodwick Dr.

知识点：单位换算。

解析：Branton Ave.：$\frac{500}{400}$ = 1.25 美元/平方英尺；Dobbs St.：$\frac{600}{450}$ = 1.33 美元/平方英尺；St. Claire Rd.：$\frac{750}{500}$ = 1.5 美元/平方英尺；Woodwick Dr.：$\frac{800}{550}$ = 1.45 美元/平方英尺。综上所述可知，St. Claire Rd. 最贵，选C。

5.17 列表数据

 例题

1. Victor decides to try three different routes to work for a period of 40 days. In the table above, he tracked whether he arrived to work late or on time each time that he used a particular route. According to the table, what is the probability that Victor took late when he used Route A?

A. $\dfrac{3}{20}$ B. $\dfrac{2}{9}$ C. $\dfrac{3}{5}$ D. $\dfrac{6}{11}$

	On time	Late	Total
Route A	5	6	11
Route B	2	10	12
Route C	6	11	17
Total	13	27	40

知识点：不独立事件的概率。

解析：Victor 选择路线 A 一共 11 天，其中迟到 6 天，则迟到的概率为 $\dfrac{6}{11}$，选 D。

2. A survey conducted on a random sample reports findings on telecommuting in non-academic jobs in the United States, with a focus on sales and computer programming. According to the table above, what is the probability that a randomly chosen job from the study is a partially remote sales job? Round to the nearest hundredth.

Telcommuting in the US job market

	Sales	Computer Programming	Other	Total
100% Remote	185	247	179	611
100% On-Site	1918	1837	1364	5119
Partially Remote (>20% remote)	1012	743	930	2685
Total	3115	2827	2473	8415

知识点：实验事件的概率。

解析：部分偏远地区的销售有 1012 人，总数为 8415 人，则随机选到部分偏远地区的销售人员的概率为 $\dfrac{1012}{8415} \approx 0.12$。

3. Geometry students participated in an activity to classify the shapes in the room by number of sides and color. The table above displays the results. If a triangle is chosen at random from this activity, what is the probability that it is blue?

A. $\dfrac{3}{16}$ B. $\dfrac{1}{8}$ C. $\dfrac{1}{2}$ D. $\dfrac{3}{4}$

	Red	Blue	Total
Triangles	1	3	4
Quadrilaterals	2	6	8
Pentagons	5	7	12
Total	8	16	24

知识点:不独立事件的概率。

解析:在选到三角形的情况下,是蓝色的概率为 $\frac{3}{4}$,故选 D。

4. A science textbook has four chapters, each with a number of skills problems and of analysis problems. A table representing this information is on the left. Based on the table, which of the following statements is true?

A. The relative frequency of analysis problems coming from chapter 4 is $\frac{4}{39}$.

B. The relative frequency of analysis problems coming from chapter 2 is $\frac{21}{89}$.

C. The relative frequency of problems in chapter 1 being skills problems is $\frac{12}{23}$.

D. The relative frequency of problems in chapter 2 being skills problems is $\frac{2}{3}$.

Chapter	Skills problems	Analysis problems	Total
Chapter 1	11	12	23
Chapter 2	10	11	21
Chapter 3	6	12	18
Chapter 4	23	4	27
Total	50	39	89

知识点:相对频率的计算。

解析:第 4 章问题分析的频数为 4,总数为 39,则相对频率为 $\frac{4}{39}$,故选 A。

5. The table above shows the most commonly spoken five languages in the world by native and non-native speakers, in millions, according to the 2013 SIL Ethnologue. If the relative frequency of Spanish non-native speakers to all non-native speakers was 4.8%, approximately how many non-native Spanish speakers, in millions, were there in 2013?

A. 20 B. 59 C. 119 D. 594

Language	Native speakers	Non-native speakers	Total
Mandarin Chinese	848	178	1026
Spanish	415	—	—
Hindi	400	200	600
English	335	—	—
Arabic	485	145	625
Total	2483	1237	3570

知识点：相对频率的应用。

解析：西班牙语的非母语使用者占非母语使用者的4.8%，非母语使用者的总数为1237人，则西班牙语的非母语使用者为1237×4.8%≈59人，故选B。

6. Donte and his friends ordered pizza for a birthday party. They asked all the guests at the party whether they wanted sauce or no sauce and whether they wanted cheese or no cheese. The results are displayed in the table above. Donte found that 1/5 of the people who wanted cheese did not want sauce. What fraction of the people who wanted sauce also wanted cheese?

A. 1/9　　　　B. 8/13　　　　C. 4/5　　　　D. 8/9

	Cheese	No cheese	Total
Sauce	—	—	18
No sauce	—	—	8
Total	20	6	26

知识点：概率的应用。

解析：在想要芝士的20人里有$\frac{1}{5}$的不想要调味汁，则在想要芝士的20人里有4人不想要调味汁，想要调味汁的有16人，所以想要调味汁又想要芝士的人占想要调味汁的$\frac{16}{18}=\frac{8}{9}$，选D。

7. Ori asked 10th and 11th graders at his school which sport they preferred between basketball and football. The table above partially shows the results. Given that 40% of 10th graders at his school prefer basketball, how many 10th graders at his school prefer football?

	10th	11th	Total
Football	—	12	—
Basketball	14	—	—
Total	—	—	156

知识点：百分数的应用。

解析：40%的十年级学生，即14名学生喜欢篮球，则60%的十年级学生喜欢足球，人数为 14÷40%×60%＝21 人。

8. Several English professors categorized the literary works from their seminars by time period and length as shown in the table above. According to the table, what percentage of those books with 500 or more pages are from the 19th century?

Time period	Fewer than 100 pages	100~499 pages	500 or more pages	Total
Old/Middle English	1	2	2	5
Neo-classical	0	1	2	3
19th century	1	7	6	14
20th century	1	0	2	3
Total	3	10	12	25

A. 17%　　　　B. 43%　　　　C. 50%　　　　D. 56%

知识点：百分数的应用。

解析：超过 500 页的一共有 12 本，其中来自 19 世纪的有 6 本，则 $\frac{6}{12} \times 100\% = 50\%$，选 C。

9. The houses in the "historic district" of a particular town are either historically protected or not. The above table partially represents these homes and whether they have foundations made from poured concrete, mortar and field stone, or a combination of both. If only 4.5% of the non-historically-protected homes have a field stone & mortar foundation, how many homes is this? Round to the nearest whole number.

House Construction in the Historic District

	Poured Concrete	Field stone & mortar	Combination	Total
Historically-protected	0	—	—	205
Non-historically-protected	—	—	18	134
Total	—	203	—	339

知识点：百分数的应用。

解析：非受保护历史遗物房屋有 134 栋，其中有石头和砂浆做地基的占 4.8%，则 134×4.8%≈6 栋。

10. Mr. Bumble delivers newspapers to his community every week. His route takes 3 hours to complete. During the first 2 weeks of delivering newspapers, he traveled a total of 100 blocks. Mr. Bumble delivers newspapers for 50 weeks each year. How many blocks does Mr. Bumble travel delivering newspapers in 1 year?

A. 1 block　　　B. 4 blocks　　　C. 50 blocks　　　D. 2500 blocks

知识点：百分数的应用。

解析：两周走了 100 个街区，则一周走 50 个，一年 50 周走 50×50=2500 个，故选 D。

5.18 散点图

例题

1. The scatter plot below shows the number of smartphone solds, N, in millions, at a certain company from 2008 to 2012, where t represents years since 2008. Which of the following best models the relationship between N and t?

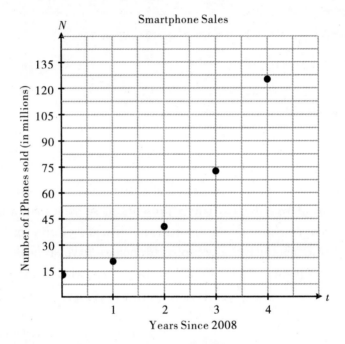

A. $N=15(0.56)^t$
B. $N=15(2.25)^t$
C. $N=11.68(1.82)^t$
D. $N=11.68(9.1)^t$

知识点：散点图的应用。

解析：由图可知，当 $t=0$ 时，$N\approx12$；当 $t=1$ 时，$N\approx22$，$\frac{22}{12}\approx1.83$，故选 C。

2. The scatter plot below shows the percent, P, of Americans that reported accessing the Internet at home via dial-up Internet service. If t represents the years since 2005, which of the following exponential equations best models the trend in the percent of dial-up users from 2005 to 2012?

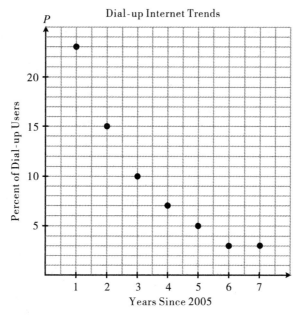

A. $P=30(0.7)^t$ B. $P=30(1.5)^t$ C. $P=-30(0.7)^t$ D. $P=-30(1.5)^t$

知识点：散点图的应用。

解析：当 $t=1$ 时，$P=23$；当 $t=2$ 时，$P=15$。综上所述，选项 A 最符合条件，故选 A。

3. The scatter plot below shows the population of St. Louis, Missouri from 1950 to 2010. Based on the line of best fit to the data shown, which of the following values is closest to the average yearly change in the population of St. Louis, Missouri?

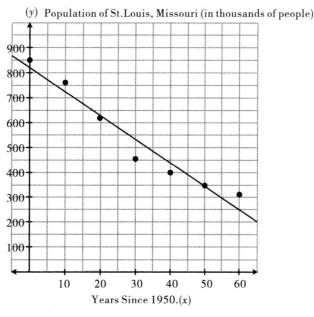

A. -9.3 thousand   B. -93.3 thousand   C. -0.11 thousand   D. -0.93 thousand

知识点：散点图的应用。

解析：观察点 $(20,625)$ 与点 $(50,350)$，每年平均的改变为 $\dfrac{350-625}{50-20}\approx -9.17$，与选项 A

最为接近,故选 A。

4. The scatter plot below shows the number of teams, t, that play in round r of a basketball tournament. For integer values of r, where $1 \leqslant r \leqslant 6$, which of the following equations best models the data?

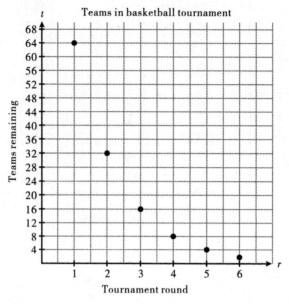

A. $t=96-32r$ B. $t=64-16r$ C. $t=128(0.5)^r$ D. $t=128(2)^r$

知识点:散点图的应用。

解析:当 $r=1$ 时,$t=64$;当 $r=2$ 时,$t=32$;当 $r=3$ 时,$t=16$。综上所述,每当 r 增加 1,t 则缩小到原来的 $\frac{1}{2}$,故选 C。

A ball was dropped from an initial height of 55 feet (ft). A motion detector recorded the maximum height, h, in feet, of the ball after the nth bounce. The results are shown in the scatterplot below.

5. Which of the following statements best describes the situation?

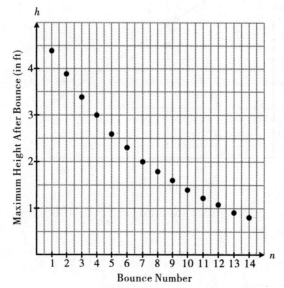

A. The maximum height of the ball decreases by 0.3 ft after each bounce.
B. The maximum height of the ball decreases by 0.5 ft after each bounce.
C. The maximum height of the ball decreases by 1% after each bounce.
D. The maximum height of the ball decreases by 12% after each bounce.

知识点：散点图的应用。

解析：当 $t=1$ 时，$h=4.4$；当 $t=2$ 时，$h=3.9$；当 $t=3$ 时，$h=3.4$；当 $t=4$ 时，$h=3$。很明显排除选项 A、B。$\frac{4.4-3.9}{4.4}\times 100\% \approx 11.4\%$，$\frac{3.9-3.4}{3.9}\times 100\% \approx 12.8\%$，所以选 D。

6. The scatter plot below shows the temperature in degrees Celsius at different depths in meters at a location in the Pacific Ocean. A function that models the data shown is:
$$f(x)=-0.12x+24.91$$
where x represents the water depth in meters, and f represents the water temperature in degrees Celsius. According to this model, at what depth will the temperature be -20 degrees Celsius?

A. 27.31 meters
B. 24.91 meters
C. 374.25 meters
D. 210 meters

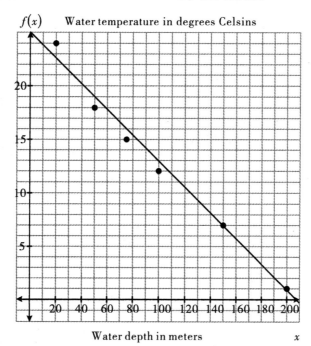

知识点：散点图的应用。

解析：当 $f(x)=-20$ 时，则 $-0.12x+24.91=-20$，解得 $x=374.25$，选 C。

7. The scatter plot below shows the costs to run a 30 second (sec) advertisement during a major sporting event from 1970 to 2010, where x is years since 1970 and c is the cost, in thousands of dollars. An exponential function that models the data is shown above. Based on the model, which of the following is a true statement?

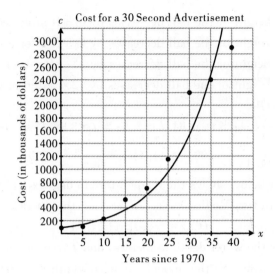

A. The cost to run a 30 sec advertisement during this sporting event in 1970 was about $1.1 million.

B. The cost to run a 30 sec advertisement during this sporting event in 2010 was about $1.1 million.

C. Between 1970 and 2010, the cost to run a 30 sec advertisement during this sporting event increased by about $110000 each year.

D. Between 1970 and 2010, the cost to run a 30 sec advertisement during this sporting event increased by about 10% each year.

知识点：散点图的应用。

解析：当 $x=0$ 时，$c=100000$；当 $x=10$ 时，$c=200000$。假设每年增长 $a\%$，则 $100000 \times (1+a\%)^{10}=200000$，$(1+a\%)^{10}=2$，所以 $\dfrac{\log 2}{\log(1+a\%)}=2$，$a\%=10\%$，选 D。

8. The scatter plot below shows the population of Florida, P, in millions, from 1900 to 2010, where t represents years since 1900. Which of the following exponential equations best models the population of Florida from 1900 to 2010?

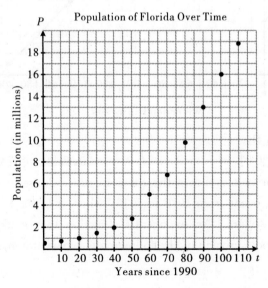

A. $P=0.710(0.53)^t$ B. $P=0.710(0.965)^t$
C. $P=0.53(1.035)^t$ D. $P=0.53(1.410)^t$

知识点：散点图的应用。

解析：当 $t=20$ 时，$P=1$；当 $t=40$ 时，$P=2$，代入可知 $P=0.53(1.035)^t$ 符合条件，选 C。

9. The scatter plot below shows the latitudes of various United States (US) cities plotted against the city's average September temperature, where is the latitude of the city, in degrees, and T is the city's average September temperature, in degrees Farenheit (℉). A line that approximates the data is shown on the graph. Which of the following statements is the best interpretation for the slope of the line of best fit in this situation?

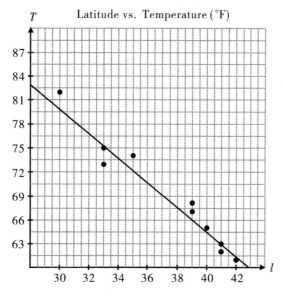

A. The average September temperature for a US city decreases by 2 ℉ for each 3 degree increase in latitude.

B. The average September temperature for a US city increases by 2 ℉ for each 3 degree increase in latitude.

C. The average September temperature for a US city decreases by 3 ℉ for each 2 degree increase in latitude.

D. The average September temperature for a US city increases by 3 ℉ for each 2 degree increase in latitude.

知识点：散点图的应用。

解析：在直线上找到两点 $(33,75)$ 以及 $(41,63)$，则斜率为 $\dfrac{63-75}{41-33}=-\dfrac{3}{2}$，即当纬度增加 2 ℉时，温度减少 3 ℉，故选 C。

10. The scatter plot below shows the number of times, s, in thousands, a video has been shared on a given day, t, after the video was initially shared. If the exponential function that best models the data is shown above, which of the following best describes the percent by which the number of shares increased each day?

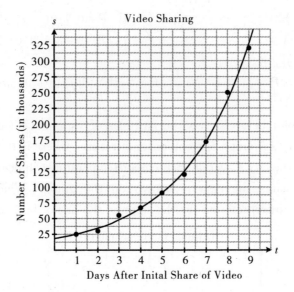

A. 5% B. 10% C. 18% D. 40%

知识点：散点图的应用。

解析：在图上找到两点(6,125)及(7,175)，则每天增长 $\frac{175-125}{125} \times 100\% = 40\%$，故选 D。

5.19 图像信息

 例题

1. The temperature, T, in degrees Celsius (℃) along a circular infrared stove measured d centimeters (cm) from the left edge of the circumference and going through the center of the stove is given by the graph below. The hottest point occurs at the center of the stove. What is the diameter of the stove in centimeters?

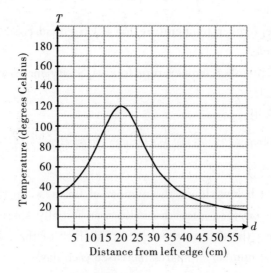

知识点:图像的理解。

解析:当离左边边缘 20 cm 时火炉温度最高,则此时为圆心,所以半径为 20 cm,直径为 40 cm。

2. An electromagnetic pulse is generated and its profile at a distance D, in micrometers (μm), is taken 1 picosecond later. The magnetic field, M, in nanotesla (nT) reaches a minimum of 4 nT at a distance of 50 μm from the source. The magnetic field reaches a maximum of 10 nT at a distance of 90 μm. Which of the following graphs in the DM-plane could represent this situation?

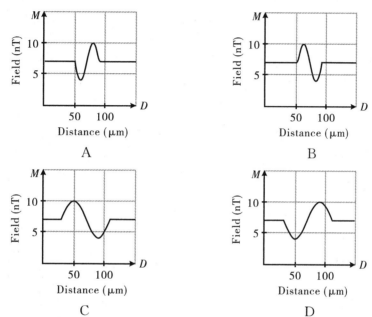

知识点:图像的理解。

解析:距离为 50 μm 时磁场为最小值,距离为 90 μm 时磁场为最大值,故选 D。

3. The graph below in the mf-plane relates the length in meters (m) of a particular thickness of guitar string to the frequency in Hertz (Hz) at which it will vibrate for a first harmonic note. By what factor does the frequency decrease between string lengths of 0.5 m and 0.6 m?

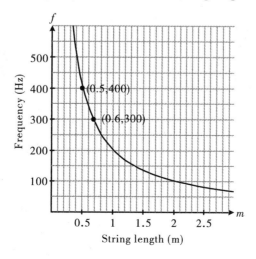

A. 0.16 B. 0.5
C. 0.6   D. 0.75

知识点：图像的理解。

解析：长度为 0.5 m 时频率为 400 Hz，长度为 0.6 m 时频率为 300 Hz，$\frac{300}{400}=0.75$，故选 D。

4. Based on the bone mass to body mass ratio of modern reptiles, paleontologists can use the fossils of the Tyrannosaurus Rex dinosaur to predict its rate of growth, r, in kilograms per year (kg/yr) at a particular age, a, in years. The rate of growth has a minimum of 50 kg/yr when the dinosaur's age is less than 1 year and greater than 29 years. Additionally, the rate of growth reaches a maximum of 600 kg/yr when a is 16 years. Which of the following graphs in the ar-plane could show this relationship?

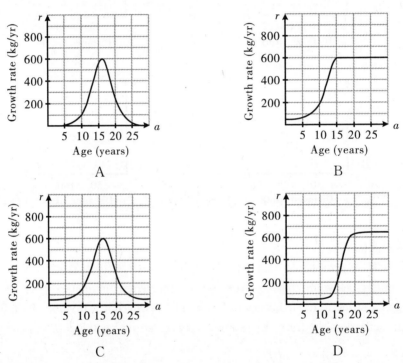

知识点：图像的理解。

解析：当恐龙小于 1 岁，大于 29 岁时，增长率为最小值 50 千克/年；当恐龙为 16 岁时，增长率为最大值 600 千克/年，故选 C。

5. A computer clock changes its voltage, v, in volts (V) over a time, t, in nanoseconds (ns) in order to control the execution of instructions. The clock starts with a voltage of 0 V, then increases to 0.1 V and stays at 0.1 V for exactly 10ns, and finally decreases to 0 V. Which of the following graphs in the tv-plane could represent this situation?

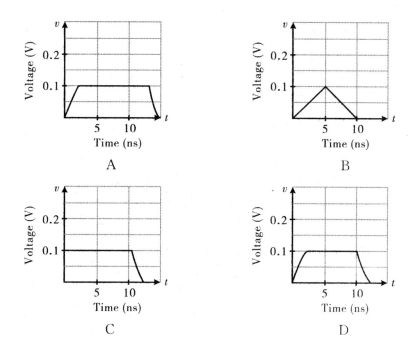

知识点：图像的理解。

解析：电压从 0 伏开始,增加到 0.1 伏,停留在 0.1 伏 10 纳秒,最后减少到 0 伏,故选 A。

6. A foreign species of insect has invaded a small island and begins to consume the island's mustard plants over a time, T, in months. The area inhabited by mustard plants, A, in acres (ac) immediately after the insect's introduction is 20 ac, and after 6 months the mustard plants disappear from the island. Which of the following graphs in the TA-plane could represent this situation?

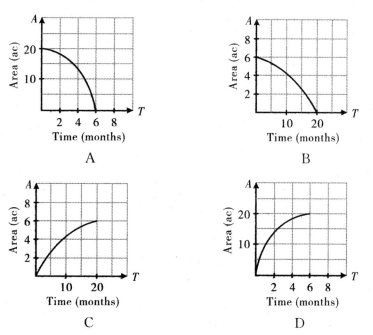

知识点：图像的理解。

解析：开始时为 20 英亩，6 个月后芥菜消失，为 0 英亩，故选 A。

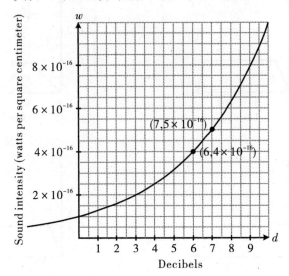

7. The graph above in the dw-plane relates the number of decibels d (dB) of a sound to the sound intensity, w, in watts per square centimeter. By what factor does the sound intensity increase between 6 and 7dB?

   A. 0.8　　　　　B. 1.25　　　　　C. $\dfrac{1 \times 10^{16}}{3}$　　　　　D. $\dfrac{2 \times 10^{16}}{7}$

   知识点：图像的理解。

   解析：6 分贝时声音强度为 4×10^{-16} 瓦特/平方厘米，7 分贝时声音强度为 5×10^{-16} 瓦特/平方厘米，则 $\dfrac{5 \times 10^{-16}}{4 \times 10^{-16}} = 1.25$，因数为 1.25，故选 B。

8. The graph below in the th-plane shows the height above ground, h, in meters (m) of a projectile t seconds (s) after it has been fired upward. To the nearest 5 meters per second, what is the absolute value of the average rate of change of height in terms of time between the time the projectile was at its highest point and the time the projectile hit the ground?

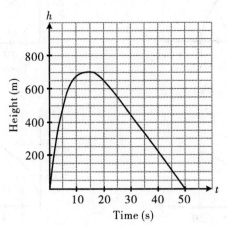

   知识点：图像的理解。

   解析：最高点的坐标为 (15,700)，落地时为 (50,0)，则平均变化率的绝对值为 $\left| \dfrac{0-700}{50-15} \right|$

=|−20|=20。

9. The rectangular floor of a playpen has a perimeter of 24 feet. Which of the following graphs in the wA-plane could represent the relationship between the width, w, in feet, and the floor area, A, in square feet, of the playpen?

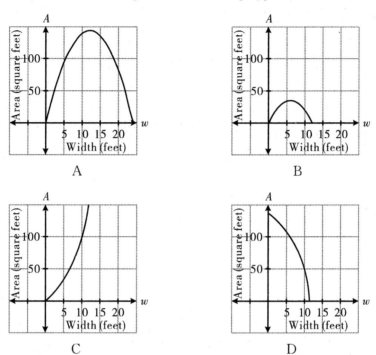

知识点:图像的理解。

解析:假设宽为 x 英尺,则长为 $(12-x)$ 英尺,面积为 $A=x(12-x)$, $A=12x-x^2=-(x-6)^2+36$,则顶点坐标为 $(6,36)$,故选 B。

10. A call option gives the purchaser the option to buy a stock in the future at a particular price known as the strike price. The dollar profit, P, of a call option is a constant negative value when the future dollar stock price, S, is less than the strike price. When the stock price is above the strike price, P increases from its constant negative value at the rate of $\$1$ per dollar of S. Which of the following graphs in the SP-plane could be the graph of a call option with a strike price of $\$15$?

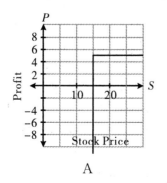

A

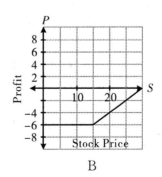

B

New SAT 非官方指南

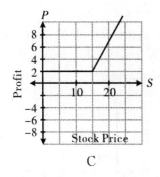
C

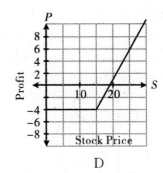
D

知识点：图像的理解。

解析：当股票价格低于执行价格时，P 为负值常量，则此时为水平直线；当股票价格高于执行价格时，P 以 1 美元的速率增加，则斜率为 1。故选 D。

5.20 线性及指数增长

 例题

1. A statistician modeled the average private law school tuition in two ways. According to both models, the tuition in 2011 was about $40000. In one model, the tuition increased by $1750 per year. In the other, the tuition increased by 5% per year. What would be the difference between these models in the year 2013?

知识点：线性及指数增长的应用。

解析：线性增长为 $40000+1750\times2=43500$，指数增长为 $40000\times(1+5\%)^2=44100$，则差为 $44100-43500=600$ 美元。

2. For the last decade, the number of insured children who had dental cleanings has been growing by 5% per year or by about 68 children per year, depending on how the growth is modeled. This year, 1760 insured children have dental cleanings. To the nearest child, what is the difference between the numbers whom the models predict will have dental cleanings 3 years from now?

知识点：线性及指数增长的应用。

解析：线性增长为 $1760+68\times3=1964$，指数增长为 $1760\times(1+5\%)^3=2037$，则差为 $2037-1964\approx73$。

3. The number of data objects stored in a company's "cloud" increased 190% per year for the first 5 years, when it reached 762 billion objects. During the next year, the company reported that 1 billion objects were being added daily. If the growth rate had not changed, how many more objects would there have been at the end of the year? Use 365 days per year.

A. 1.1 trillion objects B. 2.2 trillion objects

C. 320 trillion objects D. 397 trillion objects

知识点:线性及指数增长的应用。

解析:$(762+365×1)×10^9=1127×10^9$,则为 1.127 万亿,选 A。

4. $V(m)-V(m-1)=622$

The value, $V(m)$, in dollars of a particular house m months after purchase follows the equation given above where m is a positive integer. Which of the following statements best describes the value of the house over time?

A. The value of the house increases linearly.
B. The value of the house decreases linearly.
C. The value of the house increases exponentially.
D. The value of the house decreases exponentially.

知识点:线性及指数增长的应用。

解析:由方程 $V(m)-V(m-1)=622$ 可知,当 m 增加 1,V 增加 622,则呈线性增长,故选 A。

5. In 2000, there were 0.025 phone subscriptions per inhabitant in Africa each for mobile and fixed phones. After that, the fixed phone subscriptions steadily increased by 0.01 per 7 years, while the mobile phone subscriptions grew 48% per year. What was the total number of phone subscriptions per inhabitant in 2002?

A. 0.027   B. 0.034   C. 0.073   D. 0.083

知识点:线性及指数增长的应用。

解析:手机订阅每年增长 48%,则 2002 年为 $0.025×(1+48\%)^2=0.0548$,固定电话每 7 年增长 0.01,则两年后为 $0.025+0.00142=0.02642$,则总数为 0.083,故选 D。

6. The earnings per share of stock in a company grew 70% per year for a decade, reaching \$27 per share in 2011. Knowing that such growth is not sustainable, the adviser makes a prediction for 2014 based on the average rate of change, which was \$3 per year. To the nearest dollar, how much higher would the financial adviser's prediction be for 2014 if the adviser assumed the earnings would continue to grow 70% per year?

知识点:线性及指数增长的应用。

解析:$27×(1+70\%)^3-(27+3×3)≈97$。

7. An auto repair company is advertising on television and on the internet. It hires a statistician to poll 5000 people across the country at the beginning of every month for six months. Eight hundred people saw the advertisement on television at the beginning of the first month with an increase of 200 people each month. Also, 1000 people saw the advertisement on the internet at the beginning of the first month with an increase of x percent each month. At the beginning of the third month, there were 240 more people who saw the advertisement on the internet than on television. To the nearest percent, what is the value of x?

知识点:线性及指数增长的应用。

解析:$1000×(1+x\%)^2-(800+200×2)=240$,解方程可得 $x=20$。

8. A company bought a year of search engine optimization services (SEO) for their site. During that time, the number of visitors per month grew 20% per month, with 500 visitors the final month. After the SEO ended, the site gained 25 visitors per month. How

many fewer visitors did the site have 3 months after the SEO ended than there would have been if the number had continued to grow 20% per month?

知识点：线性及指数增长的应用。

解析：$500 \times (1+20\%)^3 - (500 + 25 \times 3) = 289$。

9. Scarlett is studying neuron degeneration in mice. One article suggests that the number of neurons remaining, $N(t)$, after t months is modeled by the following function:

$$N(t) = N_0 \cdot (1-r)^{t/\tau}$$

where is the initial number of neurons at time $t=0$, r is the degeneration rate ($0 < r < 1$), and τ is the characteristic timescale of the decay process, measured in months. If the characteristic timescale τ is 4 months, which of the following statements best describes the relationship between the number of neurons remaining and the number of months?

A. The relationship is linear because every 4 months, the number of neurons remaining decreases by a fixed amount.

B. The relationship is linear because every month, the number of neurons remaining increases by a fixed amount.

C. The relationship is exponential because every 4 months, the number of neurons remaining decreases by an amount proportional to the previous 4 months.

D. The relationship is exponential because every month, the number of neurons remaining increases by an amount proportional to the previous month.

知识点：线性及指数增长的应用。

解析：典型时标 τ 为 4 个月，则每 4 个月神经元细胞的减少数量与前 4 个月细胞数量成比例，故选 C。

10. In a particular science research database, the number of indexed genetics articles had increased by an average of 307 articles per year for several years. If there were 6000 genetics articles indexed at the end of that time, and the number of articles increased by 8% annually since then, how many more articles would be indexed than the average annual increase would predict by 2 years later? Round to the nearest article.

知识点：线性及指数增长的应用。

解析：$6000 \times (1+8\%)^2 - (6000 + 307 \times 2) = 384$。

第4部分　New SAT 写作

第6章　New SAT 作文整体介绍

6.1　New SAT 作文介绍

改革后的 SAT 考试需要考生在 50 分钟内,在阅读完一篇长达 800 字的文章之后,写出一篇分析型文章。改革后,作文分数不计入总分,成为选考科目,但是热度依然高。不仅因为不诚信考试的屡次出现,而且在申请过程中,大学招生委员会会抽调 SAT 作文来和 PS 做一定的比对,所以选考也只是一个概念。

6.2　评分标准

三个维度:Reading,Analysis,Writing。
分数区度:每个单项 1~4 分。

Reading

4 分(advanced)

The response demonstrates thorough comprehension of the source text.

The response shows an understanding of the text's central idea(s) and of most important details and how they interrelate, demonstrating a comprehensive understanding of the text.

The response is free of errors of fact or interpretation with regard to the text.

The response makes skillful use of textual evidence (quotations, paraphrases, or both), demonstrating a complete understanding of the source text.

3 分(proficient)

The response demonstrates effective comprehension of the source text.

The response shows an understanding of the text's central idea(s) and important details.

The response is free of substantive errors of fact and interpretation with regard to the text.

The response makes appropriate use of textual evidence (quotations, paraphrases, or both), demonstrating an understanding of the source text.

 Analysis

4 分(advanced)

The response offers an insightful analysis of the source text and demonstrates a sophisticated understanding of the analytical task.

The response offers a thorough, well-considered evaluation of the author's use of evidence, reasoning, and/or stylistic and persuasive elements, and/or feature(s) of the student's own choosing.

The response contains relevant, sufficient, and strategically chosen support for claim(s) or point(s) made.

The response focuses consistently on those features of the text that are most relevant to addressing the task.

3 分(proficient)

The response offers an effective analysis of the source text and demonstrates an understanding of the analytical task.

The response competently evaluates the author's use of evidence, reasoning, and/or stylistic and persuasive elements, and/or feature(s) of the student's own choosing.

The response contains relevant and sufficient support for claim(s) or point(s) made.

The response focuses primarily on those features of the text that are most relevant to addressing the task.

 Writing

4 分(Advanced)

The response is cohesive and demonstrates a highly effective use and command of language.

The response includes a precise central claim.

The response includes a skillful introduction and conclusion. The response demonstrates a deliberate and highly effective progression of ideas both within paragraphs and throughout the essay.

The response has a wide variety in sentence structures. The response demonstrates a consistent use of precise word choice. The response maintains a formal style and objective tone.

The response shows a strong command of the conventions of standard written English and is free or virtually free of errors.

3 分(proficient)

The response is mostly cohesive and demonstrates effective use and control of language.

The response includes a central claim or implicit controlling idea.

The response includes an effective introduction and conclusion. The response demonstrates a clear progression of ideas both within paragraphs and throughout the essay.

The response has variety in sentence structures. The response demonstrates some precise word choice. The response maintains a formal style and objective tone.

The response shows a good control of the conventions of standard written English and is free of significant errors that detract from the quality of writing.

第 7 章 New SAT 作文评分标准实例

Adapted from Paul Bogard, *Bag Ban Bad for Freedom and Environment*. © 2013 by The San Diego Union-Ttribune, LLC. Originally published June 13, 2013.

> As you read the passage below, consider how Paul Bogard uses
> - evidence, such as facts or examples, to support claims.
> - reasoning to develop ideas and to connect claims and evidence.
> - stylistic or persuasive elements, such as word choice or appeals to emotion, to add power to the ideas expressed.

1. Californians dodged yet another nanny-state regulation recently when the state Senate narrowly voted down a bill to ban plastic bags statewide, but the reprieve might only be temporary. Not content to tell us how much our toilets can flush or what type of light bulb to use to brighten our homes, some politicians and environmentalists are now focused on deciding for us what kind of container we can use to carry our groceries.

2. The bill, SB 405, along with companion bill AB 158 in the Assembly, would have prohibited grocery stores and convenience stores with at least $2 million in gross annual sales and 10000 square feet of retail space from providing single-use plastic or paper bags, although stores would have been allowed to sell recycled paper bags for an unspecified amount. The bill fell just three votes short of passage in the Senate—with four Democratic senators not voting—and Sen. Alex Padilla, D-Los Angeles, who sponsored the measure, has indicated that he would like to bring it up again, so expect this fight to be recycled rather than trashed.

3. While public debate over plastic bag bans often devolves into emotional pleas to save the planet or preserve marine life (and, believe me, I love sea turtles as much as the next guy), a little reason and perspective is in order.

4. According to the U.S. Environmental Protection Agency, plastic bags, sacks, and wraps of all kinds (not just grocery bags) make up only about 1.6 percent of all municipal

solid waste materials. High-density polyethylene (HDPE) bags, which are the most common kind of plastic grocery bags, make up just 0.3 percent of this total.

5. The claims that plastic bags are worse for the environment than paper bags or cotton reusable bags are dubious at best. In fact, compared to paper bags, plastic grocery bags produce fewer greenhouse gas emissions, require 70 percent less energy to make, generate 80 percent less waste, and utilize less than 4 percent of the amount of water needed to manufacture them. This makes sense because plastic bags are lighter and take up less space than paper bags.

6. Reusable bags come with their own set of problems. They, too, have a larger carbon footprint than plastic bags. Even more disconcerting are the findings of several studies that plastic bag bans lead to increased health problems due to food contamination from bacteria that remain in the reusable bags. A November 2012 statistical analysis by University of Pennsylvania law professor Jonathan Klick and George Mason University law professor and economist Joshua D. Wright found that San Francisco's plastic bag ban in 2007 resulted in a subsequent spike in hospital emergency room visits due to E. coli, salmonella, and campylobacter-related intestinal infectious diseases. The authors conclude that the ban even accounts for several additional deaths in the city each year from such infections.

7. The description of plastic grocery bags as "single-use" bags is another misnomer. The vast majority of people use them more than once, whether for lining trash bins or picking up after their dogs. (And still other bags are recycled.) Since banning plastic bags also means preventing their additional uses as trash bags and looper scoopers, one unintended consequence of the plastic bag ban would likely be an increase in plastic bag purchases for these other purposes. This is just what happened in Ireland in 2002 when a 15 Euro cent ($0.20) tax imposed on plastic shopping bags led to a 77 percent increase in the sale of plastic trash can liner bags.

8. And then there are the economic costs. The plastic bag ban would threaten the roughly 2000 California jobs in the plastic bag manufacturing and recycling industry, although, as noted in the Irish example above, they might be able to weather the storm if they can successfully switch to producing other types of plastic bags. In addition, taxpayers will have to pony up for the added bureaucracy, and the higher regulatory costs foisted upon bag manufacturers and retailers will ultimately be borne by consumers in the form of price increases.

9. Notwithstanding the aforementioned reasons why plastic bags are not, in fact, evil incarnate, environmentalists have every right to try to convince people to adopt certain beliefs or lifestyles, but they do not have the right to use government force to compel people to live the way they think best. In a free society, we are able to live our lives as we please, so long as we do not infringe upon the rights of others. That includes the right to make such fundamental decisions as "paper or plastic?"

> Write an essay in which you explain how Adam B. Summers builds an argument to persuade his audience that plastic shopping bags should not be banned. In your essay, analyze how Summers uses one or more of the features listed in the box above (or features of your own choice) to strengthen the logic and persuasiveness of his argument. Be sure that your analysis focuses on the most relevant features of the passage.
>
> Your essay should not explain whether you agree with Summer's claims, but rather explain how Summers builds an argument to persuade his audience.

7.1 阅读策略

提示:这篇文章难度中等,笔者的学生平均需要 6~8 分钟完成略读和精读。

读文章过程要注意三要素:(1) 文章主旨;(2) 主旨如何被拓展;(3) 写作风格。

7.2 分析

P1+2:关键点为 Senate narrowly voted down a bill to ban plastic bags statewide, but the reprieve might only be temporary。本段是为了引出文章的 topic,要不要禁止塑料袋的使用。

P3:关键点为 While public debate over plastic bag bans often devolves into emotional pleas to save the planet or preserve marine life, a little reason and perspective is in order。本段是文章的主旨段,提出了作者的态度,那就是废除的做法没有充分理由,所以自然地引出作者的理性分析。

P4:关键点为 1.6% solid waste;HDPE bags, which are the most common kind of plastic grocery bags, make up just 0.3% percent of this total。本段通过数字表达塑料袋,其实只造成了相对较少的污染。

P5:关键点为 comparison between plastic bags and paper bags, less greenhouse effect。通过对比说明,相比纸袋,塑料袋造成了很少的温室效应。

P6:关键点为 comparison between plastic bags and reusable bags
Carbon footprint, health problems, infectious diseases and even deaths。通过对比说明,相比可再生袋,塑料袋的污染少,对身体的有害影响也比较少。

P7:关键点为 plastic bags not single use, serve as trash bags and looper scooper。本段说明塑料袋不是所谓的用过一次就会被丢掉的袋子,事实上还有很多生活用途。

P8:关键点为 economic costs, threaten 200 jobs, regulatory costs, price increase。说明塑料袋还能带来经济效应。

P9:关键点为 environmentalists have every right to try to convince people to adopt certain beliefs or lifestyles, but they do not have the right to use government force to compel people to live the way they think best. 通过让步反驳，指出环保学家没有权利迫使老百姓放弃使用塑料袋的权利。

7.3 范文分析和评分标准

Essay 1

3/3/3

The style and features an author use can help persuade the audience if clearly used. Adam B. Summers in this essay uses factual evidence, word choice, and emotion to build his argument. In doing this, Summers successfully persuades his audience into believing "Paper or Plastic" is a personal right.

When using factual evidence, Summers further persuades his reader. Readers are often attracted to facts because they are hard evidence to proving a point. Summers touches upon how plastic bag waster makes up only 0.3 percent out of the 1.6 percent of all municipal solid waste products. By providing this fact, Summers shows the low numbered statistics which persuade the reader. The reader sees the small numbers and is immediately taking the author's side. Another use of factual evidence is when Summers discusses Ireland's problem since they have banned the use of plastic bags. By adding in the effects this had on another country, the audience realized the same situation could happen in California, causing the reader to further his mind to Summer's ideas.

The word choice Summers uses helps lure his readers in to his argument. In the first paragraph, Summers uses words such as "dodged", "narrowly", and "down". The usage of words makes the reader feel as if his is in the actual voting process of the bill, taking the rocky road in state government only to get voted down. From the start, Summers makes the audience feel involved which intrigues the reader further. In the second to the last paragraph, Summers plays with the phrases "weather the storm" and "pony up" to represent the possibilities to come if a bill banning plastic bags is passed. By telling the reader to "get ready", he puts a negative feeling to the future of the bill and persuades the reader into thinking that the future may not be something they like.

Summers also adds in personal emotion to make the reader feel connected to the author. He writes "I love sea turtle as much as the next guy" to show that he is human too and cares about nature. The claim would touch many readers who are in the same position as Summers; they love nature but think the banning of plastic bags is unreasonable. Summers connects to all readers in his audience when he futher helps …[unfinished]

评分标准

Reading 3: The write accurately paraphrases the central idea of the passage. The write

also both paraphrases and directly quotes important details from the next.

Analysis 3: The writer identifies three persuasive elements—factual evidence, word choice, and emotion—and competently evaluates how these aspects of Summers's text contribute to building his argument.

Highlight: "Summers discusses Ireland's problem since they have banned the use of plastic bags. By adding in the effects this had on another country, the audience realized the same situation could happen in California, causing the reader to further his mind to Summer's ideas." "In the second to the last paragraph, Summers plays with the phrases 'weather the storm' and 'pony up' to represent the possibilities to come if a bill banning plastic bags is passed. By telling the reader to 'get ready', he puts a negative feeling to the future of the bill and persuades the reader into thinking that the future may not be something they like."

Although these moments of analysis are effective, the response lacks the thoroughness and insight seen in responses scoring higher.

Writing 3: The response is mostly cohesive and demonstrates effective use and control of language. The introduction is brief but effectively provides a clear central claim. The rest of the response is organized according to this three-pronged structure, with each body paragraph remaining on topic. A clear progression of ideas is demonstrated both within paragraphs and throughout the responses. The writer integrates quotations and examples from the source text to connect ideas and paragraphs logically. There are a variety of sentences structures. There are some examples of precise word choice. (lure his audience; take the rocky road; make the audience feel involved)

 Essay 2

4/4/4

In Adam B. Summers's "editorial for the San Diego Union-Tribune", he argues against the possible laws hindering Californians from using plastic bags at grocery stores. He believes they would do no more harm than good, and that "a little reason and perspective is in order." By the end of this piece the reader will likely find themselves nodding in agreement with what Summers has to say, and this isn't just because he is right. Summers, like any good writer, employs tactical reasoning and persuasive devices to plead with the audience to take his side. In this article, he demonstrates many such devices.

"Plastic bags ... make up only about 1.6 percent of all municipal solid waste materials." Summers ventures, his first utilization of a cold, hard fact. The truth in the numbers is undeniable, and he cites his sources promptly, making the statement that much more authentic. Knowledge is often viewed as power, and with information as direct as a statistic, Summers is handling that power to the reader—the power to agree with him. Not only does Summers spread the facts with numbers, he also does so with trends. He talks about the price increase in Ireland, and the documented health hazards of reusable bags. He uses the truth, backed by reliable sources, to infiltrate the readers' independent mind.

His thoroughness in this regard carefully builds his argument against this piece of legislation, and this is just one of the many ways he spreads his opposition.

Additionally, Summers appeals to the ethnical and emotional side of individuals. With key phrases like "taxpayers will have to pony up" and "borne by consumers", Summers activates the nature of a human to act in their own self-interest. While one might view this as selfish, Summers reassures the reader that they are not alone in feeling this way, further contributing to his argument. With his statement that he "loves sea turtles as much as the next guy", Summers adds acceptance to those who don't care to act with regard for the environment. By putting himself beside the reader as a typical consumer, he equals them, and makes himself more likeable in the process. Appealing to environmentalists, too, Summers qualifies that they "have every right to try to convince people to adopt certain beliefs or lifestyles, but they do not have the right to use governmental force..." A statement such as this is an attempt to get readers of either persuasion on his side, and his ingenious qualification only adds to the strength of his argument. An article focusing on the choice between "paper or plastic," and how that choice might be taken away certainly seems fairly standard, but by adjusting his diction (using well known phrases and selecting words with strong connotations), Summers creates something out of the ordinary. It is with word choice such as "recycled rather than trashed" that the author reveals the legislations intent to stir up a repeat bill. Because the issue at hand is one of waste and environmental protection, his humorous diction provides a link between he and the audience, revealing not only an opportunity to laugh, but also reinforcement of the concept that Summers is trustworthy and just like everyone else. Negative words with specifically poor connotations also aid Summers in his persuasive struggle. "Reprieve" "dubious" "bureaucracy" and "evil incarnate" all depict a disparaging tone of annoyance and anger, surely helping Summers to spread his message.

It is through many rhetorical devices that Summers sells his argument. Powerful diction, qualification, ethos, pathos, logos, and informative facts all contribute to an exceptionally well-written argument. It is his utilization of these practices and more that make this article worthy of recognition. Once one reads the piece, they will be nodding along in accordance with Summers, and it isn't for no reason.

Reading 4: The writer provides a brief summary of Summers's main point in the introductory paragraph and throughout the response uses a mixture of direct quotations and paragraphs to show an understanding of the central idea and important details from the source text interrelate. Further, the writer demonstrates an understanding of how the central idea and important details interrelate by consistently relating details to the main argument of the source text.

Analysis 4: This response demonstrates a sophisticated understanding of the analytical task by offering an insightful analysis of Summers's employment of tactical reasoning and persuasive devices to plead with the audience to take his side.

The writer puts forth a thorough evaluation of Summers's use of evidence, reasoning, and stylistic and persuasive elements by continually analyzing even the smallest features of Summers's piece. For example, when citing a fact that Summers provides (Plastic bags... make up only about 1.6...), the writer focuses on the truth in the numbers as well as Summers's deliberate choice to share the fact's source and the effect doing do has on Summers's argument. The writer continues the analysis by broadening the focus to a brief but sophisticated discussion of knowledge as power and the persuasive approach of handling that power to the reader. This type of well-considered evaluation continues throughout the response, during which the writer touches on Summers's appeals to the ethical and emotional side of individuals and Summers's use of diction to create something out of the ordinary. The response is focused on relevant and strategically chosen features of the source text in support of the writer's analysis.

Writing 4: This response demonstrates highly effective command of language and cohesion. The response is highly organized and demonstrates a deliberate progression of ideas, with the writer seamlessly transitioning from point to point. Sentence structures are varied and often sophisticated (While one might view this selfish, Summers reassures the reader that they are not alone in feeling this way, further contributing to his argument). Word choice is precise without tonal missteps (tactical reasoning; his ingenious qualification only adds to the strength of his argument; disparaging tone of annoyance and anger). The response shows a strong command of the conventions of standard written English and is virtually free of errors.

第8章 New SAT 作文写作框架

分析：本章节的主要目的是通过2017年3月SAT作文真题来提炼作文的写作框架和可以借鉴的模板。研究高分范文，基本可以得出两种基本的写作结构。

框架一：流水账型

主要特点：按照顺序的方式，来逐一剖析文章的特点。此写法结构清晰，脉络清楚，但是对于写作者的自身能力有较高的要求。毕竟要做到每一段都有东西可以分析，还分析地不错，不是一件简单的事情。

框架二：层次型

主要特点：按照模块的方式来分析文章，从论证手法、写作风格、修辞手段等角度分块讨论。此写法有相对固定的写作模板和一定的写作思路。缺点是很多学生会被模板限制住，文章显得别扭。

8.1 流水账型写法分析

> Prompt
> As you read the passage below, consider how Paul Bogard uses
> - evidence, such as facts or examples, to support claims.
> - reasoning to develop ideas and to connect claims and evidence.
> - stylistic or persuasive elements, such as word choice or appeals to emotion, to add power to the ideas expressed.

8.1.1 阅读和分析

1. At my family's cabin on a Minnesota lake, I knew woods so dark that my hands disappeared before my eyes. I knew night skies in which meteors left smoky trails across sugary spreads of stars. But now, when 8 of 10 children born in the United States will never know a sky dark enough for the Milky Way, I worry we are rapidly losing night's natural darkness before realizing its worth. This winter solstice, as we cheer the days' gradual movement back toward light, let us also remember the irreplaceable value of darkness.

2. All life evolved to the steady rhythm of bright days and dark nights. Today, though, when we feel the closeness of nightfall, we reach quickly for a light switch. And too little darkness, meaning too much artificial light at night, spells trouble for all.

3. Already the World Health Organization classifies working the night shift as a probable human carcinogen, and the American Medical Association has voiced its unanimous support for "light pollution reduction efforts and glare reduction efforts at both the national and state levels." Our bodies need darkness to produce the hormone melatonin, which keeps certain cancers from developing, and our bodies need darkness for sleep. Sleep disorders have been linked to diabetes, obesity, cardiovascular disease and depression, and recent research suggests one main cause of "short sleep" is "long light." Whether we work at night or simply take our tablets, notebooks and smartphones to bed, there isn't a place for this much artificial light in our lives.

4. The rest of the world depends on darkness as well, including nocturnal and crepuscular species of birds, insects, mammals, fish and reptiles. Some examples are well known—the 400 species of birds that migrate at night in North America, the sea turtles that come ashore to lay their eggs—and some are not, such as the bats that save American farmers billions in pest control and the moths that pollinate 80% of the world's flora. Ecological light pollution is like the bulldozer of the night, wrecking habitat and disrupting ecosystems several billion years in the making. Simply put, without darkness, Earth's

ecology would collapse...

5. In today's crowded, louder, more fast-paced world, night's darkness can provide solitude, quiet and stillness, qualities increasingly in short supply. Every religious tradition has considered darkness invaluable for a soulful life, and the chance to witness the universe has inspired artists, philosophers and everyday stargazers since time began. In a world awash with electric light ... how would Van Gogh have given the world his "Starry Night"? Who knows what this vision of the night sky might inspire in each of us, in our children or grandchildren?

6. Yet all over the world, our nights are growing brighter. In the United States and Western Europe, the amount of light in the sky increases an average of about 6% every year. Computer images of the United States at night, based on NASA photographs, show that what was a very dark country as recently as the 1950s is now nearly covered with a blanket of light. Much of this light is wasted energy, which means wasted dollars. Those of us over 35 are perhaps among the last generation to have known truly dark nights. Even the northern lake where I was lucky to spend my summers has seen its darkness diminish.

7. It doesn't have to be this way. Light pollution is readily within our ability to solve, using new lighting technologies and shielding existing lights. Already, many cities and towns across North America and Europe are changing to LED streetlights, which offer dramatic possibilities for controlling wasted light. Other communities are finding success with simply turning off portions of their public lighting after midnight. Even Paris, the famed "city of light," which already turns off its monument lighting after 1 a.m., will this summer start to require its shops, offices and public buildings to turn off lights after 2 a.m. Though primarily designed to save energy, such reductions in light will also go far in addressing light pollution. But we will never truly address the problem of light pollution until we become aware of the irreplaceable value and beauty of the darkness we are losing.

Write an essay in which you explain how Paul Bogard builds an argument to persuade his audience that natural darkness should be preserved. In your essay, analyze how Bogard uses one or more of the features in the directions that precede the passage (or features of your own choice) to strengthen the logic and persuasiveness of his argument. Be sure that your analysis focuses on the most relevant features of the passage. Your essay should not explain whether you agree with Bogard's claims, but rather explain how Bogard builds an argument to persuade his audience.

分析

P1:文章第 1 段通过作者个人的 anecdote 逸闻趣事来引出 darkness 的重要性这个话题。

P2:文章第 2 段指出了现状,就是 too much artificial light。光太多,黑暗太少。

P3~P5:这 3 段介绍了 darkness 对于人类和动物的精神层面有很多帮助。

P6:第 6 段通过数据进一步呼应第 2 段,再次指出目前的世界光太多,黑暗太少。

P7：第7段展示了解决此问题的两个方法：利用新的照明技术和关闭已有的灯光，并且分别给了实例来证明可行度。

8.1.2 我带你写

In the article "*Let There Be Dark*" published in 2012, the author Paul argues that people are losing the darkness in the night and that natural darkness should be protected.

In the opening paragraph, the author describes a specific moment in his childhood when he feels the power of darkness with words "my hands disappeared before my eyes" and sees a real picture in the night using vivid words such as "meteors left smoky trails across sugary spreads of stars". With this in mind, the readers would feel a bit regretful and worried when they realize the darkness is rapidly disappearing currently. The use of number "8 out of 10" would naturally lead the reader to believe that this issue should arouse public attention.

After pointing out the underlying cause, namely, the light pollution in the second paragraph, the author uses the following two paragraphs to demonstrate the negative influence of light pollution on human beings and on other species. These two paragraphs are featured by a serious tone, with a certain number of reliable sources and scientific terms to strengthen the seriousness of the issue. For example, in paragraph three, he first mentions two authorities, "World Health Organizations" and "American Medical Association" to back up the importance of reducing light pollution. After establishing the high credibility among the readers, the author uses the diction "our" to connect him to the audience before pointing out the specific terms such as "hormone melatonin", "sleep disorder", "diabetes", "obesity" and "cardiovascular disease". Knowledge is often viewed as power, and with information as direct as this, the author is handling that power to the reader—the power to agree with him.

Not only does he spread the facts with cold fact, he also does so with examples and data in the next paragraph. In paragraph four, the author centers on the negative impact on the animals, by using both well-known species such as birds that migrate in night and little-known species such as bats and moths. After presenting these examples, Paul utilizes simile to evoke agreement from the reader about the damaging effect of artificial light. The author compares light pollution to the bulldozer, a vehicle used for knocking down buildings and makes use of a vivid verb "wreck" to form a picture in the mind of the reader.

After Paul's illustration of the impact on the physical health, he appeals to emotion by pointing out the profound value of darkness such as inner peace and serenity. More importantly, he mentions a strong fact that night is the Muse of the artists and philosophers by citing the masterpiece of Vincent Van Gogh "Starry Night" as a most convincing case. The use of rhetorical questions in the end of the paragraph effectively arouses people's second thoughts and concern for the future generations when the author uses "our children" and "grandchildren."

The word "yet" in the beginning of paragraph 6 well indicates a contrast with the previous content which focuses on the importance of night for human beings, for animals and for spiritual enjoyment. In fact, despite the necessity of darkness, it is shortening in all over the world. Paul's use of data and facts occurs throughout his article, but is most prevalent in this paragraph, where "an increase of 6% in the amount of light" and "those of us over 35" prove to be sound evidence. Noteworthy is the credible source "NASA", together with the con-notated "a blanket of light"(the word blanket, compared with layer, has a sense of undesirability).

Fortunately, in the final paragraph, the author provides all the readers who have been convinced of the significance of darkness with methods to stop the light pollution, one of which is to rely on modern technology. Successful examples around the world are listed in order to cause the reader to have confidence, such as LED streetlights. The other way is to shield existing lights. For example, the author mentions metropolises such as Paris which choose to turn off its monument lighting after 1 a.m. and will require public places to turn off light after 2 a.m. The use of this example is quite successful in that the author picks up a "nightless" city and demonstrates to us how this city contributes to the longer darkness, which prevents the readers from saying "no" to his proposal. The last sentence of this whole passage echoes the final sentence of the opening paragraph and reminds the public that only after they raise awareness about the value of "darkness" can the problem of light pollution be truly addressed.

Paul begins his argument with personal experience, combines data and terms, and finalizes with examples. He sodifies his argument and builds his argument with logic, statistics and rhetoric, allowing for a reader to be in more agreement and satisfaction of his argument.

8.1.3 写作框架提炼

开头段

Introduction

Logic, reason, and rhetoric create a strong persuasive argument. Peter utilized these tools in his article "…". The author uses many different types of evidence to support his claims and persuade his audience that _____.

中间段

Within the first several paragraphs of this article, the author offers many statistical evidence. He throws out numbers, which appeal to a logical thinking audience. He then shifts from using statistical evidence to historical evidence.

In the next few paragraphs, the author centers on _____ and backs up his claim by using examples…

Peter uses his last few paragraphs to state his claims once again. He reinforces his idea that _____.

结尾段

Great persuasive essays utilize the tools of persuasion. Goodman begins his argument with logic, combined in reason, and finalizes with rhetoric. A flow of examples propels the reader into agreement with the author. He sodifies his argument and builds his argument with logic, reason and rhetoric, allowing for a reader to be in more agreement and satisfaction of his argument.

8.2 层次性写法分析和实例

8.2.1 阅读和分析

阅读原文

Adapted from E. J. Dionne Jr., *A Call for National Service* © 2013 by Washington Post. Originally published July 3, 2013.

1. Here is the sentence in the *Declaration of Independence* we always remember: "We hold these truths to be self-evident, that all men are created equal, that they are endowed by their Creator with certain unalienable Rights, that among these are Life, Liberty and the pursuit of Happiness."

2. And here is the sentence we often forget: "And for the support of this Declaration, with a firm reliance on the protection of Divine Providence, we mutually pledge to each other our Lives, our Fortunes and our Sacred Honor."

3. This, the very last sentence of the document, is what makes the better-remembered sentence possible. One speaks of our rights. The other addresses our obligations. The freedoms we cherish are self-evident but not self-executing. The Founders pledge something "to each other", the commonly overlooked clause in the Declaration's final pronouncement.

4. We find ourselves, 237 years after the Founders declared us a new nation, in a season of discontent, even surliness, about the experiment they launched. We are sharply divided over the very meaning of our founding documents, and we are more likely to invoke the word "we" in the context of "us versus them" than in the more capacious sense that includes every single American.

5. There are no quick fixes to our sense of disconnection, but there may be a way to restore our sense of what we owe each other across the lines of class, race, background—and, yes, politics and ideology.

6. Last week, the Aspen Institute gathered a politically diverse group of Americans under the banner of the "Franklin Project," named after Ben, to declare a commitment to offering every American between the ages of 18 and 28 a chance to give a year of service to

the country. The opportunities would include service in our armed forces but also time spent educating our fellow citizens, bringing them healthcare and preventive services, working with the least advantaged among us, and conserving our environment. Service would not be compulsory, but it would be an expectation. And it just might become part of who we are.

7. The call for universal, voluntary service is being championed by retired U. S. Army Gen. Stanley McChrystal, in league with two of the country's foremost advocates of the cause, John Bridge land, who served in the George W. Bush administration, and Alan Khazei, co-founder of City Year, one of the nation's most formidable volunteer groups. The trio testifies to the non-ideological and nonpartisan nature of this cause, as did a column last week endorsing the idea from Michael Gerson, my conservative Post colleague.

8. "We've a remarkable opportunity now," McChrystal says, "to move with the American people away from an easy citizenship that does not ask something from every American yet asks a lot from a tiny few." We do, indeed, owe something to our country, and we owe an enormous debt to those who have done tour after tour in Iraq and Afghanistan.

9. McChrystal sees universal service as transformative. "It will change how we think about America and how we think about ourselves," he says. And as a former leader of an all-volunteer Army, he scoffs at the idea that giving young Americans a stipend while they serve amounts to "paid volunteerism," the phrase typically invoked by critics of service programs. "If you try to rely on unpaid volunteerism," he said, "then you limit the people who can do it … I'd like the people from Scarsdale to be paid the same as the people from East L. A. "

10. There are real challenges here. Creating the estimated 1 million service slots required to make the prospect of service truly universal will take money, from government and private philanthropy. Service, as McChrystal says, cannot just be a nice thing that well-off kids do when they get out of college. It has to draw in the least advantaged young Americans. In the process, it could open new avenues for social mobility, something the military has done for so many in the past.

11. Who knows whether the universal expectation of service would change the country as much as McChrystal hopes. But we have precious few institutions reminding us to join the Founders in pledging something to each other. We could begin by debating this proposal in a way that frees us from the poisonous assumption that even an idea involving service to others must be part of some hidden political agenda. The agenda here is entirely open. It's based on the belief that certain unalienable rights entail certain unavoidable responsibilities.

8.2.2 分析

P1: quotes from *Declaration of Independence* (the American people are born with rights).

P2: quotes again to show we have duty to protect the right, historical evidence.

P3: clarify the relation between these two quotes, responsibility as the precondition of enjoying right, not the verse.

P4: point out the division among people, a distorted definition of "we", by comparison and contrast.

P5: introduce the main purpose of this essay, to restore the lack of connection.

P6: specify the plan to include a one-year public service (18～28): armed force, educating the less-advantage group, environmental protection. (主旨段)

P7: further promote this idea by referring to those authoritative people who also champion this plan.

P8: quote the words of one supporter McChrystal who urges people to realize they owe a lot to the country and to the people who have served in the war.

P9: still quote the argument of McChrystal who casts doubt on the opponents' view that a stipend to national service is a mistake.

P10: point out the reason for the argument above, contribute to social mobility for the least advantaged group. (第7～11段是展开段)

P11: A little concession in the first sentence of the ending paragraph, to draw people's full attention to this new plan and to encourage more people to take part on the ground that duty is the basis of the personal rights. (再次重申文章主旨)

8.2.3 层次性模板提炼

📖 开头段

In " ", the author argues _____. By the end of this piece, the reader will likely find themselves nodding in agreement with what he has to say, and this isn't just because he is right. Peter, like any good writer, employs tactical reasoning and persuasive devices to plead with the audience to take his side. In this article, he demonstrates many such devices.

📖 中间段

中间第一段(论证方法)

The writer's use of examples occurs throughout his article, but is most prevalent in the beginning. Examples initially draw interest from readers. The writer then presents more appalling examples, including _____ in order to draw the attention of all the readers. He employs examples in order to infiltrate the reader's independent mind. (例子论证)

After his illustration of his examples, he makes full use of reason to convince the reader... He further builds and enhances his argument when he states that ... He also uses reason to evoke agreement within the reader's mind when he draws simple conclusions. Reason allows the author to construct upon his solid foundation of evidence that creates his argument. (道理论证)

The writer's first utilization of a cold, hard fact is presented in _____. The truth in the numbers is undeniable, and his cites his sources promptly, making the statement that much more authentic. Knowledge is often viewed as power, and with information as direct as statistic; he is handling that power to the reader—the power to agree with him. (数据论证)

中间第二段(写作风格)

Additionally, the writer appeals to the ethnical and emotional side of individuals. With phrases like _____, he activates the nature of a human to act in their own self-interest. With statement such as..., he adds acceptance to... A statement such as this is an attempt to get readers either persuasion on his side and his ingenious qualification only adds to the strength of his argument. (情感诉求)

Moreover, adjusting his diction (using well known phrases, selecting words with strong connotations), the writer creates something out of the ordinary. It is with word choice such as " " that the author reveals... His humorous diction provides a link between him and the audience, revealing not only an opportunity to laugh, but also reinforcement of the concept that... Negative words such as ... all depict a disparaging tone of annoyance and anger, surely helping Peter to spread his message. (措辞)

中间第三段(修辞手段)

Rhetoric seals the deal in Goodman's argument. After presenting the facts using logic, and making connections using reason, Goodman utilizes rhetoric to place the cherry on the top of his argument. Rhetoric is crucial in an argument because... In this case, his use of rhetoric evokes agreement from the reader. In his final stanza, after presenting all methods, the author utilizes theoretic to once again state the obvious. The writer presents his claim that...; the answer to his statement is apparent and causes the reader to side with him.

结尾段

It is through many rhetorical devices that Peter sells his argument. Powerful diction, qualification, ethos, pathos, logos, and informative facts all contribute to an exceptionally well-written argument. It is his utilization of these practices and more that make this article worthy of recognition. Once one reads the piece, he will be nodding along in accordance with Peter, and it isn't for no reason.

8.2.4 补充性评论

 精

官方指南指出，New SAT 作文不是要"全"，而是要"精"，比如如果你觉得作者某个部分的写作很精妙，你可以只对着 diction 分析。不过笔者建议大部分考生准备阶段要全，考试才有精的资本。要在自己准备模板或者写作素材时，准备各种情况的常见词汇和句型，考试的时候可以对实际情况进行实际分析，然后抽取组合写作。诸如 tone 这一个元素，就有很多关键词可以用，比如笔者就是 determine and hopeful。表现形式可有以下几种：

Positive Neutral Negative；
Benevolent Colloquial Bitter；
Compassionate Detached Disdainful；
Determined Scholarly Scornful；
Supportive Factual Sarcastic。

 思路

作为一个新手，中间第一段你要做的是去拼命看出来有哪个论证方式最明显，然后先把提前准备的套句拿上去写，比如看到了数字，立刻就拿出自己准备好的句子（the author offers many statistical evidence. He throws out numbers, which appeal to a logical thinking audience）。

中间第二段也如此，看看用词、句型等有哪些特别明显的可以套上的点，比如作者用了一个感叹句，你赶快从准备好的素材库里调出一个套句（Exclamatory sentence is used to express a wish, a desire or a command. The author's inspirational tone is initiated by the use of the imperative verb "let"）。

到了中间第三段再去写修辞手段，看看哪个文章有，就去大力吆喝吧。比如发现了类比，继续调动固定句型（The analogy, which would be accessible to every listener, draws on everyday experience and makes good common sense）。

 深入

如果想要拿更高的分数，考生需要继续去补充高阶知识，深入了解每一个模块，比如论证手法有很多种，每一种的表达和实例都要去了解。修辞手段有很多，也需要更多地去深入了解。

 点题

同时最为重要，也最容易被人忽略的就是"为什么"。当一个考生在文章中清晰指出作者是用了哪些具体的单词，或者语法手段、修辞手段的时候，很多时候却忽略了和文章主题、作者态度的一个结合。这里有一个修辞手段很重要，更重要的是指出作者为什么会选择这个修辞手段，为什么要放在这一段使用，和作者的表达意图或者态度有什么样的联系。

8.2.5 更多练习(6月真题)

A Carbon Tax Beats a Vacuum Ban

Starting in September, the European Union will ban vacuum cleaners using more than 1600 watts of power, with the limit slated to be lowered to 900 watts by 2017. This ban won't just affect a handful of the worst offenders. According to the European Commission, the average vacuum cleaner sold today uses 1800 watts.

Intended largely to reduce carbon emissions, the vacuum cleaner ban joins numerous other regulations throughout the world that severely restrict consumers' choices. Want an incandescent light bulb? Too bad they're banned. How about a gas guzzling car? Sorry, they're being squeezed out by tighter fuel economy standards.

Rules like these rub many people the wrong way because they represent government intrusion into even the most minute of personal decisions. Do we really want the government telling us what kind of vacuum cleaner or light bulb to buy? Don't policy makers have better things to think about? Backers of such regulations counter that, when people buy powerful vacuum cleaners and incandescent bulbs, they don't take into account the spillover costs they impose on others by contributing to climate change.

Fortunately, there's a better solution. A carbon tax—set to reflect the spillover costs of carbon emissions—would eliminate the need to micromanage the kinds of vacuum cleaners and light bulbs that people can buy. Instead, the tax would provide consumers with an incentive to act in a socially responsible manner by ensuring that those who operate such products pick up the tab for the climate harm they cause.

The main advantage of the carbon tax is that it leaves consumers free to decide whether to buy energy-efficient vacuum cleaners and light bulbs or whether to reduce their carbon footprint in other ways. That's a big improvement over the regulatory approach because individual consumers are in a better position than government bureaucrats to figure out the least painful way to reduce their contribution to climate change.

A carbon tax is also better targeted than vacuum cleaner bans and other regulations. Some critics of the EU's new rule claim that consumers will need to run their less powerful vacuum cleaners for longer periods of time to achieve their desired level of cleanliness, which might actually increase the amount of electricity they use. Similarly, improving fuel economy through tighter standards may increase the amount of driving that people do. These "rebound effects" might not be big enough to actually cause a net increase in emissions, but they still reduce the effectiveness of the regulations.

A carbon tax avoids these problems by directly targeting the real culprit—carbon. Under a carbon tax, there's an incentive to cut back on carbon emissions along every dimension. In other words, because tax payments are in line with actual emissions, a Prius owner who drives a lot could very well pay more than an SUV owner who hardly ever drives.

Economists of all political stripes agree on these points. In a 2011 poll of leading academic economists representing a variety of demographic backgrounds and political views, 90 percent agreed with the statement: "A tax on the carbon content of fuels would be a less expensive way to reduce carbon-dioxide emissions than would a collection of policies such as 'corporate average fuel economy' requirements for automobiles." There's no doubt that economic advisers offer similar advice when policy makers consider regulations like the vacuum cleaner ban. Unfortunately, these misguided policies often turn out to be more politically feasible than a carbon tax.

That may change going forward, however. As policy makers look to trim budgets and find additional sources of revenue, a carbon tax could represent a good compromise between conservatives and liberals—a way to address climate change while protecting consumer freedom and raising revenue that can be used to lower other taxes.

更多参考范文,可以通过扫描封底二维码,添加上海必赢公众号获得。

第 9 章　New SAT 作文高阶篇

本章节深入枚举了可供考生自由发挥的知识点,旨在帮助写作基础稳定在中上游的考生塑造个人文风,构建精密的语素识别体系,并最终冲刺高分。

- 阅读和分析

Adapted from Peter S. Goodman, *Foreign News at a Crisis Point*. © 2013 by The HuffingtonPost.com, Inc. Originally published September 25, 2013. Peter Goodman is the executive business and global news editor at TheHuffingtonPost.com.

> As you read the passage below, consider how Peter S. Goodman uses
> - evidence, such as facts or examples, to support claims.
> - reasoning to develop ideas and to connect claims and evidence.
> - stylistic or persuasive elements, such as word choice or appeals to emotion, to add power to the ideas expressed.

1. Back in 2003, *American Journalism Review* produced a census of foreign correspondents then employed by newspapers based in the United States, and found 307 full-time people. When AJR repeated the exercise in the summer of 2011, the count had dropped to 234. And even that number was significantly inflated by the inclusion of contract writers who had replaced full-time staffers.

2. In the intervening eight years, 20 American news organizations had entirely eliminated their foreign bureaus.

3. The same AJR survey zeroed in on a representative sampling of American papers

from across the country and found that the space devoted to foreign news had shrunk by 53 percent over the previous quarter-century.

4. All of this decline was playing out at a time when the U.S. was embroiled in two overseas wars, with hundreds of thousands of Americans deployed in Iraq and Afghanistan. It was happening as domestic politics grappled with the merits and consequences of a global war on terror, as a Great Recession was blamed in part on global imbalances in savings, and as world leaders debated a global trade treaty and pacts aimed at addressing climate change. It unfolded as American workers heard increasingly that their wages and job security were under assault by competition from counterparts on the other side of oceans.

5. In short, news of the world is becoming palpably more relevant to the day-to-day experiences of American readers, and it is rapidly disappearing.

6. Yet the same forces that have assailed print media, eroding foreign news along the way, may be fashioning a useful response. Several nonprofit outlets have popped up to finance foreign reporting, and a for-profit outfit, GlobalPost, has dispatched a team of 18 senior correspondents into the field, supplemented by dozens of stringers and freelancers…

7. We are intent on forging fresh platforms for user-generated content: testimonials, snapshots and video clips from readers documenting issues in need of attention. Too often these sorts of efforts wind up feeling marginal or even patronizing: "Dear peasant, here's your chance to speak to the pros about what's happening in your tiny little corner of the world." We see user-generated content as a genuine reporting tool, one that operates on the premise that we can only be in so many places at once. Crowd-sourcing is a fundamental advantage of the web, so why not embrace it as a means of piecing together a broader and more textured understanding of events?

8. We all know the power of Twitter, Facebook and other forms of social media to connect readers in one place with images and impressions from situations unfolding far away. We know the force of social media during the Arab Spring, as activists convened and reacted to changing circumstances. We get that YouTube and Vine and Instagram have become key components of the informational plumbing. Facts and insights reside on social media, waiting to be harvested by the digitally literate contemporary correspondent.

9. And yet those of us who have been engaged in foreign reporting for many years will confess to unease over many of the developments unfolding online, even as we recognize the trends are as unstoppable as globalization or the weather. Too often it seems as if professional foreign correspondents, the people paid to use their expertise while serving as informational filters, are being replaced by citizen journalists who function largely as funnels, pouring insight along with speculation, propaganda and other white noise into the mix.

10. We can celebrate the democratization of media, the breakdown of monopolies, the rise of innovative means of telling stories, and the inclusion of a diversity of voices, and still ask whether the results are making us better informed. Indeed, we have a professional

responsibility to continually ask that question while seeking to engineer new models that can channel the web in the interest of better informing readers …

11. We need to embrace the present and gear for the future. These are days in which newsrooms simply must be entrepreneurial and creative in pursuit of new means of reporting and paying for it. That makes this a particularly interesting time to be doing the work, but it also requires forthright attention to a central demand: We need to put back what the Internet has taken away. We need to turn the void into something fresh and compelling. We need to re-examine and update how we gather information and how we engage readers, while retaining the core values of serious-minded journalism.

12. This will not be easy. The resulting models are far from obvious. But the alternative—accepting ignorance and parochialism—is simply not an option.

Write an essay in which you explain how Peter S. Goodman builds an argument to persuade his audience that news organizations should increase the amount of professional foreign news coverage provided to Americans. In your essay, analyze how Goodman uses one or more of the features listed in the box above (or features of your own choice) to strengthen the logic and persuasiveness of his argument. Be sure that your analysis focuses on the most relevant features of the passage.

Your essay should not explain whether you agree with Goodman's claims, but rather explain how Goodman builds an argument to persuade his audience.

初步分析

分析 New SAT 写作素材的第一步是找出文章的论点。所谓论点，就是文章所要议论、阐述的观点，是作者要表达的主张和见解。一篇文章的论点，可以是一个或者多个。如果超出一个，那就需要明确中心论点。New SAT 写作素材的中心论点大多出现在文章开头，最后通过结尾重述或强调，以达到遥相呼应的效果。

鉴于 New SAT 写作选取的议论文素材往往摘自美国的主流报刊或名人的公众演讲，它们的论点势必鲜明直白，容易定位。不仅如此，New SAT 写作部分还设有一大隐藏型助攻——文章前后两段的方框文字，即 prompt(提示)。第一个方框内的文字提示了考生文章中可能出现的修辞方法和论证切入点；第二个方框内的文字则交代了作者的中心论点。比如，在本样题中，Prompt 2 给出了作者的论点：news organizations should increase the amount of professional foreign news coverage provided to people in the United States（美国境内的新闻机构应当扶持和增加高水准的海外新闻报道）。确定了中心论点后，我们便可以它为风向标，逐步理顺文章的逻辑链。

对已达到高阶程度的考生而言，可以不必严格按照传统步骤读完所有的段首段尾句，毕竟 New SAT 作文的素材通常比较艰深，且排版充满作者的个人风格，比如作者有时为了抒情和增强语势，会递进地给出平行意义的几个独立段落，换言之，这些段落只是为了支持同一个分论点而已，删掉任何一段都不影响理解。还有时候，作者会利用插入语、同位语、定语从句等，编织长难复合句，这就导致了一个段落有时只包含两句长句，如果要看完一头一尾的两句话就等于看完了全段,这显然无益于提升阅读理解效率。所以,建议高阶学生先大致浏览全文,然后根据段与段的关系,自行划分逻辑层次,将几个段落视为一个整体,并重点拎出这个超大段落的首尾句进行逻辑串联。

本文中第4段的第一句"all of this decline"是提示词组,而在代词 this 后的 decline 必然有所指代,一旦找到指代的内容,就能顺藤摸瓜将这些内容与第4段整合在一起。再看本文的第1~3段,不难注意到,作者使用了多个包含"减少、收缩、失去"意味的词汇:"dropped""inflated""eliminated""shrunk",有力呼应着"decline",由此可以判断,第1~4段可糅合为一段。前闭口找到后,就应该摸索后闭口了。下移到第5段,看到总结归纳的代表词 "In short",能够猜想到第5段才是第一个超大段落的末段,至此,第一个超大段落切分完毕。考虑到第1~3段在平行阐述各种 decline,段首的句子和段中的句子相比并无特殊,所以没有细究价值,直接看段末的句子即可:"In short, news of the world is becoming palpably more relevant to the day-to-day experiences of American readers, and it is rapidly disappearing."(简言之,世界新闻显然正与美国读者的日常体验变得息息相关,但这个类型的新闻在急速消失)。

以上就是第一大段落的梗概,继续往后看"Yet the same forces that have assailed print media, eroding foreign news along the way, may be fashioning a useful response." 第6段段末有省略号,代表后面有删节,所以这一段可独立作为对之前情况的反向补充(Yet 意为"但是")。段意只需看首句的含义:但是那些攻击了美国纸媒并进而削弱了海外报道的势力,其也应运而生了相关有用的对策。这句之后便是这些势力采取的对策实例,可略过。

接下去第7段的末句是反问句,"Crowd-sourcing is a fundamental advantage of the web, so why not embrace it as a means of piecing together a broader and more textured understanding of events?"(众包是网络的一个根本优势,所以何不利用该渠道为各种(社会新闻)事件拼凑出更广泛、更有质感的理解呢?)显然之后的段落作用是承接、支撑这个问句的,其中列举了各式社交媒体的发展及影响力。而第9段开头再次用了"and yet"转折,和前两个段落语义不一致,所以第三个段落群确定为第7、8段,接着只需分析这一大段落的首尾两句。首句:"We are intent on forging fresh platforms for user-generated content: testimonials, snapshots and video clips from readers documenting issues in need of attention."(我们专注为用户自主发布的信息——尤指关于某些亟须公众注意的事件的证言、快照和视频剪辑——铸建新奇的平台)。尾句:"Facts and insights reside on social media, waiting to be harvested by the digitally literate contemporary correspondent."(真相和见解蔓生在社交媒体之中,静待被精通数码设备的当代记者收割)。由此归纳后可大致了解这一大段阐述的是:和数码设备挂钩的社交媒体被赋予了传播各类有用信息的使命。

前面提过第9段有转折含义,先看首句后能明白这一段主要说的是,作者和其他从事海外报道多年的资深记者在理解线上自媒体的快速发展之余,却也忧心忡忡。再看接下去的长句前,我们先跳到第10段看看第9段和第10段是否可以无缝结合为一段,第10段的第一句:"we can … but still ask …"这个句式同时提及了某一事物的正反面,极具辩证性,所以应该是一句对以上信息的最后总结。所以,第9段和第10段并非完全一致的关系,需要割裂开看。

第10段又因为末尾有省略号(后续有删减),无法直接与后段连接,所以自成一段。第10段的"indeed"一词代表在先前的某基础上强调、重申,所以和首句重复,我们只看段首句即可:"We can celebrate the democratization of media, the breakdown of monopolies, the rise of innovative means of telling stories, and the inclusion of a diversity of voices, and still ask whether the results are making us better informed."(我们可以庆贺媒体的民主化、垄断机制的瓦解、新兴的趣味叙述手法以及百家争鸣的自由言论,但同时也得扪心自问:以上这些现象是否真的帮助我们更高效地获取了信息?)

第12段句首出现了代词"this",所以可以马上把第11段和第12段拎在一起。第12段属于议论文常见的结尾,未必和中心论点有关,功能只限于点睛,可算是无意义段落。因此,真正的结尾段落其实是第11段。高阶学生只需要看第11段的首句和尾句:"We need to embrace the present and gear for the future."(此处断句较容易产生歧义,可能有些学生会断句理解成"我们应当欣然接受送给未来的礼物和准备",而另一些学生会理解成"我们应当欣然接受当下的局面,同时也接受为未来的准备",然而,不管是以上哪种理解都不影响总体,所以不必花时间钻牛角尖。但是请考生切记:如果不确定文章某个表达的内涵,在举例和分析时也得尽量避开这个雷区,以免在 reading 和 analysis 这两个评分标准内扣分);"We need to re-examine and update how we gather information and how we engage readers, while retaining the core values of serious-minded journalism."(我们(尤指作者所在的新闻行业)需要重新审核和更新获取信息和吸引读者的方式,与此同时传承严肃新闻学的核心价值观)。

最后梳理一遍,本文的逻辑脉络如下:世界新闻正与美国读者的日常体验变得息息相关,但这个类型的新闻在急速消失,作者从该矛盾的现象切入,谈到了新兴新闻报道方式,尤其是社交媒体上用户自由发表的证言、快照和视频剪辑等。作者虽然深知这股自媒体代替传统纸媒的趋势是时代的必然,但也不禁忧虑这个进程带来的弊端,所以倡导自己所在的新闻行业重新审核和更新获取(海外)信息和吸引读者的方式,与此同时传承严肃新闻学的核心价值观。

深入分析

理解了全篇文章的逻辑架构,接下来就应该按顺序标记出全篇使用的论证手法、修辞手法和写作风格,并结合文义,探讨这些手法的作用。evidence, reasoning, persuasive elements 和 stylistic elements 这四大元素并不是孤立的,而是相互关联甚至相互重叠的,因此考生在考前冲刺阶段应建立识别和分析的体系。同时,考生也须铭记 prompt 中的提醒: Be sure that your analysis focuses on the most relevant features of the passage,在标记时可忽略琐碎无关的细节,只筛选出最具代表性、与中心论点/分论点最为相关的句子、词组和单词。

从上到下,陆续可以找到以下较有高亮价值的内容:

(1) 第1~3段:Back in 2003, found 307 full-time people, in the summer of 2011, the count had dropped to 234, in the intervening eight years, 20 American news organizations, shrunk by 53 percent over the previous quarter-century 等,以上这些片段都包含一个共性:可量化的数字。这便体现了一种论证手法——数据论证法(statistical argument)。数字往往显得权威、可靠、确凿,进而能有力支撑观点。在本文中,这些数字都旨在突出:美国新闻机构放在海外新闻板块的重心不断下滑。

(2) 第5段:In short, news of the world is becoming palpably more relevant to the day-

to-day experiences of American readers, and it is rapidly disappearing. 两个单句虽由 and 连接,但逻辑方向并不一致,相反,日益变得重要的某事物却在快速凋零,这是一个不合情理的悖论,所以可以推断,作者使用了矛盾修辞法(oxymoron),and 一词只是为了营造冲突感,增强戏剧性,我们在做阅读理解时,也千万不要乱了方寸、混淆了作者的立场。

(3) 第 7 段: Too often these sorts of efforts wind up feeling marginal or even patronizing: "Dear peasant, here's your chance to speak to the pros about what's happening in your tiny little corner of the world."这段话字里行间可以嗅到对用户自主发布渠道的讽刺,写作风格非常幽默。而与讽刺反语挂钩的修辞手法有 4 种,如 irony(常对物),sarcasm(常对人,比 irony 程度强且偏尖刻),satire(可对物、可对人,多用于讽刺和取笑某人、某想法、某机构、某体制)和 innuendo(暗讽,多依靠影射)。如此辨析下来,最符合这段文字修辞手法的应为 satire。辨析同一大类的修辞手法是考试时的一大难点,因此建议考生充分理解各大相似修辞手法的本质区别。

(4) 第 8 段"We know the force of social media during the Arab Spring, as activists convened and reacted to changing circumstances. We get that YouTube and Vine and Instagram have become key components of the informational plumbing."议论文分析包含三个密不可分的要素:论点、论据和论证。虽然 New SAT 写作的要求聚焦于找出作者的论点并分析作者的各种论证手法,但论据也被默认为论证的一种基础,即举例论证(exemplification)。在摘选的文段中,分别举了两个例子——阿拉伯之春事件和年轻人群体耳熟能详的几大社交娱乐网站。这些例子或影响力深远到街巷皆知,或贴近生活,因此都有助于读者快速匹配自己的知识库,并领会作者意图。

(5) 同样在第 8 段,"Facts and insights reside on social media, waiting to be harvested by the digitally literate contemporary correspondent."这一句中,reside on(居住在、驻守在),wait(等待),harvest(收割)这三个动词运用得非常精妙,作者运用了移位修饰修辞法(transferred epithet)将 facts and insights 这两个本来没有生命的物体与常描绘活物的动词相搭配,将它们比作富含养分、待人收割的粮食作物,也生动形象地将社交媒体勾勒为一片蕴藏着丰富事实资料以及公众观点的开放式沃土。

(6) "We need to put back what the Internet has taken away. We need to turn the void into something fresh and compelling. We need to re-examine and update how we gather information and how we engage readers, while retaining the core values of serious-minded journalism."这段话的每句句首和句式都一样,运用了排比(parallelism)及首语重复(anaphora)的修辞手法,将一个句子的开头单词或短语在随后的句子中重复多遍,层层推进语势,充满情感张力,呼吁新闻行业在保留严肃端正的价值观基础上,寻回失落的辉煌,摒弃落后的理念,改革信息采集和自我推广的模式。

(7) 第 12 段"But the alternative—accepting ignorance and parochialism—is simply not an option."其中故意用了冗笔的修辞手法(pleonasm),加入了看似重合多余的词组"the alternative",以此补充了非此即彼的含义,凸显出别无选择的危机感,同时,富有节奏的语序也让整个收尾更富张力。

(8) 作者全篇用了许多 we,从第一人称的视角提出问题、阐释观点,力求与读者站在一边,产生共鸣。

我带你写

一共分为三步走：意译出中心论点——→根据全文大意概括文章的行文思路——→按一定的空间顺序罗列增加了作者说服力的修辞手法、写作风格等其他元素。

首先，有了中心论点的蓝本，我们只需要用 paraphrase（同义转述）的方法将该论点进行改写，然后附在自己 essay 的首段，切记：不能直接复制原论点。即使没有头绪如何大幅地提升论点的表达，至少可以进行同义词替换和词序调换，比如：将 news organizations should increase the amount of professional foreign news coverage provided to people in the United States 改为 news agencies ought to provide more professional foreign news coverage for people in America，以上沿用了原表达的句式和主干词汇，平实却不失大方。

如果想要展示更强的写作功底，可以更灵活地删减和扩充语义，或者改变句式。建议学生先标记两种词汇，第一步，区分关键名词，关键名词通常本身是固定的专用术语，或者在文中被作者重复了多次，关键名词可以保留不做改动，如果要冒险改动，必须确信自己已透彻地理解了作者对该名词的精准定义，比如在这里 professional foreign news coverage 可以视为关键名词，如果想要更改，可以把 professional 替换为 quality，exemplary，paragons of 等。第二步，标记可改的词和词组，在例句中，有更改余地的包括：(1) should＝ought to，might as well，had better，除了词组以外，含义相同的句式也可供选择：should＝it is necessary/essential/imperative for sb. to do sth.；it is necessary/essential/imperative that sb. (should) do sth. 虚拟语气；或者 it is incumbent (up)on sb./sth. to do sth；(2) increase the amount of＝increase the number of/increase/augment，"增加"一词也可引申为"更好地促进、支持、强化、使……充沛、有活力"等意思，因此可以联想到相关词汇 boost，support，reinforce，invigorate，buttress。继续联想，还可以结合文义，使用有关"复兴、复苏、改革"之类的动词，如 reboot、restore、revive、refresh 等；(3) people in the United States＝local Americans、domestic audience 等。

接下来，试试用以上的诀窍，来翻译并整合前两个小节内的提示，完成后两步。

知识补充（论证手法）

1. 数据论证（statistical argument）

用权威、确凿的数字支持论点。例如上文中第1～3段的统计数据。

2. 道理论证（reasoning）/引用论证（quotation）

道理论证——运用讲道理的方法，通过经典著作中的精辟见解、古今中外名人名言及被人们公认的科学原理、定理、公式等来证明观点。由于道理论证所引用的材料都是被客观实际所证实的科学结论，或是被人们所公认的道理，因此具有理论的权威性和思想的深刻性，具有不可辩驳的力量和说服力。引用认证是道理论证的一种，即引用名人名言或名人的观点等作为论据，引经据典地分析问题、说明道理。引用论证的作用包括：引用先贤名言、格言警句，可以增强论证的说服力和权威性；引用名人佚事、奇闻趣事，可以增强论证的趣味性，吸引读者往下读。但使用以上两种论证方法时要注意：一定要持严谨的科学态度，不可错漏曲解，更不能断章取义。

3. 归纳论证（inductive argument）/演绎论证（deductive argument）

归纳论证是两种方向相反的论证方法。前者也叫"事实论证"，是用列举具体事例来论证一般结论的方法；后者也叫"理论论证"，是先提出一个一般原理或结论进而论证个别事例的方法。记忆方法：归纳论证是从特殊证明一般，演绎论证是从一般证明特殊。

4. 类比论证（analogical argument）

类比论证是一种通过已知事物（或事例）与跟该事物（或事例）有某些相同特点的事物（或事例）进行比较类推从而证明论点的论证方法。其中，"具有某些相同特点"是这种论证方法成立的必须前提。例如：鲁迅在《未有天才之前》中曾说道："幼稚对于老成，有如孩子对于老人，决没有什么耻辱。"在这句话中，幼稚和孩子是一对具有相同特点的事物，老成和老人是一对具有相同特点的事物。记忆方法：类比论证是一种从特殊到特殊的论证方法。

5. 比喻论证（metaphorical argument）

比喻论证是用人们熟知的事物做比喻来证明论点的方法。值得一提的是，类比和比喻有相近之处：类比论证的主体事物和客体事物之间有相似点，比喻论证的本体事物和喻体事物之间也有相似点；类比能形象生动地证明论点，而议论文中的比喻也有使抽象事物具体化，深奥的道理通俗化的作用。正由于有这些相近之处，有些学生难免会混淆这两种修辞手法。但类比和比喻毕竟是不同的，它们有许多根本的区别。

首先，比喻和类比是两个不同的概念，虽然两者都含有一个"比"字，但含义不同。比喻中的"比"是"比拟"的意思，而类比中的"比"是"比较"的意思，所谓"类比"，就是"比较类推"。

其次，比喻的本体和喻体之间的相似点只有一个；类比的主体和客体之间进行比较类推的相似点，则不限于一个。比喻中如果出现了几个喻体，那么这些喻体只分别与本体有比拟的相似点，没有共同的比拟的相似点，而类比中的所有客体与主体都有共同的类比的相似点。

再次，比喻和被比喻的两个事物必须在其整体上极其不同，比如把"平凡的我"比作"浩瀚星空中的一颗星"；而类比中的主体和客体的两个事物在整体上可以是相同的，比如类比各个时代的王权，王权都代表统治的高级阶层。

最后，比喻只能依据本体和喻体的相似点进行比拟，而类比在依据主体和客体的相似点进行充分比较的基础上，还可以依据相异点进行比较，从而得出主体事物的某些性质有甚于客体事物相应的某些性质的结论。

6. 对比论证（contrastive argument）

拿正反两方面的论点或论据做对比，在对比中证明论点。比如"A城市为了治理空气污染颁布了车辆限牌政策，B城市没有颁布该政策"。经过对这两个城市空气污染指数长达半年的观察，可以对比后得知车辆限牌政策究竟有无起效，进而论证这个政策是否值得推广。

7. 因果论证（argument via cause and effect）

它通过分析事理，揭示论点和论据之间的因果关系来证明论点。因果论证可以用因证果，或以果证因，还可以因果互证。

8. 经验论证（empirical argument）

基于自身的人生阅历、生活常识对某事物做出判断。比如在本样题中，作者Peter S. Goodman基于自己在美国新闻行业的多年从业经验，以及身为内部人士的观察，提出了一系列心得总结，让读者心服口服。

练习（结合 AP 写作选择题）

AP 英语语言与写作考试和 New SAT 的写作部分交集甚多，都结合了学生的阅读能力和写作能力，要求学生能快速并有目的性地读懂相关材料，并根据所读材料或日常积累的知识及生活经历，写出目的性明确的文章。同时，考生在能读懂并分析阅读材料中的各种修辞手法的同时，也需要能在自己的文章中应用一些修辞手法。可见两种考试都期望考生精通各种修辞手法，了解文章的写作风格，并理解这些语言上的处理所能达成的目的。因此，通过历年的 AP 英语语言与写作真题的练习，对 New SAT 写作大有裨益。大家可搜寻 AP 英语语言与写作的真题自行练习。

• 阅读和分析

Adapted from *Why Literature Matters* by Dana Gioia. © 2005 by The New York Times Company. Originally published April 10, 2005.

> As you read the passage below, consider how Dana Gioia uses
> - evidence, such as facts or examples, to support claims.
> - reasoning to develop ideas and to connect claims and evidence.
> - stylistic or persuasive elements, such as word choice or appeals to emotion, to add power to the ideas expressed.

1. Strange thing has happened in the American arts during the past quarter century. While income rose to unforeseen levels, college attendance ballooned, and access to information increased enormously, the interest young Americans showed in the arts—and especially literature—actually diminished.

2. According to the 2002 Survey of Public Participation in the Arts, a population study designed and commissioned by the National Endowment for the Arts (and executed by the US Bureau of the Census), arts participation by Americans has declined for eight of the nine major forms that are measured … The declines have been most severe among younger adults (ages 18~24). The most worrisome finding in the 2002 study, however, is the declining percentage of Americans, especially young adults, reading literature.

3. That individuals at a time of crucial intellectual and emotional development bypass the joys and challenges of literature is a troubling trend. If it were true that they substituted histories, biographies, or political works for literature, one might not worry. But book reading of any kind is falling as well.

4. That such a longstanding and fundamental cultural activity should slip so swiftly, especially among young adults, signifies deep transformations in contemporary life. To call attention to the trend, the Arts Endowment issued the reading portion of the Survey as a separate report, *Reading at Risk: A Survey of Literary Reading in America*.

5. The decline in reading has consequences that go beyond literature. The significance of reading has become a persistent theme in the business world. The February issue of

Wired magazine, for example, sketches a new set of mental skills and habits proper to the 21st century, aptitudes decidedly literary in character: not "linear, logical, analytical talents," author Daniel Pink states, but "the ability to create artistic and emotional beauty, to detect patterns and opportunities, to craft a satisfying narrative." When asked what kind of talents they like to see in management positions, business leaders consistently set imagination, creativity, and higher-order thinking at the top.

6. Ironically, the value of reading and the intellectual faculties that it inculcates appear most clearly as active and engaged literacy declines. There is now a growing awareness of the consequences of nonreading to the workplace. In 2001 the National Association of Manufacturers polled its members on skill deficiencies among employees. Among hourly workers, poor reading skills ranked second, and 38 percent of employers complained that local schools inadequately taught reading comprehension.

7. The decline of reading is also taking its toll in the civic sphere... A 2003 study of 15-to-26-year-olds' civic knowledge by the National Conference of State Legislatures concluded, "Young people do not understand the ideals of citizenship ... and their appreciation and support of American democracy is limited."

8. It is probably no surprise that declining rates of literary reading coincide with declining levels of historical and political awareness among young people. One of the surprising findings of *Reading at Risk* was that literary readers are markedly more civically engaged than nonreaders, scoring two to four times more likely to perform charity work, visit a museum, or attend a sporting event. One reason for their higher social and cultural interactions may lie in the kind of civic and historical knowledge that comes with literary reading...

9. The evidence of literature's importance to civic, personal, and economic health is too strong to ignore. The decline of literary reading foreshadows serious long-term social and economic problems, and it is time to bring literature and the other arts into discussions of public policy. Libraries, schools, and public agencies do noble work, but addressing the reading issue will require the leadership of politicians and the business community as well...

10. Reading is not a timeless, universal capability. Advanced literacy is a specific intellectual skill and social habit that depends on a great many educational, cultural, and economic factors. As more Americans lose this capability, our nation becomes less informed, active, and independent-minded. These are not the qualities that a free, innovative, or productive society can afford to lose.

Write an essay in which you explain how Dana Gioia builds an argument to persuade his audience that the decline of reading in America will have a negative effect on society. In your essay, analyze how Gioia uses one or more of the features in the directions that precede the passage (or features of your own choice) to strengthen the logic and persuasiveness of his argument. Be sure that your analysis focuses on the most relevant features of the passage.

Your essay should not explain whether you agree with Gioia's claims, but rather explain how Gioia builds an argument to persuade his audience.

初步分析

第一步依然是根据 prompt 的提示浓缩全文的中心论点："the decline of reading in America will have a negative effect on society"(美国国民的阅读量下降会对社会产生消极的影响)。我们需要围绕着这一论点抽丝剥茧找到逻辑主线。为了高效地提炼全篇大意，这里依旧沿用划分超大段落的方法。第 1 段的"diminished"，第 2 段的"declined"，第 3 段的"falling"，都意味着"下降，减少"，由此可以判断三个段落在陈述同一个趋势，所以将它们合成为一段。先看段首句："Strange thing has happened in the American arts during the past quarter century."(在过去的 25 年中，美国的文艺界发生了奇怪的事)。作为段首句，却没有展开是怎样的怪事，所以继续看第二句："While income rose to unforeseen levels, college attendance ballooned, and access to information increased enormously, the interest young Americans showed in the arts—and especially literature—actually diminished."(当收入上涨到空前之高，大学入学率不断膨胀，信息获取的权限显著增加，美国的年轻人对艺术——尤其是文学——显示的兴趣却大不如前了)。再看段尾句，发现是 but 开头，理应与前一句连接才能语义完整，所以直接分析最后两句："If it were true that they substituted histories, biographies, or political works for literature, one might not worry. But book reading of any kind is falling as well."(假使文学书籍的地位只是被历史小说、人物传记或政治作品所取代，那倒也不用觉得忧虑，可惜事实上所有类别的书籍阅读量都在一路下跌)。综上所述，第一超大段落的中心思想是：虽然人们的生活水平、文化层次和信息获取程度走高，但是美国的年轻人日益将文学和其他类别的书籍束之高阁。

第 4 段独立成段，承上启下，既阐明了年轻人阅读量下降这个趋势折射了当代生活的深刻转型，也介绍了美国国家艺术基金会为应对这一现象做出的调研，第 5~8 段都是调研的成果。

第 5 段段首句"The decline in reading has consequences that go beyond literature."(阅读量的下降远不止会削弱文学素养)。而第 7 段段首句用类似的句子结构以及提示词"also"呼应了第 5 段，又点出"The decline of reading is also taking its toll in the civic sphere"(阅读量下降还对公民的社会参与度造成了不良影响)。因此，第 5、6 段为第三超大段落。第 8 段可看到和 civic sphere 互相匹配的 social interaction，所以第 7、8 段为第四超大段落。这两个超大段落分别揭露了阅读量下降对商界上层管理与基层运作，以及公民的社会参与度的不利影响。

第9段提到了"literature's importance to civic, personal, and economic health"(文学对于公民社会参与度、个人健康和经济发展的重要性),从正面总结了第5~8段,所以独立成段。本段中心思想还需要看尾句:"Libraries, schools, and public agencies do noble work, but addressing the reading issue will require the leadership of politicians and the business community as well."(图书馆、学校、公共机构固然正在履行自己神圣的义务,但要解决阅读量下降的问题还需要政治家和工商业界的领导)。

第10段最后自成一段,作者选择了气势磅礴的论调,居高展望未来,警示读者不改变现状的后果,以此感召读者发起行动,共同维护构建一个自由、创新且多产的社会。"As more Americans lose this capability, our nation becomes less informed, active, and independent-minded. These are not the qualities that a free, innovative, or productive society can afford to lose."文章的结尾部分,作者警醒道,除非阅读能受到更多的重视,否则美国整体将变得见闻狭隘、消极且丧失独立意识。

最后梳理后,本文的行文思路如下:虽然美国国民的生活水平、文化层次和信息获取程度走高,但是本国的年轻人日益将文学和其他类别的书籍束之高阁。作者由此开始关注该现象并展开了思考。诚然,现代生活的根本性变化带动了阅读量的下降,但美国国家艺术基金会依然发布了一个调研,希望告诫公众阅读量下降的危害,包括妨碍商界上层管理与基层运作以及降低公民的社会参与度。综上所述,为了促进公民社会参与度、个人健康发展和经济良性发展,政治家和工商业界需要挑起重担,带领民众走出这个泥沼,也只有这样,才能构建一个自由、创新且多产的美国社会。

深入分析

以下为有价值的文章亮点:

(1) 全篇首句"Strange thing has happened in the American arts during the past quarter century"设置了悬念,吸引读者随着作者一起去探寻 what strange thing?

(2) 第1段"While income rose to unforeseen levels, college attendance ballooned, and access to information increased enormously, the interest young Americans showed in the arts—and especially literature—actually diminished."作者运用矛盾修辞手法(oxymoron),将收入的增长、大学入学率的上升与美国年轻人对艺术及文学兴趣的下降放在一起进行对比,目的在于凸显读者比例日益下降这个问题的讽刺性和严峻性。

(3) 第2段的 "eight of the nine major forms that are measured""younger adults (ages 18~24)"和第6段的 "ranked second""38 percent of employers"都呈现了非常精确的数字,这些数据的论证有效地让读者认识到阅读量的全面下降以及阅读量下降对企业员工的不良影响。

(4) 第5段的 "The February issue of Wired magazine, for example, sketches a new set of mental skills and habits proper to the 21st century, aptitudes decidedly literary in character: not 'linear, logical, analytical talents,' author Daniel Pink states, but "the ability to create artistic and emotional beauty, to detect patterns and opportunities, to craft a satisfying narrative." 第7段的 "A 2003 study of 15-to-26-year-olds' civic knowledge by the National Conference of State Legislatures concluded, 'Young people do not understand the ideals of citizenship … and their appreciation and support of American democracy is

limited.'"都用了引证的论证方式,借权威的杂志、调研夯实了阅读对职业、对公民社会参与度的巨大影响。

(5) 文章的第5~8段,都用反面的口吻指摘了阅读量下降的弊端,而第9段则用正面的口吻肯定了阅读的益处,如此正反兼蓄的论述展现了缜密性,异常有说服力。

(6) 第10段"As more Americans lose this capability, our nation becomes less informed, active, and independent-minded. These are not the qualities that a free, innovative, or productive society can afford to lose."通过这个假设式预言,作者得以激发读者的危机感和国家荣誉感,在情感上感召读者去行动,并再次彰显了之前所提观点的重要性。

(7) 通篇看下来,可以感觉到作者的文风含蓄,比如"As more Americans lose this capability, our nation becomes less informed, active, and independent-minded."中"less"一词是曲意修辞(litotes)的体现,即用否定表达肯定的意思,委婉地指出一旦美国国民失去阅读能力,整个国家都将陷入信息闭塞、停滞不前且无独立意识的泥潭。再比如"Libraries, schools, and public agencies do noble work, but addressing the reading issue will require the leadership of politicians and the business community as well.""If it were true that they substituted histories, biographies, or political works for literature, one might not worry. But book reading of any kind is falling as well."这些句子都是先扬后抑,以温和的让步姿态开场,渐渐过渡到事物的消极面。

我带你写

同上篇,先同义转述中心论点:the decline of reading in America will have a negative effect on society。decline of reading是关键名词最好不变;have a negative effect on= affect, imperil, pose a threat to, put/place…in jeopardy, put…at stake等。

接下来,试试用以上的诀窍来翻译并整合前两个小节内的提示,完成后两步。

知识补充

写作风格(writing style)由众多有机部分共同构成,其中以下四部分最为核心。

1. 措辞(diction)

措辞即prompt中提到的choice of word,指遣词造句的技巧。分为正式措辞和非正式措辞,但考虑到New SAT写作素材的出处大多来自权威的作家、演说家等,必然是正式居多。其中,运用措辞技巧时,应格外注意以下三个元素:

(1) 内涵词(loaded words)

顾名思义,内涵词是指承载着丰富内涵的短语、单词。可能对应的修辞手法有:双关、讽喻、暗讽、隽语等。使用内涵词可塑造多重表达意境,引导读者反复咀嚼文字深意,加深共鸣。

(2) 消极词汇(negative words)

此处所指的消极词汇并非对应语言学中的passive vocabulary(可以思考后推断出含义但无法熟练运用的词汇),而是指带来消极负面情绪的用词,比如贬义词。消极词汇的作用是暗示作者的态度和立场,奠定文章的基调。

(3) 幽默感(sense of humor)

幽默的措辞往往可以用善意调侃的笔触生动刻画出人生百态,让人发笑,让人难忘,让人深思。同时,幽默的措辞可以增加严肃话题的趣味性和可读性,让读者在会心一笑的同时也领悟真谛。

2. 口吻态度(tone)

众所周知,议论文的目的是说服读者接受作者的某些观点和主张,所以理解作者的态度对分析议论文尤其重要。态度口吻与措辞相辅相成,联系紧密。

态度口吻从广义上可以分为正面的(positive)、负面的(negative)和中立的(neutral)。再细分的话,常见有:正式的(formal)、非正式的(informal)、亲密的(intimate)、庄严的(solemn)、忧郁的(somber)、戏谑的(playful)、严肃的(serious)、讽刺的(ironic)、居高临下屈尊的(condescending)、不表态的(uncertain)、客观的(objective)、主观的(subjective)、乐观的(optimistic)、悲观的(pessimistic)、密切关注的(concerned)、有争议的(contentious)、有偏见的(biased)、不赞同的(disagreed)、持怀疑态度的(skeptical/incredulous/doubtful)、冷漠的(indifferent)、尖锐的(pointed)、袒护的(defensive)、批评的(critical)、妥协的(compromising)、保守的(reserved)、赞许的(consenting)、以事实为依据的(factual)、蔑视的(disparaging)、愤慨的(indignant)等。

3. 句型(sentence type)

句型从侧面也能反映出作者的文风。以下举几个文学作品常出现的句式:

(1) 祈使句(imperative sentence)表示请求、命令、叮嘱、希望、警告等,语气较为强烈,常用来呼吁读者发起某种行动。例如:Watch your steps.(走路小心。——警告)。

(2) 感叹句(exclamatory sentence)常用来表示喜、怒、哀、乐以及惊异等强烈的感情。例如:How I missed Vivian! 我多么想念薇薇安啊!

(3) 英语反问句的特点是"无疑而问",用疑问句(interrogative)的形式表示确定(assertion)的意思,以加强语气、增强表达效果。句末一般打问号,有的也可打感叹号。反问的形式有两种:用肯定的形式表示否定、用否定的形式表示肯定。例句:What a sunny day! Why don't we go shopping today? 今天天气真晴朗,我们何不出门逛逛街呢?

(4) 反义疑问句(question tags)有时带有感情色彩,表示惊奇、愤怒、讽刺、不服气等。例如:You call this a day's work, don't you? 你也好意思说这就是你一天的工作,不是吗?

(5) 强调句(emphatic sentence)可以通过强调对句子中的某个部分来表达作者的意愿或情感。例如:It was to you and not anyone else that I lent the money. 我只借钱给你,不借给其他人。

(6) 被动句(passive sentence)的功能有:促使信息均匀分布、实现语篇连贯、保持句式结构平衡、突出行为动作的施事、突出被动行为本身或被动行为产生的结果、突出行为的受事、详细阐明行为的施事、传达礼貌和委婉意图、表达客观性、制造悬念、形成对偶和构成排比,因此一般用于正式文体(科普文章、新闻报道、法律文件、官方声明等)。例如:The euro was inspired by the idea of creating "a country called Europe". 欧元诞生于"欧洲一体化"的设想。

(7) 警句(epigram),一般是一句话或一段引语,用来激励和告诉当事人某些道理,提醒人们要在生活中时刻保持某种精神品格。如:Few, save the poor, feel for the poor. 几乎没有人拯救穷人,同情穷人(提醒人们要去拯救和同情穷人)。

4. 情感共鸣(emotional appeal)

能撩拨读者心弦的文章,其作者必然提前了解了读者的心理以及情感特征,并将这些特征注入写作方式中,从而让听众产生心理共鸣,此外,作者还会通过带有倾向性或暗示性的语句向读者施加某种信仰和情感,来激起他们的感情并最终促使他们发起行动。简单说来,就是"投其所好,动之以情"。

- 阅读和分析

本篇阅读文章选自 Christopher Hitchens 于 2009 年发表在 Vanity Fair 上的一篇社论文 *The Lovely Stones*,该文章与 New SAT 写作时的阅读素材难度相仿,且作为样题进行分析。中心论点设置为:作者敦促大英博物馆将帕特农神庙的真迹归还给希腊。

> As you read the passage below, consider how Christopher Hitchens uses
> - evidence, such as facts or examples, to support claims.
> - reasoning to develop ideas and to connect claims and evidence.
> - stylistic or persuasive elements, such as word choice or appeals to emotion, to add power to the ideas expressed.

1. The great classicist A. W. Lawrence once remarked of the Parthenon that it is "the one building in the world which may be assessed as absolutely right."

2. Not that the beauty and symmetry of the Parthenon have not been abused and perverted and mutilated. Five centuries after the birth of Christianity the Parthenon was closed and desolated. It was then "converted" into a Christian church, before being transformed a thousand years later into a mosque—complete with minaret at the southwest corner—after the Turkish conquest of the Byzantine Empire. Turkish forces also used it for centuries as a garrison and an arsenal, with the tragic result that in 1687, when Christian Venice attacked the Ottoman Turks, a powder magazine was detonated and huge damage inflicted on the structure. Most horrible of all, perhaps, the Acropolis was made to fly a Nazi flag during the German occupation of Athens. I once had the privilege of shaking the hand of Manolis Glezos, the man who climbed up and tore the swastika down, thus giving the signal for a Greek revolt against Hitler.

3. The damage done by the ages to the building, and by past empires and occupations, cannot all be put right. But there is one desecration and dilapidation that can at least be partially undone. Early in the 19th century, Britain's ambassador to the Ottoman Empire, Lord Elgin, sent a wrecking crew to the Turkish-occupied territory of Greece, where it sawed off approximately half of the adornment of the Parthenon and carried it away. As with all things Greek, there were three elements to this, the most lavish and beautiful sculptural treasury in human history. Under the direction of the artistic genius Phidias, the temple had two massive pediments decorated with the figures of Pallas Athena, Poseidon, and the gods of the sun and the moon. It then had a series of 92 high-relief panels, or metopes, depicting a succession of mythical and historical battles. The most intricate element was the frieze, carved in bas-relief, which showed the gods, humans, and animals that made up the annual Pan-Athens procession: there were 192 equestrian warriors and auxiliaries featured, which happens to be the exact number of the city's heroes who fell at

the Battle of Marathon. Experts differ on precisely what story is being told here, but the frieze was quite clearly carved as a continuous narrative. Except that half the cast of the tale is still in Bloomsbury, in London, having been sold well below cost by Elgin to the British government in 1816 for $2.2 million in today's currency to pay off his many debts.

4. Ever since Lord Byron wrote his excoriating attacks on Elgin's colonial looting, first in *Childe Harold's Pilgrimage* (1812) and then in *The Curse of Minerva* (1815), there has been a bitter argument about the legitimacy of the British Museum's deal. I've written a whole book about this controversy and would just make this one point. If the Mona Lisa had been sawed in two during the Napoleonic Wars and the separated halves had been acquired by different museums in, say, St. Petersburg and Lisbon, would there not be a general wish to see what they might look like if re-united? If you think my analogy is overdrawn, consider this: the body of the goddess Iris is at present in London, while her head is in Athens. The front part of the torso of Poseidon is in London, and the rear part is in Athens. And so on. This is grotesque.

5. It is unfortunately true that the city allowed itself to become very dirty and polluted in the 20th century, and as a result the remaining sculptures and statues on the Parthenon were nastily eroded by "acid rain." And it's also true that the museum built on the Acropolis in the 19th century, a trifling place of a mere 1450 square meters, was pathetically unsuited to the task of housing or displaying the work of Phidias. But gradually and now impressively, the Greeks have been living up to their responsibilities. Beginning in 1992, the endangered marbles were removed from the temple, given careful cleaning with ultraviolet and infra-red lasers, and placed in a climate-controlled interior. Alas, they can never all be repositioned on the Parthenon itself, because, though the atmospheric pollution is now better controlled, Lord Elgin's goons succeeded in smashing many of the entablatures that held the sculptures in place. That leaves us with the next best thing, which turns out to be rather better than one had hoped.

6. About a thousand feet southeast of the temple, the astonishing new Acropolis Museum will open on June 20. With 10 times the space of the old repository, it will be able to display all the marvels that go with the temples on top of the hill. Most important, it will be able to show, for the first time in centuries, how the Parthenon sculptures looked to the citizens of old.

7. The Acropolis Museum has hit on the happy idea of exhibiting, for as long as following that precedent is too much to hope for, its own original sculptures with the London-held pieces represented by beautifully copied casts. This has two effects: It allows the visitor to follow the frieze round the four walls of a core "cella" and see the sculpted tale unfold (there, you suddenly notice, is the "lowing heifer" from Keats's *Ode on a Grecian Urn*). And it creates a natural thirst to see the actual re-assembly completed. So, far from emptying or weakening a museum, this controversy has instead created another one, which is destined to be among Europe's finest galleries. And one day, surely, there will be an agreement to do the right thing by the world's most "right" structure.

初步理解

乍看之下，这篇文章相较之前的样题难度陡升，但撇除其中的大量专业术语后，我们能发现，它和其他 New SAT 写作素材一样，都遵循以下基本结构：呈现一个问题——分析问题背景——呼吁某种行动。因此，我们在通读文章时可以标注陌生单词，如果这些单词出现次数不超过 1 次，则默认为次要信息不做深究；如果出现次数超过 3 次，才视作关键信息，应结合上下文语境推测大致的词义。考虑到这篇文章的内容难度较大，但段落较少，所以逐段进行理解，不予切分超大段落群。

在第 1 段中，作者先借助了名人的评价引出了本文的讨论对象——帕特农神庙。

在第 2 段和第 3 段中，我们能觉察到一系列和"破坏、损毁、玷污"相关的单词交织出现，如 "abused" "perverted" "mutilated" "damage" "desecration" "dilapidation" "sawed off"，由此可以推断这两段都在按时间顺序细数帕特农神庙曾遭受过的不幸。其中第 2 段主要叙述了帕特农神庙先后被关闭、被荒废、被改建为基督教教堂、被土耳其军队用作军队工事、被炸弹损毁和被纳粹占领。第 3 段，则在"The damage done by the ages to the building"（帕特农神庙早期被各个时代烙上的伤痕）基础上，从首句"But there is one desecration and dilapidation that can at least be partially undone"过渡到近代一件本可以避免的劣迹：在 19 世纪时以埃尔金为首的一伙英国人强行锯下并掠夺了神殿里将近一半的装饰性雕塑作品。之后大段文字都在描绘被掠夺的艺术品的极高工艺和欣赏价值。这段出现了大量和建筑艺术相关的专业词汇，包括山形墙饰品（pediment）、雕带（frieze）、大起伏/小起伏（high-relief/bas-relif）、柱间壁（metope）等，但出现次数不超过 3 次，因此可以不必细究这些专业词汇，而是将注意力放在归纳主旨大意上。第 3 段段末，作者强调了这条雕带上的浮雕讲述了一个连贯的故事（a continuous narrative），但有一半被卖到了伦敦，暗示了完璧归赵的必要性。

在第 4 段中，作者用了两次类比让读者更直观地了解到上段那笔交易的荒谬。首先，他把帕特农神庙比作公认的艺术结晶——蒙娜丽莎肖像画。他假设如果蒙娜丽莎被一分为二，人们肯定会想把这两半拼合在一起，以此来说明同样作为建筑的结晶，帕特农神庙也同样有必要保留其完整性。接着，作者又高瞻远瞩地想到，或许会有读者质疑帕特农神庙和蒙娜丽莎的价值没有可比性。于是用了更直接的同类类比，将帕特农神庙的现状比作身首异处的彩虹女神雕像、惨遭截肢的海王波塞冬雕像。

在第 5 段中，作者欲扬先抑，先承认了希腊确实曾经自甘堕落，任其雕塑被风吹雨打，接着话锋一转开始反驳，用具体事例证明希腊人已经意识到了自己的责任，并开始花大成本去保护那些艺术作品。

在第 6 段中，作者继续摆出更多事实来呼应上段的分论点（希腊人意识到了责任并着手保护起艺术品），比如计划在神殿附近开一家阿克罗波利斯博物馆展示神殿的雕塑。

最后在第 7 段中，作者兵不血刃地暗示：大英博物馆虽然能继续装傻充愣死撑着不归还抢占的帕特农神庙部分，但阿克罗波利斯博物馆已经打算办一个展览，一边展出自己收藏的一半真迹，一边用仿品代替被英国抢走的另一半真迹。如此一来，参观者自然而然会渴望看到完整的真迹。最后，作者展望道：有朝一日，英国政府终将屈服于人民群众的施压，让帕特农神庙的真迹重回故土。

最后梳理一遍全文思路：在文章开头，作者借助各种耳熟能详的历史典故描绘出帕特农神庙饱经风霜的历史。接着，从不可逆的历史烙印转到了本可避免的一场人为灾难：在 19

世纪时以埃尔金为首的一伙英国人强行锯下并掠夺了神殿里将近一半的装饰性雕塑作品，并在之后以极其低廉的价格卖给了大英博物馆抵债。但这笔交易除了价格不符合艺术品的原有价值外，意义上也十分荒谬——因为这笔交易活生生割裂开了一件原本完整的伟大艺术品。虽然希腊人曾经自甘堕落，任由帕特农神庙的雕塑被风吹雨打，但现在已经意识到了自己的责任，并开始花大成本去保护那些艺术作品，比如计划在神殿附近开一家阿克罗波利斯博物馆展示神殿的雕塑。在此大背景下，大英博物馆虽然能继续装傻充愣死撑着不归还抢占的帕特农神庙部分，但随着该博物馆的展览，参观者自然而然会渴望看到完整的真迹，因此作者坚信有朝一日，英国政府终将屈服于人民群众的施压，让帕特农神庙的真迹重回故土。

深入分析

以下为有价值的文章亮点：

（1）第1段中，作者运用了引用手法（quotation）介绍了文章的描写对象。有些考生会误以为此处运用了暗引（allusion）修辞手法，其实不然，暗引修辞手法引用的东西包括典故、谚语、成语、格言和俗语等。引用出处最多的是《圣经》故事以及希腊、罗马神话、《伊索寓言》和某些源远流长的谚语、格言等，而 A. W. Lawrence 只是一个近代的古典建筑学及雕塑专家。他提出的评论作为印证。

（2）在文章第2段，作者才算是运用了暗引（allusion）的手法，罗列了一系列历史典故。其中提到了神庙在基督教诞生的五个世纪后被废弃一事，暗示帕特农神庙比基督教诞生还要早足足500年之多，突出了神庙的历史悠久。之后，作者指出神庙还曾卷入过第二次世界大战中，他凭借经验论证法（empirical argument），用与历史名人握过手的亲身经验增加了典故的可信度。这一段落中，即使是一个不熟悉历史的人，也会对诸如"基督教""拜占庭""纳粹"等专有名词产生共鸣，同时，第2段中作者精心埋下了许多引导性的词汇，如"tragic result""huge damage""most horrible of all"等，这些词不仅折射了作者自己的立场，也巧妙地唤起了读者的恻隐之心，使他们在目睹神庙经历了那么多波折后，由衷对其产生敬畏和珍惜的情感。

（3）第3段中，曾提到雕带上的浮雕讲述了一个连贯的故事，且一半被卖到了英国伦敦。作者既从理性的角度跟读者进行了道理论证（故事只剩一半了，根本让人读不懂啊），也采用了矛盾修辞手法（oxymoron）营造出这一现象的不合理性。此外，这一段中，还补充道那条雕带当时是被贱卖用来抵债的荒诞桥段"half the cast of the tale is still in Bloomsbury, in London, having been sold well below cost by Elgin to the British government in 1816 for \$2.2 million in today's currency to pay off his many debts"，旨在用讽刺的修辞手法（satire），点出这笔交易的可笑。

（4）第4段用了一系列的类比论证（analogical argument），进一步强调交易的不合理性。作者分别把帕特农神庙遗迹等同于被锯成两半的蒙娜丽莎、身首异处的彩虹女神雕塑和惨遭截肢的海王波塞冬雕像，巧妙地将读者对以上三件知名艺术品的崇敬和爱护转移到了帕特农神庙上，并让其对大英博物馆霸占帕特农神庙部分遗迹的自私行径嗤之以鼻。

（5）第5段中，作者谈到希腊政府正努力从污染中拯救神庙时用了尖锐的反语修辞（irony）。作者在第5段感谢了锯下雕像的埃尔金，因为多亏了他，这些雕像才得以留在英国不受希腊空气的污染。这段话充斥着浓浓的讽刺意味，作者用这种幽默的方式犀利地指出比起解决环境对神庙的影响,更重要的是让神庙变得完整。

(6) 第 5 段和第 6 段,运用了大量的举例论证(exemplification)来支撑希腊人正担负起自己保护艺术品的职责。

(7) 第 7 段,"And one day, surely, there will be an agreement to do the right thing by the world's most 'right' structure."与开头第 1 段夸帕特农神庙是"the one building in the world which may be assessed as absolutely right."首尾呼应,通过"right"一词一语双关,重申我们有义务还帕特农神庙一个公道。

我带你写

以下是一位曾在 New SAT 写作考试中摘得 11 分高分的学生,围绕该样题写的范文,供考生借鉴参考:

Christopher Hitchens establishes his credibility by mentioning in P4 that he has already "written a whole book about" the controversy between Britain and Greece over "the lovely stones", and in the passage, he expresses his opinion as a justice seeker angered by the immoral actions done by Britain. The purpose of the passage is exhorting the British Museum to return the relic of Parthenon to its homeland; Hitchens tries to achieve this purpose by employing historical allusions and acrimonious diction to appeal to pathos, inserting analogy to appeal to logos, and adopting a sarcastic tone to magnify the irrationality of Britain's doings.

In the opening of P2, Hitchens states that "the beauty and symmetry of the Parthenon" have been "abused and perverted and mutilated", using contrary diction to emphasize the unjust treatments that the Parthenon received over centuries, seeking readers' sympathy. Hitchens then alludes to history, in which the Parthenon was desolated, converted into a Christian church, transformed into a mosque, inflicted with huge damage, and even bore the humiliation of flying a Nazi flag. By portraying the unjust treatment that the Parthenon, "the building in the world which may be assessed as absolutely right", received, Hitchens arouse his audience's pity. He also inserts a personal anecdote of shaking hand with the man who tore the swastika down to credit his assertion and establishes reliability for himself.

In P3, Hitchens first introduces Elgin's action of "desecration and dilapidation"—robbing the Parthenon of half of its adornment. Hitchens devotes a series of descriptive sentences on the various adornments in the Parthenon, which were all "sawed off" by Elgin's crew. The contrast between the verb "sawed off" and the magnificence of the Parthenon's adornments draws reader's attention on the unjust behavior of Elgin's crew. Hitchens invites his audience to feel his rage more intimately by employing the analogy of Mona Lisa being "sawed in two" and "the separated halves" being "acquired by different museums" in St. Petersburg and London. This analogy allows the general audience who is more familiar with Mona Lisa, to imagine what it is like if Mona Lisa got the same treatment as the Parthenon. Hitchens convinces the readers that Britain is committing a "grotesque" wrongdoing which deprives visitors of the privilege of seeing a complete work of art.

Towards the end of the passage, Hitchens adopts a sarcastic tone in order to convince his readers of the importance of restoring a complete assembly in Athens. He mentions Elgin's goons' action of "smashing many of the entablatures that held the sculptures in place", reminding the readers of Elgin's doing of sawing off sculptures mentioned in the previous paragraph. In the last sentence however, Hitchens ends on a sarcastic note by commenting that Elgin's action "leaves us with the next best thing" because it protected the sculptures from the "acid rain" in Athens. Then in P6 and P7, Hitchens depicts "the astonishing new Acropolis Museum" and emphasizes that the new museum is now able to show "how the Parthenon sculptures looked to the citizens of old" through representing "London-held" pieces with "beautifully copied casts". However, there is no doubt that copied casts can never outshine the originals. Thus, Hitchens infers that the new museum "creates a natural thirst to see the actual assembly completed". He speaks from visitors' standpoint and calls for Britain to return the sculptures Elgin took from the Parthenon.

In the concluding sentence, Hitchens reasserts the purpose of the passage, implying that it is Britain's responsibility to do "the world's most right sculpture" justice and help create a complete assembly of the Parthenon in Athens for the benefits of general visitors.

知识补充：修辞手法 & 自选写作特点

修辞格（figures of speech）是提高语言表达效果的语言艺术。它能使语言生动形象、具体活泼，给人以美的享受。英语修辞格种类繁多，在此分为音韵修辞格、词义修辞格和句法修辞格。

1. 音韵修辞格（phonological rhetorical devices）

音韵修辞格是利用词语的语音特点创造出来的修辞手法，它主要包括拟声（onomatopoeia）、头韵（alliteration）、半谐音（assonance）和尾韵（consonance）。音韵修辞格具有音乐的节奏感，可增强语言的表现力。

（1）拟声法（onomatopoeia）是模仿自然界各种声音的修辞手法。例如：
She closed the window with a bang.
她砰的一声关上了窗户。
When John asked Mary to marry him, her heart went pit-a-pat.
当约翰向玛丽求婚时，她的心扑扑地跳。

（2）头韵法（alliteration）是在一个词组或一个诗行中，有两个以上彼此靠近的词，其开头的音节（或其他重读音节）具有同样的字母或声音，通常是辅音字母相同。许多英语绕口令把头韵法用到了极致。例如：
While we were walking, we were watching window washers' wash Washington's windows with warm washing water. 在走路时，我们看着清洁窗户的工人用暖水清洗华盛顿的窗户。

此外，还有一系列常见的词组（表示并列或对比居多），如：

boom and bust	经济繁荣与萧条
safe and sound	平平安安
green as grass	幼稚无知

now or never	机不可失,时不再来
with might and main	竭尽全力
from top to toe	从头到脚
first and foremost	首先

(3) 半谐音(assonance)是指重复某个发音相同或相似的音节,也称准押韵和元韵,是指一组词、一句话或一行诗中同一元音重复出现。例如:

On their fifth game, he beat her fair and square.

在第五局比赛中,他正大光明地打败了她。

All roads lead to Rome.

条条大路通罗马。

(4) 尾韵(consonance)是指相同词尾辅音在一组词、一句话或一行诗中重复出现,具有悦耳的节奏感。例如:

My object in living is to unite my vocation and avocation.

我生活的目标就是将我的职业和爱好结合在一起。

Health is better than wealth.

健康胜过财富。

2. 词义修辞格(semantic rhetorical devices)

词义修辞格主要借助语义的联想和语言的变化等特点创造出来的修辞手法。它们主要包括明喻(simile)、隐喻(metaphor)、转喻(metonymy)、提喻(synecdoche)、暗引(allusion)、换喻(antonomasia)、通感(synaesthesia)、拟人(personification)、类比(analogy)、双关(pun)、夸张(hyperbole)、婉辞(euphemism)、反语(irony)、逆喻(oxymoron)和轭式搭配(zeugma)等。

(1) 第一大类:比喻类。包含 6 种修辞手法,即明喻(simile)、隐喻(metaphor)、转喻(metonymy)、提喻(synecdoche)、暗引(allusion)和换喻(antonomasia)。

人们生活在自然界,有许多共同的经历、感受和概念可以互相分享置换,而这样一种置换的过程就统称为比喻修辞。以上 6 种修辞手法虽然都属于比喻修辞的大类,但各自也存在区别。

• 明喻(simile)是将具有共性的不同事物做对比。这种共性不是事物的自然属性,只存在于人们的意识中。英语中的明喻与汉语的明喻基本相同,用某一事物或情境来比拟另一个事物或情境,其本体和喻体均同时出现在句中,在形式上是相对应的。标志词常用 like, as, seem, as if, as though, similar to, such as 等。例如:

He was like a wounded animal desperate to escape the hunter's aim.

他像一头受伤的野兽,不顾一切要逃脱猎人的追捕。

She looked as if she had just stepped out of a fairytale and brushed against me like a princess.

她看上去好像刚从一个童话故事中走出来,像公主一样与我擦肩而过。

• 隐喻(metaphor),也称暗喻,有汉语中隐喻、借喻及拟物的特点,即把甲事物当作乙事物来描写,利用某些单词进行含蓄的比喻,此时这些单词已经不再是字面上的意思了。例如:

German planes rained down bombs, shells and bullets.

炸弹、炮弹和子弹像暴雨一样从德国人的飞机上倾泻而下。

All the world's a stage, and all the men and women merely players.

整个世界就是一个舞台,所有的男男女女都只是舞台上的选手。

• 转喻(metonymy),也称借喻,不直接说出所要说的事物,而使用另一个与之相关的事物名称。两种不同事物并不相似,但又密不可分,因而常用其中一种事物名称代替另一种,但前提条件是甲必须与乙在本质上有相似之处。比如:以容器代替内容,以工具和材料代替事物,以作者代替作品,以具体事物代替抽象概念,以特定的建筑和场所代表机构等。例如:

Governments tend to have more muscle to suppress the criticism they dislike.

政府倾向于花更多的力气去镇压自己不喜欢的评论。

Word came that the president himself was coming to inspect them.

有消息传来,总统要亲自来视察他们。

• 提喻(synecdoche),又称举隅法,具有"牵一发而动全身"的功能。提喻法或以部分代替全体,或以全体代替部分,或以特殊代替一般,或以一般代替特殊,或以抽象代替具体,或以具体代替抽象。往往因微见著,在提到某人或某物时,不直呼其名,而是用与其密不可分的东西来代替。例如:

There are about 200 hands working in my uncle's chemical plant.

我叔叔的化学工厂约有 200 名工人。

French is the most beautiful tongue in the world.

法语是世界上最美的语言。

• 暗引(allusion)与汉语的暗引相似。其特点是不注明来源和出处,一般引用人们熟知的关键词或词组,将其融合编织在作者的话语中。引用的东西包括典故、谚语、成语、格言和俗语等。英语引用最多的是源出《圣经》故事以及希腊神话、罗马神话、《伊索寓言》和某些源远流长的谚语、格言等。例如:

Vanity is his Achilles' heel.

虚荣自负是他的致命伤。

It's a Catch-22-situation without experience you can't get a job and without a job you can't get experience.

这是一个无解的死循环——没有经验你就找不到工作,而找不到工作就无从累积经验。

• 换喻(antonomasia),也称换称,指用形容词、头衔、绰号或称呼等代替姓名或称谓,或者用专有名词代替普通名词。换喻中的专有名词通常来源自宗教、古代及当代的历史和文学,这是换喻和提喻最大的不同。但换喻往往只指代名词,适用范围比起暗引窄。如:

The Iron Lady——撒切尔夫人

The King of Soccer——贝利

The King of Pop——迈克尔·杰克逊

Man of Steel——斯大林

Solomon——聪明人

Judas——叛徒

Hitler——暴君

Uncle Tom——与白人妥协顺应的黑人

(2) 第二大类:联想类。包含 7 种:通感(synaesthesia)、拟人(personification)、类比

（analogy）、双关（pun/paronomasia）、讽喻（allegory）、移位修饰（transferred epithet）和象征（symbolism）。

• 通感（synaesthesia），也称通觉、联觉、移觉或连带感觉，这种修辞法在描述客观事物时，用形象的语言使感觉转移，将人的视觉、听觉、嗅觉、触觉和味觉等不同感觉互相沟通、交错，彼此挪移转换，使意象更为活泼、新奇。例如：

What a noisy scarf.
这围巾太鲜艳了。
Peter savored the song's melody bit by bit.
彼得仔细品茗着这首歌的旋律。

• 拟人（personification）与汉语中的拟人手法完全相同，就是赋予物以人的言语属性。这种拟人化的修辞手法读起来使人感到特别形象生动、富有情趣。例如：

The stars danced gracefully in the moonlit sky.
群星在月光照耀的天穹中翩然起舞。
The fire ran wild.
火势迅速蔓延。

• 类比（analogy）是指将两个本质上不同的事物就其共同点进行比较，通常借助简单熟悉的事物进行延伸，深入浅出地说明某种复杂的情况或道理。例如：

Gas is to car as wood is to fire.
油对汽车而言就如同木头之于火。
Telling someone you have a BlackBerry is like announcing that you drive a Yugo.
告诉别人你拥有一台黑莓手机就跟宣布你还在开一辆80年代的南斯拉夫牌汽车一样。

• 双关（pun/paronomasia）是利用一个词、一句话或一个语言片段的双重含义，借题发挥出多种解释，旁敲侧击，从而达到意想不到的滑稽效果。双关可分为谐音双关（homophonic puns）和语义双关（homographic puns）。前者是利用词意根本不同的谐音词构成的，后者是利用一词多义的特点来构成的。双关往往会同时表达双重意思：一个是表面的，一是隐含的，并且以隐含的意思为主，恰当地运用这种手法会使语言生动有趣，达到由此及彼的效果。例如：

What does that lawyer do after he dies? —Lie still.
那个律师死后会干什么？——躺着仍说鬼话。
Reading while sunbathing makes you well red.
在晒日光浴时看书能让你变得肤色古铜且又博学。

• 讽喻（allegory）富有寓言性，假借过去或别处的事例，传达暗示、影射或者讥讽现世各种现象的含义。具有双重性，表层含义与真正意味的是两回事。例如：

Make the hay while the sun shines.
莫失良机，趁热打铁。
It's time to turn plough into sword.
到了该努力的时候了。

• 移位修饰（transferred epithet），是将仅可用于修饰某种东西的词汇移植修饰到另类东西上的一种语言使用手法，使风马牛不相及的成分凑在一起，反而使得语言简练凝缩，形象生动。例如：

He lay in bed, smoking his thinking pipe.
他躺在床上,抽烟思考。
He left as soon as the baking interview completed.
备受煎熬的面试一结束他便急速离开。

• 象征(symbolism)是指通过联系类似的或传统意义上代表某事物的某个具体形象,使人产生联想,从而表现与之相联系的某种抽象的概念、思想、感情,表现作品主题的艺术创作手法。象征手法通常体现在暗喻和讽喻之中,因此考生在下定义时,只需在象征或"两喻"中二选一。例如:

Life is a roller-coaster.
生活就像过山车。(暗喻)
Sorry this meal isn't much, John. We didn't have time to kill the fatted calf.
约翰,很抱歉只有粗茶淡饭,我们来不及设宴欢迎你。(讽喻)

(3) 第三大类:强弱化语气类。包含4种:夸张(hyperbole)、含蓄陈述(understatement)、婉辞(euphemism)和曲意(litotes)。

• 夸张(hyperbole)与汉语的夸张完全相同,都是为了表达深刻的感受,抒发强烈的感情,通过故意夸大事实来给人留下深刻的印象。夸张运用丰富的想象、过激的言词渲染和装饰客观事物,可以加强语势、提升表达效果,以达到强调的目的。例如:

I'm so busy trying to accomplish ten million things at once.
我正同时忙着处理数不清的事务。
Your dog is so ugly, we had to pay the fleas to live on him.
你的狗长得太丑,连跳蚤都不愿意寄生在它身上。

• 含蓄陈述(Understatement),也称降调陈述、低调陈述,是一种较弱的反语形式。含蓄陈述所带有的否定标记并非是为了否定某个观点,而只是为了淡化语义,暗示字面义与言下义之间的差异。含蓄陈述还可以用来表达说话人的愿望、想法和见解,引起较肯定的情感;不具敌意和威胁、体现谅解,较少蔑视。在含蓄陈述中,有时会使用减缩手法,即使用 a bit, scarcely, hardly, rather, almost, pretty 等低调词(downtoners)来代替 very, extremely 等程度副词,故意降低事物程度、范围和结果的好坏。但是,只有当说话者持一种谨慎态度而使这类副词带上明显的修辞色彩时,它们才算得上是含蓄陈述。否则,就只是一些普通副词而已。这就要求我们从字里行间去挖掘说话者言语中所蕴含的真正语言色彩。例如:

He is no mean opponent in the coming debate.
他是之后辩论赛的一个劲敌。

• 婉辞(euphemism)是指用温和的、间接的词语代替生硬粗俗或避讳的词语,以避免直接说出不愉快的事实,冒犯别人或者造成令人窘迫沮丧的局面。例如:

He is out visiting the necessary.
他出去方便一下。
His relation with his wife has not been fortunate.
他与妻子关系不融洽。

• 曲意(litotes)是指利用否定的形式,表达肯定的意思。例如:
War is not healthy for children and other living things.
战争对儿童和其他生物来说是危险的。

Einstein is not a bad mathematician.

爱因斯坦是一个出色的数学家。

（4）第四大类：讽刺幽默类。包含4种：反语（irony）、讥讽（sarcasm）、讽刺（satire）和暗讽（innuendo）。

• 反语（irony）是指用相反意义的词来表达意思，通常比较诙谐和温和，如指责某人过失、错误时，却用赞同过失的说法，而在表扬时则用近乎责难的说法。用含蓄的褒义词语来表示其反面的意义，从而使本义更加幽默，更加讽刺。反语一般需借助特定的上下文和语境才能被正确理解。例如：

The marriage counselor recently got a divorce.

这位婚姻顾问最近离了婚。

It would be a fine thing indeed not knowing what time it was in the morning.

早上没有时间观念还真是一件好事啊！

• 讥讽（sarcasm），该修辞的特点是尖刻，往往蓄意中伤或讥讽。例如：

Well, of course, I knew that gentlemen like you carry only large notes.

啊，当然，我知道像您这样的先生只带大面额的票子。

• 讽刺（satire）可用来泛指反语和讥讽这两类修辞手法，但本身更常用来讽刺社会现象、体制政策或一些人，但针对事居多。例如：

Marriage is the chief cause of divorce.

离婚的首要原因在于结婚。

If this is going to be a Christian nation that doesn't help the poor, either we have to pretend that Jesus was just as selfish as we are, or we've got to acknowledge that He commanded us to love the poor and serve the needy without condition and then admit that we just don't want to do it.

如果这个国家变成一个不体恤贫苦民众的基督教国度，我们要么只能假装耶稣跟我们一样自私，要么就只得承认耶稣的确命令我们无条件地去爱护穷人并服务有需要的人，但之后坦言我们就是不想那么干。

• 暗讽（innuendo）是一种温和的反语，往往通过比较隐晦曲折的方式表达对所提及的某事某物的不同意和不赞赏。例如：

The weatherman said it would be worm tomorrow. He must take his readings in a bathroom.

那个天气预报员说明天天气会很"软"和，他的语文肯定是体育老师教的。

He is one candidate in this race who does not have a drinking problem.

他是这场竞选中唯一一个没有酗酒问题的候选人。

（5）第五大类：矛盾修辞。主要有4种：逆喻（oxymoron）、对立（antithesis）、隽语（paradox）和轭式搭配（zeugma）。

• 逆喻（oxymoron）也称反意法，指用两种不相调和的特征形容同一个事物，以不协调的搭配使读者领悟句中微妙的含义。与汉语中的反映辞格类似，都是将相互矛盾的概念和判断巧妙地联系在一起，以便相互映衬，突出事物的特点，表达复杂的思想感情和意味深长的哲理。矛盾修辞手法在英语中常见，但在汉语中很少见。如：sweet sorrow 忧喜参半（不是甜蜜的悲伤）；proud humility 不卑不亢（不是骄傲的谦卑）。例如：

I like a smuggler. He is the only honest thief.

我喜欢走私犯,他们是唯一一类诚实的小偷。

I like humanity, but I loathe persons.

我喜欢人性,但我厌恶人类。

• 对立(antithesis)也称对照、对比、对偶,有时也可用对照(contrast)同义替换,这种修辞将意义完全相反的语句放在对等的短语或语法结构中排在一起做对比,在比较和衬托之中突出不同事物的矛盾性。例如:

Give me liberty, or give me death.

不自由,毋宁死。

Pride hurts, modesty benefits.

满招损,谦受益。

United we stand, divided we fall.

合则存,分则亡。

• 隽语(paradox)是一种貌似矛盾,但包含一定哲理的说法。例如:

More haste, less speed.

欲速则不达。

Ignorance is strength.

无知即力量。

• 轭式搭配(zeugma)指用一个词(动词、形容词或介词)与两个以上的在意义上不相干的名词搭配。它用词简练、饶有风趣,可以使语言活泼、富有幽默感。例如:

He lost his coat and his temper.

他丢了自己的大衣并发起了脾气。

You held your breath and the door for me.

请你屏息以待,为我留着门。

3. 句法修辞格(syntactical rhetorical devices)

句法修辞格主要是指通过句子结构的均衡布局或者突出重点创造出来的修辞手法。这类辞格主要包括重复叠言(rhetorical repetition)、排比(parallelism)、修辞疑问(rhetorical question)、倒装(hyperbaton/inversion/anastrophe)、换置(hypallage)、冗笔(pleonasm)、仿拟(parody)、渐进(climax)、渐降(anticlimax)、仿词(nonce word)和顿呼(apostrophe)。

(1) 重复叠言(rhetorical repetition),这种修辞法是指在特定的语境中,将相同的结构、相同的意义词组成句子重叠使用,以增强语气和力量。其中包括联珠(anadiplosis)、首语重复(anaphora)、重言(hendiadys)、同义反复(tautology)和连词叠用(polysyndeton)。

• 联珠(anadiplosis):将一个或一组单词重复多遍,例如:

Men in great place are thrice servants: servants of state, servants of fame, and servants of business.

位居高位的人同时侍奉着三个主人:国家、名望和生意。

• 首语重复(anaphora):将一个句子的开头单词或短语,在随后的句子中重复多遍,例句:

We shall fight on the seas and oceans, we shall fight on the beaches, we shall fight on the landing grounds, we shall fight in the fields and in the streets, we shall fight in the hills.

我们将在远洋上战斗,我们将在沙滩上战斗,我们将在降落坪战斗,我们将在田野和街巷中战斗,我们将在山丘上战斗。

• 重言(hendiadys):用 and 连接两个名词,以代替一个形容词和一个名词,比如例句中的 voice and supplication,代替 supplicatory voice,例如:

I love the Lord, because he has heard my voice and supplication.

我敬爱主,因为他能聆听到我的心声和祈祷。

• 同义反复(tautology):用不同的单词、短语或句子重复同一个意思,例如:

With malice toward none, with charity for all.

不要以怨恨相对,应以慈悲为怀。

• 连词叠用(polysyndeton):在一组单词、短语或从句中,连续使用某个连词,比如在例句中,连续使用 and,给人一种一气呵成的感觉。例如:

And every living substance was destroyed which was upon the face of the ground, both man, and cattle, and the creeping things, and the fowl of the heaven; and they were destroyed from the earth: and Noah only remained alive, and they that were with him in the ark.

每一个生活在地球表面的活物,包括人、牲畜、爬行动物和天空的飞鸟都尽数被毁灭了,在地球上不复存在,只有诺亚本人和方舟里的物种幸存了下来。

(2) 排比(parallelism),这种修辞法是把两个或两个以上的结构大体相同或相似、意思相关、语气一致的短语或句子排列成串,形成一个整体。例如:

No one can be perfectly free till all are free; no one can be perfectly moral till all are moral; no one can be perfectly happy till all are happy.

所有的人自由后,才能完全自由;所有的人都有道德,才能完全合乎道德;所有的人都幸福了,才能真正幸福。

(3) 修辞疑问(rhetorical question),它与疑问句的不同在于它并不以得到答复为目的,而是以疑问为手段,取得修辞上的效果,其特点是:肯定问句表示强烈的否定,而否定问句表示强烈的肯定。它的答案往往是不言而喻的。例如:

The gods, they say, give breath, and they take it away. But the same could be said-could it not?

人都说老天爷把气赐予生灵,又把气夺走。不过这话用在小小的逗号上,何尝不是如此?

How was it possible to walk for an hour through the woods and see nothing worth of note?

怎么可能在森林中游走了一小时却没见到任何值得一提的风景呢?

(4) 倒装(hyperbaton/inversion/anastrophe),一种像倒装或逆序的修辞方法,使用与正装语序相偏离的方法,从而产生一种效果。

Then come the climax of the trial.

接着迎来了审判的高潮。

Up went the balloon into the cloudless sky.

气球腾空而起,飘入万里无云的蓝天。

（5）换置(hypallage)，和移位修饰法相似，但需要交换两个单词的位置，交换之后的句子符合语法，但不一定符合逻辑，作用同移位修饰法，都是用来增加趣味性和活泼性的。

Apply water to the wound. —Apply the wound to water.

（6）冗笔(pleonasm)：使用多余的单词来丰富句子的含义，例如：

No one, rich or poor, will be excepted.

（7）仿拟(parody)，是一种模仿名言、警句、谚语，改动其中部分词语，从而使其产生新意的修辞。例如：

A friend in need is a friend to be avoided.

一个急需帮助的朋友，是一个急需避开的朋友。

To smoke or not to smoke, that is a question.

抽烟还是不抽烟，这是一个问题。

（8）渐进(climax)，这种修辞是将一系列词语按照意念的大小、轻重、深浅、高低等逐层渐进，最后达到顶点，可以增强语势，逐渐加深读者印象。例如：

Eye had not seen nor ear heard, and nothing had touched his heart of stone.

眼不见耳不闻，没有什么能打动他铁石般的心肠。

（9）渐降(anticlimax)，与climax相反的一种修辞法，将一系列词语由大到小、由强到弱地排列。例如：

The duties of a soldier are to protect his country and peel potatoes.

一个士兵的职责除了保卫国土，还有削土豆。

（10）仿词(nonce word)，为了某种特殊需要而临时创造的、没有得到普遍使用的新词。英语仿词是对言语常规的一种变异，其原型可以是某一名词、口头禅、成语、谚语或名言。这种修辞方法的生成手段主要是换词，就是改动替换原型中的部分词语，可能是原型中的名词、动词、形容词、副词、介词、连词或某一部分结构，把它们融合在自己的语句中，以增强文字的感染力和表现力。仿词具有语言生动、明快机智、辛辣锐利的特点，具有别具一格的修辞功能。

（11）顿呼(apostrophe)，是指在演说、抒情文章中或诗歌中突然用第二人称对不在场的人或对拟人的事物发出呼语的一种修辞方式。演说者或文章作者在难以控制自己的强烈感情时突然中断自己的思路，把话语直接转向不在场的、已死去了的人或拟人的事物，似乎他们就在眼前，并与他们对话或请求，他们做讲演者所讲内容的见证人。讲话人或文章作者在使用这一修辞格时情绪激动达到了最高潮，因而这种修辞格具有很强的感染力。必须指出，用第二人称对事物发出呼语（即顿呼），实际上也是使事物人格化的一种拟人手法。例如：

England! Awake! Awake! Awake!

英格兰！醒醒！醒醒！醒醒！

Frailty, thy name is woman!

脆弱，你的名字是女人！

4. 自选写作特点

除了修辞手法，New SAT写作考试也明确允许其他"features of your own choice"（自选写作特点）。在此，笔者简要罗列出了10个常见的写作特点及其对应术语：

（1）设置悬念(cliffhanger setting)。

（2）欲扬结合（combination of praise and criticism）。

(3) 铺垫（bedding）。

(4) 烘托渲染（foreshadow/set off ... by contrast）。

(5) 虚实相生（nihility and reality/feints and ambushes）。

(6) 承上启下（form a connecting link between the preceding and the following）。

(7) 开门见山（come straight to the point）。

(8) 卒章显志（signpost in closing）。

(9) 托物寓意（display implication through objects）。

(10) 咏物抒情（express feelings through chanting）。

以上这些写作特点虽不属于四大指定元素的范畴，但经常能借助结构上的变动，达到某些文学艺术效果，供考生在分析时穿插提及。